Speaking Lives,
Authoring Texts

Speaking Lives, Authoring Texts

Three African American Women's Oral Slave Narratives

EDITED BY
DoVeanna S. Fulton Minor
AND
Reginald H. Pitts

STATE UNIVERSITY OF NEW YORK PRESS

Published by State University of New York Press, Albany

© 2010 State University of New York

For information, contact State University of New York Press, Albany, NY
www.sunypress.edu

Production by Dana Foote
Marketing by Michael Campochiaro

Library of Congress Cataloging-in-Publication Data

Speaking lives, authoring texts : three African American women's oral slave narratives /
edited by DoVeanna S. Fulton Minor and Reginald H. Pitts.
    p. cm.
Includes bibliographical references.
ISBN 978-1-4384-2965-6 (hbk. : alk. paper) — ISBN 978-1-4384-2964-9 (pbk. : alk.
paper) 1. Picquet, Louisa, b. 1828? 2. Jackson, Mattie J. 3. Dubois, Silvia, 1788 or
9–1889. 4. Women slaves—United States—Biography. 5. Slavery—United States—
History—19th century. I. Fulton Minor, DoVeanna S. II. Pitts, Reginald H. III. Picquet,
Louisa, b. 1828? Louisa Picquet, the octoroon, or, inside views of southern domestic life.
IV. Jackson, Mattie J. Story of Mattie J. Jackson. V. Larison, Cornelius Wilson, 1837–1910.
Silvia Dubois.
    E444.S73 2010
    306.3'62092—dc22

                                                                    2009012

10 9 8 7 6 5 4 3 2 1

For Black women who have spoken up throughout the ages.

CONTENTS

ILLUSTRATIONS

ACKNOWLEDGMENTS

This volume honors African American women who determinedly used their voices to document history in spite of living in a society that dismissed and ignored their views and lives.

We absolutely must begin our acknowledgments by expressing the strongest appreciation to P. Gabrielle Foreman for having the insight and excitement to introduce each of us to the other. Gabrielle understood the strengths each of us brought to this project and foresaw this rich combination.

We would like to acknowledge and thank The University of Alabama and Arizona State University for supporting this research.

The careful and nuanced readings of our anonymous reviewers helped shape this volume. Verner Mitchell and Jürgen Grandt read multiple versions of the manuscript and offered prudent and cogent commentary. We are indebted to William L. Andrews for suggesting that this book should be used as a companion to DoVeanna's first book, *Speaking Power*.

We greatly appreciate the assistance of archivists at the Hunterdon County Historical Society; the National Archives in College Park, Maryland; the Massachusetts Archives at Columbia Point, Boston; the New Jersey State Library and State Archives in Trenton, New Jersey; the St. Charles County Historical Society of St. Charles, Missouri; the Lawrence History Center and the Lawrence Public Library in Lawrence, Massachusetts; and the Historical Society of Princeton, New Jersey. Louise Sandberg of the Special Collections Room of the Lawrence Public Library in Lawrence, Massachusetts, Barbara Brown, collections manager of the Lawrence History Center, and Damarys

Ramos, senior clerk for the City of Lawrence provided invaluable assistance to complete this work. The photograph of Sylvia Dubois and her daughter, Elizabeth Alexander, is reprinted courtesy of the Hunterdon County Historical Society. We are grateful for their permission to reprint it in this volume.

Very able research assistance was provided by Deadja Baker, Savannah Carroll, Aysha Labon, Markus Harris, and Iris Minor. Reg would like to also gratefully acknowledge the work of Kathy Flynn, consummate genealogist and historian, in searching out the site of Henry and Louisa Picquet's gravesite in New Richmond, Ohio, and sharing the information, as well as her successful attempts in involving the New Richmond Historical Society to more closely investigate and commemorate the lives of the Picquets and other African American residents of New Richmond. Leslie Miller's careful and meticulous clerical assistance was significant to preparing the manuscript for publication. Leslie, thank you for very quickly and efficiently whipping this project into shape. Stephanie Freeman brought us through the home stretch. We appreciate your work, Stephanie.

We are extremely grateful to our editor, Larin McLaughlin of State University of New York Press, and her assistant Andrew Kenyon. Larin's encouragement and patience kept this project on track. Andrew's quick response to questions sped along the process of preparing this manuscript for publication. We also appreciate Pat Hadley-Miller, whose copyediting expertise greatly improved this work. Because of her keen eyes, many errors and flaws were avoided. Any remaining imperfections are wholly our responsibility. We extend our warmest gratitude to production editor, Dana Foote of State University of New York Press. As the project coordinator for this volume, she held our feet to the fire for meeting deadlines and ensured this project came to completion. Dana, thank you for your unfailing clarity and good humor.

DoVeanna would like to thank Reginald for finding this project interesting enough that he never hesitated to collaborate on it. Because of his astounding gift as a historical researcher, Reginald made this book much more than it would have been. DoVeanna thanks her family for their consistent support and encouragement. Her parents, Doveanna R. Garner, and William and Alberta Fulton, have generously nurtured her work and ambitions. In your own unique way, each of you has taught her the values of speaking and listening. She wishes to express deep gratitude to her husband, Deon Minor, and son, Israel, for their sacrifice and devotion. They endured long hours with her absence for the good of this project. Deon, you are the reason.

Reg would like to thank DoVeanna for bringing this project to his attention, and is honored to have been given the chance to work with her in bringing the stories of these three women to light; he admires her steadfastness, vision, and scholarship. Reg would also like to thank his fellow firefighters at the LaMott Fire Company No. 1 of Cheltenham Township, Montgomery County, Pennsylvania, for allowing the use of the company computer in order to type up his share of the narrative at times when the computer was not being used for other tasks; and also many thanks to his daughter Kaari for not yawning or rolling her eyes when her old man would read off portions of the manuscript to her, or to anyone else in earshot.

INTRODUCTION

Speaking Lives, Authoring Texts:
African American Women's Voices Raised for Freedom

From the outset of their enterprises, Louisa Picquet, Mattie Jackson, and Sylvia Dubois probably never imagined their life stories would be read and studied more than a century after they related them. Picquet and Jackson told their stories to reach specific pecuniary objectives, while Dubois diffidently related her narrative in response to Cornelius W. Larison's request. Yet Dubois's response reflects an overarching attitude held by many women as ordinary individuals who know the value of lived experience, particularly the experiences of devalued, dismissed people. Dubois proclaims, "Most of folks think that niggers ain't no account but, if you think what I tell you is worth publishing, I will be glad if you do it. 'T won't do me no good but maybe 't will somebody else. I've lived a good while, and have seen a good deal, and if I should tell you all I've seen, it would make the hair stand up all over your head" (150–51). Implicit in her statement is the confirmation that her experience is worth knowing and may offer lessons for others. In spite of the pejorative value that she realizes many Americans hold for African Americans, Dubois acknowledges Larison's appreciation of her life. Moreover, she suggests both the scenes she witnessed and the manner in which she will construct her narrative are so powerful that readers/listeners will experience a physical reaction. All three women display conscious narrative power: the power of experiential testimony, oral manifestation, and commitment to and

1

demand for justice by African American women. Without the benefits and privilege of reading and writing literacy (and in collaboration, sometimes uneasy, with amanuenses), these women left documents of their lives and of the challenges of African American women to make their voices heard. This volume ensures that early-twenty-first-century readers "hear" these voices to gain not only historical knowledge, but to understand the dynamics of literacy and self-representation and locate oral narratives in the spectrum and tradition of African American literary production.

Speaking Lives is an edited volume of three orally related nineteenth-century African American women's slave experiences, *Louisa Picquet, The Octoroon: A Tale of Southern Slave Life* (1861), *The Story of Mattie J. Jackson* (1866), and *Silvia Dubois, A Biografy of The Slav Who Whipt Her Mistress and Gand Her Fredom* (1883). Because these are oral texts, scholars have failed to sufficiently study and consider them in the genre of slave narratives. As a form of writing, slave narratives have received considerable scholarly attention, particularly in the last thirty years. According to Charles Davis and Henry Louis Gates Jr., slave narratives allowed ex-slaves to "write themselves into being" by exercising the act of literacy, thereby evidencing intellectual abilities that refuted arguments for Black inferiority. However, this concentration on written slave narratives obscures and dismisses the significance of oral slave narratives, thousands of which were recorded by amanuenses from the antebellum period through the Great Depression.[1] In fact, oral narratives were so prolific that Philip Gould confirms, "Abolitionist newspapers and periodicals published and reviewed as many, if not more, oral testimonies against slavery and ex-slave speeches as 'written' narratives" (20). Davis's and Gates's claim is representative of the focus of much of the scholarly research on and textual recoveries of African American lives and literary works in the last few decades. Many of the recently published oral slave narratives are considered as only oral history, without acknowledging their literary value. Publication of volumes like *Slave Narratives: A Folk History of Slavery in the United States from Interviews with Former Slaves* (2008), a collection of oral narratives recorded by writers of the Federal Writer's Project in the 1930s; Norman Yetman's *When I Was a Slave: Memoirs from the Slave Narrative Collection* (2002), and Alan B. Govenar's *African American Frontiers: Slave Narratives and Oral Histories* (2000) include oral narratives to explicate historical records of African American experiences. Alternately, McCarthy's and Doughton's *From Bondage to Belonging: The Worcester Slave Narratives* (2007) and David W. Blight's *A Slave No More: Two Men Who Escaped to Freedom, Including Their Own Narratives of Emancipation* (2007) showcase narratives written by ex-slaves that have seen scant scholarly attention or have been recently recovered. Although the authors and editors of these volumes appreciate the literariness of their respective narratives, they do not include any oral narratives.

This concentration on written slave narratives obscures and dismisses the significance of oral slave narratives as texts *authored* by their narrators. Examining the plethora of critical analysis of Frederick Douglass's *Narrative of the Life of Fredrick Douglass* and Harriet Jacobs's *Incidents in the Life of Slave Girl,* John Ernest notes this separation of studying slave narratives as historical texts (content) or literary rhetoric (style). Ernest argues, "to separate style from content is to undermine the authority of the slave narrative *as a text* and of the writers of slave narratives *as authors*" (emphasis in original, 224). Although Ernest focuses on written texts, his point is relevant for orally related narratives, too. By ignoring oral narratives, not only do scholars of African American literature silence a substantial number of voices, multiple conceptualizations of identity and representations of resistance to injustice are elided in favor of literary representations that do not fully reflect the multiplicity of African American lives and experiences as well as the manifold rhetorical styles found in African American oral traditions.

This volume brings together three slave narratives orally transmitted by women who—under various circumstances—escaped physical slavery and the discursive bondage of illiteracy. At the center of each of these liberating acts is the practice of Black feminist orality, which is discussed in DoVeanna S. Fulton's *Speaking Power: Black Feminist Orality in Women's Narratives of Slavery.*[2] Fulton explains,

> On one level, Black feminist orality can be understood as related to the African American women's tradition of "sass" in which one responds with independence, knowing, and force to an individual in authority. On another level, Black feminist orality is a more abstract notion with features of circularity and multiplicity that counter the hegemony of writing. Black feminist orality in these texts demonstrates a combination of theory and practice commonly identified in Black women's work. (13)

This volume counters the idea of oral histories as merely "anecdotal" tales. Rather, it shows a fundamental function of oral histories as frameworks through which Black women view themselves and the world in which they live. These frameworks are crucial to their identity development and to social and cultural analyses. "These narrators demonstrate a speaking subject's ability to theorize concepts and language within a writing environment that could silence non-writers," posits Fulton, "Picquet's, [Jackson's, and Dubois's] narratives diffuse the primacy of Western logic and writing as the definitive form of intellectual communication" (26). Instead they substantiate the power of orality as a pragmatic philosophical approach to survival and self-representation.

The editors of *Speaking Lives* are indebted to the *Schomburg Library of Nineteenth-Century Black Women Writers* series (1988) in which each of these narratives was reprinted. However, the circumstance of their separate publications obviates their significance to one another and the impact of orality in African American literary study. Each of the editors of the Schomburg editions analyzes the narratives with different approaches. In his introduction to the Schomburg edition of *Louisa Picquet*, Anthony G. Barthelemy insightfully identifies the omissions and avoidances of personal details offered by ex-slaves in oral narratives. Barthelemy writes, "In their narratives, events are reported, but the personal lives are withheld or veiled in a struggle to preserve their already compromised privacy" (xxxv). Barthelemy recognizes the contentious relationship between Picquet and her interviewer demonstrated by her resistance to his invasive questions. Yet he states, "The fact that Picquet's is not *really* a narrative does not diminish the importance of her omissions" (emphasis added, xli). This statement suggests that the question and answer structure of the text and its as-told-to nature undermines Picquet's position as the author of her story. In his introduction to *Six Women's Slave Narratives,* in which *The Story of Mattie J. Jackson* is published, William Andrews finds, "Perhaps the most dramatic scenes in the autobiographies of Jackson, [Lucy A.] Delaney, and [Annie L.] Burton are those that depict the herculean (and usually successful) efforts of slave mothers to keep their families together in slavery or to reunite them after emancipation" (xxxi). Jared Lobdell, editor of the *Sylvia Dubois* Schomburg edition, is primarily concerned with confirming or refuting the historical record that Dubois relates. As an alternative to approaching these narratives from different standpoints,

Speaking Lives concentrates on their major commonality, namely, oral as-told-to narrative, which proves the capacity of orality to control textual representations and establishes Picquet, Jackson, and Dubois as genuine authors of their texts.

In presenting these narratives, the editors have endeavored to maintain, as much as possible, the integrity of the original texts; thus, notes and comments by amanuenses remain, as does unique punctuation that demonstrates textual dynamisms.[3] In this manner, each narrator's voice remains undisturbed, substantiating Fulton's argument that "African American women consistently employed African American oral traditions . . . to relate not only the pain, degradation and oppression of slavery, but also to celebrate the subversions, struggles, and triumphs of Black experience in the midst of slavery and afterwards" (3). These oral traditions are the foundation of a literary tradition grounded in African American lived experiences. The experiences in these narratives reveal the means by which these women develop self-defined identities, challenge injustice, and articulate political and civil rights as they tell their life stories and authorize their texts. The narratives in this volume exemplify this discursive practice of resistance and self-representation through orality born of struggles to articulate and own themselves via African American oral traditions.

AFRICAN AMERICAN ORAL TRADITIONS FUNDAMENTAL TO BLACK FEMINIST ORALITY

Oral traditions are central to African American culture and are seen in many forms with multivalent qualities. Through Spirituals, works songs, folktales, speeches, and oral ethnographies, African Americans protested injustice and created a record of the "peculiar institution" that contradicted the master narrative of benign slavery with slaves who were both intellectually inferior and unable to adopt the behaviors and values of Western civilization. The musical form of this oral discourse, seen chiefly in Spirituals and works songs, grew out of the slave experience of pain and struggle. African American slaves first created the sacred music known as Spirituals in rural spaces of plantation slave communities. In opposition to their owners who forbade slave worship, African American slaves met in "praise houses" or "hush harbors," which might have been a cabin in the slave quarters or even a secluded area under a tree in the woods. These clandestine places became sacred spaces where slaves worshipped stealthily but freely. Frederick Douglass believed "that the mere hearing of those songs would do more to impress some minds with the horrible character of slavery, than the reading of whole volumes of philosophy on the subject could do" (57). More than fifty years later, W. E. B. Du Bois called Spirituals "sorrow songs" that expressed the soul of African American slaves and were "not simply . . . the sole American music, but . . . the most beautiful expression of human experience born this side the seas" (156). Representing a worldview that sees little distinction between the sacred and the secular, enslaved African Americans sang Spirituals to transcend their physical environment when laboring in plantation fields and homes as well as meeting for worship.

Spirituals are a uniquely African American art form in that they are grounded in oral traditions from West and Central African cultures and the American experience of the slave institution.[4] Spirituals combined works songs of slaves, field hollers, and Christian hymns. Robert Darden maintains, "It is important to remember that both the field hollers and work songs could also be religious at the same time. As in Africa, the slave made no distinction between the 'religious' and 'non-religious' aspects of his or her life" (44). Works songs wed sound and movement to produce labor and were performed where work was done, in field and domestic spaces. They are reflective of a political economy based on subjugation and repression. Field hollers—shouts, solo exclamations, half-sung, half-yelled, half-yodeled fragments of songs, sometimes sung in falsetto—could be heard during the limited free time slaves enjoyed and were used to communicate messages, make one's presence known, or just to express emotion. These oral traditions provided emotional outlets manifest in music and are the foundation of later forms of Blues, Jazz, and Gospel.

Although many enslaved Africans adopted the tenets of Christianity for moral and spiritual guidance, their religious worship practices and beliefs reflected African rhythms, structures, and worldviews. For instance, many Spirituals are adaptations of Protestant lined-out hymns in which one person leads with the words of the song and the group repeats the line in drawn out melody. This practice was particularly effective for African American oral culture, for not only were oral traditions central to African American slave culture, but with the prohibition of literacy, a person did not have to read in order to participate in musical worship.

In the African American Spiritual tradition, hymns are infused with distinctly African characteristics. These elements include: call and response, which demonstrates a relationship between the leader and the group; complex rhythms with syncopation and polyrhythms of hand-clapping, foot-tapping, exclamations, and percussive sounds; often a five-note pentatonic scale that is African-based as opposed to the eight-note scale found in much of European music; an existentialist religious outlook concerned with day-to-day lived experience; abstractions that are made concrete such as death viewed in everyday experience; a lack of distance between God, Jesus, the Holy Spirit and humans, which, though blasphemous by European standards, is reflective of an African worldview of gods not being "Sunday gods" but involved in everyday situations; and a philosophy in which feeling takes priority over meaning, that is, religion is not only a philosophical or theological system, it is an emotional experience as well.[5]

The significance of the African aspects of Spirituals culminates in the yearning for liberation they express. The oral tradition of Spirituals is embedded in the slave experience and the desire for freedom and deliverance—freedom to own the self, to worship and live autonomously, and deliverance from the dehumanizing practices of forced labor, rape, familial separation, and arbitrary violence of slavery. Some Spirituals contain lyrics explicitly about freedom, like the traditional song "Oh Freedom." Other lyrics are more covert and implicit, such as biblical stories of deliverance and freedom often sung to express faith in ultimate justice. The complexity of these allusions renders powerful speech acts of agency and insurgence. For example, "Mary Don You Weep" combines two seemingly disparate stories, Jesus' resurrection of Lazarus in the New Testament, and the Old Testament's story of the Israelite's deliverance from Egyptian slavery—a situation commonly paralleled with African American enslavement—in a celebration of life (freedom) and triumph of justice (defeat of an enemy):

Mary, don you weep and Martha don you moan.
Mary, don you weep and Martha don you moan.
Pharaoh's army got drown-ded,
  Oh Mary don you weep.

I thinks every day and I wish I could,
Stan on de rock whar Moses stood.
Oh Pharaoh's army got drown-ded,
    Oh Mary don you weep. (Ward 5)

The lyrics are consoling, celebratory, and subversive. Rather than the seeming incongruence of the biblical stories, the song combines resurrection of the body with active insurgent resistance to oppression. With the subjective "I" the lines "I thinks every day an I wish I could, / Stan on de rock whar Moses stood," suggest slaves take an active role in the defeat of slavery. Just as Moses was empowered by God to destroy Pharaoh and his army, so, too, does this Spiritual express a desire for, and calls enslaved African Americans to be agents in, slavery's abolition. This philosophical multivalent quality of Spirituals pervades both Louisa Picquet's and Mattie Jackson's narratives. These narrators demonstrate their cognizance of double-voiced language that, like "Mary Don You Weep," expresses faith in divine retribution for slavery's injustices and illustrates subjective resistance to those injustices.

For women, this orality became an effective medium to express both their own demands for liberation and to relate a history that placed themselves at the center of representations and experiences they conveyed. In spite of the work of abolitionists and women's rights activists, generally women and African Americans—African American women in particular—were excluded from the public sphere in which they could have told their stories. Moreover, large-scale illiteracy among antebellum Africans precluded writing history, even in the private forms of letters and diaries used by white women. Yet Black women able to read and write still incorporated oral traditions into their texts, showing the fluidity of orality and its power to inform.

For African American women the power to read and write did not supersede the power of orality. Maria W. Stewart exemplified this merging of writing and orality in speeches for freedom. Stewart was the first African American woman to speak before a mixed-gender audience and to leave texts of her speeches. She was much more than an abolitionist, as she addressed varied subjects like religion, anticolonization, political and economic exploitation, Black self-determination, and women's rights. Like many nineteenth-century African American abolitionists, Stewart's discourse displayed a fundamental concern with Black civil rights and self-determination. Moreover, by choosing to present her views to "promiscu-ous" audiences, Stewart's oratory marked her radical resistance to gender and racial circumscriptions. Editors Carol B. Conaway and Kristin Waters contend, "[Stewart] can be seen to stand squarely in the camp of radical politics, carefully traversing the dangerous terrain of limited speech for women and blacks with a message of uplift but also of treasonous rebellion. As someone whose work is beginning to command its own canon of inter-pretation, her sophisticated analysis is emerging as the founding voice of black feminist theory" (5). In the genre of the slave narrative, African Amer-ican women employed orality for empowerment as well. Harriet Jacobs's *Incidents in the Life of a Slave Girl,* the only book-length slave narrative authored by a Black woman, uses a form of orality, found in written and as-told-to narratives, in which history is passed on orally.

Prohibitions against reading and writing literacy disregarded or failed to recognize other forms of literacy, forms that facilitated slave agency, resistance, and freedom. Oral literacy—that is, the capacity to verbalize and understand uses of the voice for self-expression and to represent the world—provided a cogent means for slaves and ex-slaves to challenge authority and for empower-ment both in slavery and freedom. Oral literacy includes employing and com-prehending various orally discursive practices and styles like repetition, intonation, inflection, rhyme, alliteration, parallelism, and even inversion and omission. Although many narratives were actually written by ex-slaves them-selves, many others were orally dictated to amanuenses and published in the abolitionist press. In spite of laws against literacy, by 1860 thousands of slave narratives had been published.[6] Although Douglass's *Narrative* is considered the paradigmatic slave narrative because it contains the most famous example of a man who attained freedom through reading and writing, oral literacy, too, serves a significant function in the *Narrative.* A case in point is the pref-ace written by William Lloyd Garrison, in which the abolitionist relates his initial encounter with Douglass at an antislavery convention when Douglass gives a speech on his slave experience. While he admits Douglass "gave utter-ance to many noble thoughts and thrilling reflections," Garrison's description of the incident places himself at the center of the action and the subsequent audience fervor, thereby minimizing Douglass's agency (Douglass 35). At the end of the *Narrative,* Douglass writes of the same incident; however, his description attests to both his oral literacy and sophisticated literary skills.

Douglass's narration omits Garrison's role (his name is never mentioned) and locates Douglass as the initiator and author of his oratory. In this instance Douglass uses his literary skills to refuse Garrison's exploitation and assert authority over himself and his work. Instead of understanding that oral literacy works in tandem with reading and writing literacy, scholars have privileged Douglass's reading and writing literacy over his oral literacy skills. Elizabeth McHenry observes, "The limited definition of black literacy associated with Frederick Douglass fails to take into account the extent to which the spoken word offered many black Americans access to written texts" (13). African American women had to face comparable struggles for authorship, and similar assertions of authority are found in the narratives in this volume.[7]

Ex-slave women without sufficient writing skills to produce their own narratives employed oral literacy skills that were, in Bernice Johnson Reagon's words, "learned in the womb" from their foremothers. Lack of reading and writing literacy did not keep these women silent or in chains. Oral literacy offered generations of women in Black communities an effective instrument to educate and arm their daughters and granddaughters for survival in a world in which, as Audre Lorde proclaims, "we were never meant to survive" (42). McHenry corroborates the value of oral literacy. She finds, "Many early nineteenth-century literary societies endorsed a broader notion of oral literacy that did not valorize the power of formal or individualized literacy over communal knowledge" (13). Just as Harriet Jacobs's appropriation of her grandmother's oral history enhanced her narrative, the narrative experiences of Louisa Picquet, Mattie J. Jackson, and Sylvia Dubois contain speech acts of resistance and liberation in both their real-life and rhetorical experiences.[8] Although the three narratives were recorded by three different amanuenses, the narrative subjects illustrate how nonliterate freedwomen used orality to control the representation of their lives and to express their strength, perseverance, and humanity. The varied circumstances and structures of each text demonstrate the mediation of African American women's voices and how they have resisted and/or negotiated that mediation.

The unique relationship each narrator had with her amanuensis is a factor in her voice mediation and points to the method of "speaking in tongues," as articulated by Mae Henderson, that African American women writers consistently employ. Henderson uses the phase "speaking in tongues" to denote both glossolalia—the ability given by the Holy Spirit to speak in unknown languages—and heteroglossia—a discourse that communicates in known multiple languages simultaneously—to analyze writings by Black women that "account for racial difference within gender identity and gender difference within racial identity. . . . Through the multiple voices that enunciate her complex subjectivity, the black woman writer not only speaks familiarly in the discourse of the other(s), but as Other she is in contestorial dialogue with the hegemonic dominant and subdominant or 'ambiguously (non)hegemonic' discourses" (120). Like Black women writers, Picquet, Jackson, and Dubois, as speaking subjects, "speak in tongues," yet their voices are mediated by amanuenses who are hegemonic (Hiram Mattison and C. W. Larison) and (non)hegemonic (L. S. Thompson). These amanuenses' intercessions in the narratives vary in degrees. It is through the orality in these texts that we hear "the multiple voices that enunciate [their] complex subjectivit[ies]." These narratives offer examples of nonliterate Black women's negotiated mediation and their self-assertion through—and sometimes despite—scribes who have their own subjective aims. The ex-slave women of these narratives are in dialogue with their amanuenses and the larger society whose social constructs of race, gender, and class marginalize them. At times their language can be unknown to the interviewer. Other times they speak in multiple languages, which offer multivalent narrativity that seemingly satisfies inquiries of one audience while speaking more covertly to another.

Louisa Picquet, The Octoroon: A Tale of Southern Slave Life (1861)

In 1860, Louisa Picquet traveled throughout Ohio and New York to raise money to purchase her mother's freedom.[9] She agreed to relate her life story to publish a slave narrative for fundraising purposes and as a tool for the abolitionist cause. Louisa was born some time around 1830 to a mulatto slave woman, Elizabeth Ramsey, and her white owner on a plantation in Lexington County, South Carolina, just outside the capital city of Columbia. Elizabeth was a house slave, a seamstress, who was evidently a quadroon, or of one-fourth African ancestry, and was lighter-skinned than most slaves. Working as a domestic slave, Elizabeth was probably under the constant scrutiny of her owner, a man Picquet refers to in the narrative as "John"

Randolph, but who was more likely James Hunter Randolph (1792–1869), a lawyer and planter farming with his father Isaac Fitz Randolph in Columbia during this period.[10] Still in her infancy, Louisa and her mother were sold because baby Louisa looked too much like the mistress's child. Later when Louisa was thirteen she and her mother were sold separately, her mother as a cook to a Mr. Horton of Texas, Louisa as a concubine to a Mr. Williams of New Orleans. At Williams's death Louisa and her children were freed, after which the family moved to Cincinnati, Ohio. Louisa gave birth to four children fathered by Williams, but only two survived enslavement. One child died soon after the family moved to Cincinnati, leaving only her daughter, Elizabeth—named for her absent grandmother—alive. Three years after arriving in Cincinnati, Louisa married Henry Picquet, a single father raising his four-year-old daughter, Harriet. A native of Augusta, Georgia, Henry was the eldest (but only son) of five mulatto children of an Alsatian-born farmer and gunsmith by one of his slaves. After being freed, Henry and his family moved to Cincinnati. Together Louisa and Henry produced Sarah and Thomas. Later Henry joined the Union army and served in Tennessee. After the end of the war, Henry, claiming service-related injuries, spent almost fifteen years in an attempt to receive a military pension, which was ultimately granted. During that period, the Picquet family moved from Cincinnati to the town of New Richmond, Ohio where they would live for the rest of their lives. Louisa received his military pension until her death in 1896.[11]

Louisa Picquet has a question and answer structure that allows the interviewer, Hiram Mattison, a white Methodist minister, to determine the nature of the questions. Mattison's questions reveal his preoccupation with miscegenation and the abuse, both sexual and physical, of slave women. With his initial description of Picquet, Mattison conflates illiteracy with slavery, and femininity with whiteness. He writes, "A certain menial-like diffidence, her plantation expression and pronunciation, her inability to read or write, together with her familiarity with and readiness in describing plantation scenes and sorrows, all attest the truthfulness of her declaration that she has been most of her life a slave . . . But, notwithstanding the fair complexion and lady-like bearing of Mrs. Picquet, she is of African descent on her mother's side" (45). For Mattison, Picquet's illiteracy verifies her status as slave, even as her whiteness and "lady-like" behavior contradict her blackness. From the start, Picquet's body and self are a paradox Mattison simply

cannot resolve. Picquet's octoroon status firmly situates her within the realm
P. Gabrielle Foreman delineates as "Mulatto/a-ness[,] . . . a representational
trope [that] often designates a discursive mobility and simultaneity that can
raise questions of racial epistemology, while it also functions as a juridical
term that constrains citizenship by ante- and postbellum law and force"
(506). Thus for Mattison, and presumably his readers, Picquet's octoroon
status and body crosses color-line boundaries—and in fact destabilizes those
boundaries—yet maintains and reinscribes assumptions of limited Black
intellectual capacity.

To tell her story Picquet must wade through his preconceptions with
Black feminist oral literacy superior to Mattison's written literacy. Using
what Zora Neale Hurston called "featherbed resistance," Picquet cunningly
both answers and evades the questions in a discursive manner that permits
her own subjective representation. In the introduction to her folklore collection, *Mules and Men*, Hurston uses this term to describe the manner in
which African Americans resist cultural, communal, and psychological intrusion, penetration, and appropriation by whites. She explains, "The theory
behind our tactics: 'The white man is always trying to know into somebody's
business. All right, I'll set something outside the door of my mind for him to
play with and handle. He can read my writing but he sho' can't read my
mind'" (2). With Picquet's "featherbed resistance" Mattison reads the writing
of her cultural body but, as the narrative reveals, he fails to read—and comprehend—her will and agency to control her representation and to obtain
her mother's freedom. These textual dynamics expose the practice by which a
nonliterate freedwoman wrests narrative agency from the amanuensis and
creates a subjective representation.

Picquet chooses to evade Mattison's intrusive questions regarding physical abuse. For example, Mattison asks, "Did your master ever whip you?"
(46). Picquet answers, "Oh, very often: sometimes he would be drunk, and
real funny, and would not whip me then. He had two or three kinds of
drunks. Sometimes he would begin to fight at the front door, and fight
everything he come to. At other times he would be real funny" (46). Clearly,
Mattison's question demands a response that describes Picquet's whippings
in detail. However, not only does Picquet not describe the whippings, or
their number, for that would leave the impression of a passive victim, she
conveys her master's (Mr. Cook's) character and uses language that strongly

suggests how actively she resisted him. By relating Cook's intemperance, Picquet constructs an immoral image of him, which is particularly significant given the concern and activism of temperance advocates during this period.

In fact, in the same issue of the *Cincinnati Gazette,* the newspaper in which Picquet's notice announcing the manumission of her mother appears, a chapter of a serialized temperance novel, *A Tale of New England Life: A Mother and Her Son or Sowing and Reaping* is published. The object of the temperance movement was to promote moderate consumption of alcoholic beverages or total abstinence. Temperance activists identified the root cause of social crises like spousal abuse, indolence, and domestic impoverishment as stemming from the "demon drink." For many white abolitionists and temperance advocates—although these groups were not mutually inclusive—slaveholding and drunkenness occasioned similar disapprobations; both constituted transgressions of Christian principles. Even though the *Gazette* was not exclusively concerned with abolition and temperance, its pages reveal the editor's sympathy with these movements. The readers of *Louisa Picquet,* who, it is safe to assume, were potentially the audience for the *Gazette,* and, therefore, interested in abolition *and* temperance, would find Cook's inebriation vulgar and disgraceful.

Picquet rhetorically controls the narrative by using the word "fight," implying two or more persons in active combat, instead of "whip" (which Mattison uses), and illustrating her rejection of the victim status Mattison would ascribe to her. She dismisses Cook's threatening image with her description of him as "real funny." Instead of fear and terror, Cook inspires Picquet's disdain and contempt. This exchange displays Picquet's integrity and strength more effectively than either Cook's menace or Mattison's literary intrusion.

Picquet asserts her agenda throughout the narrative in spite of Mattison's often vacuous inquiries that trivialize her experience and objectify her. Throughout the text he often intercepts Picquet's detailed narration of emotional experiences that fail to meet his abolitionist agenda. Rebecca Anne Ferguson finds that "such disruptions of what was probably a much fuller conversation show Mattison determined to report only the facts he considers relevant to his agenda and sometimes less responsive to all that Picquet might have wanted to tell" (60–61). While recounting the sales and separation of her mother and herself, Mattison asks, "It seems like a dream, don't it?" (56). She replies, "No; it seems fresh in my memory when I think of it—no longer than yesterday" (56). She goes on to describe how her mother prayed for her while she was on the auction block, and says, "I often thought her prayers followed me, for I never could forget her. Whenever I wanted any thing [sic] real bad after that, my mother was always sure to appear to me in a dream that night, and have plenty to give me, always" (56). Picquet refuses to trivialize and temper the gravity and import of the emotions caused by the forced separation. The reality of the auction block produces the dream of maternal sustenance. She redefines the word "dream"—which Mattison uses to depict something lost and intangible— and imbues it with strength and immediacy that emphasize her connection to her mother rather than the separation. Picquet's language exemplifies African characteristics of oral tradition in which abstract concepts take on concrete qualities. For Picquet, her mother's prayers stand in for the missing mother. That mother materializes in dreams and sustains Picquet in reality. Her emphasis on the maternal bond that remains in spite of the physical severing is a discursive maneuver to promote her self-representational agenda, which is to increase the sales of her narrative in order to raise money to buy her mother's freedom. Thus, the intangible dream becomes the tangible reality: the boon of freedom.

Extraliterary forms of prayer, song, and humor spiritually sustained slave women to assert agency, empowerment, and freedom. When Picquet is troubled by her position as Williams's mistress and fears divine retribution for her sins, Williams entreats her that as long as she maintains her fidelity to him God would not hold her responsible. With more theological perception than Williams suspects, Picquet dismisses his entreaty and "begin[s] then to pray that he might die, so that I might get religion; and then I promise the Lord one night, faithful, in prayer, if he would just take him out of the way, I'd get religion and be true to Him as long as I lived" (59). Soon after this prayer Williams contracts a lingering illness that proves fatal. Picquet's confidence in the power of prayer supersedes her fear of Williams's wrath. She maintains the very faithfulness and fidelity insisted on by Williams, only she is faithful to herself and her beliefs, not to him. Even though she is sympathetic to Williams's plight, she never regrets praying for his death, and instead prays for his redemption before death. For Picquet freedom for the soul through religious conversion is only possible with physical freedom from slavery. It is significant to note that her desire for freedom is articulated in the context of spirituality.

Picquet's emphasis on redemption places the narrative in the tradition of spiritual narratives. In addition to her journey to freedom, Picquet narrates her journey to religious conversion. At Williams's death, Picquet and her children were emancipated, and around 1847 she moved to Cincinnati, Ohio, where she married Henry Picquet in September 1850 at the Zion Baptist Church. The officiating minister was the Reverend Wallace Shelton. Louisa Picquet's religious conversion came as a result of attending a meeting at Zion Baptist Church, where Shelton pastored. Zion Baptist, the second oldest African American church in Cincinnati, and Shelton took a firm anti-slavery stance in which Picquet found solace. When Mattison inquires if Zion communed with slaveholders, she firmly replies, "*No sir; they will not.* The Union Baptist Church does. When white ministers come from the South, they let them break the bread of Communion; but in our church, if they come there, they don't do it, unless they come with a lie in their mouth. . . . No slaveholder, or apologist for slavery, can preach in that church; that was the foundation when they first started" (emphasis in original, 65). Zion's abolitionist policy informed and sustained Picquet's spirituality. Zion nurtured a culture of resistance in which Picquet eagerly participated. The members risked their lives for freedom, not only for themselves, for others as well. Perhaps because this image does not fit his agenda Mattison fails to probe the fact that Picquet was actively involved in the Underground Railroad, hiding in her home from authorities fugitive slaves. She was a personal friend of Levi Coffin, one of the foremost Underground Railroad agents, and received his endorsement for her fundraising mission at the outset. As a result of the 1850 Fugitive Slave Act, which required citizens to assist in the recapture of escaped slaves, church services offered forums to warn fugitives and disseminate information. Picquet's description of this antislavery activity amounts to her chronicle of African Americans performing their civic duties; as one hundred years later Martin Luther King Jr. declared, they had "a moral responsibility to disobey unjust laws" (1857).

Picquet's narrative demonstrates the relationship between spirituality and freedom. Yolanda Pierce contends, "The courage and the liberty to speak, preach, evangelize, and witness in word and in letter are at the heart of the sanctification experience" (93). When the mental and emotional strain of her mother's enslavement overwhelms Picquet—what she calls a "troubling" in her spirit—prayer and her commitment to follow Christ provide relief and inspire action. She declares, "I prayed hard that night. . . . And the moment I believe that the Lord would relieve me, the burden went right off; and I felt as light as if I was right up in the air" (64). After this conversion Picquet begins to search in earnest for her mother and work to free her. Her description mirrors other descriptions of sanctification experience—the religious experience in which a person feels consecration and possession by God and sometimes includes speaking in tongues as glossolalia (unknown language)—about which Pierce writes. Yet the promise of heaven in the afterlife does not preclude Picquet from striving for what Douglass called "the heaven of freedom" on earth (113). Although Picquet recognizes her conversion and adherence to Christianity will ensure reunion with her mother after death, the prospect of eternal reunion does not negate the desire for freedom and meeting her mother in this life. "Sanctification's promise," Pierce maintains, "is not located in some future time and place, but in the now" (98). The belief of freedom in eternity and freedom from sin inspires the determination for freedom on earth. Consequently, unlike traditional spiritual narratives that "[foreswear] the temporal to revere the eternal," in Picquet's text the temporal is not dismissed in favor of the eternal (Moody 104–05). The temporal is made possible because of the eternal. In this instance, Black feminist orality, manifested in prayer and faith, empowers Picquet to achieve freedom for her mother, her children, and herself. Thus Picquet "speaks in tongues" to both readers interested in her religious conversion and those who understand that physical liberation is necessary for and sustains spiritual redemption.

The Story of Mattie J. Jackson (1866)

Mattie Jane Jackson was nineteen when she brought her eleven-year-old half-brother to Lawrence, Massachusetts to live with his father (once known as George Brown, but after escaping from slavery, was known as John G. Thompson), and stepmother, Lucy Susan Prophet Schuyler Thompson. Thompson had recently lost her last child, a Civil War soldier, and no doubt was more than curious about meeting her new husband's eldest surviving stepdaughter. In 1866, Jackson, a nonliterate twenty-year-old ex-slave woman, related her slave experiences to her stepmother who, as the title page informs us, went by the title Dr. L. S. Thompson. The resultant narrative can be viewed as these women's act of bonding—each was looking for something—Jackson for her father and trying to finish her education, Thompson to regain a family. The primary purpose of publishing the narrative was to raise funds for Jackson's education. Evidence shows she was able to finish her education and move back home to St. Louis, rejoining her mother, Ellen, and her mother's third husband, Sam Adams. The 1870 Census lists the Adams's household as including Mattie (called Martha) and the missing Jackson sister Hester. Ellen Adams appears in the 1880 census with her married daughter "Mattie Dyer."[12]

Jackson (sometimes she appears in the public record as Martha) in 1869 married William Reed Dyer, a native of Warrenton, Missouri, who was employed as a porter on steamboats plying the Mississippi River.[13] Eventually, they moved into their own home in the city of St. Louis. Out of their eight children, only four boys and a girl reached maturity. Her eldest son was William Henry Dyer. He worked as an elevator operator at the St. Louis City Hall and died before he was forty, leaving a widow and three children.

Jackson remembered Lucy Thompson and named one son after her stepmother's last surviving child: Arthur Thomas Dyer became a cook on a Pullman dining car and lived in Denver and Chicago. Married twice, Arthur had a son named for his father by his first wife. Another son, Albert L. Dyer, went to Idaho and died young. Jackson's youngest surviving child, Warren Charles Dyer who, despite a lifetime spent working on factory assembly lines, held U.S Patent #1,437,296 for a "bathing appliance," essentially a back scrubber. Warren died in St. Louis in 1945. Her only daughter, Edith, married an oil field worker named Milton C. Slaughter and lived in Alton, Illinois, just upriver from St. Louis, where she ran a boardinghouse. They soon separated, and Edith, employed as a seamstress and domestic, moved back to St. Louis, dying of tuberculosis at a young age.

There were four grandchildren, two of whom served in World War I. A great-grandson, after being rebuffed in repeated attempts to enlist in the Marines after Pearl Harbor, subsequently served in the United States Army during World War II. Marrying twice, his only child by his first marriage was the last direct descendant of Mattie Jackson. Willetta Dyer Reed, a thirty-seven-year-old administrator for the Census Bureau, known as a poet, community activist, gourmet cook and caterer, died childless in Los Angeles in 1981.[14]

Through Jackson's narrative, we see slavery in St. Louis, just before the end of the Civil War. Her description of the taking of Camp Jackson by Union soldiers, for instance, provides a unique perspective of military action from an enslaved woman's point of view, a perspective that was at odds with her slave mistress's view. "I told my mistress that the Union soldiers were coming to take the camp," Jackson states (108). "She replied that it was false, that it was General Kelly [*sic*] coming to reinforce Gen. Foster. In a few moments the alarm was heard. I told Mrs. L. the Unionist had fired upon the rebels. She replied it was only the salute of Gen. Kelley [*sic*]. At night her husband came home with the news that Camp Jackson was taken and all the soldiers prisoners" (108). She continues, "there was not a word passed that escaped our listening ears. My mother and myself could read enough to make out the news in the papers. The Union soldiers took much delight in tossing a paper over the fence to us. It aggravated my mistress very much. My mother used to sit up nights and read to keep posted about the war" (108). Not only is Jackson better informed than her mistress, she has a more realistic outlook on the war than Mrs. Lewis as well. This battle was the first major Civil War action in Missouri and was the only combat operation that took place within the boundaries of St. Louis.[15] Jackson offers a historical narrative from the vantage point of enslaved Black women and foregrounds their political consciousness. Moreover, her account suggests various levels of literacy among slaves and that enslaved African Americans were more literate and informed than what has been previously thought.

Jackson begins the narrative with a description of her paternal heritage and her parents' marriage and forced separation due to slavery. Jackson tells of her family's multiple attempts to escape and eventual recapture. The narrative concentrates on the machinations Jackson and her family endure to obtain freedom. Both Jackson and Thompson assume positions as authors of the text through discursive means—Thompson as the actual literate writer, and Jackson through the orality expressed in her critique of slavery and slave mistresses and her projection of a virtuous young woman striving for self-improvement and personal growth.

Thompson's authorship is plainly stated on the title page, "Written and Arranged by Dr. L. S. Thompson (formerly Mrs. Schuyler,) as given by

Mattie." In addition to the authority Thompson claims through literacy, conveyed with the phrase "written and arranged by," she assumes added credibility and authority as a professional with the title of doctor and use of initials. The formality indicated through the initials is compounded by the parenthetical note, "formerly Mrs. Schuyler." First, the phrase (printed in small type) is the only indication of Thompson's gender, and thus disrupts the reader's assumption that the author is male. Second, the title, "Mrs.," signifies respectability. The transition from "Mrs." to "Dr." suggests the narrative is produced by an upwardly mobile, respectable, educated woman who, the reader later learns, is also African American. Joycelyn Moody contends, "*The Story of Mattie J. Jackson* is indeed a narrative that 'tests' readers' amenability to accepting the discursive authority of a nineteenth-century black woman" (124).

Jackson's stepmother was herself a formidable woman. Born Lucy Susan Prophet in the western Massachusetts town of Rutland, she was the daughter of a family of African Americans and Native Americans of the Pequod tribe who inhabited the Connecticut River valley. Evidence suggests she learned to read and write in the common schools of her hometown where she earned her title of "Doctor" due to her knowledge of herbal remedies used for medical purposes. She moved to Worcester, Massachusetts, and, sometime around 1837, married the Reverend Peter Schuyler, originally from Albany, New York, and an itinerant preacher in the African Methodist Episcopal Church. He joined her medical practice, and was known as an "Indian Doctor."[16]

Of their seven children, only two survived their father, who died circa 1850, Rodney J., about aged eleven, and Arthur Thomas, about aged three. Rodney Schuyler evidently did not long survive his father, and Lucy was soon left alone with her youngest son. This situation did not stop her from being involved in antislavery activity in and around the city of Worcester, and subsequently in the city of Lawrence, Massachusetts, where they moved circa 1855. In 1857, when Lewis Sweet brought his wife, child and slave woman Betty from Tennessee to Lawrence, Lucy Schuyler engaged a local attorney to serve a writ of habeas corpus on Betty, who had allegedly expressed a desire to stay in the free North. The Sweets also engaged local counsel and the matter was brought before Chief Justice Lemuel Shaw, who declared that Betty, having been brought into a free state, was herself free;

and as a free woman, if she wished to return to Tennessee with the Sweets, she could do so as a free woman.

During this time Dr. Schuyler met an escaped slave from St. Louis, where he had been known as George Brown. As George Brown, he had married Ellen Turner Jackson, thus becoming stepfather to Mattie Jackson and her youngest sister Hester (or Esther), but after the birth of their son George, Jr., Brown escaped from slavery, making his way to Massachusetts, where he changed his name to John G. Thompson. He was working as a barber in a local hotel when he married Dr. Schuyler in 1860, and settled into a house at 292 Common Street in Lawrence. For some time, she advertised her treatments and medicines in the local newspapers.[17]

With the organization of the 54th Massachusetts Infantry (Colored) in 1863, Arthur T. Schuyler—not yet sixteen years of age—falsified his age and enlisted in Company C on March 4, 1863. He served through the war, fighting at the battle of Fort Wagner (depicted in the film *Glory*), among other places. When he returned home in September of 1865, he was dying from tuberculosis, which took his life the following April. He was just eighteen years old.[18]

During this period John Thompson discovered that his son George, whom he had last seen in St. Louis years before, was alive and well. It was doubtless with the desire to reconstitute a family unit that the Thompsons sent word to Ellen Turner Adams of their whereabouts and to send the eleven-year-old boy to Massachusetts, with his big sister Mattie as chaperone.

In her narrative Mattie Jackson's discursive authority surpasses Lucy Thompson's in narrative agency and rhetorical control. Although Jackson cannot write, both she and Thompson reiterate several times that Jackson can read and has produced the narrative to finance her continued education. Jackson "advises all, young, middle age or old, in a free country to learn to read and write . . . Manage your own secrets, and divulge them by the silent language of your own pen" (119). The narrative acts as a vehicle by which Jackson can follow her own advice to control and construct her representation. In addition to Moody's suggestion that "[t]he narrative emphasis of *The Story* is less on the skills Jackson lacks than on those she virtuously pursues" (107), the narrative underscores the skill of orality Jackson already possesses and sustains the text through the episodes of abuse she chooses to relate and how she relates them.

Similar to Sylvia Dubois, Mattie Jackson performed a physical act that signaled the end of her acceptance of abuse. Both Dubois's and Jackson's acts are reminiscent of Frederick Douglass's fight with Mr. Covey.[19] Jackson shows her resistance to physical abuse in the proceeding passage:

> One evening, after I had attended to my usual duties, and I supposed all was complete, [Mrs. Lewis], in a terrible range [*sic*], declared I should be punished that night. I did not know the cause, neither did she. She went immediately and selected a switch. She placed it in the corner of the room to await the return of her husband at night for him to whip me. As I was not pleased with the idea of a whipping, I bent the switch in the shape of a W, which is the first letter of his name. (109–10)

Jackson's switch bending is a speech act in which she subverts both the mistress's and master's authorities. First, by destroying the switch, the mistress is undermined in her attempt to have Jackson whipped. Then, by specifically creating the letter W, she signifies that the switch is intended for Mr. Lewis. Furthermore, Jackson's recognition of the significance of the W implies her realization that an inverted W is an M, which is the first letter of her name; and therefore indicates the power reversal involved in her assertion of agency. This is, then, a dual signifying act that accentuates Jackson's physical and rhetorical authority. She effectively puts her signature on this discursive and physical act of resistance. In slavery, then, Jackson's literacy (however marginal) is a vehicle for knowledge and communication for both obtaining freedom and asserting physical autonomy.

The foundation of Jackson's physical and rhetorical resistance, and thus her Black feminist orality, does not emerge from a vacuum but is the example of her mother's unrelenting desire for freedom and demands for justice and equality. In narrated instance after instance, Ellen Turner Jackson heroically attempts escapes and protects her children, physically and with cunning manipulation. She reads newspapers learning the latest military events and public policy changes, actions for which she gains Mr. Lewis's enmity: "He hated my mother in consequence for her desire for freedom, and her endeavors to teach her children the right way as far as her ability would allow. He also held charge against her for reading the papers and understanding political affairs" (113). Although Jackson holds titular ownership, the narrative could just as easily be titled "The Story of Ellen Turner Jackson." In fact the initial impetus for publication is Ellen's, not Jackson's. "I had previously told my step-mother my story," Jackson explains, "and how often my own mother had wished she could have it published" (125). Ellen Turner Jackson's paradigmatic struggles reflect the pain and burdens many mothers experience and from which they strive to shield their children. "When our children are involved," Blanche Radford Curry declares, "the suffering and injustices that racism places on them are often heavier for mothers to bear than the agony and burdens of racism on ourselves" (132). Mattie Jackson's courage to speak, fight, and write is maternally inspired. Her mothers (Ellen Turner Jackson and Lucy Schuyler Thompson) are living examples who speak in multiple forms of resistance and authority. Their lived experiences provide Mattie Jackson with "critical understandings," which Suzanne C. Carothers identifies as daily living performance that teaches "such things as achieving independence, taking on responsibility, feeling confident," fighting for freedom, human dignity, and equality (237). In short, Mattie Jackson's narrative demonstrates that her skillful "speaking in tongues" comes out of the theory and practice performances exemplified in her mothers' lives.

Sylvia Dubois (Now 116 Years Old), A Biography of the Slave Who Whipped Her Mistress and Gained Her Freedom (1883)

During most of the nineteenth century, Sylvia Dubois (pronounced "Doo-Boyce") was notorious on central New Jersey's Sourland Mountain as a hard-drinking, fist-fighting barfly: stocky and muscular, loud and profane, she brooked opposition from no one, and, evidence suggests, everyone knew it.[20] Children ran from her; her adult neighbors tended to give her a wide berth, even in her old age. She was a tough woman who once owned and operated an unlicensed tavern where drunkenness and gambling, as well as other nefarious activities, were alleged to have occurred; and as an old woman, she walked the dusty roads going to market in the small Jersey crossroad market towns of Wertsville and Flagtown and Blawenberg, selling produce and other truck goods from her small farm until her advanced years.

The narrative of Sylvia Dubois was recorded by Dr. Cornelius Wilson Larison in 1883, when she was said to be 116 years old. However, since Dubois's two youngest daughters Elizabeth (1825) and Rachel (1827) were born when she would have been around sixty years old, it is not unreasonable to suspect that Dubois was stretching the truth in giving her age to Dr. Larison. Although it seems likely she was not as old as Larsion represented, Dubois's significantly advanced age was unmistakable.[21] Larison, a graduate of what is now Bucknell University, started out as a country schoolteacher before qualifying as a physician; he continued his interest in education, organizing the Academy of Arts and Sciences at Ringoes, New Jersey. Dr. Larison was a man of many interests and was well known as an aficionado of local history. He interviewed Dubois as part of his desire to record the history of his "native county" that included "the doings of the great and the small, the rich and the poor, the proud and the humble, the exalted and the abject, the virtuous and the vicious, the frugal and the squalid" (181). For Larison, Dubois fell into the second category of each of these pairs.

Dubois was born into slavery on New Jersey's Sourland Mountain sometime between 1768 and 1789. Her mother purchased her and her children's freedom with a loan from Dominicus Dubois when Sylvia was only two years old. Unfortunately, when her mother failed to repay the loan, she and her children became Dubois's slaves. In order to regain their freedom, she sought work outside of Great Bend, Pennsylvania, where she left her children with Dominicus Dubois, who ran both a tavern and a ferry. Left without her mother's protection, young Sylvia suffered tremendous abuse from her mistress, Mrs. Elizabeth Scudder Dubois, who used a variety of tools to abuse the young girl. After enduring years of abuse, Sylvia retaliated with her fists to triumph over Mrs. Dubois.

Although the title of the narrative states that it was this altercation that led to her freedom, Sylvia's manumission may have occurred because of her interaction with Dominicus Dubois, not her dealings with his wife. Sylvia gave birth to a daughter she named Judith, sometime in either 1806 or 1807. Historian Marc Mappen suggests that Dominicus Dubois was the father of the child, which would easily explain Elizabeth Dubois's animosity toward Sylvia. Sylvia's testimony supports this suspicion. She states, "I tried to please him, and he tried to please me; and we got along together pretty well" (155). Mappen writes, "It occurs to the modern reader that [Dominicus] Dubois had a sexual relationship with Sylvia Dubois, which would explain his leniency, his wife's savagery and perhaps even the child that suddenly appears in the narrative" (51). This notion increases the complexity of Sylvia's act of resistance. Her actions intimate that not only did she refuse to accept Elizabeth's abuse, she may have also rejected the secondary position Dominicus had assigned her.

As remarkable as her physical resistance was, Sylvia Dubois's survival in freedom was more remarkable. According to her narrative, the fight with her mistress prompted Dubois's master to manumit her and force her to leave the tavern he owned and in which she worked. Her only option was to walk, carrying her baby daughter, Judith, from "Great Bend on the Susquehanna" (just south of the New York–Pennsylvania state line at Binghamton) back to the Sourlands—a distance of 165 miles traveling contemporary highways and, without roads, a much more difficult expanse to cover in the early nineteenth century. She recounts, "sometimes I didn't see a person for half a day; sometimes I didn't get half enough to eat, and never had any bed to sleep in; I just slept anywhere. My baby was about a year and a half old, and I had to carry it all the way. The wood was full of panthers, bears, wildcats, and wolves; I often saw 'em in the daytime, and always heard 'em howling in the night" (166).[22] On her journey, she repelled a white man who demanded to know who she belonged to and where she was going. Unequivocally, Dubois responded, "I'm no man's nigger—I belong to God—I belong to no man . . . I'm free. I go where I please" (167). Then, carefully setting her baby down, she raised her fists and prepared to fight. This incident is indicative of her unwavering courage and confidence in the power of her voice and body to defend herself and her child.

When she returned to New Jersey, Dubois worked for a time as a domestic in the nearby town of Princeton, particularly for the wealthy Tulane family for whom Tulane University is named. She subsequently returned to Sourland Mountain where she worked with her maternal grandfather, Harry "Put" Compton, a Revolutionary War veteran who owned property on the mountain at a crossroads called Cedar Summit at the intersection of two market routes. Around 1812, Compton opened "Put's Old House," or "Put's Tavern," an unlicensed taproom notorious for nefarious and illegal activity, including cockfighting and gambling.[23] After Compton grew too old and feeble to operate the establishment, Sylvia Dubois moved with her two youngest daughters to Put's Tavern, where she ran the establishment, dealing with both the law (as personified by the Hunterdon County Sheriff's Office, the tax assessor of Amwell Township, and the county court in Flemington), and her neighbors (those "damned democrats"), who she suspected burned down the tavern sometime around 1841, leaving her virtually destitute.

Dubois died in 1888; however, she did not perish as a result of the devastating "Great Blizzard of 1888," which in two days dumped an immense amount of snow on the Atlantic Seaboard from Canada south to Philadelphia, although contemporary reports attributed her death due to this event.[24] She survived the blizzard and lived two more months as reported in the following:

> Sylvia Dubois is at last really dead. So, at least, the *Hopewell Herald* announces. She died last Sunday morning [May 27, 1888] at her residence on Sourland Mountain, not of old age but of erysipelatous [*sic*] inflammation; aged 122. She leaves two daughters, respectively 94 and 73 years old. Her burial was from the African church, on the mountain; Rev. W. H. Pitman conducting the exercises.[25]

As with other dictated narratives, the authorship of the text is complicated by the roles of the amanuensis and ex-slave. In the case of Sylvia Dubois's narrative, authorship is even more complex because Larison writes the narrative following the rules of spelling advocated by the Committee on the Reform of English Spelling. The purpose of this reform movement was to modify written English so that the written text would reflect the sound of its oral manifestation. *Speaking Lives* includes the original and a translation into standard English. According to Larison, this system of phonetic spelling conveys Dubois's voice and intentions more clearly than standard English spelling. Larison's intervention with the phonetic spelling stands between Dubois and the reader. He insists the narrative was recorded in this manner to represent Dubois's speech and character more fully. However, the awkwardness of the spelling contributed to the dismissal of the narrative by scholars for many years, thereby, rendering Dubois mute. Yet the narrative exemplifies Black feminist orality through Dubois's unique command of language in spite of Larison's attempt at standardization.

Larison's questions suggest he intended to record a narrative that documented folk life—customs, practices, foodways, entertainment—among
slaves in New Jersey, much in the same way that many narratives collected in
the 1930s by interviewers of the Works Progress Administration were constructed. This narrative construction reveals interviewers were unconcerned
with the ex-slave's person, her or his personal feelings, perceptions, and reac-
tions to her or his experiences. However, Dubois undermines Larison's intentions and expresses her own concerns. For instance, even though he
seemingly wants to truncate discussions of injustice and violence by local
whites toward the African American population, Dubois repeatedly indicts
"them damned democrats" for setting fire to her home and stealing her property. She acknowledges that those without money receive no justice; the
entire legal system ignores the poor and disenfranchised. Her descriptions of
beatings suffered by Blacks leave powerful images that even Larison cannot
dismiss. She reiterates, "My God, how they licked 'em—cut the hide all in
gashes" (171). Despite her willingness to engage in physical confrontation,
Dubois condemns unjust violence. She exposes the brutality against enslaved
and free people of color in the *North* and counters myths about northern
brotherly love and Christian charity. Her return to this subject, even when it
seems Larison would like to move on, suggests another example of "speaking
in tongues" in which Dubois speaks around the impediment of Larison and
insists on being heard.

By her own testimony and Larison's narration of local lore, Sylvia
Dubois is a folk hero in the tradition of "bad men" and "bad women" in
African America folklore. She relates her experiences in humorous language
that displays the ability of slave women to view and represent past experiences with wit and levity. Rather than detract from the seriousness of the situation, this humorous attitude reinforces their agency and triumph.
Through the use of humor, Dubois controls the construction of the narrative
and affects the reader's response to it. Although white writers like Harriet
Beecher Stowe and Mark Twain depict humorous situations involving slave
women, they fail to portray humor that solicits readers' identification with
these women.[26] Unfortunately, the absurdity of these depictions ridicule
slave women and diminish their humanity. Contrarily, Dubois's narrative
humor substantiates her authority and celebrates resistance. Her narrative

corroborates Michele Najilis's observation that "being able to laugh at one's tragedies presupposes the formation of a pretty solid identity."[27] Thus, humorous representations of slave experience by former slave women demonstrate Black women's complex identities and allow readers to laugh with, instead of at, Black women.

ORALITY, AUTHORITY, AND AUTHORSHIP

Despite Picquet's, Jackson's, and Dubois's empowerment through oral resistance, the use of orality is problematized by the fact that *Louisa Picquet, The Story of Mattie J. Jackson*, and *Silvia Dubois* are ultimately written by the amanuenses, Mattison, Thompson, and Larison. Mark Reinhardt queries, "When assessing the politics and legacy of fugitive slave cases, what weight should be given to the matters of slave agency and voice?" (85).[28] Although none of these women was a fugitive slave at the time their narratives were recorded, this is a crucial question contemporary readers must not dismiss in favor of literary recovery and historical revisionism. In *Louisa Picquet*, Picquet's voice gets lost or silenced in the second half of the narrative. It is Mattison who directs the reader's attention to the proceeding events in Picquet's life and, although there are some instances related in Picquet's voice, for the most part Mattison's narrative voice is privileged over hers. Similarly, in the description of the events at and patrons of Put's Tavern in his "Gleanings," Larison sits in moral judgment of Dubois, clearly evincing his class and racial biases.

Yet as mediators Mattison, Larison, and Thompson employed differing approaches that are evident in the narratives and that, alternately, violate or nurture the ex-slave woman's voice. When Picquet discusses the letters she and her mother exchanged Mattison consistently undermines her claims to literacy with parenthetical asides. For instance, Picquet states, "I wrote a letter," and in parentheses Mattison records, "got one written" (66). Although we may never know the extent of Picquet's literacy, historical evidence proves her writing skills were sufficient to complete legal documents. In her husband's attempts to get his Army pension, she wrote statements and letters and signed his name, as he was nonliterate. These documents confused the Washington bureaucrats, who noted, "Well, he says he's illiterate, and signs with an 'X,' but here's this letter he wrote and signed with his full name! What's up with this?"[29] Conversely, although Larison uses phonetic spelling, he maintains the integrity of Dubois's voice. He consistently addresses her respectfully as Mrs. Dubois and avoids writing dialect but faithfully (and phonetically) relates the colloquialisms and idioms she uses. Thompson, on the other hand, not only writes the narrative in Jackson's first-person voice, she supports Jackson's current literacy skills and the educational enterprise for which the narrative is produced. The narrative proper ends with Jackson's assertion, "When I complete my education, if my life is spared, I shall endeavor to publish further details of our history in another volume from my own pen" (127). Jackson's goal "to publish further details of *our* history" suggests she aims to write not just another autobiography—she plans to be the mediating voice for others as well. Clearly the Jackson-Thompson team is more supportive and equitable than the Picquet-Mattison and Dubois-Larison dyads. Of Jackson and Thompson, Moody contends, "The amanuensis-author and her narrator-subject may signal different socioeconomic classes, but their purposes, like their synchronous 'voices' derive from their common race, religion, and gender and converge for a common sacred good" (124). Contrarily, *Louisa Picquet* demonstrates Mattison's intentions were at odds with Picquet's subjective purposes. Mattison's position as privileged white male pervades his antislavery views to the extent that he becomes more than mediator; he is voyeur to Picquet's Black woman's life and body.

This dilemma presents itself in other narratives written by amanuenses and has caused the texts to be ignored as part of African American literary tradition.[30] Narratives recorded by interviewers inherently raise questions around the narrator's voice and textual interests, particularly when we consider the racial and gendered dynamics between interviewer and interviewee. As Sharon Ann Musher points out, these dynamics not only affect how narrators respond to questions, they can determine what questions are asked in the first place.[31] Certainly Mattison's prurient questions reflect his privileged racial and gender status in relation to Picquet. Yet Picquet's responses anticipate Gloria Anzaldua's "Third World Woman['s]" declaration, "We are done being cushions for your projected fears. We are tired of being your sacrificial lambs and scapegoats" (318). In spite of Mattison's voyeuristic mediation, Picquet wrests narrative agency from him to authorize her text in which her experiences are not the scapegoat for Mattison's sexual fantasy but are subjective representations of the struggles and triumphs, pains and joys of her life. Even as Mattison and Larison, either purposefully or mistakenly, tried to misrepresent them, Picquet and Dubois rhetorically seized their texts and left indelible marks inscribed upon the minds of successive readers.

Marginal literacy forced these women to rely on amanuenses to write their narratives. Marginal literacy did not force them to accept objectification. Notwithstanding their literacy skills, Picquet's, Jackson's, and Dubois's mediated voices hold the power of resistant subjects determinedly maintaining the integrity of themselves and their families. They speak to us almost one hundred and fifty years later about not just Black slave women's subjugation. In using orality, they speak of Black women's multiple agentive means to control their lives and representations, especially when those representations are mediated. These narratives expand the breadth of writings by African American women. These voices, raised for freedom and education, demand our attention without prejudice or preference for written literacy. In speaking, these women author their personal narratives to right injustice and advance knowledge and freedom.

NOTES

Excerpts of this introduction were previously published in DoVeanna Fulton's *Speaking Power: Black Feminist Orality in Women's Narratives of Slavery* and her encyclopedia entry "Spirituals."

1. Critic John Ernest maintains, "Most students interested in American literary history, then, and many of their teachers, will encounter fewer than a handful of narratives that will represent a genre that includes an estimated 6,000 texts—including books, periodical publications, and oral histories and interviews" (218).

2. See Fulton (2–19).

3. The original publication of *Silvia Dubois* was phonetically written and produced with diacritical symbols. For this reason, the original text included in this volume is a facsimile of the original publication. The editors have standardized the spelling of Sylvia when used, except in the title of the narrative.

4. In the preface to the pioneering volume *The Books of American Negro Spirituals,* James Weldon Johnson vehemently argues for the uniqueness of Spirituals that enslaved Africans in America developed. Johnson emphatically states, "The Spirituals are purely and solely the creation of the American Negro" (50).

5. Arnold Shaw enumerates these elements in his book *Black Popular Music* (9–10).

6. In her unprecedented study of slave narratives, *The Slave Narrative,* Marion Wilson Starling documents 6,006 slave narratives published separately, in anthologies, and in antislavery newspapers and periodicals. See Starling (339–50).

7. Evidence suggests Harriet Jacobs first considered allowing Harriet Beecher Stowe, author of *Uncle Tom's Cabin,* to write her story. Regrettably, Stowe revealed Jacobs's personal information to her employer and thus violated Jacobs's confidence. Following this circumstance Jacobs decided to write her own narrative and later chose Lydia Maria Child as editor. See Yellin (119–40). Unfortunately, for almost a century Child was thought to be the writer of *Incidents* and Jacobs was not known or acknowledged as the author.

8. Fulton argues that Jacobs's inclusion of her grandmother's oral history is a form of orality that is significant to her representation of Black women in *Incidents.* See Fulton (30–32).

9. The original publication of Piquet's narrative includes two distinctly different subtitles. The complete title on the cover page is *Louisa Picquet, The Octoroon: A Tale of Southern Slave Life.* The inside title page reads: *Louisa Picquet, The Octoroon; or the Inside Views of Southern Domestic Life.* This subtitle underscores the prurient nature of Mattison's interest in Picquet's experience.

10. Although both Mattison and Picquet try to link Randolph to the illustrious Randolphs of Virginia, this branch of the family originated in Monmouth County, New Jersey, and went South after the end of the American Revolution. See Christian and Randolph (84).

11. Pension Records for Henry Picquet, Private, Company K, 42nd United States Colored Troops, National Archives, Washington, D.C.

12. 1870 Federal Census, St. Louis Township, St. Louis County, Missouri, Sheet No. 32, lines 15–18. 1880 Federal Census, 3rd Ward, City of St. Louis, Enumeration District 148, Sheet No. 7, lines 30–37.

13. The marriage certificate found in the St. Louis County Marriage Records (14:45) reads:

> This certifies that Read Dyer [*sic*] of the county of St. Louis in the state of Missouri and Martha Jackson of the county of St. Louis in the state of Missouri were by me joined together in holy matrimony on the twenty-seventh day of July in the year of Our Lord one thousand eight hundred and sixty-nine. In presence of [blank]
>
> Gary Mathis, pastor M. E. Zion Church.

Filed and recorded August 14th 1869—Julius Conrad, Recorder.

14. The information on the Dyer family found in the previous paragraphs were compiled from various sources, including census enumeration of population for the city of St. Louis for 1870, 1880 and 1900; death certificates issued by the Missouri Department of Health in Jefferson City, Missouri, for the following:

"Ester" Diggs, died June 20, 1920, certificate no. 15994

Edith Dyer, died December 30, 1915, certificate no. 38652

Warren Dyer, died July 20, 1945, certificate no. 21859

The probate records of the estate of William Reed Dyer, filed in St. Charles County Probate Court, April 30, 1913 (courtesy of St. Charles Historical Society, St. Charles, MO). Information on Willetta Reed Dyer can be found at "Community Organizer Dies," Los Angeles Sentinel, February 12, 1981, p. A–5.

15. See McPherson (290–94) and "Civil War History in St. Louis: The Gateway to the West Played a Pivotal Role in the Clash."

16. See "Another Slave Case in Boston."

17. Information on Dr. Lucy S. Thompson compiled from information supplied by Louise Sandberg, of the Special Collections Room of the Lawrence Public Library, Lawrence, Massachusetts, Barbara Brown, Collections Manager, Lawrence History Center, Lawrence, Massachusetts, and Damarys Ramos, Senior Clerk, City of Lawrence, Lawrence, Massachusetts.

18. See Massachusetts Adjutant General, Emilio, and Massachusetts Archives.

19. In his 1845 *Narrative of the Life of Frederick Douglass,* it is following his physical defeat of his master, Mr. Covey, that Douglass *feels* free and then initiates his escape. This triumph "rekindled the few expiring embers of freedom, and revived within me a sense of my own manhood" (113). Although Dubois's act mirrors Douglass's, physical combat was not a commonly pursued route to freedom for slave women. Jackson's switch-bending act is more discursive and symbolic than either Dubois's or Douglass's acts.

20. Sourland "Mountain" is a heavily wooded and rocky volcanic ridge only about six hundred feet above sea level; it is called "Mountain" as it rises steeply from the flat land surrounding it, so that it looms in the distance from such neighboring towns as Princeton, Flemington, and Lambertville. For more on the Mountain, its people, and its past see Luce.

21. Jared Lobdell's archival investigations call into question Larison's confirmation of Dubois's assertion that she was born two days after Richard Compton, whose birth was documented in the Compton family Bible. However, Lobdell's results are as inconclusive as Larison's are questionable. For example, in trying to calculate Dubois's age, Lobdell speculates, "it might be argued, she was ten years old when

Monmouth was fought, and that, too, would make her birth date fall in late 1767 or early 1768. This, however, is not entirely independent evidence, since the same person who told her that Richard Compton was born in 1768 could well have told her that the Battle of Monmouth was fought in 1778" (8). Not only is Lobdell's speculation merely a guess, it conveys his consistent refusal to credit Dubois with a trustworthy historical memory.

22. This incident is validated by the obituary of Judith—or Mrs. Judith Roberts, as she later became known—published in the Princeton *Press,* January 17, 1891: "When quite an infant her mother brought her from Great Bend on the Susquehanna, walking nearly all the journey (with the exception of a lift upon a raft of those days,) with her little one in her arms." The story is also corroborated by successive census returns that put Judith's year of birth around 1806 or 1807 and place of birth as Pennsylvania. Her life stands in contrast to that of her mother and sisters. For example, census returns show she was literate whereas her mother and siblings were not and, instead of living a rowdy life on Sourland Mountain, Judith married early to Charles Roberts, "a very respectable man," by whom she had at least six children. She lived in a small two-story home on John Street in Princeton's African American community—less than ten miles from Put's Tavern, but a world away in daily habits. Judith Roberts was described as "a remarkable woman, shrewd and sensible, and having a very retentive memory." Unfortunately, Judith did not have someone like C. W. Larison to record her story.

23. Hunterdon County property records substantiate Harry Compton's ownership of the property Dubois mentions: Philip Servis and Mary, his wife of Hopewell Township, Hunterdon [now Mercer] County, NJ to Harry Compton, "a black man" of [now East] Amwell Township, Hunterdon County, NJ, a parcel of land situated in Amwell Township, dated February 28, 1812, recorded April 12, 1816, Hunterdon County Deed Book 24:322; Abraham Kise and Hannah his wife of Montgomery Township, Somerset County, NJ to Harry Compton, "a free black man," of [now East] Amwell Township, Hunterdon County, NJ, a contiguous parcel of land in Amwell Township, dated [August 27,] 1813, recorded April 12, 1816, Hunterdon County Deed Book 24:323.

24. See newspaper articles in *Hunterdon County Democrat,* March 27, 1888.

25. This obituary appears in the Princeton, New Jersey *Press,* June 2, 1888.

26. In her novel, *Uncle Tom's Cabin* Harriet Beecher Stowe depicts Aunt Chloe as a sassy Black woman whose speech is humorous because it imitates whites even as it is in dialect. Similarly, Twain's short story "A True Story" features Aunt Rachel, whose quips and wit are underscored by her dialect. For more of Stowe's and Twain's depictions of humorous Black women see Mullen (255) and Fulton (53–54).

27. See Margaret Randall's *Sandino's Daughters Revisited* (64).

28. We thank Joycelyn Moody for pointing us to both Mark Reinhardt's essay and Sharon Ann Musher's article and presenting a thoroughly insightful response to not only this essay but all those presented at the "Speaking Power, Writing Past Pain in U.S. Black Women's Autobiographies" session at the MESEA conference, Pamplona, Spain, 2006.

29. This circumstance is detailed in "Deposition of Henry Picquet, dated 27 June 1887, in Pension Records of Henry Picquet, late Unassigned Troops, 42nd United States Colored Troops, National Archives." Henry Picquet answers the question: "When did you first make an application for a pension and are you literate," by saying, " . . . I cannot read much and cannot write at all. I never signed any paper but with a mark. But often times my wife has always signed my name when it was necessary and I asked her to do it. I cannot say that my first application was read over to me or not. I did not sign my name to it."

30. The *Narrative of Sojourner Truth* is a case in point; there, the relationship between Truth and her amanuensis, Olive Gilbert, is a significant factor in appreciating the narrative. See Fulton (24–26).

31. In her examination of interviews collected by the Federal Writers' Project in the late 1930s, Musher compares the questionnaires used by interviewers that were developed by John Lomax, director of the Folklore Division of the Writers' Project, and Sterling Brown, director of the Office of Negro Affairs. Lomax, self-described as "upper crust of poor white trash," was more interested in collecting folklore of a dying generation, and his questions were meant to elicit material on "daily life, folk songs, and superstitious practices" of slave life (8). Brown, on the other hand, was an African American poet and scholar who "did not believe that the interviews with ex-slaves should document primarily the daily practices of a people nearing extinction, but rather that they should record individuals' responses to varying conditions of slavery and freedom," and thus constructed "questions focused on both ex-slaves' historical experiences and on their perceptions of that past" (9–10).

WORKS CITED

Andzaldua, Gloria. "Speaking in Tongues: A Letter to Third World Women." *The Longman Anthology of Women's Literature*. Ed. Mary K. DeShazer. New York: Longman, 2001. 316–23.

"Another Slave Case in Boston." *Liberator* 11 Nov. 1857: 132.

Barthelemy, Anthony G. Introduction. *Collected Black Women's Narratives.* New York: Oxford UP, 1988. xxix–xlviii.

Carothers, Suzanne C. "Catching Sense: Learning from Our Mothers To Be Black and Female." *Uncertain Terms: Negotiating Gender in American Culture.* Eds. Faye Ginsburg and Anna Lowenhaupt Tsing. Boston: Beacon, 1990. 232–47.

Christian, Louise A., and Howard S. Fitz Randolph. *The Descendants of Edward Fitz Randolph and Elizabeth Blossom, 1630–1950.* East Orange, NJ: Louise A. Christian, 1950.

"Civil War History in St. Louis: The Gateway to the West Played a Pivotal Role in the Clash." 16 December 2008. http://www.explorestlouis.com/media/pressKit/civilWarAttractions.asp.

Conaway, Carol B., and Kristin Waters. Introduction. *Black Women's Intellectual Traditions: Speaking Their Minds.* Burlington, VT: U of Vermont P, 2007. 1–10.

Curry, Blanche Radford. "Mothers Confronting Racism: Transforming the Lives of Our Children and Others." *Everyday Acts Against Racism: Raising Children in a Multiracial World.* Ed., Maureen T. Reddy. Seattle: Seal, 1996. 132–43.

Darden, Robert. *People Get Ready!: A New History of Black Gospel Music.* New York: Continuum, 2004.

Davis, Charles T., and Henry Louis Gates Jr., eds. "The Language of Slavery." Introduction. *The Slave's Narrative.* New York: Oxford UP, 1985. xi–xxxiv.

Du Bois, W. E. B. *Souls of Black Folk.* (1903). New York: Dover, 1994.

Douglass, Frederick. *Narrative of the Life of Frederick Douglass, An American Slave, Written by Himself.* (1845). New York: Penguin, 1982.

Ellenberger, Matthew. "Illuminating the Lesser Lights: Notes in the Life of Albert Clinton Horton." *Southwestern Historical Quarterly* 88 (1985): 363–86.

Emilio, Luis Fenollosa. *History of the Fifty-Fourth Regiment of Massachusetts Volunteer Infantry, 1863–1865.* Boston: Boston Book, 1894.

Ernest, John. "Beyond Douglass and Jacobs." *The Cambridge Companion to the African American Slave Narrative.* Ed. Audry Fisch. New York: Cambridge UP, 2007. 218–31.

Federal Writers' Project. *Slave Narratives: A Folk History of Slavery in the United States from Interviews with Former Slaves.* Washington, DC: Library of Congress, 2008.

Ferguson, Rebecca Anne. "The Mulatta Text and the Muted Voice in *Louisa Picquet the Octoroon:* Revising the Genre of the Slave Narrative." Diss. Marquette U, 1995.

Foreman, P. Gabrielle. "Who's Your Mama? 'White' Mulatta Genealogies, Early Photography, and Anti-Passing Narratives of Slavery and Freedom." *American Literary History* 14 (2002): 505–39.

Fulton, DoVeanna S. *Speaking Power: Black Feminist Orality in Women's Narratives of Slavery.* Albany: State U of New York P, 2006.

———. "Spirituals." *Writing African American Women: An Encyclopedia of Literature by and about Women of Color.* Ed. Elizabeth Ann Beaulieu. Westport, CT: Greenwood Publishing Group, 2006. 816–20.

Gilbert, Olive. *Narrative of Sojourner Truth.* (1850). New York: Vintage, 1993.

Gould, Philip. "The Rise, Development, and Circulation of the Slave Narrative." *The Cambridge Companion to the African American Slave Narrative.* Ed. Audry Fisch. New York: Cambridge UP, 2007. 11–27.

Govenar, Alan B. *African American Frontiers: Slave Narratives and Oral Histories.* Santa Barbara, CA: ABC-CLIO, 2000.

Henderson, Mae. "Speaking in Tongues: Dialogics, Dialectics, and the Black Women Writer's Literary Tradition." *Reading Black, Reading Feminist: A Critical Anthology.* Ed. Henry Louis Gates Jr. New York: Meridian, 1990. 116–42.

Hurston, Zora Neale. *Mules and Men.* 1935. New York: Harper Perennial, 1990.

Jacobs, Harriet A. *Incidents in the Life of a Slave Girl, Written by Herself.* (1861). Cambridge: Harvard UP, 1987.

Johnson, James Weldon. "From Preface to *The Books of American Negro Spirituals.*" *Signifyin(g), Sanctifyin', and Slam Dunking: A Reader in African American Expressive Culture.* Ed. Gena Dagel Caponi. Amherst: U of Mass P, 1999. 45–71.

King, Martin Luther Jr. "Letter from Birmingham Jail." 1964. *The Norton Anthology of African American Literature.* Eds. Henry Louis Gates Jr., et al. New York: Norton, 1977. 1854–1866.

Lobdell, Jared C. Introduction. *Silvia Dubois, A Biografy of The Slav who Whipt Her Mistress and Gand Her Fredom.* By C. W. Larison, MD. New York: Oxford UP, 1988. 3–25.

Lorde, Audre. *Sister Outsider: Essays and Speeches.* Berkeley: Crossings Press, 1984.

Luce, T. J. *New Jersey's Sourland Mountain.* Princeton: Sourland Planning Initiative, 2005.

Mappen, Marc. *Jerseyana: The Underside of Jersey History.* New Brunswick: Rutgers University Press, 1992.

Massachusetts Adjutant General. *Massachusetts Soldiers, Sailors, and Marines in the Civil War.* 9 vols. Boston: Norwood, 1931.

Massachusetts Archives. *Massachusetts Deaths for 1866.* 192:169.

McCarthy, B. Eugene, and Thomas L. Doughton. *From Bondage to Belonging: The Worcester Slave Narratives.* Amherst: U of Mass P, 2007.

McHenry, Elizabeth. *Forgotten Readers: Recovering the Lost History of African American Literary Societies.* Durham: Duke UP, 2002.

McPherson, James M. *Battle Cry of Freedom: The American Civil War.* (1988). London: Penguin, 1990.

Moody, Joycelyn. *"Sentimental Confessions": Spiritual Narratives of Nineteenth-Century African American Women.* Athens, GA: U of Georgia P, 2001.

Mullen, Harryette. "Runaway Tongue: Resistant Orality in *Uncle Tom's Cabin, Our Nig, Incidents in the Life of a Slave Girl,* and *Beloved.*" *The Culture of Sentiment: Race, Gender, and Sentimentality in Nineteenth-Century America.* Ed. Shirley Samuels. New York: Oxford UP, 1992. 244–64.

Musher, Sharon Ann. "Contesting 'The Way the Almighty Wants It': Crafting Memories of Ex-Slaves in the Slave Narrative Collection." *American Quarterly* 53 (2001): 1–31.

Pierce, Yolanda. *Hell Without Fires: Slavery, Christianity, and the Antebellum Spiritual Narrative.* Gainesville: UP of Florida, 2005.

Randall, Margaret. *Sandino's Daughters Revisited: Feminism in Nicaragua.* New Brunswick: Rutgers UP, 1994.

Reagon, Bernice Johnson. *We'll Understand It Better By and By: Pioneering African American Gospel Composers.* Washington: Smithsonian Institution, 1992.

Reinhardt, Mark. "Who Speaks for Margaret Garner? Slavery, Silence, and the Politics of Ventriloquism." *Critical Inquiry* 29 (2002): 81–119.

Shaw, Arnold. *Black Popular Music: From the Spirituals, Minstrels, and Ragtime to Soul, Disco, and Hip-Hop.* New York: Schirmer, 1986.

Starling, Marion Wilson. *The Slave Narrative: Its Place in American History.* Boston: G. K. Hall, 1981.

Stowe, Harriet Beecher. *Uncle Tom's Cabin: or Life Among the Lowly.* (1852). New York: Harper & Row, 1965.

Twain, Mark. "A True Story." 1874. *Mark Twain: Collected Tales, Sketches, Speeches, and Essays, 1852–1890.* New York: Library Classics of the United States, 1992. 578–82.

Vansant, Nicholas. *Work Here, Rest Hereafter, or the Life and Character of Rev. Hiram Mattison.* New York: N. Tibbals & Son, 1870.

Ward, Jerry W. Jr. *Trouble the Water: 250 Years of African American Poetry.* New York: Mentor, 1997.

Weiss, Harry B. *Country Doctor: Cornelius Wilson Larison of Ringoes, Hunterdon County, New Jersey, 1837-1910; Physician, Farmer, Educator, Author, Editor, Publisher and Exponent of Phonetic Spelling.* Trenton: New Jersey Agricultural Society, 1953.

Yellin, Jean Fagan. *Harriet Jacobs: A Life.* New York: Basic Civitas, 2004.

CHRONOLOGY OF
LOUISA PICQUET

Circa 1828—Louisa is born near Columbia, South Carolina to fifteen-year-old Elizabeth Ramsey, a quadroon slave seamstress and "Mr. Randolph," a slave owner (probably James Hunter Randolph). Approximately two months after the birth, as Mrs. Randolph is displeased with the fact that the new slave baby resembled her youngest child, Elizabeth and baby Louisa are sold to David R. Cook of Jasper County, Georgia.

Circa 1828–1841—Elizabeth and Louisa live on the Cook Plantation; Elizabeth has three more children, but only one, the youngest boy, John, born circa 1841, survives childhood. Cook gets into trouble with his creditors and flees with his slaves to Mobile, Alabama where Louisa works as a nursemaid and domestic help for merchant Thomas M. English and for Mr. "Bachelor" whose wife runs the boardinghouse where David Cook stays.

Circa 1841—Cook's creditors catch up with him in Mobile and his slaves are sold to settle his outstanding debts. Thirteen-year-old Louisa is sold to a Mr. (John) Williams of New Orleans, while Elizabeth and John were sold to Colonel Albert Clinton Horton of Wharton, Texas.

1841–1847—Louisa becomes Williams's concubine and bears him four children, including a daughter, Elizabeth "Eliza" Williams, born 1842. Two children die in infancy.

1847 (February 16)—John Williams, aged 50, dies in New Orleans; Louisa stays in Williams's house until his brother tells her that he will no longer pay the rent; she moves her children to stay temporarily with a friend, a Black woman named Helen Hopkins, while Williams's brother takes the furniture from the house, sells it at a secondhand furniture store, and gives the money to Louisa, who in turn uses the money to go to Cincinnati, Ohio.

1847–1850—Louisa, calling herself Louisa Williams, takes in washing for income in Cincinnati; one of her children dies; Louisa meets Henry Picquet.

1850 (September 15)—Henry Picquet and Louisa Williams are married in Zion Baptist Church in Cincinnati by the Reverend Wallace Shelton; they make their home in the Fourth Ward of Cincinnati with his daughter Harriet, aged four, and her daughter Eliza, aged eight; Henry Picquet goes to work at the Carlisle Building at Fourth and Walnut streets in Cincinnati as a janitor.

1852—Louisa gives birth to Sarah Picquet born in Cincinnati.

1856—Louisa gives birth to Thomas Picquet born in Cincinnati.

1858—Louisa finds out her mother is alive and well on Colonel A. C. Horton's Sycamore Grove plantation on Caney Creek in Wharton County, Texas, and immediately commences corresponding with her, and also with Colonel Horton as to the possibility of redeeming her mother from slavery. The price is set at one thousand dollars "or an exchange of property of equal value."

1859–1860—Louisa tries to save money and determines that she would do better to solicit funds from various charitable donors. She starts in Cincinnati and goes from town to town, first in southern Ohio, and then north to Xenia, Oberlin, and subsequently Cleveland. In Cleveland, it was suggested that she go to Buffalo, New York. From Buffalo, she goes to New York City and meets the Reverend Hiram Mattison, a Methodist minister and antislavery agitator. She travels with Mattison soliciting funds, and soon returns to Cincinnati. Ultimately, she is successful in raising nine hundred dollars and sends for her mother.

1860 (October 13)—Louisa Picquet places a notice in the Cincinnati *Daily Gazette* announcing that her mother has safely arrived in Cincinnati.

1861—Hiram Mattison publishes his pamphlet "Louisa Picquet, the Octoroon: Or Inside Views of Southern Domestic Life."

1864 (September 8)—Henry Picquet enlists in the Union Army and is sent first to Camp Delaware, Ohio, and then, after completing basic training, is sent to Nashville, Tennessee. He serves first in Company E, 17th United States Colored Troops; he is placed on detached duty as an officer's orderly, and then subsequently reassigned to Company K, 42nd United States Colored Troops. He starts complaining of various physical ills, including a hernia, rheumatism, and neuralgia.

1865 (May 25)—Henry Picquet receives a medical discharge from the service.

1867—Henry Picquet's physical ills preclude him from working full time at his previous job at the Carlisle Building, and Louisa Picquet becomes "the sole support of the household." The family moves from Cincinnati to New Richmond, Ohio, about fifteen miles away.

1870–1885—Henry Picquet applies several times for a Veterans' Invalid Pension for injuries incurred while in the Army; he is rejected three times during this period.

1885 (June 9)—Henry Picquet is awarded a Veterans' Pension for six dollars a month.

1889 (December 13)—Henry Picquet dies in New Richmond, Ohio.

1890 (March 18)—Louisa Picquet receives a Widow's Pension based on her late husband's service-related disability; she receives twelve dollars a month.

1896 (June 11)—Louisa Picquet dies in New Richmond, Ohio.

LOUISA PICQUET, THE OCTOROON:

A Tale of Southern Slave Life.

BY REV. H. MATTISON, A. M.,
PASTOR OF UNION CHAPEL, NEW YORK.

A TALE OF SOUTHERN SLAVE LIFE.

BY REV. H. MATTISON, A. M.,
PASTOR OF UNION CHAPEL, NEW YORK.

NEW YORK:
PUBLISHED BY THE AUTHOR, Nos. 5 & 7 MERCER STREET.
1861.

FRONTISPIECE OF THE ORIGINAL PUBLICATION OF
LOUISA PICQUET, THE OCTOROON (1861)

CHAPTER I.
ILLUSTRIOUS BIRTH AND PARENTAGE

LOUISA PICQUET, the subject of the following narrative, was born in Columbia, South Carolina, and is apparently about thirty-three years of age. She is a little above the medium height, easy and graceful in her manners, of fair complexion and rosy cheeks, with dark eyes, a flowing head of hair with no perceptible inclination to curl, and every appearance, at first view, of an accomplished white lady.[1] No one, not apprised of the fact, would suspect that she had a drop of African blood in her veins; indeed, few will believe it, at first, even when told of it.

But a few minutes' conversation with her will convince almost anyone that she has, at least, spent most of her life in the South. A certain menial-like diffidence, her plantation expression and pronunciation, her inability to read or write, together with her familiarity with and readiness in describing plantation scenes and sorrows, all attest the truthfulness of her declaration that she has been most of her life a slave. Besides, her artless simplicity and sincerity are sufficient to dissipate the last doubt. No candid person can talk with her without becoming fully convinced that she is a truthful, conscientious, and Christian woman. She is now, and has been for the last eight years, a member of the Zion Baptist Church in Cincinnati, Ohio, of which Rev. Wallace Shelton is now (May, 1860) the pastor.

But, notwithstanding the fair complexion and lady-like bearing of Mrs. Picquet, she is of African descent on her mother's side—an octoroon, or eighth blood—and, consequently, one of the four millions in this land of Bibles, and churches, and ministers, and "liberty," who "have *no rights that white men are bound to respect.*"

The story of her wrongs and sorrows will be recited, to a large extent, in her own language, as taken from her lips by the writer, in Buffalo, N. Y., in May, 1860.

CHAPTER II.
LOOKS TOO MUCH LIKE MADAME RANDOLPH'S CHILDREN, AND IS SOLD OUT OF THE FAMILY

"I was born in Columbia, South Carolina. My mother's name was Elizabeth. She was a slave owned by John Randolph,[2] and was a seamstress in his family. She was fifteen years old when I was born. Mother's mistress had a child only two weeks older than me. Mother's master, Mr. Randolph, was my father. So mother told me. She was forbid to tell who was my father, but I looked so much like Madame Randolph's baby that she got dissatisfied, and mother had to be sold. Then mother and me was sent to Georgia, and sold. I was a baby—don't remember at all, but suppose I was about two months old, maybe older."

CHAPTER III.
THE SECOND MASTER FAILS AND HIS SLAVES ARE SCATTERED

"Then I was sold to Georgia, Mr. Cook bought mother and me. When mother first went to Georgia she was a nurse, and suckled Madame Cook's child, with me. Afterward, she was a cook. I was a nurse. I always had plenty to do. Fast as one child would be walkin', then I would have another one to nurse."

Question (by the writer).—"Did your master ever whip you?"

Answer.—"Oh, very often; sometimes he would be drunk, and real funny, and would not whip me then. He had two or three kinds of drunks. Sometimes he would begin to fight at the front door, and fight everything he come to. At other times he would be real funny."

Q.—"He was a planter, was he?"

A.—"Yes; he had a large cotton plantation, and warehouse where he kept all the cotton in, and stores up the country, in a little town—Monticello—and then he had some in Georgia. He used to give such big parties, and everything, that he broke up. Then his creditors came, you know, and took all the property; and then he run off with my mother and me, and five other slaves, to Mobile, and hired us all out. He was goin' to have enough to wait on him, for he could not wait on his self. I was hired out to Mr. English. He was a real good man; I wouldn't care if I belonged to him, if I had to belong to any body. I'd like to swap Mr. Cook for him. Mr. English and his wife were very clever to me. They never whipped me. Mother had a little baby sister when we first went to Mobile—a little girl just running round. She died in Alabama. She had one before that, while she was in Georgia; but they all died but me and my brother, the oldest and the youngest."

Q.—"Had she any one she called her husband while she was in Georgia?"

A.—"No."

Q.—"Had she in Mobile?"

A.—"No."

Q.—"Had she any children while she lived in Mobile?"

A.—"None but my brother, the baby when we were all sold."

Q.—"Who was the father of your brother, the baby you speak of?"

A.—"I don't know, except Mr. Cook was. Mother had three children while Mr. Cook owned her."

Q—"Was your mother white?"

A.—"Yes, she pretty white; not white enough for white people. She have long hair, but it was kinda wavy."

Q.—"Were you hired out in Mobile?"

Q.—"Yes; with Mr. English."

CHAPTER IV.
A WHITE SLAVE LOVE ADVENTURE

"While I was living in Mobile, a gentleman there owned a colored man that was more white than I am. He was about my age. He had no beard; just a young man, might have been nineteen or twenty. His master was not married, but had a girl belong to him, a very light girl he bought from Charleston; he bought her for himself, though he kept her boarding out.

"This colored man I spoke of used to drive out when his master's sisters wanted to go out. They often came to Mr. English's with them, and ring the bell. There I met him often at the door before I knew he was colored, and when he found out I was colored, he was always very polite, and say, 'Good morning, miss,' and ask if the ladies was in. Then, after he got acquainted, he used to come and see me Sundays. He wanted me to marry him, and I liked him very well, and would have had him if he had not run off."

Q.—"How came he to run off?"

A.—"You see Mr.—³ kept that girl, but never go where she was; but, whenever he want to see her he send for her to the office. And this young man who wanted me had to go always and tell that girl, and go with her to the office, whenever his master wanted him to.

"Then this man had another waitman, one was perfectly white and the other jet black; and the black one got jealous of the other one, and thought his master thought more of his other servant, the white one. (He did think more of him.) So the two had a falling out; and, to seek revenge, the dark one told the master he see something which he did not see—that the other one was out walking with this girl. He knew (that is, the black one) that his master would whip him (the light one) for that, when he would not whip him for anything else. That night his master had not sent for her, and, of course, he thought it might be true.

"Then he ask T—about it, and he denied it, but the owner believed it. Then he whipped him awfully, soon as he came to the office that morning; and sent for the girl, and whipped her, and sent her off to New Orleans.

"Then the partner of this man, he spoke to T—afterward, and told him he would go away. He was an Englishman, or Scotchman. He came out that way—was not raised there. He never would own a slave. He felt sorry T— was whipped so, and told him he would go away. His first excuse was he had no money, and the next was on account of being acquainted with me. Then the man inquire what kind of looking girl I was, and told him if I was white as he represented there would be no difficulty at all about getting away, and he would let him have money for both of us to go away.

"Then he told me what this gentleman said to him, and that he had the money from this gentleman, and wanted me to go away with him. Well, I knew that he could neither read nor write, and was afraid that we would be caught, and so I dare not go. We had about two hours' talk then, but when he found out I would not go, he said he must go; he had the money, and all his arrangements made. That's the last I saw of him. I suppose T—left that night. 'Twas not very long after that I went to Mr. Bachelor's to live, and we were all sold."

We shall hear of this fugitive T—again, further on in our narrative.

CHAPTER V.
INTRIGUES OF A MARRIED "SOUTHERN GENTLEMAN"

Q.—"Did Mr. Cook always treat *you* well, as to any insults?"

A.—"No. After we went to Mobile, I went to Mr. Bachelor's, after I was at Mr. English's, and Mr. Cook was boarding there. I was a little girl, not fourteen years old. One day Mr. Cook told me I must come to his room that night, and take care of him. He said he was sick, and he want me and another slave girl to come to his room and take care of him. In the afternoon he went to his room, and said he was sick. I was afraid to go there that night, and I told Mrs. Bachelor what Mr. Cook said to me. Then she whispered with her sister, Mrs. Simpson, and then told me I need not go. She said she would go up and see Mr. Cook, and have someone else go and take care of him. Then I went up after Mrs. Bachelor, not to let him see me, and listen to the door. Mrs. Bachelor went in and ask him how he done. She said, 'I heard you was sick, and I thought I would come up and see if there was anything serious.' He groaned, and seemed to get worse than ever—told how bad he felt about his head, and one thing an'other. Then her reply was, that she would have some water put on to bathe his feet and some mustard, and have one of the boys come up and take care of him. She went right on in that way, without his asking, and smooth it off in that way, so as not to let on that she thought anything, at the same time clearing me.

"Then he thanked her very kindly. So she went down, and had the water sent up. Then, pretty soon, he sent down by the boy, to tell me to bring up some more *mustard.* Then Mrs. Bachelor, she understood it, and *she* took up the mustard herself. Then the boy stay with him all night, and just about daylight he come down. When he come down he come to the room (you see, I slept in Mrs. Bachelor's room)—he call me and says, 'Your massa, Henry, says you must take him up a fresh pitcher of water;' and Mrs. Bachelor told him to go and take it up himself; that I was busy.

Q.—"Were you hired to Mrs. Bachelor then?"

A.—"I don't know. I was workin' there; it might have been in part for his board, for aught I know. Mrs. Bachelor kept boarding-house. She was Scotch; came from Scotland."

Q.—"Well, what happened next?"

A.—"I didn't go up till breakfast-time. At breakfast-time I had to take his breakfast up to his room, on a waiter. He had not got up yet—I take the waiter up to the bed. Well, him thinking that all the boarders gone down, talk rather louder than he would if he'd a thought they were there. The door was open wide enough for a person to come in.

"Then he order me, in a sort of commanding way (I don't want to tell what he said), and told me to shut the door. At the same time he was kind a raising up out of the bed; then I began to cry; but before I had time to shut the door, a gentleman walk out of another room close by, picking his nails, and looking in the room as he passed on. Then Mr. Cook turned it off very cute. He said. 'What you stand there crying for, you dam' fool? Go 'long down stairs, and get me some more salt.' Same time he had not taste his breakfast, to see whether he want any salt, or not. That was to blind with that gentleman, because he see me there crying, or heard me, or something. Then I was very glad to get out to get the salt, but still I knew I should have to come back again, and it would not be much better. Then I went down to get the salt, and Mrs. Bachelor caught my looks, and spoke and said, 'Louisa, one of the boys will take that salt up, I want you a minute.' Then I thought she was the best friend I had in the world. She had such a nice way of turning off things. Then I didn't go up till that day, some time. He did not come down, but call out of the window for me to bring him up a pitcher of water. Then I brought the water up, and he want to know why I did not come up with the salt. I told him the reason, that Mrs. Bachelor said she wanted me, and sent it up by one of the boys. Then he said he wanted me to understand that I belong to him, and not to Mrs. Bachelor—that when he called, or wanted me, I was not to consult with Mrs. Bachelor, or any person else.

"Then he told me I must come up in his room that night; if I didn't he'd give me hell in the mornin'. Then I promised him I would, for I was afraid to say anything else. Then he forbid me sayin' anything to Mrs. Bachelor about what he said to me—you see there where he got me. Then I came to conclusion he could not do anything but whip me—he could not kill me for it; an' I made up my mind to take the whippin'. So I didn't go that night.

"Then in the mornin' he want to know why I didn't come up, and I told him I forget it. Then he said, I don't believe you forgot it; but if you forget that, I won't forget what I told you. So he whip me, so that I won't forget another time.

Q.—"Well, how did he whip you?"

A.—"With the cowhide."

Q.—"Around your shoulders, or how?"

A.—"That day he did."

Q.—"How were you dressed—with thin clothes, or how?"

A.—"Oh, very thin; with low-neck'd dress. In the summertime we never wore but two pieces—only the one under, and the blue homespun over. It is a striped cloth they make in Georgia just for the colored people. All the time he was whippin' me I kept sayin' I forgot it, and promisin' I would come another time."

Q.—"Did he whip you hard, so as to raise marks?"

A.—"Oh yes. He never whip me in his life but what he leave the mark on, I was dressed so thin. He kept asking me, all the time he was whippin' me, if I intended to mind him. Of course I told him I would, because I was gettin' a whippin'. At the same time, I did not mean to go to his room; but only did it so that he would stop whippin' me. He want to know what I was afraid of— if I could not sleep as well there as anywhere else? Of course I told him, yes, sir; and that I wan't afraid of anything. At the same time, I was afraid of him; but I wouldn't tell him. Then he let me go. Then, as luck would have it, he got playin' cards with some gentlemen after dinner, about two or three o'clock, and never stop all night; so I thought from appearance of things in the mornin'. They were playin' and drinkin' together all night; so I did not go to his room till mornin'. I had my excuse all made up—because he had company, and I was waitin' and got to sleep. At the same time I didn't intend, and expect to take another whippin' in the mornin'.

"Then, in the mornin', I went up to call him to breakfast; and, as I knock at the door to call him, to tell him that breakfast was ready, he told me to come in. He came to the door, and I smelt his breath, and see from the way he spoke to me that he had been drinkin'. He told me to come in, that he had somethin' for me. At the same time, he took hold of my hand, and kind a pull me, and put a whole handful of half-dollars in my hand. Then I knew he was drunk, but it surprise me so that I didn't know what to think. At the same time, he was holdin' on to me, and askin' me if I would come back. I told him, yes. But I thought he was so drunk he would forget, and so I have all that money. I never had any money but copper and five cents before; and, of course, my hand full of half-dollars looked to me like a fortune. I thought he had got it that night playin' cards. I went on, then, down stairs; and in the afternoon, when he got a little sober, he ask me what I done with that money. First I ask him, what money? I thought he would forget it, and didn't let on that I knew anything about it. Then he said, that money I let you have this mornin'. Then I knew he had not forgot.

"Then, you see, I had seen a flowered muslin dress in the store several times, and I take a fancy to it; I thought it look beautiful. It was perfectly white, with a little pink leaf all over it. So I went to the store, and ask the man what's the price of it. Then he told me, but I could not reckon it, so I lay the money out, and told him to give just as many yards as I had half-dollars. Then he told me that would be too large a pattern for me; but I told him, no, I wanted a nice full dress. That was the largest pattern I ever had afore, or since. Then I told Mr. Cook I put the money away, and could not find it. I had sense enough to know he would not dare tell anyone that he gave me the money, and would hardly dare to whip me for it. Then he say no more about it, only he told me to come up there that night. He said he want to see some more about that money; he didn't believe I lost it. Then I told Mrs. Bachelor that I guess I'd have to go up stairs that night; and ask her what I should do. She was the best friend I had; but she could not interfere no more, because if she did he'd know that I told her. Then she said she had no patience with him—he was the meanest man she ever saw. She abused him then a great deal, before her sister and before me. Then she said the best plan would be to keep out of his way, and if he called me, not to answer. I was to keep in her room that evening as much as possible.

"Well, about tea-time he wanted water. That was sent up. Then he wanted to know where I was; he wanted a button sewed on his wristband. Then Mrs. Bachelor sent him word that, if he could not find me, to send the shirt down, and her sister, or one of the girls, would put a button on for him, if he was in a hurry. The shirt came down, and the button was sewed on. I suppose he just took the button off for an excuse. Then, when they went up with the shirt, he sent word down that, when I came, I must come up and get his boots and black them. He did not care about waitin' so long for them in the mornin'. He thought I'd give out somewhere. Then, about bedtime, he call one of the boys to know if they told me about the boots; and they said they hadn't seen me. I was all the time in Mrs. Bachelor's room, but none of them knew it. I sewed the button on, but he didn't know it. Then he pretended to be mad because I was gone out at night, and she excuse me, and said, perhaps I had gone out with some children, and got to playin', and didn't know it was so late. He was mad, and told her his wife never allowed me to go out nights, and she must not; and allowed he would give me a floggin' for it. He said I knew better than to go out. He thought I was out, or, perhaps, he thought it was a trick to keep me from him and that made him so mad.

"In the mornin' he came down, and want to know where I was. You see, I'd made up my mind to take the whippin'. I knew he would not kill me, and I'd get over it the same as I had before. So I told him I was down stairs asleep.

"Then he came to me in the ironin'-room, down stairs, where I was, and whip me with the cowhide, naked, so I 'spect I'll take some of the marks with me to the grave. One of them I know I will." (Here Mrs. P. declines explaining further how he whipped her, though she had told our hostess where this was written; but it is too horrible and indelicate to be read in a civilized country.) Mrs. P. then proceeds, "He was very mad, and whipped me awfully. That was the worst whippin' I ever had."

Q.—"Did he cut through your skin?"

A.—"Oh yes; in a good many places. I don't believe he would whip me much worse, if I struck his wife or children; and I didn't do anything. He pretended it was because I was out, but I knew what it was for. When he came out of the room, after he had whipped me, he said, to make Mrs. Bachelor believe, 'I'll be bound she won't go out another time without permission.' Then, when he was whippin' me so awfully, I made up my mind 'twas of no use, and I'd go, and not be whipped anymore; and told him so. I saw he was bent on it, and I could not get Mrs. Bachelor to protect me anymore. Then he went away, and that was the last I ever saw him. That very day, about noon, we was taken by the sheriff, and was all sold the next mornin'. I tell you I was glad when I heard I was taken off to be sold, because of what I escape; but I jump out of the fryin'-pan in to the fire. Mrs. Bachelor said it was a good thing, when I went away."

Q.—"Where was Mrs. Cook all this time?"

A.—"She was up the country, in Georgia, with a sister of hers. When he failed in Georgia, he sent her up to her sister. I suppose she was willing to do it; she must have understood it."

Q.—"How many children had she?"

A.—"I could not tell; they had a lot of them. I know I been nursin' all my life up to that time."

CHAPTER VI.
THE FAMILY SOLD AT AUCTION—
LOUISA BOUGHT BY A "NEW ORLEANS GENTLEMAN,"
AND WHAT CAME OF IT

Q.—"How did you say you come to be sold?"

A.—"Well, you see, Mr. Cook made great parties, and go off to watering-places, and get in debt, and had to break up [fail], and then he took us to Mobile, and hired the most of us out, so the men he owe should not find us, and sell us for the debt. Then, after a while, the sheriff came from Georgia after Mr. Cook's debts, and found us all, and took us to auction, and sold us. My mother and brother was sold to Texas, and I was sold to New Orleans."

Q.—"How old were you, then?"

A.—"Well, I don't know exactly, but the auctioneer said I wasn't quite fourteen. I didn't know myself."

Q.—"How old was your brother?"

A.—"I suppose he was about two months old. He was little bit of baby."

Q.—"Where were you sold?"

A.—"In the city of Mobile."

Q.—"In a yard? In the city?"

A.—"No. They put all the men in one room, and all the women in another; and then whoever want to buy come and examine, and ask you whole lot of questions. They began to take the clothes off of me, and a gentleman said they needn't do that, and told them to take me out. He said he knew I was a virtuous girl, and he'd buy me, anyhow. He didn't strip me, only just under my shoulders."

Q.—"Were there any others there white like you?"

A.—"Oh yes, plenty of them. There was only Lucy of our lot, but others!"

Q.—"Were others stripped and examined?"

A.—"Well, not quite naked, but just same."

Q.—"You say the gentleman told them to 'take you out.' What did he mean by that?"

A.—"Why, take me out of the *room* where the women and girls were kept; where they examine them—out where the auctioneer sold us."

Q.—"Where was that? In the street, or in a yard?"

A.—"At the market, where the block is?"

Q.—"What block?"

A.—"My! don't you know? The stand, where we have to get up?"

Q.—"Did you get up on the stand?"

A.—"Why, of course; we all have to get up to be seen."

Q.—"What else do you remember about it?"

A.—"Well, they first begin at upward of six hundred for me, and then some bid fifty more, and some twenty-five more, and that way."

Q.—"Do you remember anything the auctioneer said about you when he sold you?"

A.—"Well, he said he could not recommend me for anything else only that I was a good-lookin' girl, and a good nurse, and kind and affectionate to children; but I was never used to any hard work. He told them they could see that. My hair was quite short, and the auctioneer spoke about it, but said, 'You see it good quality, and give it a little time, it will grow out again.' You see Mr. Cook had my hair cut off. My hair grew fast, and look so much better than Mr. Cook's daughter, and he fancy I had better hair than his daughter, and so he had it cut off to make a difference."

Q.—"Well, how did they sell you and your mother? That is, which was sold first?"

A.—"Mother was put up the first of our folks. She was sold for splendid cook, and Mr. Horton, from Texas, bought her and the baby, my brother. Then Henry, the carriage-driver, was put up, and Mr. Horton bought him, and then two field-hands, Jim and Mary. The women there tend mills and drive ox wagons, and plough, just like men. Then I was sold next. Mr. Horton run me up to fourteen hundred dollars. He wanted I should go with my mother. Then someone said 'fifty.' Then Mr. Williams allowed that he did not care what they bid, he was going to have me anyhow. Then he bid fifteen hundred. Mr. Horton said 'twas no use to bid any more, and I was sold to Mr. Williams. I went right to New Orleans then."

Q.—"Who was Mr. Williams?"

A.—"I didn't know then, only he lived in New Orleans. Him and his wife had parted, some way—he had three children, boys. When I was going away I heard someone cryin', and prayin' the Lord to go with her only daughter, and protect me. I felt pretty bad then, but hadn't no time only to say good-bye. I wanted to go back and get the dress I bought with the half-dollars, I thought a good deal of that; but Mr. Williams would not let me go back and get it. He said he'd get me plenty of nice dresses. Then I thought mother could cut it up and make dresses for my brother, the baby. I knew she could not wear it; and I had a thought, too, that she'd have it to remember me."

Q.—"It seems like a dream, don't it?"

A.—"No; it seems fresh in my memory when I think of it—no longer than yesterday. Mother was right on her knees, with her hands up, prayin' to the Lord for me. She didn't care who saw her: the people all lookin' at her. I often thought her prayers followed me, for I never could forget her. Whenever I wanted anything real bad after that, my mother was always sure to appear to me in a dream that night, and have plenty to give me, always."

Q.—"Have you never seen her since?"

A.—"No, never since that time. I went to New Orleans, and she went to Texas. So I understood."

Q.—"Well, how was it with you after Mr. Williams bought you?"

A.—"Well, he took me right away to New Orleans."

Q.—"How did you go?"

A.—"In a boat, down the river. Mr. Williams told me what he bought me for, soon as we started for New Orleans. He said he was getting old, and when he saw me he thought he'd buy me, and end his days with me. He said if I behave myself he'd treat me well: but, if not, he'd whip me almost to death."

Q.—"How old was he?"

A.—"He was over forty; I guess pretty near fifty. He was gray headed. That's the reason he was always so jealous. He never let me go out anywhere."

Q.—"Did you never go to church?"

A.—"No, sir; I never darken a church door from the time he bought me till after he died. I used to ask him to let me go to church. He would accuse me of some object, and said there was more rascality done there than anywhere else. He'd sometimes say, 'Go on, I guess you've made your arrangements; go on, I'll catch up with you.' But I never dare go once."

Q.—"Had you any children while in New Orleans?"

A.—"Yes; I had four."

Q.—"Who was their father?"

A.—"Mr. Williams."

Q.—"Was it known that he was living with you?"

A.—"Everybody knew I was housekeeper, but he never let on that he was the father of my children. I did all the work in his house—nobody there but me and the children."

Q.—"What children?"

A.—"My children and his. You see he had three sons."

Q.—"How old were his children when you went there?"

A.—"I guess the youngest was nine years old. When he had company, gentlemen folks, he took them to the hotel. He never have no gentlemen company home. Sometimes he would come and knock, if he stay out later than usual time; and if I did not let him in in a minute, when I would be asleep, he'd come in and take the light, and look under the bed, and in the wardrobe, and all over, and then ask me why I did not let him in sooner. I did not know what it meant till I learnt his ways."

Q.—"Were your children mulattoes?"

A.—"No, sir! They were all white. They look just like him. The neighbors all see that. After a while he got so disagreeable that I told him, one day, I wished he would sell me, or 'put me in his pocket'—that's the way we say— because I had no peace at all. I rather die than live in that way. Then he got awful mad, and said nothin' but death should separate us; and, if I run off, he'd blow my brains out. Then I thought, if that be the way, all I could do was just to pray for him to die."

Q.—"Where did you learn to pray?"

A.—"I first begin to pray when I was in Georgia, about whippin'—that the Lord would make them forget it, and not whip me: and it seems if when I pray I did not get so hard whippin'."

CHAPTER VII.
INSIDE VIEWS OF ANOTHER SOUTHERN FAMILY

Q.—"Did you feel that you were doing right in living, as you did, with Mr. Williams?"

A.—"No; when I was a little girl in Georgia the madame, Mrs. Cook, used to read the Bible, and explain it to us. One night she read the commandments about stealin', and committin' adultery. They made a great impression on my mind. I knew what stealin' was, but I did not know what adultery was. Then I asked her the meanin'. She did not want to answer for a good while. I suppose I was so small she hated to tell me, but I kept on askin'. Then she said, 'You see *Lucy*, how many children she's got?' I told her yes. Then she said she did not know the father of any of them children, and said when folks had children that way they must be married like *she* (Mrs. Cook) was to her husband. It was adultery to stay with anyone without bein' married—that was the meanin' of it."

Q.—"Who was this Lucy?"

A.—"She was a seamstress in Mrs. Cook's family."

Q.—"What was her color?"

A.—"Right white—light hair and blue eyes. All her children were right white."

Q.—"And was *she* a slave?"

A.—"Yes, sir."

Q.—"How many children had she?"

A.—"Five or six in Georgia, and one after she went to Mobile."

Q.—"And had she no husband?"

A.—"No, sir; never had a husband in her life."

Q.—"Do not the slave women usually have husbands, or those they call their husbands?"

A.—"Yes, sir; some of them do; but some of them do not. They can't have any husbands, because their masters have them all the time."

Q.—"How did you say it was with Lucy?"

A.—"She sew in the house all day, and then go to her room, off, at night."

Q.—"What became of her?"

A.—"Well, she was sold the day I was, in Mobile, and got free after a while; and each of the white men bought his child. Mr. Moore bought his, and Mr. Hale bought his; and then the others, that their fathers would not own, her relations bought and set free."

Q.—"Who do you mean by her relations?"

A.—"Why Lucy's sister Judy, and Mr.—[4] who kept her. I tell you how he did: He bought Elcy, Lucy's sister, first, and lived with her till she died. He had her learn to read and write, and taught her music, and done first rate by her. Then, when Elcy died, he bought her sister, Judy, and is livin' with her yet. Then, when they heard that Lucy was sold, all her sisters and brothers unite, sent on and bought her, and set her free."

CHAPTER VIII.
OCTOROON LIFE IN NEW ORLEANS

Q.—"Well, now tell me about your life in New Orleans."

A.—"Well, when Mr. Williams bought me he told me where I was goin', to New Orleans, and what he bought me for. Then I thought of what Mrs. Cook told me; and I thought, now I shall be committin' adultery, and there's no chance for me, and I'll have to die and be lost. Then I had this trouble with him and my soul the whole time."

Q.—"Did you ever say anything to him about this trouble?"

A.—"Yes, sir; I told him often. Then he would dam' at it. He said *he* had all that to answer for himself. If I was only true to him, then I could get religion—that needn't hinder me from gettin' religion. But I knew better than that. I thought it was of no use to be prayin', and livin' in sin.

"I begin then to pray that he might die, so that I might get religion; and then I promise the Lord one night, faithful, in prayer, if he would just take him out of the way, I'd get religion and be true to Him as long as I lived. If Mr. Williams only knew *that*, and get up out of his grave, he'd beat me half to death. Then it was some time before he got sick. Then, when he did get sick, he was sick nearly a year. Then he begin to get good, and talked kind to me. I could see there was a change in him. He was not all the time accusin' me of other people. Then, when I saw that he was sufferin' so, I begin to get sorry, and begin to pray that he might get religion first before he died. I felt sorry to see him die in his sins. I pray for him to have religion, when I did not have it myself. I thought if he got religion and then died, I knew that I could get religion.

"It seems he did get religion, because he was so much changed in his way; but he said he wanted to see his way clearer."

Q.—"Was he rich?"

A.—"Oh no, sir. He had to borrow some of the money of his brother to buy me."

Q.—"What kind of a house did you live in?"

A.—"Why, it was a rented house. When he got up, one mornin', I got him up in a chair by the fire—it was cold weather—then he told me he was goin' to die, and that he could not live; and he said that if I would promise him that I would go to New York, he would leave me and the children free. He was then writin' to a table—had a little table to the side of him. Then he told me how to conduct myself, and not to live as I had lived with him, with any person. He told me to come out this way (North), and not to let anyone know who I was, or that I was colored. He said no person would know it, if I didn't tell it; and, if I conducted myself right, someone would want to marry me, but warned me not to marry anyone but a mechanic—someone who had trade, and was able to take care of me and the children."

Q.—"How many children had you then?"

A.—"Only two. I had four, but two had died. Then I promised him to go to New York. Then he said, just as soon as he died I must go right to New York; and he said he would leave me the things. He hadn't any thing to leave me but the things."

Q.—"What things?"

A.—"The things in the house—the beds, and tables, and such things."

CHAPTER IX.
DEATH OF HER THIRD OWNER, AND ESCAPE OF LOUISA

"Then, in about a month or three weeks, he died. I didn't cry nor nothin', for I was glad he was dead; for I thought I could have some peace and happiness then. I was left *free*, and that made me so glad I could hardly believe it myself.

"Then, on Sunday, I dressed myself and went out to go to church; and that was the first time I had been to church in six years. I used to go to the colored church in Georgia, with my mother, in the afternoon. When I got there, to the church in New Orleans, the minister talked just as though he knew all about me, and talked about the vows I had made to the Lord about my husband. Then I said in my mind, he wan't my husband; but then I determined to go there to church. Then I asked the people what church it was, and they said, a Methodist church. Then Mr. Williams' brother came, and told me I must go out of that house, because he would not pay the rent. Then a woman there, a friend of mine, let me come in one of her rooms. She was very kind to me, and used to give me victuals when I did not know where to get it."

Q.—"Who was this woman?"

A.—"Her name was Helen Hopkins; she was a colored woman that used to take in washing. I never knew how it was that she was so kind to me. I always thought it was the Lord takin' care of the widow and the fatherless.

"One day I met Mr. Williams' brother, and he asked me what I was doin'; and I told him, nothin'. He said that by rights I belonged to him, because his brother had not paid him the money that he borrowed to help buy me. Mr. Williams—John Williams—had said before that he would give me somethin' for the children. Then he asked me why I did not go away, as his brother told me. Then I told him it was because I had not money enough to go with, and asked him to give me some. Then he said I had better thank God for my freedom; and that his brother had got enough from him. Then I told this friend of mine, who had given me victuals, and she advised me to get away as soon as I could.

"Then Mr. John Williams sent the things I had to a secondhand furniture store, and sold them all; and I took the money and my two children, and went to Cincinnati. I had just money enough to get there, and a little bit over."

Q.—"What made you stop at Cincinnati?"

A.—"Because I had no money to go further; and I met all my friends there that I knew, when I was small, in Georgia. One of them was a Mrs. Nelson who was once a slave in Georgia with my mother. Her husband had bought her, and she was livin' with him in Cincinnati. I went right to her house. Then, when I saw her free, and was free myself, I began to think more about my mother."

Q.—"When had you seen your mother last?"

A.—"At the auction, where we were all sold. It is now 'most twenty years ago."

Q.—"Had you never heard from her?"

A.—"Yes. I had one letter from her when I was in New Orleans. Mr. Williams read the letter to me, and told me that my mother wanted me to send her some tea and sugar. That was just like the mornin' we parted. It grieved me so to think that she was where she could have no sugar and tea. She could always get it in Georgia, if she had to take in workin' and do it at night. But I had no money, and could not send her anything; and I felt bad to think my mother could not have any of these things. Whenever I set down to eat ever since, I always think of my mother. When Mr. Williams was sick, before he died, he promised me, if he ever got up off from that bed, he would buy my mother, and set us all free. But he never did it."

Q.—"Are the two children you brought with you from New Orleans now living?"

A.—"No; one of them died soon after I got to Cincinnati. I have only one of them livin'—a daughter, about eighteen years old."

Q.—"Is she as white as you are?"

A.—"Oh yes; a great deal whiter."

CHAPTER X.
STILL ANOTHER SOUTHERN HOUSEHOLD

Q.—"Have you any other children?"

A.—"Yes; three others. I been in Cincinnati near twelve years. Three years after I came there, I married Mr. Picquet, my husband."

Q.—"Is he a white man or colored?"

A.—"He's a mulatto. His mother is brown skin, and his father white, and that makes a mulatto, you know."

Q.—"Who was his father?"

A.—"He was a Frenchman, in Georgia. He bought my husband's mother, and live with her public. I knew all about it there, before I left Georgia. She had four other children beside my husband."

Q.—"Were they all slaves?"

A.—"Yes. They all belong to Mr. Picquet, but he never uses them as slaves. They are his children."

Q.—"How did they get free?"

A.—"Why, when he got married, he sent them all to Cincinnati, the mother and five children. It would be unpleasant for them all to stay there together (*i.e.*, his wife, and concubine and her children)."

Q.—"Had your husband ever been married before?"

A.—"Yes; he married a slave-woman there."

Q.—"How do the slaves get married?"

A.—"In a general way they ask the owners, and the owner says yes; and they get married."

Q.—"Do they have a minister to marry them out on the plantations?"

A.—"No; not one out of three plantations. They ask the master, and then have little bit of frolic, and sometimes they don't have that."

CHAPTER XI.
DOMESTIC PURITY IN GEORGIA

Q.—"How was it with Henry, your husband?"

A.—"Why, he hired Eliza, and rented a house, and put her in. She was a slave-woman, and took in washin'.'"

Q.—"How came they to part?"

A.—"Why, you see, she belong to heirs, and the property was sold for the money to be divided. Then a gentleman in Macon bought Eliza for himself. Then Henry felt so bad about it that, pretty soon, he went to see her. He went there with the intention of buyin' her and her baby, which was Henry's. Mr. Picquet, Henry's father, was goin' to let him have the money. So, when he got there, he found it different from what he expected. He found he could not have her any more for his wife. You see, the gentleman had bought her for himself. So my husband writ to his father that he could not get his wife, but he could buy the child. Then his father, Mr. Picquet, sent on the money, and he bought the child, and brought it away. It was about three months old, and he raised it on a bottle, work all day, and then worry with the child all night."

Q.—"Is that child yet living?"

A.—"Oh yes; she is livin' with us in Cincinnati, and the smartest one we got too. She is about thirteen or fourteen."

Q.—"Is she as white as your children?"

A.—"Oh no; she is the darkest one in the house. But her hair is straight, only little bit wavy."

CHAPTER XII.
THE LONG-LOST MOTHER HEARD FROM

Q.—"How came you to find out where your mother was?"

A.—"Well, I hear she was in Texas, and I keep writin' to Texas, and supposed it was one place, but never got no answer. But I kept prayin', and always believed that I should see her or hear from her, before I died."

Q.—"You kept up praying all this time, did you?"

A.—"Yes; but when I came to Cincinnati, I thought more about my mother—to think I was free, and so many others that I knew in Georgia, and she was still in slavery! It was a great weight on my mind; and I thought if I could get religion I should certainly meet her in heaven, for I knew she was a Christian woman. I had thought of it very often, and thought how often I had told the Lord I would serve him and had not done so, till I was almost afraid to make another promise. Then I made up my mind to serve the Lord. I had often been to the Methodist meeting there, when there was great excitement; but I never went up to be prayed for. I thought it was a sin if I did not go up in the right way.

"But I kept feelin' worse in my mind. Everything I had ever done all came up before me. I felt as if I could not look up; my eyes were fixed on the ground. In the evenin'—Sunday evenin'—I went to meetin' in the Zion Baptist Church. Mr. Shelton was preachin'. After he got through, they was singin'; I felt troubled all through it. Then I went up to the altar with others. I made up my mind that I would never hold up my head again on this earth till the Lord converted me. I prayed hard enough that night. My husband was so mortified to think I prayed so loud, and made so much noise; but I told him, Henry, I have to die for myself, and it did not set me back at all. But I did not get rid of the burden I felt till near daylight that night, or next mornin'. I was prayin' nearly all night, and near mornin' I felt worse, as if I would die; and I tried to wake Henry up, but I could not wake him at all. It seemed as if I had not time. All my long prayers had gone to just the one word, 'Lord, have mercy!' and I could not say anything but that. And the moment I believe that the Lord would relieve me, the burden went right off; and I felt as light as if I was right up in the air. And it seemed as if there was light in the room. Then, the next Sunday, I joined the church, and the Sunday after was baptized. That was eight years ago, going on nine. I been in that church ever since."

Q.—"Is your husband a professor of religion?"

A.—"Yes; he belongs to the same church. He experienced religion in Georgia."

Q.—"How about the two daughters?"

A.—"Elizabeth, my daughter, belongs to the same church. My husband's daughter, Harriet, does not belong to any church."

Q.—"Does your church commune with slaveholders?"

A.—"*No, sir; they will not.* The Union Baptist Church does. When white ministers come there from the South, they let them break the bread at the Communion; but in our church, if they come there, they don't do it, unless they come with a lie in their mouth. They ask them if they believe in slavery, or apologize for it, and if they do, then they don't preach there. No slaveholder, or apologist for slavery, can preach in that church; that was the foundation when they first started."

Q.—"Well, how did you find out where your mother was?"

A.—"Well, I have made it a business for about eleven years, to inquire of everyone I saw, almost, about my mother. If any fugitives came through, I made it my business to get to see them, and inquire. A great many fugitives come through Cincinnati. I have had lots of them in my house.

"One time a colored woman came there, real genteel, and ask to board. I thought she was a runaway slave, though she tried to make me believe she was free. Her name was Mary White. She was there two or three weeks, and I notice she never went out only on Sunday evenin's. One afternoon she went to our church, and heard it give out by the preacher, that if any of the friends knew of a woman by the name of Mary White, to tell her to be on the lookout, for the hell-hounds were after her up to one of the hotels. Then she spring up, and came to where I was and told me. That night we darken up the house, and a Quaker friend came there and had her fixed up; and next day she was on her way to Canada. After that I got a couple of letters from her, returning thanks to us all for helpin' her on her way. She was in a sheriff's family in Canada, and was doing well."

Q.—"Now tell me how you found your mother?"

A.—"I used to take in washin', and one day a gentleman, Mr. B., a good friend of ours in Cincinnati, sent some shirts there to be done up, and said he was goin' to Texas. Then my husband inquired, and found out that he knew Mr. Horton, in Texas, and told us what kind of a lookin' man he was. Then I remembered how he looked when he bought my mother in Mobile, and I knew it was the same man. Then he told us how to send a letter, and where to mail it. [There is a kink about mailing a letter, so as to have it reach a slave, that we never before dreamed of; but Mrs. P. does not wish it published, for fear it will hinder her from getting her letters.] Then I wrote a letter [got one written], and in three weeks I had a letter from my mother."

Q.—"What became of the first letter you had from your mother, while you were in New Orleans?"

A.—"I never saw that. Mr. Williams only told me he got it, and what was in it. I only knew she was in Texas. I thought it was all Texas."

Q.—"Have you the first letter you received from your mother?"

A.—"Yes; up stairs. Shall I go and get it?"

Here the letter was brought. It is on a tough blue paper, well soiled and worn, but yet quite legible. The following chapter contains an exact copy.

CHAPTER XIII.
LETTER FROM A SLAVE MOTHER

"Wharton, March 8, 1859

"My Dear Daughter,

"I a gane take my pen in hand to drop you a few lines.

"I have written to you twice, but I hav not yet received an answer from you I can not imagin why you do not writ I feel very much troubel I fear you hav not recived my letters or you would hav written; I sent to my little grand children a ring also a button in my first letter I want you to writ to me on recept of this letter, whether you hav ever received the letters and presents or not I said in my letter to you that Col. Horton would let you have me for 1000 dol. or a woman that could fill my place; I think you could get one cheaper where you are[5] that would fill my place than to pay him the money; I am anxios to hav you to make this trade. you hav no Idea what my feelings are. I hav not spent one happy moment since I received your kind letter. it is true I was more than rejoyest to hear from you my Dear child; but my feelings on this subject are in Expressible. no one but a mother can tell my feelings. in regard to your Brother John Col. Horton is willing for you to hav him for a boy a fifteen years old or fifteen hundred dol I think that 1000 dollars is too much for me you must writ very kind to Col Horton and try to Get me for less money; I think you can change his Price by writing Kindly to him aske him in a kind manner to let you hav me for less I think you can soften his heart and he will let you hav me for less than he has offered me to you for.

"you Brother John sends his love to you and 100 kisses to your little son; Kiss my Dear little children 100 times for me particuler Elizabeth say to her that she must writ to her grand mar ofton; I want you to hav your ambrotipe taken also your children and send them to me I would giv this world to see you and my sweet little children; may God bless you my Dear child and protect you is my prayer.

"Your affectionate mother,

"Elizabeth Ramsey.

"direct your letter to Gov. A. C. Horton Wharton Wharton contey texas."

The reader will understand that the brother John, mentioned in this letter, was the "baby" sold with the mother some twenty years ago, in Mobile, whose slips were made of Louisa's pink dress bought with the half-dollars. Louisa's mother never would take the name of Randolph or Cook—the name of her owner—as other slaves do, so she still sticks to her first name of Ramsey, as when she lived in South Carolina thirty-five years ago.

This letter is dated at Wharton. Mrs. P. says it is "in the country, where they go in the winter, and live at Matagorda in the summer." By looking upon a map of Texas it may be seen that Matagorda is at the mouth of the Colorado River, on the Gulf of Mexico; and Wharton about forty miles northwest, on the same river, both in Southern Texas.

Another friend. Mrs. Ramsey now lives with Arthur, the coachman, who was sold at the same time with her in Mobile, as her husband. The letter is, of course, written by some white person, and is printed exactly as it is written.

There is a fact worth recording in regard to the first letter that reaches Mrs. Ramsey. It is thus described by Mrs. Picquet:

"I had been tryin' hard to find out where my mother was twelve years, after I came to Cincinnati; and when I get that letter written,

I just put my trust in the Lord to go with it. I had tried so long, and could not get no word at all. I prayed to the Lord to go with each seal. There was three envelopes: one to take the letter to my friend at St. Louis, to mail the letter that was in it to Matagorda for me. That letter was directed to the postmaster in Texas; and a letter to him in it, asking him, if Col. Horton was alive, to send it to him, and, if not, to send it to some of his children. And I prayed the Lord that he would work in the hearts of the man in St. Louis, and the postmaster at Matagorda, that my letter might reach my mother.

"In that letter I ask Mr. Horton if he would please to read it to my mother, to let her know that I was yet alive; and, if he did not feel disposed to read it to her, would he be so kind as to drop me a few lines, just to let me know if she was alive; and, if she was dead, how long ago, and how she died; and, if she was livin', if she was well, and how she looked—just to ease my mind, for I had been weighed down with sorrow to see her for many years. I told him I had no silver nor gold to pay him; but I trust the Lord would reward him for his kindness, if he would do that much for me. I told him I had great faith in the Lord; and I would pray that his last days might be his best. I tell him if she was livin', and he would sell her, I would try to buy her. If I thought she would die the next week, it would be a great comfort for me to have her here to bury her."

Thus it seems that the Lord did go with the letter, and that Mrs. Horton read the letter to Louisa's mother. She then wrote two letters, but they did not reach Mrs. P. One of them, the one containing the button and the ring, was afterward found in the post-office in Matagorda, by Mrs. Ramsey. It was probably either not stamped, or not properly directed.

As soon as Mrs. P. got the first letter from her mother, she wrote two letters back, one to her mother, and the other to Mr. Horton, and both dated and mailed as before. In a short time she received another from her mother, written but a few days after the first received by Mrs. P.; and as it throws some additional light upon the question whether or not slaves have any proper affection for their offspring, we transcribe and print that also.

SECOND LETTER FROM THE SLAVE MOTHER

"Warton, Warton County, March 13, '59.

"My Dear Daughter,

"Your very kind and affectionate letters dated at St. Louis, One in January the other in Febuary has been received and contents partickularly notist, I had them read often creating in me both Sorrow and Joy. Joy that you were living & a doing wel so far as the comforts of this world are concerned and you seem to have a bright prospect in the World to come, this the brightest of all other prospects, If a Person should gain the whole world & lose there Soul they have lost all, My Dear Daughter you say a great deal to me about instructing your Brother in his duty, I endeavor to set a good example before him it is all that I can do John is a good disposed Boy & a favorite with his Master, Arthur, Jim & Mary are all members of the Babtist Church, they are all well and a doing well, In your first letter you spoke of trying to purchase me & your Brother, the proposition was made to you to exchang Property of equal value, or to take One Thousand Dollars for me, & Fifteen Hundred for your Brother this may seem an extravagant price to you but it is not an average price for Servants, I know of nothing on this earth that would gratify me so much as to meet with My Dear & only daughter, I fear that I should not be able to retain my senses on account of the great Joy it would create in me, But time alone will develup whether this meeting will tak plase on earth or not Hope keeps the soul alive, but my Dear Daughter if this should not be our happy lot, I pray God that we may be able to hold fast to the end, & be the Happy recipients of the promise made to the faithful. There will be no parting there, but we shall live in the immediate presence and smiles of our God. It is not in our power to comply with your request in regard to the Degeurrotypes this tim, we shall move to Matagorda shortly, there I can comply with your request. Arthur, Jim, Mary and your brother desire to be very kindly remembered to you, Answer this at as early a date as convenient Direct your letter to Goven A. C. Horton, Matagorda, Texas.

"May God guide and protect you through Life, & Finally save You in Heaven is the prayer of your affectionate mother,

"Elizabeth Ramsey."

Before this second letter was received Mrs. P. writes to Mr. Horton, reminding him that her mother was growing old, and that it would be better for him to sell her cheaper, and buy a younger person. In answer to this letter the following was received from Mr. Horton himself.

CHAPTER XIV.
LETTER FROM THE OWNER OF ELIZABETH

MATAGORDA, June 17, 1859.

"LOUISA,

"I have your favor of 16th April last, and contents duly noticed.

"You seem to think that I ask you too much for your mother. Money would not induce me to sell her, were it not for existing circumstances. You know that she is as fine a washer, cook, and ironer as there is in the United States. It's true she is getting old, but she carries her age well, and looks as young as she did twenty years ago. I only ask you to place another of her quality and qualifications in her stead. You can not complain of this, if it's not of your power to comply with the terms. I write you to come and see her, and I pledge myself you shall not be molested either directly or indirectly, but protected to the utmost extent.

"I send you by this mail a Daguerreotype likeness of your mother and brother, which I hope you will receive. Your mother received yours in a damaged condition. Your mother and all your acquaintance are in fine health, and desire to be remembered, and would be pleased to see you.

"Respec'y yours,

"A. C. HORTON."

The Daguerreotype mentioned above was duly received, in perfect order, and is now in the hands of Mrs. Picquet. They are both taken on one plate, mother and son, and are set forth in their best possible gear, to impress us in the north with the superior condition of the slave over the free colored people.

Just here might come in a chapter more romantic and thrilling than any thing as yet narrated in this pamphlet, but, for reasons that we must not name, it must remain unprinted for the present. The time may come, and we hope soon will come, when it may be published without prejudice to any party or interest.

From the date of the last of the preceding letters, Mrs. Picquet has received letters from her mother nearly every month, but nothing further from Mr. Horton himself, though Mrs. P. has often written him, importuning him to take less for her mother. At length, in March, 1860, she wrote to Mrs. Horton, appealing to her regard for her own mother, to talk to Col. Horton, her husband, and see if he would take less than one thousand dollars for Mrs. Ramsey. Of the results of this appeal we shall learn hereafter.

CHAPTER XV.
PRIVATE EFFORTS TO BUY THE MOTHER

Mrs. Picquet's first plan was to draw her husband's wages two years in advance. He was in the employ of Mr. John Carlisle, of Cincinnati, and was willing to have the fruit of his labor thus taken in advance to restore his mother-in-law to freedom, and to the embrace of her daughter. But how were they to live these two years? The two years' labor would only amount to about five hundred dollars, at most; and how to get the remaining five hundred dollars, and take care of themselves and family at the same time, was the insurmountable difficulty. Mrs. P. was anxious to sell everything she had to help buy the mother, but all she had on earth would bring but little. For one whole year Mrs. P. saved every penny she could, even denying herself many of the comforts of life; and the amount of all this rigid economy was only sixty dollars saved. By this time she began to be discouraged. She talked with friends, and they advised her to go out and solicit money for the purpose. This she was reluctant to do. She had her family of four young children to care for, as well as her husband; had never traveled, except from New Orleans to Cincinnati, and dreaded to go out for such a purpose. She knew that many were abroad soliciting money for such purposes, and feared it would be in vain for her to make the attempt. But her mother was in bondage, and she resolved to make the attempt at all hazards.

The Press of Cincinnati gave the effort their encouragement. The *Daily Gazette* of Saturday, March 10, contained the following:

"TO THE BENEVOLENT OF CINCINNATI"

"Louisa Picquet, though to all appearance white, is, nevertheless, a colored woman. She was born a slave, and has a mother and brother now in slavery in Texas. She is personally known to me. She is in our midst, appealing for aid to buy her mother out of slavery. Let our citizens respond to her appeal.

JAMES POINDEXTER,
"of Zion Baptist Church."

This Mr. Poindexter, it seems, was not then in active service, as pastor of the church, though still residing there.

The *Journal and Messenger* of March 16, contained the following editorial notice: "Louisa Picquet, formerly a slave, but with a complexion as white almost as that of any person, is now visiting villages in this State [Ohio], soliciting aid to purchase her mother, who is a slave in Texas. She is a member of Zion Baptist Church, in this city, is well recommended; and is, no doubt, worthy of public sympathy and benevolence."

Mrs. P. accordingly procured a subscription-book, pasted the above notices into the front of it, and started out in Cincinnati first. A well-known "Friend," in Cincinnati, recommended her as follows, on a blank leaf:

"The bearer of this, Louisa Picquet, I believe to be a very worthy, pious woman. Would recommend her to the sympathy of the friends of humanity, in aiding her to redeem her mother from slavery."

LEVI COFFIN
"Cincinnati, 15th 12th mo., 1860."

Similar recommendations were inserted by JOSEPH EMERY.

CHAPTER XVI.
SOLICITING HELP ABROAD TO BUY A MOTHER

Thus fitted for her undertaking, Mrs. P. started out in Cincinnati first, and obtained subscriptions to the amount of about three hundred dollars.

Among them was one by JOHN CARLISLE, Esq. (the gentleman in whose employ Mr. Picquet has been for years), amounting to fifty dollars. A Mr. W. Mills gave ten dollars, P. Wilson twenty dollars, and many others in Cincinnati five dollars each.

Mrs. P. then went to Lebanon, Ohio, to see Hon. Thomas Corwin, but he had gone to Washington; but his nephew, Matthias Corwin, took her book, and wrote as follows in it:

"I hereby certify that I have known the bearer, Louisa Picquet, for the last ten years. She comes to Lebanon to ask aid to purchase her mother, who is now a slave in Texas. I have no doubt but the money that is given will be faithfully applied to that purpose.

M. CORWIN.

"Lebanon, January 28, 1860."

A Mr. Suydam went one way in Lebanon with Mrs. Picquet and the book, and Mr. Corwin another, and between them raised a nice little sum; but the book does not show where that subscription ends, and the next village begins. Mr. Corwin then gave her a letter to some member of the legislature, at Columbus, where she obtained $121. She next visited Dayton, Springfield, Xenia, Urbana, and Wellington, in all of which places she obtained more or less help, though the amounts were generally small.

CHAPTER XVII.
LOUISA IS IDENTIFIED IN OHIO
BY A FELLOW-TRAVELER

"While in Ohio, going from Xenia to Springfield in the cars," says Mrs. P., "I was expecting a letter to be left in the cook-house, at the depot, for me. I had got my seat in the cars, and wanted to leave a message with the cook about the letter. A gentleman was goin' out, and I stopped him, and asked him if he'd be kind enough to take this message to the cook. He did so, and came back and told me what the cook said; and then took a seat about five or six seats back of me, on the opposite side. As he took his seat, a lady asked him, thinkin' he knew all about me, how that woman got along raisin' money to buy her mother? He asked her, what woman? She said, that colored woman you was speakin' to just now. He told her she was mistaken; he was not speakin' to any colored woman. She insisted on it that he was. He told her, no; it was that lady in front, who was givin' him some directions about a letter—and was pointin' toward me.

Just at that time I was turnin' round to hand my book to a gentleman sittin' just behind me. The moment the first gentleman saw my face there, he asked a gentleman before him if I didn't come from Mobile, Alabama. He said he believed I did. He asked if my mother's name wan't Elizabeth? He laughed, and said, yes, I believe that's the name.

"Then the first gentleman came to me, and, after speakin' and bowin', he asked me if I knew him? I told him I did not know—perhaps I did—his face looked familiar to me; thinkin' it was some one I had seen in travelin' around in askin' for money. He said, 'were you ever in Mobile?' I told him, yes; and he wanted to know if my mother's name was Elizabeth Ramsey?' I told him it was. Then he wanted to know if I ever lived with Mr. English, in Mobile? I told him, yes. He then said he knew me well; and that his name was Bolden. He is a Baptist preacher now, but was not a preacher then. He was goin' up to Springfield, to organize a church: so I heard on the cars. Then he turned to the other gentleman, and said, 'I know this lady well. I knew her when she lived at Mr. English's, in Mobile.' He told what a fine woman my mother was, and said he knew the day I was sold; and said it had been twenty years. He even spoke to me about Lucy, and told how white she was, and her children; and asked me what ever became of her. I told him she was sold in Mobile; but afterward her friends bought her up, and her children."

CHAPTER XVIII.
VISIT TO OBERLIN, AND SOME OF THE "RESCUERS:" AND THENCE TO NEW YORK

She next went to Oberlin, where she met with most cheering encouragement. Hon. Mr. Plumb (one of the "Rescuers," we believe,) took hold of the matter with great spirit. The Wesleyan Methodist Church took a collection of $14.92; the Congregational Church, $99.58; and the Episcopal Church, *ninety-five cents!* Other private subscriptions brought the amount collected in Oberlin up to $135; for which a draft was sent on to Mr. W. T. Drake, banker, Cincinnati. She then visited Penfield, Litchfield, Medina, and other small places, collecting small amounts (all of which are carefully entered in the subscription-book), and finally went to Cleveland. Here she received $9.62 at the door of the Baptist Church, in the morning on the Sabbath, and $17.14 in a collection in the First Congregational Church, in the evening.

At Cleveland Mrs. P. was advised to visit Buffalo, where the General Conference of the Methodist Episcopal Church was in session. The Baptist minister in Cleveland wrote a letter to another Baptist minister in Buffalo, and a Mr. Day wrote another to Rev. Mr. Hill, a delegate to the General Conference.

Mrs. Picquet then went on to Buffalo and delivered one of her letters, but received so little encouragement, owing, doubtless, to the interest upon the subject of slavery then pending in the General Conference, that she concluded to go on to New York.

Mr. Henry R. Smith, of Cleveland, had been very active in Mrs. P.'s behalf while she was in that city, and had given her letters to Henry Ward Beecher and others in New York. On reaching that city she met with excellent encouragement, so that, in a few days, she collected $223 there; $55.70 of this was collected at the Anniversary of the American Anti-slavery Society, at the Cooper Institute.

CHAPTER XIX.
AN UNEXPECTED MEETING

While in New York, Mrs. P. was going from the Brooklyn Ferry to 29th Street, where she stopped. On her way up, between Fulton Street and the Park, she saw a man on the top of the omnibus, with the driver. He looked at her earnestly, and she at him, and knew him in a moment. He then got off and walked along to her, and said, "You must excuse me," but asked her name, and if she did not live at English's, in Mobile. She told him she did, and who she was. Then he told her he had been in New York ever since he ran away; that no one ever thought he was colored, as he said, "I just ranked in here." Mrs. P. wanted to know who he married. He laughed, and said, "You know I would never marry any but a white girl." He told Mrs. P. he had four children, and would like her to see them; and if she would wait in the Park he would bring them down there. He did not wish to have his wife see Mrs. P., as she was there raising money, and if—'s wife should hear of the interview, it would be natural for her to wish to know where he knew Mrs. P., and thus the fact of his being of African descent, and once a slave, might get out.

Mrs. P. walked in the Park awhile, till—went home, got three of his children, and came down in an omnibus with them, and stopped, and went into the Park. Mrs. P. says they were very pretty children. "Pretty dressed too," says Mrs. P.; "I think the mother must be very tasty woman. The two oldest were *very* white, girls. The youngest was a boy, dressed in little pants and sack, and a hat with feathers in it. He was a brunette, and I laughed, and said, 'That one has the stain on it.' He laughed, and said the family often laughed about, it, but little did they think what was the real cause of it. The family of his wife would often joke about it, and say they guessed his wife was frightened by a nigger; and he said, 'There's many a truth told in joke.'"

Here Mrs. P. added, "Now, it is astonishing, in the South, the white men run after the colored women, their own and others; but if a colored man speak to a white woman they want to shoot him." Mrs. P. promised to keep the matter secret, lest it might break up a family, or one of our white citizens in New York might be remanded back to slavery. And so they parted; but not till he had given her $5 to help purchase her mother. It was put down in the book by Mr.—, and stands here before us as we write, "Cash, $5." This is the young man who wished Louisa to run away from Mobile with him, twenty years ago.

CHAPTER XX.
RETURN TO BUFFALO—CALLS UPON "M"

While in New York Mrs. P.'s attention was directed to the writer, who was then in Buffalo, though our whereabouts was not known by the parties directing. Neither did they know our address. They sent her, therefore, to the Colored Orphan Asylum, on 43d Street, to ascertain our address. Here she met with Mr. Wm. E. Davis, who has charge of the Asylum, and is a communicant at Union Chapel, one of the best of men, and a practical Abolitionist. He and others there gave her seven dollars for the object, and also gave her a letter to the writer, at Buffalo. This was the first we had known of the case.

On looking over the subscription list, and the certificates of deposits and drafts which Mrs. P. had in possession, obtained in New York, and elsewhere, it was evident that it was a clear case, and, after deducting her expenses in travel (an account of which she had carefully kept by the aid of a little boy), together with what would be necessary to take her to her home in Cincinnati, and to get her mother from Matagorda, Texas, it would require at least one hundred and fifty dollars more than had as yet been subscribed.

CHAPTER XXI.
SUSPECTED AND REPULSED BY A "FRIEND OF THE COLORED PEOPLE"

When Mrs. P. first came to Buffalo, she had brought a letter to Rev. Mr.—, a Baptist minister residing there, and also one to Rev. Mr. Hill, a delegate from the Erie Conference; but for some cause they could not then aid her, as she had hoped. She accordingly passed on to New York; but, on her return Mr. Hill seemed disposed to do something for her, if he could, and for this purpose introduced her to Rev. Henry Slicer, a delegate from the East Baltimore Conference, in hope of getting him to bring up the matter in the Conference. Mr. S. looked sternly at Mrs. P., and with an imperious air said, "*You* a colored woman? You're no Negro. Where did you come from? If you are a Negro, where are your free papers to show it?" At the same time, looking over her book of letters, he asked, "Who wrote these letters? Where is the envelope that came on them, to show the postmark? You've got no envelope here." Then he handed back the book and papers, and said he could not do anything about it. As he went away he looked at Mr. Hill and said, "She's no Negro;" and thus ended the assistance from Rev. Henry Slicer.

CHAPTER XXII.
LOUISA IS INDORSED AFRESH FROM CINCINNATI

Being thus repulsed, and virtually accused of being an impostor, Mrs. P. felt deeply grieved, as any sensitive and virtuous woman would; but she made no reply, except to say that she believed she had one of the envelopes at the house where she was stopping. She had not thought to keep and show them as a proof that she was not an impostor, and this was the first time they had been called for; for the reader must understand that begging was new business to her, and that she had not resorted to it till all hope of getting her mother free by any other means had fled forever.

The fact of this cold repulse and alleged suspicion becoming known H. H. Mattison, Esq., of Buffalo (a relative of the writer), told Mrs. P. to go to his house and remain till her case could be brought before the Conference. He then went to the telegraph office and telegraphed to Evans & Co., Bankers, Cincinnati, to whom Mrs. P. had referred him, to know if Mrs. P. resided there, and everything was as she represented.[6]

The telegraph operator kindly sent the message (amounting to nearly three dollars) gratuitously, and the next mail brought the following letter from W. T. Drake, Esq., of the firm of Evans & Co., and one of the first subscribers upon Mrs. Picquet's book:

EVANS & CO., BANKERS

JASON EVANS}   {H. W. HUGHES
BRIGGS SMITH}   {W. T. DRAKE
CINCINNATI, 22nd May, 1860.
"H. H. Mattison, Esq., Buffalo, N. York.

"*Dear Sir,*—I am in receipt of your telegram of 21st inst., and hasten to reply.

"I *know* Mrs. Picquet has a mother in bondage in Texas, for whom she is trying to raise sufficient money to purchase her freedom.

"I know, also, Mrs. Picquet to be a truthful, and, I trust, Christian woman. You can, therefore, place the utmost confidence in her representations to you.

"I cordially commend her to your charity, in assisting her in the humane and filial endeavor of purchasing a mother from the curse of slavery.

"A mother! Who would not brave any danger, toil, and hardship for that dear name!

"I am, very truly,
"W. T. DRAKE.

"I have just seen the husband of Mrs. Picquet. He hands me two letters from Mrs. P.'s mother, received since she has been gone. Will you please hand them to her, after reading. The master of this woman has agreed to take $100 less than his former price."

The two accompanying letters referred to will be found in the following chapter.

CHAPTER XXIII.
MORE LETTERS FROM THE MOTHER

"April 15th '60.

"Dear Daughter,

"I have been looking for some time for a letter from you.

"I wrote to you on the business you wrote to me a bout; I have never herd if you received the letter or not.

"I received a letter from you that was written to Mrs. Horton a few days since. She red it and then sent it to me. I ask her what she would do for us. She said that she was willing for him to take less

"I had a talk with Col Horton yesterday he told me that he would not take less than nine hundred dollars & no less this is hard but we can not help it so you must make your self easy & dont fret any more than you can help.

"I would help you but my Situation is such that I cant.

"You must come and see me soon your brother was well when I heard from him last kiss my little grand children for me your affectionate mother,

"ELIZABETH RAMSEY."

"MATAGORDA, April 21, 1860.

"Dear Daughter,

"I received your kind & affectionate letter, & was glad to hear that you was well, & getting along very well. I was sorry to learn that you were disappointed in raising the amount of money required to purchase me. In a conversation with my master on the subject he says he is willing to take a woman in exchange for me, of my age and capasity or he will under the circumstances take nine hundred dollars in *cash* for me he says he would not part with me except under existing circumstances. he also says that money cannot buy either Arthur or John he is a training John to take charge of one of his

Plantations he has unlimited confidence in him & will not part with him untel death parts them. I should be very happy to see you My Dear Daughter as well as my Grandchildren. I hope there will be a way provided for us to meet on earth once more before we die. Cant you come and see us My Master will give all the protection you require whilst with us. This you may rest assured of. Your Brother John is well and desires to be very kindly remembered to you. Arthur wishes to be kindly remembered to you.

"Farewell My Dear Daughter. May God protect you from All evil, is the prayer of your affectionate Mother.

Elizabeth Ramsey.

This Arthur, it must be remembered, is the coachman sold with Mrs. Ramsey in Mobile, and bought by Col. Horton twenty years before; and John is the "baby" sold with its mother—the brother of Mrs. Picquet. Arthur is now, and has long been, Mrs. Ramsey's husband; and yet he is entirely willing she should go, if she can only be "free;" and she is willing to leave her husband and son forever, if she can only enjoy the precious boon of freedom. Oh, how sweet is LIBERTY! The Daguerreotype shows John to be as white as one in a hundred of our white fellow-citizens.

These two letters we took to Mrs. P., as directed, and read them to her; and the tide of emotion they created in her bosom, we can never describe. Joy, mingled with intense sorrow—the one, to learn that her mother could be bought for $100 less than the former price; and sorrow, to learn, at the same time, that *her brother could not be bought out of bondage at any price.* These two conflicting currents seemed to sweep over her soul in a mingled flood of joy and sorrow.

But all this only showed the importance of every proper effort to restore the mother to freedom, even if the brother was obliged to remain in life-long bondage.

CHAPTER XXIV.
METHODIST GENERAL CONFERENCE— CALLING UPON THE BISHOPS

The next evening we took Mrs. P., and went to the Bishops' rooms to see what arrangement could be made for bringing the matter up in the conference the next morning. They received us kindly, and expressed the utmost willingness to have it brought up, and the balance of the money raised. Bishop JANES gave a donation at once, and Bishops BAKER and SCOTT subsequently.

Bishop BAKER was to preside the next morning, and either he or Bishop SCOTT suggested that anyone might bring up the matter as a privileged question, as soon as the audience was sufficiently large to secure the object.

We went to the conference room next morning, and spoke to one or two delegates, who seemed to have good excuses for declining. We then called upon Dr. E. O. HAVEN, editor of *Zion's Herald,* Boston, and a delegate; and introduced him to Mrs. Picquet.

He was not quite as incredulous as Rev. H. SLICER; but heard her brief story with deep interest and emotion, and at once consented to bring up the matter in the conference the first fitting opportunity. But the effort to do so failed, on account of the extreme sensitiveness on the slavery question, lest it should be thought the case was brought in to exert an influence upon that question, which was then pending before the conference. The only way, therefore, to do anything was by private application. Accordingly, we took Mrs. P.'s book, and collected what we could ($68.80), and she returned home to Cincinnati.

This left still wanting, as near as we could calculate, some eighty or ninety dollars to make up the $900, and the amount necessary to purchase her mother, and bring her from Matagorda to Cincinnati.

CHAPTER XXV.
NEW DIFFICULTIES ENCOUNTERED—
THE MOTHER STILL IN BONDAGE

Upon returning to Cincinnati, Mrs. P. proceeded to collect the subscriptions made in that city, amounting to some $300, cheered by the fond hope of yet meeting her long-lost mother once more in this world. But some of the subscribers had died, others had moved away, and still others were tardy about paying what they had subscribed; so that the last we heard of the matter (which was by letter from Mr. Coffin, mentioned on page 33, a highly respectable citizen of Cincinnati), Mrs. P. was almost in despair about ever succeeding in her filial undertaking.

We learned this fact, however, that every dollar that had thus far been given for the object was deposited with Messrs. Evans & Co., bankers, Cincinnati, and would be sacredly kept for that purpose till enough was obtained to accomplish the object. We had hoped to be able to close with a chapter entitled, *"The long-lost mother restored to her daughter,"* but are as yet denied this satisfaction.

And now, reader, you have the narrative, closed, as we are obliged to close it after all that has been done, under a cloud of disappointment and gloom. The mother and brother are yet toiling in bondage in Texas; and the daughter weeping, and praying, and begging to obtain the amount yet needful to release the mother, at least, from her life-long oppression. Ought the object to fail for lack of about three hundred dollars? May not this pamphlet fall into the hands of some who can sympathize with this daughter of affliction and victim of relentless oppression, and will rejoice in the opportunity of doing *something* to help alleviate her sorrow? That there is no imposition or deception about it you must be perfectly satisfied. Mrs. P. is a child of God, a sister in Christ, as is also her mother. She loves her *mother* as you love yours, if living; and wishes not only to see her, but to bring her from the house of bondage to a land of freedom.

Should any of our readers be willing to contribute to this object, as we hope many will, let them inclose, if it be but a single dollar, either to Evans & Co., bankers, Cincinnati, Ohio, or to Rev. H. Mattison, care of Mason Brothers, New York City, by whom all such gifts will be sacredly donated to the object for which they are contributed. And as soon as the amount is made up, and the slave-mother released, the public will be duly notified; and all donors, whose address we have, especially informed of the happy conclusion of this hitherto sad and dark narrative.

CHAPTER XXVI.
CONCLUSION AND MORAL OF THE WHOLE STORY

The reader has, no doubt, been impressed with the main features of this artless and truthful story, as he has perused it; and will need little aid in retaining in dark outline upon the pages of memory the abhorrent picture which it presents. There are a few points, however, to which we deem it important to call special attention, as we now close the narration:

I.—And first, let it be remembered that this is *no fiction*. It is a plain, unvarnished story, from the lips of one who has spent her life in the South; has seen and known all that she asserts; and has no motive for exaggeration or falsehood. On the other hand, the very worst things in the narrative are those which she recited with the least apparent satisfaction. And the manner in which they were referred to, in their recital, showed conclusively that they were not and could not have been inventions to serve a purpose. Of all that has ever been published respecting the actual workings of slavery in the South, nothing has ever appeared that was worthy of more implicit confidence in all its details than the preceding pages. Though unable to read or write, Mrs. P. has an excellent memory; is decidedly intelligent; and, more than all, is deeply pious and conscientious. All that she has said, therefore, is worthy of the most implicit belief.

II.—The darkest and most prominent feature of the whole narrative is *the deep moral corruption* which it reveals in the families concerned, resulting from the institution of slavery.

1. At the outset (p. 2), we find the mother of Mrs. P., Elizabeth, through no fault of her own, a "seamstress," or concubine, in the family of John Randolph, who becomes the father of Louisa. Then there is trouble in the family, and Elizabeth and her young babe, like Hagar of old, must leave the patriarchal mansion in South Carolina for a home among strangers in Georgia.

2. Then she has three more *quadroon* children, while Mr. Cook owned her; but no husband, either black or white (p. 4).

3. She has another child while in Mobile (the brother now in Texas), who is as white as Louisa; but no husband (p. 4).

4. We have the case of Lucy, the seamstress of Mr. Cook, with her "light hair and blue eyes," and her six or seven white children; but no husband (p. 16).

5. We have the cases of Elcy and Judy, kept by Mr.___ (p. 17).

6. Next we have the very "gentlemanly" conduct of Mr. Cook, a married man, toward Louisa, while in Mobile (p. 6–11). And yet all this is tolerated even by Mrs. Bachelor, the friend of Louisa, inasmuch as the loathsome wretch was not at once driven from beneath her roof. What kind of a home

would such a man find of it in a New England or Ohio family? And yet he remains in peace, and associates with the family of Mrs. B., in Mobile, as a "gentleman," as a matter of course. Though foiled by her in his designs upon this poor slave-child, he is, nevertheless, recognized as a "gentleman," and admitted to female society, as if he were as pure as Joseph! What, we ask, must be the moral atmosphere in which such monsters can live and breathe?

7. We have the "gentleman" in Mobile, with his "very light girl bought from Carolina for himself," which he kept "boarding out."

8. We have the "gentleman from New Orleans," who is too poor to pay his debts, but can borrow money of his brother to buy Louisa, as a concubine, at the age of fourteen; and with whom she lives, as slave and mistress, till she becomes the mother of six children, of whom he is the father.

9. We have the case of Mr. Picquet, the father of the husband of Louisa, who bought Elizabeth, and lived with her till she became the mother of five children—all of whom (following the condition of the mother, according to the slave laws,) were slaves.

Thus it is that we have near 300,000 mulattoes in the Slave States; to a great extent the contributions of slaveholders and their sons to the common stock of southern chattels.

10. Finally, we see the wife of Henry, Mr. Picquet, Jr., and his babe, taken from him, a "gentleman" having "bought her for himself"; and the bereft husband is obliged to buy his own child, and rear it alone as best he can, while his wife, as the result of a desperate act, for which few under the circumstances will blame her, ends her days upon the gallows.

And all this in the brief narrative of a single individual who has been but a few years behind the scenes. There is not a family mentioned, from first to last, that does not reek with fornication and adultery. It turns up as naturally, and is mentioned with as little specialty, as walrus beef in the narrative of the Arctic Expedition, or macaroni in a tour in Italy.

Now, if such are the glimpses of southern domestic life which a single brief narrative reveals, what must the remainder be, which is hidden from our "Abolition" eyes? Alas for those telltale mulatto, and quadroon, and octoroon faces! They stand out unimpeached, and still augmenting as God's testimony to the deep moral pollution of the Slave States. We may shudder at the "heathenism" of a Turkish harem, and send missionaries to convert the Mohammedans; we may stand aghast at the idea of twenty thousand Syrian women sold to supply the harems of the Mussulmans, and pour out our money like water to relieve or release them; but wherein is all this a whit worse than what is constantly practiced, with scarce a word of unfavorable comment, in our own "Christian" (?) land? If there is any difference, it is certainly in favor of the Turk; for neither his concubines nor his children by them are *slaves;* while, in this country, our chivalrous "southern gentlemen" beget thousands of slaves; and hundreds of the children of our free white citizens are sold in the southern slave markets every year.

III.—The failure of Mr. Cook, with his large cotton plantation, and the subsequent sale of his slaves by the sheriff (probably to pay some "conservative" New York merchant), illustrates the "happy condition" of these slaves who have such "kind masters," but are, nevertheless, liable to be sold for debt at the auction-block, not only upon the death of their master, but at any time during his life; and then, as in this case, brothers and sisters, parents and children, wives and husbands (if there be any such), must part to meet no more in this world.

"But these," says one, "are the *evils* of slavery, to which I am as much opposed as you are." Verily, they are the "evils," but they are just such "evils" as necessarily belong to the system, and inhere in it, and without which slavery never did and never can exist. While the tree stands it will bear just these fruits, and no other. To sustain the system, therefore, or to practice under or apologize for it, is virtually to abet all its abominations. There is no escape from this conclusion.

What, then, is the duty of the American citizen who loves his country—the Christian citizen, especially? Ought he not to set his face against this giant wrong in every possible way? Can he even hold his peace concerning it, and be innocent? Ought he not to use all his influence, socially, ecclesiastically, and politically, to undermine and destroy it? Should he not speak and write against it, pray and protest against it, give and vote against it, till it shall wither under the just indignation of an enlightened and humane people? And, if a minister, an editor, especially, is it not his solemn duty to open his mouth for the dumb, and plead the cause of the oppressed?

May the Lord arouse this guilty nation to a sense of its deep and unwashed guilt, and bring us to repentance and reformation before the republic shall crumble beneath the weight of our accumulated crimes, and He who led Israel out of Egypt, by his sore judgments, shall arise for the sighing of the millions whom we hold in chains, and shall pour out his fury upon us to our utter confusion and ruin!

Since the preceding was stereotyped, the following has been sent us, marked in the *Cincinnati Daily Gazette* of October 15, 1860:

NOTICE—The undersigned takes this the first opportunity of expressing her thanks to those ladies and gentlemen residing in Cincinnati and elsewhere, that having accomplished through their kind aid the freedom of her mother, Elizabeth Ramsey, from slavery, by paying to her owner, Mr. A. C. Horton, of Texas, cash in hand, the sum of $900, collected by myself in small sums from different individuals, residing in this city and States of Ohio and New York.

I beg leave further to express my gratitude by thanking you all for your kindness, which will be engraved on my heart until death. My mother also desires to say that she is also most grateful to you all, and that if any of those friends who have assisted her to her freedom, feel disposed to call on her at my residence on Third Street, near Race (No. 135), she will be happy to see them, and thank them personally.
Very respectfully, yours, etc.
LOUISA PICQUET.
Cincinnati, October 13, 1860.

So the poor old mother is free at last! and the miserable wretch who bought her twenty years ago for perhaps $600, and has had her labor for twenty long years, now receives his $900 for her old and calloused flesh and bones. And yet he is probably a member of the Methodist Episcopal Church, South, and makes loud profession of piety! May Heaven save the heathen from the curse of such a Christianity!

CHAPTER XXVII.
SLAVE-BURNING, OR THE "BARBARISM OF SLAVERY"

We often hear pathetic appeals for money to send missionaries to the heathen, who burn widows on funeral piles, or throw their children into the Ganges; but the *suttee* was long since abolished in India; and so far as we know there is but one place on earth where human beings are burned alive. That place is the Slave States of America!

The following is from the *St. Louis Democrat* of July 20, 1859; it relates to a slave-burning that had recently taken place at Marshall, Missouri:

"The Negro was stripped to his waist, and barefooted. He looked the picture of despair; but there was no sympathy felt for him at the moment. Presently, the fire began to surge up in flames around him, and its effects were soon made visible in the futile attempts of the poor wretch to move his feet. As the flames gathered about his limbs and body, he commenced the most frantic shrieks, and appeals for mercy, for death, for water. He seized his chains; they were hot, and burned the flesh off his hands. He would drop them and catch at them again and again. Then he would repeat his cries; but all to no purpose. In a few moments he was a charred mass, bones and flesh alike burned into a powder."

Read also the following description of a similar scene in Mississippi, from the *Natchez Free Trader,* 1858:

"The victim was chained to a tree, faggots were placed around him, while he showed the greatest indifference. When the chivalry had arranged the pile, in reply to a question, if he had anything to say, he is reported to have warned all slaves to take example by him, and asked the prayers of those around. He then asked for a drink of water, and after quaffing it said, "Now set fire, I am ready to go in peace." When the flames began to burn him, in his agony he showed gigantic strength, and actually forced the staple from the tree, and bounded from the burning mass. But he instantly fell pierced with rifle balls, and then his body was thrown into the flames and consumed, to show that no such being had ever existed. Nearly four thousand slaves from the neighboring plantations were present as at a moral lesson written in characters of hell fire. Numerous speeches were made by the magistrates and ministers of religion (facetiously so called) to the slaves, warning them that the same fate awaited them if they proved rebellious to their owners."

Read also the following, taken from the *Alton* (Ill.) *Telegraph* of April 30, 1836; it is part of an account of a slave-burning published in that paper under that date:

"All was silent as death when the executioners were piling wood around their victim. He said not a word, until feeling that the flames had seized upon him. He then uttered an awful howl, attempting to sing and pray, then hung his head, and suffered in silence, except in the following instance: After the flames had surrounded their prey, his eyes burned out of his head, and his mouth seemingly parched to a cinder, someone in the crowd, more compassionate than the rest, proposed to put an end to his misery by shooting him, when it was replied, 'that it would be of no use, since he was already out of pain.' 'No, no,' said the wretch, 'I am not, I am suffering as much as ever; shoot me, shoot me.' 'No, no,' said one of the fiends who was standing about the sacrifice they were roasting, 'he shall not be shot. *I would sooner slacken the fire, if that would increase his misery,*' and the man who said this was, as we understand, an officer of justice.

"If anyone wishes evidence of other Negroes being burned in the State of Missouri, I can furnish it—evidence of the burning of eight Negroes within the last ten years, and innumerable instances of Negroes being burned throughout the Slave States.

GILBERT J. GREENE.

"Tarrytown, N. Y., August 21, 1860."

Sometime in the early part of 1860, Mr. Davis, of Mississippi, publicly denied that slaves were ever burned alive at the South. This denial led to the collection of quite an amount of testimony upon the subject, most of which was published in the *New York Tribune.* We subjoin a few of these testimonies:

The editor of *Hayneville* (Ala.), *Chronicle* very justly observes:

"It is questionable whether burning Negroes by whites has any better effect than to brutalize the feeling of a community. Several have already been burned in Montgomery County, without, it seems, decreasing crime among them."

Here it is stated by an Alabama editor that "several" negroes have already been burned in Montgomery County. Several in *a single county.*

Our next witness is a Mr. Poe, a native of Richmond, Va., and afterward a resident of Hamilton County, Ohio, where he was a highly respected ruling elder in the Presbyterian Church. In a letter written about twenty years since, upon the subject of slavery, he says: "In Goochland County, Virginia, an overseer tied a slave to a tree, flogged him again and again with great severity, then piled brush around him, set it on fire, and burned him to death. The overseer was tried and imprisoned. The whole transaction may be found on the records of the court."

The late John Parrish, of Philadelphia, an eminent minister of the Society of Friends, traveled through the Slave States on a religious mission, early in this century, and on his return published a pamphlet entitled "Remarks on the Slavery of the Black People." Among other instances of cruel punishment, he states that a slave "was burned to death at a stake in Charleston, surrounded by a multitude of spectators, some of whom were people of the first rank; . . . the poor object was heard to cry, as long as he could breathe, 'not guilty—not guilty!'"

In the year 1836, a man of color was arrested in St. Louis for some offense, but was rescued by one Mackintosh, a free man of color, a steward on board a steamboat. On his way to the jail, in order to effect his escape, he stabbed and killed one of his captors. The wife and children of the murdered man excited the rage of the people by their lamentations, the jail was surrounded, the murderer demanded, and given up. He was led into the woods, on the then outskirts of the city, but near the spot where the court-house was afterward built, brush wood and green wood was piled about him, and fire set to the heap, in presence of a concourse of two or three thousand of the citizens of St. Louis. The poor wretch was from twenty minutes to half an hour in dying, during which he was praying or singing hymns in a calm voice. When his legs were consumed, the trunk disappeared in the blazing pile. "There," said a bystander, "it is over with him; he does not feel any more now." "Yes, I do," answered a steady voice from out of the flames.

A correspondent of the *Cincinnati Herald,* in July, 1845, writes to that paper that, not long before, some slaves near Oakland Cottage, Mississippi, were emancipated by the will of their master. For some reason the will was not carried out, and the slaves, exasperated by the delay, and fearful of being cheated out of the property in themselves, left them by their master, set on fire the house of the overseer, and a white child was lost in the flames. The incendiaries, eight or nine in number, were seized by the neighbors, and two of them immediately hanged. The rest were confined in a log-house, and chained to the floor. A torch was then put to the building, and the miserable creatures roasted by a slow fire, while the air was rent with their cries.

"I have just received," writes a correspondent of the *N. O. Picayune,* at Jackson, Mississippi, on the 25th of December, 1855, "the particulars of a most horrid affair just transpired at Lexington, in this State. A young lady of the neighborhood was assaulted, on a lonely road, by a slave, who attempted to violate her person. She was rescued, however, before he had accomplished his purpose, and after being deposited in a place of safety, the alarm was raised, and a hunt for the Negro who had fled, was instituted. He was soon found, and execution was speedy. He was taken into Lexington, chained to a stake, and burned alive.

The *Montgomery* (Ala.) *Mail* of April 3, 1856, says, "We learn that the negro who murdered Mr. Capeheart, was burned to death yesterday at Mount Meigs. He acknowledged himself guilty."

The *Union Springs* (Ala.) *Gazette* of the 23d of December, 1858, gives the particulars of the murder of a Mr. J. by his slave-boy Mitford. He had been whipped, and chained up from Saturday to Monday, and, when released by his master, seized an axe and killed him. The Negro made no attempt to escape, and no resistance when taken. A public meeting was called on Wednesday to consider the case, and, by a unanimous vote of the assembly, it was resolved to burn him alive. "That evening," continues the *Gazette,* "at three o'clock, in the presence of five hundred persons, he was chained to a tree and burned."

They closed their pleasant Christmas holidays of 1858 in the same way in Troy, Ky. On the first day of last year, 1859, at the annual negro sales at Troy, Mr. James Calaway, the brother-in-law of one Simon B. Thornhill, who, it seems, had been murdered by a slave in revenge for some punishment, mounted a box in the street, and exhorted the people to do speedy justice upon the murderer, and closed by saying, "All that feel as I do, will follow me." Eight hundred or a thousand followed him. They went to the jail, took out the prisoner, and in the jail-yard itself, drove down a stake, to which they chained him hand and feet. Fine split wood was piled around him, and he was miserably burned to death. "He gave," says a correspondent of the *Maysville* (Ky.) *Eagle*, "some of the most hideous screams I ever heard come from any human being."

The *Vicksburg Sun* of Saturday, March 31, 1860, says that a negro man belonging to Mr. Woodfolk, on Deer Creek, was recently burned at the stake for the murder of a negro woman. All the negroes on that and the adjoining plantations witnessed the burning. "His fate was decreed by a council of *highly respectable gentlemen.*"

In 1856, Dr. Parsons, of Boston, a gentleman of unquestionable character, published a little work of travels at the South. He copies from the *Sumter* (Ala.) *Whig* an account of a recent burning of a slave in that county. "Dave," the slave, belonged to James D. Thornton, was accused of having murdered a daughter of his mistress, and, after his arrest, confessed his guilt. Thornton and his friends took him from the jail by a stratagem, and bore him off in triumph. "They left in high glee," says the *Whig*, and carried their prisoner to the appointed place of sacrifice. Here he was "tied to a stake, with fat light wood piled around him, and the torch was applied in the presence of two thousand persons, who had met there to witness the novel scene." There were, it seems, some rumors afloat, that "Dave" was tortured, but these, the *Whig* declares, were "entirely untrue." So, burning men alive is *not* torture in Alabama. An inquiring mind, which is not sensitive, might seek to know what is.

Dr. Parsons gives another instance which occurred not long before his visit in Georgia, the particulars of which he received from eye-witnesses. A slave had received from his mistress some punishment of great severity, when he seized a hatchet, and, as he supposed, killed her, though she afterward recovered. On committing the deed, he ran at once to the court-house and surrendered himself to justice. Justice in civilized countries would have been hanging. In Georgia, it was this: The slave was given to the mob, who first gave him fifty lashes a day for five days to prepare him for what was to follow. On the following Sunday, he was taken from the jail, and suspended, naked, by his two hands, from the limb of a large oak-tree near the court-house. A fire made of hard-pine shavings was kindled beneath him, and "then the clear bright flames quickly ascended, curling about the limbs, encircling the body, scorching the nerves, crushing the fibers, charring the flesh—and, in mortal anguish, he was (in the words of an eye-witness) 'sweating as it were, great drops of blood.'" But before life was entirely extinguished, the lungs, the heart, the liver, were cut and torn from the body, with knives fastened upon poles, and with these quivering organs elevated above the crowd, the executioners shouted, "So shall it be done to the slave that murders his mistress."

On the 7th of January, 1857, three years ago, Mr. John Kingsley, of Portsmouth, Ohio, wrote to the *Antislavery Standard* of this city that he was the week before in Carter County, Ky., where he saw a Negro tied to a stake, a pile of dry wood heaped about him, and set on fire. The man belonged to one Wm. McMinnis, of that county, and was suspected of planning an insurrection. He was first whipped, 200 lashes, but denied his guilt. Fire was then tried, and, though not burned to death, he died next day. Mr. Kingsley, unable to remain and witness the sufferings of the agonized creature, rode away and attempted to excite the neighbors to a rescue; he was told to mind his own business.

BIG RAPIDS, Mecosta Co., Mich., March 28, 1860.

In the township of Extra, in Ashley County, Arkansas, the discovery was made, that a widow named Hill, and a slave woman, belonging to J. L. M__, Esq., who lived with her, had been murdered, and the house burned to conceal the deed. The alarm soon spread, and an investigation was instituted by Mr. M__, in connection with many of the leading citizens. Suspicion fell upon a slave named Ike, belonging to a man named Perdue. Ike was whipped nearly to death, in order to extort from him a confession, but he persisted in denying any knowledge of the affair. Mr. M__ then poured upon his bleeding back *spirits of turpentine,* and set it on fire! Ike then confessed that he and a Negro named Jack, belonging to J. F. Norrell, were hired by one Miller to assist in performing the deed. One fact, however, greatly invalidated this testimony, and that was, that Mr. M__ and Mr. Norrell were deadly enemies, and Ike must have known that nothing could have pleased Mr. M__ more than to convict Jack, thus subjecting his most bitter enemy to a loss of a favorite slave, worth twelve or fifteen hundred dollars. Jack was, however, immediately arrested and brought before the regulators, and certain circumstances seeming in some degree to corroborate Ike's statement, stakes were driven into the ground, and the two slaves chained to them. A large quantity of *fat pine* was piled around them and J. L. M__ set it on *fire!* In a few minutes, nothing but charred and blackened corpses remained. A subscription was circulated to indemnify the owners for their losses.

Mr. Norrell told me that when the flames were rising ten feet above Jack's head, he said to the dying slave, "I have raised you, Jack, and I never caught you in a lie. You are going to die! nothing can save you; and now, tell me truly, as you hope for heaven, are you guilty?" Jack answered from the flames, "Master, I don't know any more about it than you do." Mr. Norrell and all his family believed Jack to have been innocent, and shed tears as they spoke of him.

The act of burning turpentine upon the lacerated back, I had from the lips of Mr. M__ himself, who rather boasted of his ingenuity in thus eliciting testimony when ordinary means had failed.

I have given true names and can give the names of more than one hundred men in the vicinity, and I am ready at any time to make affidavit to what I have stated.

CORYDON E. FULLER.

Such is the barbarism of slavery. And let no man say that these "evils" of slavery are no part of the system, and not justly chargeable to it. As well may we expect drunkenness without broils and litigation, and idleness and destitution, as to expect to hold men and women in slavery without scourgings, and thumb-screws, and murder, and almost every species of torture.

God never made a man to be a slave, and no measure of cruelty can reduce an immortal spirit, made in the image of God, to entire submission to life-long bondage. Hence, while slavery exists, chains, and thumb-screws, and slave-maiming, and slave-burnings must exist, as the *only* means by which one race can be kept in a state of even partial submission to another. And even with all these terrors before them, the wonder is that the slaves do not arise, and assert their freedom at all hazards.

NOTES

The following notes are those of Hiram Mattison and are printed in the original publication.

1. The cut on the outside title-page is a tolerable representation of the features of Mrs. P., though by no means a flattering picture.

2. What "John Randolph" this was, we know not; but suppose it was not the celebrated "John Randolph of Roanoke," though it may have been, and probably was, one of the same family. A gentleman in Xenia, Ohio, told Mrs. P. that if she

could only make it out that her mother was one of John Randolph's slaves, there was money somewhere, now, of John Randolph's estate, to buy her mother and brother.

3. Mrs. P. dare not have *any* of these names published, as all the parties are still living.

4. We have the name, but Mrs. P. dare not have it published, as the parties are still living, and she fears they might shoot her.

5. For particular reasons the letter was dated at St. Louis, where so many slaves are bought for Texas and Alabama; and this letter came first to St. Louis, and was forwarded by a friend to Cincinnati. Thus all the letters come and go.

6. The object of this movement on the part of Mr. Mattison was not to satisfy the writer, or himself; but to procure fresh testimony from original sources, to either convince or silence such incredulous subjects as Rev. H. Slicer.

CHRONOLOGY OF
MATTIE J. JACKSON

1847 (January)—Mattie J. (Martha Jane) Jackson born St. Louis, Missouri, on the plantation of Charles Canory, second of three daughters of Westley Jackson and Ellen Turner.

1850 (September 20)—Esther G. Jackson born to Westley and Ellen.

1851—Westley Jackson is sold; runs away to Chicago, where he becomes a minister of the Gospel and "died before the War."

Circa 1853—Ellen takes her two surviving daughters Mattie and Esther and attempts to run away; they are caught and sold to William J. Lewis of St. Louis.

Circa 1854—George Brown meets Ellen Turner, their son George born 1855.

Circa 1857—George Brown runs away to Canada; changes his name to John G. Thompson; moves to Lawrence, Massachusetts, working as a barber. He meets Dr. Lucy Prophet Schuyler (b. 1813, Rutland, Massachusetts), an "Indian Doctor" (a botanical physician using herbal remedies), the widow of Dr. Peter Schuyler, a botanical physician and itinerant Methodist preacher. Peter and Lucy Schuyler had seven children, but their second son Arthur lived the longest. Arthur falsified his age to enlist in the 54th Massachusetts Infantry. Arthur served out his two-year term, but came home suffering from tuberculosis—he died at nineteen. After hearing "that [Ellen] and children had per-

95

ished in the woods while endeavoring to make their escape" (this was in error), John and Lucy subsequently marry August 26, 1860, and live in Lawrence.

Late 1850s—Dr. Lucy Thompson is a conductor on the Underground Railroad and is involved in a number of court cases involving runaway slaves, despite the fact that she, Mattie's stepfather, and her son Arthur Schuyler make up fully fifty percent of the total African American population of the city of Lawrence.

1861—Union troops under Brigadier General Nathaniel Lyon occupy St. Louis; Mattie goes to them after being beaten by her master; when Lewis comes to get her, Lyon, a committed Abolitionist originally from Connecticut, "immediately arrest[s] Mr. L and [gives] him one hundred lashes with the cow-hide so they might identify him by a scarred back, as well as his slaves." After Lewis recovers, he treats Ellen and her remaining children terribly; she and her children run away and hide in the city of St. Louis, but are found out, recaptured and sold to a Captain "Tirrell."

Circa 1862—Samuel Adams meets Ellen Turner (Brown); on the day set for their wedding (March 18), Captain "Tirrell" takes Ellen, Mattie, Esther, and George and spirits them to Louisville, Kentucky, where they are sold to different owners.

Circa 1863—Not quite sixteen years old, Arthur Schuyler falsifies his age to enlist in the 54th Massachusetts Infantry. He serves his two-year term but comes home suffering from tuberculosis. Arthur dies at nineteen.

1863—After various misadventures, Mattie makes her way to Indianapolis, Indiana.

1865 (May)—Esther Jackson escapes from slavery; a few weeks later, Ellen Turner Brown and her son George also escape to Indianapolis, where Mattie had settled in the boardinghouse of a Mrs. Harris.

1865 (September?)—Samuel Adams and Ellen Turner Brown marry in St. Louis; Mattie returns and works for the Canory family in Bremen, Missouri (now included within the boundaries of the city of St. Louis).

1866—George Brown, now known as John G. Thompson, contacts Mattie's aunt in St. Louis as to the whereabouts of his family; upon finding out that his one son George is still alive, he requests that he be sent to Lawrence, Massachusetts. Major John Howe, a former mayor of St. Louis, advances the carfare for George and Mattie to go to Lawrence.

1866 (April 11)—Mattie and George arrive in Lawrence.

Before 1869—Mattie returns to St. Louis and lives with her mother, stepfather, and sister, according to the 1870 Federal Census. George remains in Lawrence with his father and stepmother, changing his name to Thompson.

1869 (July 27)—Mattie marries William Reed Dyer (born Warrenton, Missouri, February 1846), a porter on Mississippi River steamboats, in St. Louis. They would have nine children, of whom five would reach maturity.

1870 (July)—William H. Dyer, the eldest son of Mattie and William, born in St. Louis. He would become an elevator operator at St. Louis City Hall. He would marry Birdie Sneed and have a son and three daughters.

1873 (October 15)—Esther Jackson marries Charles Diggs in St. Louis; they would have nine children but only two would survive childhood.

1875 (May 13)—Arthur Thomas Dyer, son of William and Mattie, born in St. Louis. Arthur is named for Lucy Thompson's last surviving son, Arthur T. Schuyler. Arthur Dyer would become a dining car chef on the Michigan Central Railroad. He would marry at least twice and have one son.

1875 (May 25)—Samuel Adams dies in St. Louis.

1877—Albert L. Dyer, son of William and Mattie, born in St. Louis; he would die before his twenty-first birthday.

1877—George Brown Thompson dies in Lawrence, Massachusetts.

1878—Edith A. Dyer, the only surviving daughter of William and Mattie, is born in St. Louis. She would move to Alton, Illinois, where she would run a boardinghouse. In 1907, she married Milton C. Slaughter, a Texas-born oil field worker and day laborer; they would have no children.

1881 (March 20)—Lucy Thompson dies in Lawrence, Massachusetts. Her age at death is listed as sixty-eight years and five days, which would make her birth date March 15, 1813 (census records show either

1814 or 1815)—this fact is of some interest as this is also Harriet E. Wilson's (author of *Our Nig*) birthday (1825).

1882 (August 10)—Warren Charles Dyer, youngest son of William and Mattie, born in St. Louis. He would work as a laborer in factories and, in 1922, receive U.S. Patent 1,437,296 for a "bathing appliance"—a device used to scrub one's back. He would marry at least three times but produce no children.

1882—John G. Thompson dies in Lawrence, Massachusetts.

1893 (May 9)—Ellen Turner Adams dies in St. Louis.

1895—William and Mattie Dyer move to the town of Dardenne, Missouri, about thirty-five miles from St. Louis. They own improved real estate both in Dardenne and the neighboring community of O'Fallon, Missouri.

1910 (February 5)—Mattie Jackson Dyer dies in Dardenne, aged sixty-three.

1912 (July 27)—William Reed Dyer dies in Dardenne, aged sixty-six.

1921 (June 21)—Esther Jackson Diggs dies in St. Louis, aged seventy.

THE STORY OF
MATTIE J. JACKSON;

*Her Parentage—Experience of Eighteen Years in Slavery—
Incidents During the War—Her Escape from Slavery.*

A True Story.

WRITTEN AND ARRANGED BY
DR. L. S. THOMPSON
(FORMERLY MRS. SCHUYLER,)
AS GIVEN BY MATTIE.

Lawrence:
Printed at Sentinel Office, 123 Essex Street.
1866.

PREFACE

The object in publishing this book is to gain sympathy from the earnest friends of those who have been bound down by a dominant race in circumstances over which they had no control—a butt of ridicule and a mark of oppression; over whom weary ages of degradation have passed. As the links have been broken and the shackles fallen from them through the unwearied efforts of our beloved martyr President Lincoln, as one I feel it a duty to improve the mind, and have ever had a thirst for education to fill that vacuum for which the soul has ever yearned since my earliest remembrance.

Thus I ask you to buy my little book to aid me in obtaining an education, that I may be enabled to do some good in behalf of the elevation of my emancipated brothers and sisters. I have now arrived at the age of twenty. As the first dawn of morning has passed, and the meridian of life is approaching, I know of no other way to speedily gain my object than through the aid and patronage of the friends of humanity.

NOTE Miss Jackson sustains a high moral character—has been much respected since she has been in Lawrence. She is from St. Louis, Missouri, and arrived here on the 11th of April, 1866. To gain the wish of the heart is utterly impossible without more means than she can obtain otherwise. Her friends have borne her expenses to Lawrence, and have and are still willing to render her aid as far their limited means will allow. She was in the same condition of all the neglected and oppressed. Her personal requirements are amply supplied. She now only craves the means to clothe and qualify the intellect. My humble prayer is that she may meet with unlimited success.

This young lady is highly worthy of all the aid our kind friends feel a duty to bestow upon her. She purposes lecturing and relating her story; and I trust she may render due satisfaction and bear some humble part in removing doubts indulged by the prejudices against the natural genius and talent of our race. May God give her grace and speed her on her way.

Respectfully yours,

L. S. T.

MATTIE'S STORY

My ancestors were transported from Africa to America at the time the slave trade flourished in the Eastern States. I cannot give dates, as my progenitors, being slaves, had no means of keeping them. By all accounts my great grand-father was captured and brought from Africa. His original name I never learned. His master's name was Jackson, and he resided in the State of New York. My grandfather was born in the same State, and also remained a slave for some length of time, when he was emancipated, his master presenting him with quite an amount of property. He was true, honest and responsible, and this present was given him as a reward. He was much encouraged by the cheering prospect of better days. A better condition of things now presented itself. As he possessed a large share of confidence, he came to the conclusion, as he was free, that he was capable of selecting his own residence and manage his own affairs with prudence and economy. But, alas, his hopes were soon blighted. More heart rending sorrow and degradation awaited him. He was earnestly invited by a white decoyer to relinquish his former design and accompany him to Missouri and join him in speculation and become wealthy. As partners, they embarked on board a schooner for St. Charles, Mo. On the passage, my grandfather was seized with a fever, and for a while was totally unconscious. When he regained his reason he found himself, near his journey's end, divested of his free papers and all others. On his arrival at St. Charles he was seized by a huge, surly looking slaveholder who claimed him as his property. The contract had previously been concluded by his Judas-like friend, who had received the bounty. Oh, what a sad disappoint-ment. After serving for thirty years to be thrust again into bondage where a deeper degradation and sorrow and hopeless toil were to be his portion for the remaining years of his existence. In deep despair and overwhelmed with grief, he made his escape to the woods, determined to put an end to his sor-rows by perishing with cold and hunger. His master immediately pursued him, and in twenty-four hours found him with hands and feet frost-bitten, in consequence of which he lost the use of his fingers and toes, and was thenceforth of little use to his new master. He remained with him, however, and married a woman in the same station in life. They lived as happily as their circumstances would permit. As Providence alloted, they only had one son, which was my father, Westly Jackson. He had a deep affection for his family, which the slave ever cherishes for his dear ones. He had no other link to fasten him to the human family but his fervent love for those who were bound to him by love and sympathy in their wrongs and sufferings. My grandfather remained in the same family until his death. My father, Westly Jackson, married, at the age of twenty-two, a girl owned by James Harris, named Ellen Turner. Nothing of importance occurred until three years after their marriage, when her master, Harris failed through the extravagance and mismanagement of his wife, who was a great spendthrift and a dreaded terror to the poor slaves and all others with whom she associated in common circumstances, consequently the entire stock was sold by the sheriff to a trader residing in Virginia. On account of the good reputation my mother sustained as a worthy servant and excellent cook, a tyrannical and much dreaded slaveholder watched for an opportunity to purchase her, but fortunately arrived a few moments too late, and she was bid off in too poor a condition of health to remain long a subject of banter and speculation. Her husband was allowed to carefully lift her down from the block and accompany her to her new master's, Charles Canory, who treated her very kindly while she remained in his family. Mr. Canory resided in St. Charles County for five years after he purchased my mother. During that time my father and mother were in the same neighborhood, but a short distance from each other. But another trial awaited them. Her master removed twenty miles away to a village called Bremen, near St. Louis, Mo. My father, thereafter, visited my mother once a week, walking the distance every Saturday evening and returning on Sunday evening. But through all her trials and deprivations her trust and confidence was in Him who rescued his faithful followers from the fiery furnace and the lion's den, and led Moses through the Red Sea. Her trust and confidence was in Jesus. She relied on His precious promises and ever found Him a present help in every time of need. Two years after this separation my father was sold and separated from us, but previous to his delivery to his new master he made his escape to a free State. My mother was then left with two children. She had three during the time they were permitted to remain together, and buried one. Their names were Sarah Ann, Mattie Jane and Esther J. When my father left I was about three years of age, yet I can well remember the little kindnesses my father used to bestow upon us, and the deep affection and fondness he manifested for us. I shall never forget the bitter anguish of my parents' hearts, the sighs they uttered or the profusion of tears which coursed down their sable cheeks. O, what a horrid scene, but he was not her's, for cruel hands had separated them.

> The strongest tie of earthly joy that bound the aching heart—
> His love was e'er a joyous light that o'er the pathway shone—
> A fountain gushing ever new amid life's desert wild—
> His slightest word was a sweet tone of music round her heart—
> Their lives a streamlet blent in one. O, Father, must they part?
> They tore him from her circling arms, her last and fond embrace—
> O never again can her sad eyes gaze upon his mournful face.
> It is not strange these bitter sighs are constant bursting forth.
> Amid mirth and glee and revelry she never took a part,
> She was a mother left alone with sorrow in her heart.

But my mother was conscious some time previous of the change that was to take place with my father, and if he was sold in the immediate vicinity he would be likely to be sold again at their will, and she concluded to assist him to make his escape from bondage. Though the parting was painful, it afforded her solace in the contemplation of her husband becoming a free man, and cherishing a hope that her little family, through the aid of some angel of mercy, might be enabled to make their escape also, and meet to part no more on earth. My father came to spend the night with us, according to his usual custom. It was the last time, and sadness brooded upon his brow. It was the only opportunity he had to make his escape without suspicion and detection, as he was immediately to fall into the hands of a new master. He had never been sold from the place of his birth before, and was determined never to be sold again if God would verify his promise. My father was not educated, but was a preacher, and administered the Word of God according to the dictation and revelation of the spirit. His former master had allowed him the privilege of holding meetings in the village within the limits of his pass on the Sundays when he visited my mother. But on this Saturday evening he arrived and gave us all his farewell kiss, and hurried away. My mother's people were aware of my father's intention, but rather than spare my mother, and for fear she might be detected, they secreted his escape. His master called a number of times and enquired for him and strongly pressed my mother to give him an account of my father, but she never gave it. We waited patiently, hoping to learn if he succeeded in gaining his freedom. Many anxious weeks and months passed before we could get any tidings from him, until at length my mother heard that he was in Chicago, a free man and preaching the Gospel. He made every effort to get his family, but all in vain. The spirit of slavery so strongly existed that letters could not reach her; they were all destroyed. My parents had never learned the rescuing scheme of the underground railroad which had borne so many thousands to the standard of freedom and victories. They knew no other resource than to depend upon their own chance in running away and secreting themselves. If caught they were in a worse condition than before.

THEIR ATTEMPT TO MAKE THEIR ESCAPE

Two years after my father's departure, my mother, with her two children, my sister and myself, attempted to make her escape. After traveling two days we reached Illinois. We slept in the woods at night. I believe my mother had food to supply us but fasted herself. But the advertisement had reached there before us, and loafers were already in search of us, and as soon as we were discovered on the brink of the river one of the spies made enquiries respecting her suspicious appearance. She was aware that she was arrested, consequently she gave a true account of herself—that she was in search of her husband. We were then destitute of any articles of clothing excepting our wearing apparel. Mother had become so weary that she was compelled to leave our package of clothing on the way. We were taken back to St. Louis and committed to prison and remained there one week, after which they put us in Linch's trader's yard, where we remained about four weeks. We were then sold to William Lewis. Mr. Lewis was a very severe master, and inflicted such punishment upon us as he thought proper. However, I only remember one severe contest Mr. Lewis had with my mother. For some slight offence Mrs. Lewis became offended and was tartly and loudly reprimanding her, when Mr. L. came in and rashly felled her to the floor with his fist. But his wife was constantly pulling our ears, snapping us with her thimble, rapping us on the head and sides of it. It appeared impossible to please her. When we first went to Mr. L.'s they had a cowhide which she used to inflict on a little slave girl she previously owned, nearly every night. This was done to learn the little girl to wake early to wait on her children. But my mother was a cook, as I before stated, and was in the habit of roasting meats and toasting bread. As they stinted us for food my mother roasted the cowhide. It was rather poor picking, but it was the last cowhide my mother ever had an opportunity to cook while we remained in his family. Mr. L. soon moved about six miles from the city, and entered in partnership with his brother-in-law. The servants were then divided and distributed in both families. It unfortunately fell to my lot to live with Mrs. Larry, my mistress' sister, which rendered my condition worse than the first. My master even disapproved of my ill treatment and took me to another place; the place my mother resided before my father's escape. After a short time Mr. Lewis again returned to the city. My mother still remained as cook in his family. After six years' absence of my father my mother married again a man by the name of George Brown, and lived with her second husband about four years, and had two children, when he was sold for requesting a different kind and enough food. His master considered it a great insult, and declared he would sell him. But previous to this insult, as he called it, my step-father was foreman in Mr. L.'s tobacco factory. He was trusty and of good moral habits, and was calculated to bring the highest price in the human market; therefore the excuse to sell him for the above offence was only a plot. The morning this offence occurred, Mr. L. bid my father to remain in the kitchen till he had taken his breakfast. After pulling his ears and slapping his face bade him come to the factory; but instead of going to the factory he went to Canada. Thus my poor mother was again left alone with two more children added to her misery and sorrow to toil on her weary pilgrimage.

> Racked with agony and pain she was left alone again,
> With a purpose nought could move
> And the zeal of woman's love,
> Down she knelt in agony
> To ask the Lord to clear the way.

> True she said O gracious Lord,
> True and faithful is thy word;
> But the humblest, poorest, may
> Eat the crumbs they cast away.

Though nine long years had passed
Without one glimmering light of day
She never did forget to pray
And has not yet though whips and chains are cast away.

For thus said the blessed Lord,
I will verify my word;
By the faith that has not failed,
Thou hast asked and shall prevail.

We remained but a short time at the same residence when Mr. Lewis moved again to the country. Soon after, my little brother was taken sick in consequence of being confined in a box in which my mother was obliged to keep him. If permitted to creep around the floor her mistress thought it would take too much time to attend to him. He was two years old and never walked. His limbs were perfectly paralyzed for want of exercise. We now saw him gradually failing, but was not allowed to render him due attention. Even the morning he died she was compelled to attend to her usual work. She watched over him for three months by night and attended to her domestic affairs by day. The night previous to his death we were aware he could not survive through the approaching day, but it made no impression on my mistress until she came into the kitchen and saw his life fast ebbing away, then she put on a sad countenance for fear of being exposed, and told my mother to take the child to her room, where he only lived one hour. When she found he was dead she ordered grave clothes to be brought and gave my mother time to bury him. O that morning, that solemn morning. It appears to me that when that little spirit departed as though all heaven rejoiced and angels veiled their faces.

My mother too in concert joined,—
Her mingled praise with them combined.
Her little saint had gone to God
Who saved him with his precious blood.

Who said "Suffer little children to come unto me and forbid them not."

The Soldiers, and Our Treatment During the War

Soon after the war commenced the rebel soldiers encamped near Mr. Lewis' residence, and remained there one week. They were then ordered by General Lyons to surrender, but they refused. There were seven thousand Union and seven hundred rebel soldiers. The Union soldiers surrounded the camp and took them and exhibited them through the city and then confined them in prison. I told my mistress that the Union soldiers were coming to take the camp. She replied that it was false, that it was General Kelly coming to re-enforce Gen. Frost. In a few moments the alarm was heard. I told Mrs. L. the Unionists had fired upon the rebels. She replied it was only the salute of Gen. Kelley. At night her husband came home with the news that Camp Jackson was taken and all the soldiers prisoners. Mrs. Lewis asked how the Union soldiers could take seven hundred men when they only numbered the same. Mr. L. replied they had seven thousand. She was much astonished, and cast her eye around to us for fear we might hear her. Her suspicion was correct; there was not a word passed that escaped our listening ears. My mother and myself could read enough to make out the news in the papers. The Union soldiers took much delight in tossing a paper over the fence to us. It aggravated my mistress very much. My mother used to sit up nights and read to keep posted about the war. In a few days my mistress came down to the kitchen again with another bitter complaint that it was a sad affair that the Unionists had taken their delicate citizens who had enlisted and made prisoners of them—that they were babes. My mother reminded her of taking Fort Sumpter and Major Anderson and serving them the same and that turn about was fair play. She then hastened to her room with the speed of a deer, nearly unhinging every door in her flight, replying as she went that the Niggers and Yankees were seeking to take the country. One day, after she had visited the kitchen to superintend some domestic affairs, as she pretended, she became very angry without a word being passed, and said—"I think it has come to a pretty pass, that old Lincoln, with his long legs, an old rail splitter, wishes to put the Niggers on an equality with the whites; that her children should never be on an equal footing with a Nigger. She had rather see them dead." As my mother made no reply to her remarks, she stopped talking, and commenced venting her spite on my companion servant. On one occasion Mr. Lewis searched my mother's room and found a picture of President Lincoln, cut from a newspaper, hanging in her room. He asked her what she was doing with old Lincoln's picture. She replied it was there because she liked it. He then knocked her down three times, and sent her to the trader's yard for a month as punishment. My mistress indulged some hopes till the victory of New Orleans, when she heard the famous Union song sang to the tune of Yankee Doodle:

The rebels swore that New Orleans never should be taken,
But if the Yankees came so near they should not save their bacon.
That's the way they blustered when they thought they were so
   handy,
But Farragut steamed up one day and gave them Doodle Dandy.

Ben. Butler then was ordered down to regulate the city;
He made the rebels walk a chalk, and was not that a pity?
That's the way to serve them out—that's the way to treat them,
They must not go and put on airs after we have beat them.

He made the rebel banks shell out and pay the loyal people,
He made them keep the city clean from pig's sty to church steeple.
That's the way Columbia speaks, let all men believe her;
That's the way Columbia speaks instead of yellow fever.

He sent the saucy women up and made them treat us well
He helped the poor and snubbed the rich; they thought he was the
   devil,
Bully for Ben. Butler, then, they thought he was so handy;
Bully for Ben Butler then,—Yankee Doodle Dandy.

The days of sadness for mistress were days of joy for us. We shouted and laughed to the top of our voices. My mistress was more enraged than ever— nothing pleased her. One evening, after I had attended to my usual duties, and I supposed all was complete, she, in a terrible range, declared I should be punished that night. I did not know the cause, neither did she. She went immediately and selected a switch. She placed it in the corner of the room to await the return of her husband at night for him to whip me. As I was not pleased with the idea of a whipping I bent the switch in the shape of W, which was the first letter of his name, and after I had attended to the dining room my fellow servant and myself walked away and stopped with an aunt of mine during the night. In the morning we made our way to the Arsenal, but could gain no admission. While we were wandering about seeking protection, the girl's father overtook us and persuaded us to return home. We finally complied. All was quiet. Not a word was spoken respecting our sudden departure. All went on as usual. I was permitted to attend to my work without interruption until three weeks after. One morning I entered Mrs. Lewis' room, and she was in a room adjoining, complaining of something I had neglected. Mr. L. then enquired if I had done my work. I told him I had. She then flew into a rage and told him I was saucy, and to strike me, and he immediately gave me a severe blow with a stick of wood, which inflicted a deep wound upon my head. The blood ran over my clothing, which gave me a frightful appearance. Mr. Lewis then ordered me to change my clothing immediately. As I did not obey he became more enraged, and pulled me into another room and threw me on the floor, placed his knee on my stomach, slapped me on the face and beat me with his fist, and would have punished me more had not my mother interfered. He then told her to go away or he would compel her to, but she remained until he left me. I struggled mightily, and stood him a good test for a while, but he was fast conquering me when my mother came. He was aware my mother could usually defend herself against one man, and both of us would overpower him, so after giving his wife strict orders to take me up stairs and keep me there, he took his carriage and drove away. But she forgot it, as usual. She was highly gratified with my appropriate treatment, as she called it, and retired to her room, leaving me to myself. I then went to my mother and told her I was going away. She bid me go, and added "May the Lord help you." I started for the Arsenal again and succeeded in gaining admittance and seeing the Adjutant. He ordered me to go to another tent, where there was a woman in similar circumstances, cooking. When the General found I was there he sent me to the boarding house. I remained there three weeks, and when I went I wore the same stained clothing as when I was so severely punished, which has left a mark on my head which will ever remind me of my treatment while in slavery. Thanks be to God, though tortured by wrong and goaded by oppression, the hearts that would madden with misery have broken the iron yoke.

MR. LEWIS CALLS AT THE BOARDING HOUSE

At the expiration of three weeks Mr. Lewis called at my boarding house, accompanied by his brother-in-law, and enquired for me, and the General informed him where I was. He then told me my mother was very anxious for me to come home, and I returned. The General had ordered Mr. Lewis to call at headquarters, when he told him if he had treated me right I would not have been compelled to seek protection of him; that my first appearance was sufficient proof of his cruelty. Mr. L. promised to take me home and treat me kindly. Instead of fulfilling his promise he carried me to the trader's yard, where, to my great surprise, I found my mother. She had been there during my absence, where she was kept for fear she would find me and take my brother and sister and make her escape. There was so much excitement at that time, (1861), by the Union soldiers rendering the fugitives shelter and protection, he was aware that if she applied to them, as he did not fulfill his promise in my case, he would stand a poor chance. If my mother made application to them for protection they would learn that he did not return me home, and immediately detect the intrigue. After I was safely secured in the trader's yard, Mr. L. took my mother home. I remained in the yard three months. Near the termination of the time of my confinement I was passing by the office when the cook of the Arsenal saw and recognized me and informed the General that Mr. L. had disobeyed his orders, and had put me in the trader's yard instead of taking me home. The General immediately arrested Mr. L. and gave him one hundred lashes with the cow-hide, so that they might identify him by a scarred back, as well as his slaves. My mother had the pleasure of washing his stained clothes, otherwise it would not have been known. My master was compelled to pay three thousand dollars and let me out. He then put me to service, where I remained seven months, after which he came in great haste and took me into the city and put me into the trader's yard again. After he received the punishment he treated my mother and the children worse than ever, which caused her to take her children and secrete themselves in the city, and would have remained undetected had it not been for a traitor who pledged himself to keep the secret. But King Whiskey fired up his brain one evening, and out popped the secret. My mother and sister were consequently taken and committed to the trader's yard. My little brother was then eight years of age, my sister sixteen, and myself eighteen. We remained there two weeks, when a rough looking man, called Capt. Tirrell, came to the yard and enquired for our family. After he had examined us he remarked that we were a fine looking family, and bid us retire. In about two hours he returned, at the edge of the evening, with a covered wagon, and took my mother and brother and sister and left me. My mother refused to go without me, and told him she would raise an alarm. He advised her to remain as quiet as possible. At length she was compelled to go. When she entered the wagon there was a man standing behind with his hands on each side of the wagon to prevent her from making her escape. She sprang to her feet and gave this man a desperate blow, and leaping to the ground she made an alarm. The watchmen came to her assistance immediately, and there was quite a number of Union policemen guarding the city at that time, who rendered her due justice as far as possible. This was before the emancipation proclamation was issued. After she leaped from the wagon they drove on, taking her children to the boat. The police questioned my mother. She told them that Capt. Tirrell had put her children on board the boat, and was going to take them to Memphis and sell them into hard slavery. They accompanied her to the boat, and arrived just as they were casting off. The police ordered them to stop and immediately deliver up the children, who had been secreted in the Captain's private apartment. They were brought forth and returned. Slave speculation was forbidden in St. Louis at that time. The Union soldiers had possession of the city, but their power was limited to the suppression of the selling of slaves to go out of the city. Considerable smuggling was done, however, by pretending Unionism, which was the case with our family.

RELEASED FROM THE TRADER'S YARD AND TAKEN TO HER NEW MASTER

Immediately after dinner my mother called for me to accompany her to our new home, the residence of the Captain, together with my brother and sister. We fared very well while we were there. Mrs. Tirrell was insane, and my mother had charge of the house. We remained there four months. The Captain came home only once a week and he never troubled us for fear we might desert him. His intention was to smuggle us away before the State became free. That was the understanding when he bought us of Mr. Lewis, as it was not much of an object to purchase slaves while the proclamation was pending, and they likely to lose all their property; but they would, for a trifle purchase a whole family of four or five persons to send out of the State. Kentucky paid as much, or more than ever, for slaves. As they pretended to take no part in the rebellion they supposed they would be allowed to keep them without interference. Consequently the Captain's intention was to keep as quiet as possible till the excitement concerning us was over, and he could get us off without detection. Mr. Lewis would rather have disposed of us for nothing than have seen us free. He hated my mother in consequence of her desire for freedom, and her endeavors to teach her children the right way as far as her ability would allow. He also held a charge against her for reading the papers and understanding political affairs. When he found he was to lose his slaves he could not bear the idea of her being free. He thought it too hard, as she had raised so many tempests for him, to see her free and under her own control. He had tantalized her in every possible way to humiliate and annoy her; yet while he could demand her services he appreciated and placed perfect confidence in mother and family. None but a fiendish slaveholder could have rended an honest Christian heart in such a manner as this.

Though it was her sad and weary lot to toil in slavery
But one thing cheered her weary soul
When almost in despair
That she could gain a sure relief in attitude of prayer

CAPT. TIRRELL REMOVES THE FAMILY— ANOTHER STRATEGY

One day the Captain commenced complaining of the expense of so large a family, and proposed to my mother that we should work out and he take part of the pay. My mother told him she would need what she earned for my little brother's support. Finally the Captain consented, and I was the first to be disposed of. The Captain took me in his buggy and carried me to the Depot, and I was put into a Union family, where I remained five months.

Previous to my leaving, however, my mother and the Captain entered into a contract—he agreeing not to sell us, and mother agreeing not to make her escape. While she was carrying out her promise in good faith, he was plotting to separate us. We were all divided except mother and my little brother, who remained together. My sister remained with one of the rebels, but was tolerably treated. We all fared very well; but it was only the calm before the rending tornado. Captain T. was Captain of the boat to Memphis, from which the Union soldiers had rescued us. He commenced as a deck hand on the boat, then attained a higher position, and continued to advance until he became her Captain. At length he came in possession of slaves. Then his accomplishments were complete. He was a very severe slave master. Those mushroom slaveholders are much dreaded, as their severity knows no bounds.

Bondage and torture, scourges and chains
Placed on our backs indelible stains.

I stated previously, in relating a sketch of my mother's history, that she was married twice, and both husbands were to be sold and made their escape. They both gained their freedom. One was living,—the other died before the war. Both made every effort to find us, but to no purpose. It was some years before we got a correct account of her second husband, and he had no account of her, except once he heard that mother and children had perished in the woods while endeavoring to make their escape. In a few years after his arrival in the free States he married again.

When about sixteen years of age, while residing with her original master, my mother became acquainted with a young man, Mr. Adams, residing in a neighboring family, whom she much respected; but he was soon sold, and she lost trace of him entirely, as was the common occurrence with friends and companions though united by the nearest ties. When my mother arrived at Captain Tirrell's, after leaving the boat, in her excitement she scarce observed anything except her little group so miraculously saved from perhaps a final separation in this world. She at length observed that the servant who was waiting to take her to the Captain's residence in the country was the same man with whom she formed the acquaintance when sixteen years old, and they again renewed their acquaintance. He had been married and buried his wife. It appeared that his wife had been in Captain Tirrell's family many years, and he also, for some time. They had a number of children, and Capt. Tirrell had sold them down South. This cruel blow, assisted by severe flogging and other ill treatment, rendered the mother insane, and finally caused her death.

In agony close to her bosom she pressed,
The life of her heart, the child of her breast—
Oh love from its tenderness gathering might
Had strengthened her soul for declining age.

But she is free. Yes, she has gone from the land of the slave;
The hand of oppression must rest in the grave.
The blood hounds have missed the scent of her way,
The hunter is rifled and foiled of his prey.

After my mother had left the Captain to take care of herself and child, according to agreement with the Captain, she became engaged to Mr. Adams. He had bought himself previously for a large price. After they became acquainted, the Captain had an excellent opportunity of carrying out his stratagem. He commenced bestowing charity upon Mr. Adams. As he had purchased himself, and Capt. T. had agreed not to sell my mother, they had decided to marry at an early day. They hired a house in the city and were to commence housekeeping immediately. The Captain made him a number of presents and seemed much pleased with the arrangement. The day previous to the one set for the marriage, while they were setting their house in order, a man called and enquired for a nurse, pretending he wanted one of us. Mother was absent; he said he would call again, but he never came. On Wednesday evening we attended a protracted meeting. After we had returned home and retired, a loud rap was heard at the door. My Aunt enquired who was there. The reply was, "Open the door or I will break it down." In a moment in rushed seven men, four watchmen and three traders and ordered mother to take my brother and me and follow them, which she hastened to do as fast as possible, but we were not allowed time to put on our usual attire. They thrust us into a close carriage. For fear of my mother alarming the citizens they threw her to the ground and choked her until she was nearly strangled, then pushed her into a coach. The night was dark and dreary; the stars refused to shine, the moon to shed her light.

> 'Tis not strange the heavenly orbs
> In silence blushed neath Nature's sable garb
> When woman's gagged and rashly torn away
> Without blemish and without crime.
> Unheeded by God's holy word:—
> Unloose the fetters, break the chain,
> And make my people free again,
> And let them breath pure freedom's air
> And her rich bounty freely share.
> Let Eutopia stretch her bleeding hands abroad;
> Her cry of anguish finds redress from God.

We were hurried along the streets. The inhabitants heard our cries and rushed to their doors, but our carriage being perfectly tight, and the alarm so sudden, that we were at the jail before they could give us any relief. There were strong Union men and officers in the city, and if they could have been informed of the human smuggling they would have released us. But oh, that horrid, dilapidated prison, with its dim lights and dingy walls, again presented itself to our view. My sister was there first, and we were thrust in and remained there until three o'clock the following afternoon. Could we have notified the police we should have been released, but no opportunity was given us. It appears that this kidnapping had been in contemplation from the time we were before taken and returned; and Captain Tirrell's kindness to mother,—his benevolence towards Mr. Adams in assisting him to furnish his house,—his generosity in letting us work for ourselves,—his approbation in regard to the contemplated marriage was only a trap. Thus instead of a wedding Thursday evening, we were hurled across the ferry to Albany Court House and to Kentucky through the rain and without our outer garments. My mother had lost her bonnet and shawl in the struggle while being thrust in the coach, consequently she had no protection from the storm, and the rest of us were in similar circumstances. I believe we passed through Springfield. I think it was the first stopping place after we left East St. Louis, and we were put on board the cars and secreted in the gentlemen's smoking car, in which there were only a few rebels. We arrived in Springfield about twelve o'clock at night. When we took the cars it was dark, bleak and cold. It was the 18th of March, and as we were without bonnets and clothing to shield us from the sleet and wind, we suffered intensely. The old trader, for fear that mother might make her escape, carried my brother, nine years of age, from one train to the other. We then took the cars for Albany, and arrived at eight o'clock in the morning. We were then carried on the ferry in a wagon. There was another family in the wagon, in the same condition. We landed at Portland, from thence to Louisville, and were put into John Clark's trader's yard, and sold out separately, except my mother and little brother, who were sold together. Mother remained in the trader's yard two weeks, my sister six, myself four.

THE FARE AT THEIR NEW HOMES

Mother was sold to Captain Plasio. My sister to Benj. Board, and myself to Capt. Ephraim Frisbee. The man who bought my mother was a Spaniard. After she had been there a short time he tried to have my mother let my brother stop at his saloon, a very dissipated place, to wait upon his miserable crew, but my mother objected. In spite of her objections he took him down to try him, but some Union soldiers called at the saloon, and noticing that he was very small, they questioned him, and my brother, child like, divulged the whole matter. The Captain, fearful of being betrayed and losing his property, let him continue with my mother. The Captain paid eight hundred dollars for my mother and brother. We were all sold for extravagant prices. My sister, aged sixteen, was sold for eight hundred and fifty dollars; I was sold for nine hundred dollars. This was in 1863. My mother was cook and fared very well. My sister was sold to a single gentleman, whose intended took charge of her until they were married, after which they took her to her home. She was her waiter, and fared as well as could be expected. I fared worse than either of the family. I was not allowed enough to eat, exposed to the cold, and not allowed through the cold winter to thoroughly warm myself once a month. The house was very large, and I could gain no access to the fire. I was kept constantly at work of the heaviest kind,—compelled to move heavy trunks and boxes,—many times to wash till ten and twelve o'clock at night. There were three deaths in the family while I remained there, and the entire burden was put upon me. I often felt to exclaim as the Children of Israel did: "O Lord, my burden is greater than I can bear." I was then seventeen years of age. My health has been impaired from that time to the present. I have a severe pain in my side by the slightest over exertion. In the Winter I suffer intensely with cold, and cannot get warm unless in a room heated to eighty degrees. I am infirm and burdened with the influence of slavery, whose impress will ever remain on my mind and body. For six months I tried to make my escape. I used to rise at four o'clock in the morning to find some one to assist me, and at last I succeeded. I was allowed two hours once in two weeks to go and return three miles. I could contrive no other way than to improve one of these opportunities, in which I was finally successful. I became acquainted with some persons who assisted slaves to escape by the underground railroad. They were colored people. I was to pretend going to church, and the man who was to assist and introduce me to the proper parties was to linger on the street opposite the house, and I was to follow at a short distance. On Sunday evening I begged leave to attend church, which was reluctantly granted if I completed all my work, which was no easy task. It appeared as if my mistress used every possible exertion to delay me from church, and I concluded that her old cloven-footed companion had impressed his intentions on her mind. Finally, when I was ready to start, my mistress took a notion to go out to ride, and desired me to dress her little boy, and then get ready for church. Extensive hoops were then worn, and as I had attached my whole wardrobe under mine by a cord around my waist, it required considerable dexterity and no small amount of maneuvering to hide the fact from my mistress. While attending to the child I had managed to stand in one corner of the room, for fear she might come in contact with me and thus discover that my hoops were not so elastic as they usually are. I endeavored to conceal my excitement by backing and edging very genteelly out of the door. I had nine pieces of clothing thus concealed on my person, and as the string which fastened them was small it caused me considerable discomfort. To my great satisfaction I at last passed into the street, and my master and mistress drove down the street in great haste and were soon out of sight. I saw my guide patiently awaiting me. I followed him at a distance until we arrived at the church, and there met two young ladies, one of whom handed me a pass and told me to follow them at a square's distance. It was now twilight. There was a company of soldiers about to take passage across the ferry, and I followed. I showed my pass, and proceeded up the stairs on the boat. While thus ascending the stairs, the cord which held my bundle of clothing broke, and my feet became entangled in my wardrobe, but by proceeding, the first step released one foot and the next the other. This was observed only by a few soldiers, who were too deeply engaged in their own affairs to interfere with mine. I seated myself in a remote corner of the boat, and in a few moments I landed on free soil for the first time in my life, except when hurled through Albany and Springfield at the time of our capture. I was now under my own control. The cars were waiting in Jefferson City for the passengers for Indianapolis, where we arrived about nine o'clock.

MATTIE IN INDIANAPOLIS—THE GLORY OF FREEDOM— PRESIDENT LINCOLN'S REMAINS EXHIBITED

My first business, after my arrival at Indianapolis was to find a boarding place in which I at once succeeded, and in a few hours thereafter was at a place of service of my own choice. I had always been under the yoke of oppression, compelled to submit to its laws, and not allowed to advance a rod from the house, or even out of call, without a severe punishment. Now this constant fear and restless yearning was over. It appeared as though I had emerged into a new world, or had never lived in the old one before. The people I lived with were Unionists, and became immediately interested in teaching and encouraging me in my literary advancement and all other important improvements, which precisely met the natural desires for which my soul had ever yearned since my earliest recollection. I could read a little, but was not allowed to learn in slavery. I was obliged to pay twenty-five cents for every letter written for me. I now began to feel that as I was free I could learn to write, as well as others; consequently Mrs. Harris, the lady with whom I lived, volunteered to assist me. I was soon enabled to write quite a legible hand, which I find a great convenience. I would advise all, young, middle aged or old, in a free country to learn to read and write. If this little book should fall into the hands of one deficient of the important knowledge of writing, I hope they will remember the old maxim:—"Never too old to learn." Manage your own secrets, and divulge them by the silent language of your own pen. Had our blessed President considered it too humiliating to learn in advanced years, our race would yet have remained under the galling yoke of oppression. After I had been with Mrs. Harris seven months, the joyful news came of the surrender of Lee's army and the capture of Richmond.

> Whilst the country's hearts were throbbing,
>   Filled with joy for victories won;
> Whilst the stars and stripes were waving
>   O'er each cottage, ship and dome,
> Came upon like winged lightning
>   Words that turned each joy to dread,
> Froze with horror as we listened:
>   Our beloved chieftain, Lincoln's dead
>
> War's dark clouds has long held o'er us,
>   They have rolled their gloomy fold's away,
> And all the world is anxious, waiting
>   For that promised peaceful day.
> But that fearful blow inflicted,
>   Fell on his devoted head,
> And from every town and hamlet
>   Came the cry our Chieftain's dead.
>
> Weep, weep, O bleeding nation
>   For the patriot spirit fled,
> All untold our country's future—
>   Buried with the silent dead.
> God of battles, God of nations to our country send relief
> Turn each lamentation into joy whilst we mourn our murdered
>   chief.

On the Saturday after the assassination of the President there was a meeting held on the Common, and a vote taken to have the President's body brought through Indianapolis, for the people to see his dear dead face. The vote was taken by raising the hands, and when the question was put in favor of it a thousand black hands were extended in the air, seemingly higher and more visible than all the rest. Nor were their hands alone raised, for in their deep sorrow and gloom they raised their hearts to God, for well they knew that He, through martyred blood, had made them free. It was some time before the remains reached Indianapolis, as it was near the last of the route. The body was placed in the centre of the hall of the State House, and we marched in by fours, and divided into two on each side of the casket, and passed directly through the hall. It was very rainy,—nothing but umbrellas were to be seen in any direction. The multitude were passing in and out from eight o'clock in the morning till four o'clock in the afternoon. His body remained until twelve o'clock in the evening, many distinguished persons visiting it, when amid the booming of cannon, it moved on its way to Springfield, its final resting-place. The death of the President was like an electric shock to my soul. I could not feel convinced of his death until I gazed upon his remains, and heard the last roll of the muffled drum and the farewell boom of the cannon. I was then convinced that though we were left to the tender mercies of God, we were without a leader.

Gone, gone is our chieftain,
The tried and the true;
The grief of our nation the world never knew.
We mourn as a nation has never yet mourned;
The foe to our freedom more deeply has scorned.

In the height of his glory in manhood's full prime,
Our country's preserver through darkest of time;
A merciful being, whose kindness all shared
Shown mercy to others. Why was he not spared?

The lover of Justice, the friend of the slave,
He struck at oppression and made it a grave;
He spoke for our bond-men, and chains from them fell,
By making them soldiers they served our land well.

Because he had spoken from sea unto sea
Glad tidings go heavenward, our country is free,
And angels I'm thinking looked down from above,
With sweet smiles approving his great works of love.

His name with the honor forever will live,
And time to his laurels new lustre will give;

He lived so unselfish, so loyal and true,
That his deeds will shine brighter at every view.

Then honor and cherish the name of the brave,
The champion of freedom, the friend to the slave,
The far-sighted statesman who saw a fair end,
When north land and south land one flag shall defend.

Rest, rest, fallen chieftain, thy labors are o'er,
For thee mourns a nation as never before;
Farewell honored chieftain whom millions adore,
Farewell gentle spirit, whom heaven has won.

SISTER LOST—MOTHER'S ESCAPE

In two or three weeks after the body of the President was carried through, my sister made her escape, but by some means we entirely lost trace of her. We heard she was in a free State. In three months my mother also escaped. She rose quite early in the morning, took my little brother, and arrived at my place of service in the afternoon. I was much surprised, and asked my mother how she came there. She could scarcely tell me for weeping, but I soon found out the mystery. After so many long years and so many attempts, for this was her seventh, she at last succeeded, and we were now all free. My mother had been a slave for more than forty-three years, and liberty was very sweet to her. The sound of freedom was music in our ears; the air was pure and fragrant; the genial rays of the glorious sun burst forth with a new lustre upon us, and all creation resounded in responses of praise to the author and creator of him who proclaimed life and freedom to the slave. I was overjoyed with my personal freedom, but the joy at my mother's escape was greater than anything I had ever known. It was a joy that reaches beyond the tide and anchors in the harbor of eternal rest. While in oppression, this eternal life-preserver had continually wafted her toward the land of freedom, which she was confident of gaining, whatever might betide. Our joy that we were permitted to mingle together our earthly bliss in glorious strains of freedom was indescribable. My mother responded with the children of Israel,—"The Lord is my strength and my song. The Lord is a man of war, and the Lord is his name." We left Indianapolis the day after my mother arrived, and took the cars at eleven o'clock the following evening for St. Louis, my native State. We were then free, and instead of being hurried along, bare headed and half naked, through cars and boats, by a brutal master with a bill of sale in his pocket, we were our own, comfortably clothed, and having the true emblems of freedom.

MOTHER'S MARRIAGE

It appeared to me that the city presented an entirely new aspect. The reader will remember that my mother was engaged to be married on the evening after we were kidnapped, and that Mr. Adams, her intended, had prepared the house for the occasion. We now went in search of him. He had moved about five miles into the country. He had carefully preserved his furniture and was patiently awaiting our return. We were gone two years and four months. The clothing and furniture which we had collected were all destroyed. It was over a year after we left St. Louis before we heard from there. We went immediately from the cars to my aunt's, and from there went to Mr. Adams' residence and took him by surprise. They were married in a week after our return. My mother is comfortably situated on a small farm with a kind and affectionate companion, with whom she had formed an early acquaintance, and from whom she had been severed by the ruthless hand of Wrong; but by the divine hand of Justice they were now reunited forever.

MATTIE MEETS HER OLD MASTER—GOES TO SERVICE—IS SENT FOR BY HER STEP-FATHER IN LAWRENCE, MASS.

In a short time I had selected a place of service, and was improving my studies in a small way. The place I engaged was in the family where I was born, where my mother lived when my father Jackson made his escape. Although Mr. Canory's family were always kind to us, I felt a great difference between freedom and slavery. After I had been there a short time my step-father sent for me and my half brother to come to Lawrence. He had been waiting ever since the State was free, hoping to get some account of us. He had been informed, previously, that mother, in trying to make her escape, had perished by the way, and the children also, but he was never satisfied. He was aware that my aunt was permanently in St. Louis, as her master had given her family their freedom twenty years previous. She was formerly owned by Major Howe, harness and leather dealer, yet residing in St. Louis. And long may he live and his good works follow him and his posterity forever. My father well knew the deception of the rebels, and was determined to persevere until he had obtained a satisfactory account of his family. A gentleman moved directly from Lawrence to St. Louis, who made particular enquiries for us, and even called at my aunt's. We then heard directly from my father, and commenced correspondence. He had not heard directly from us since he made his escape, which was nine years. He had never heard of his little son who my mother was compelled by Mrs. Lewis to confine in a box. He was born eight months after he left. As soon as possible after my mother consented to let my little brother go to his father he sent means to assist us to make preparations for our journey to the North. At first he only sent for his little son. My mother was anxious about sending him alone. He was only eleven years old, and perfectly unused to traveling, and had never been away from his mother. Finally my father came to the conclusion that, as my mother had endured such extreme hardships and sufferings during the nine years he was not permitted to participate or render her any assistance, that it would afford him much pleasure in sending for us both, bearing our expenses and making us as comfortable as his means would allow. Money was sent us, and our kind friend, Mr. Howe, obtained our tickets and voluntarily assisted us in starting. We left for the North on Monday, April 9th, and arrived safe and sound, on the 11th. We found my step-father's residence about six o'clock in the evening. He was not expecting us till the next day. Our meeting is better imagined than told. I cannot describe it. His little son was only two years old when he left, and I was eleven, and we never expected to meet him again this side of eternity. It was Freedom that brought us together. My father was comfortably situated in a nice white cottage, containing some eight rooms, all well furnished, and attached to it was a fine garden. His wife, who is a physician, was absent, but returned on the following day. The people were kind and friendly. They informed me there was no other colored family in the city, but my step-mother was continually crowded with friends and customers without distinction. My step-mother had buried her only son, who returned from the war in a decline. The white friends were all in deep sympathy with them. I felt immediately at home among such kind and friendly people, and have never felt homesick, except when I think of my poor mother's farewell embrace when she accompanied us to the cars. As soon as my step-mother had arrived, and our excitement was over, they commenced calculating upon placing me in the Sabbath school at the church where my mother belonged. On the next Sabbath I accompanied her and joined the Sabbath school, she occupying a side seat about middle way up the house. I was not reminded of my color except by an occasional loafer or the Irish, usually the colored man's enemy. I was never permitted to attend a white church before, or ride in any public conveyance without being placed in a car for the especial purpose; and in the street cars we were not permitted to ride at all, either South or West. Here I ride where I please, without the slightest remark, except from the ignorant. Many ask me if I am contented. They can imagine by the above contrast. My brother and myself entered the public school, and found a host of interested friends and formed many dear acquaintances whom I shall never forget. After attending school a month the term closed. I advanced in my studies as fast as could be expected. I never attended school but one month before. I needed more attention than my kind teacher could possibly bestow upon me, encumbered as she was by so many small children. Mother then proposed my entering some select school and placing myself entirely under its discipline and influence. I was much pleased with the idea, but as they had already been to so much expense for me, I could not wish to place them under any heavier contribution. I had previously told my step-mother my story, and how often my own mother had wished she could have it published. I did not imagine she could find time to write and arrange it, but she immediately proposed writing and publishing the entire story, by the sale of which I might obtain the aid towards completing my studies. I am glad I came to the old Bay State, the people of which the rebels hate with an extreme hatred. I found it just such a place as I had imagined by the appearance of the soldiers and the kindness they manifested.

New England, that blessed land,
All in a happy Union band;
They with the needy share their bread
And teach the weak the Word of God.

We never heard from my sister Hester, who made her escape from Kentucky, except when she was on the cars, though we have no doubt she succeeded in gaining her freedom.

SUMMARY

On my return to St. Louis I met my old master, Lewis, who strove so hard to sell us away that he might avoid seeing us free, on the street. He was so surprised that before he was aware of it he dropped a bow. My mother met Mrs. Lewis, her old mistress, with a large basket on her arm, trudging to market. It appeared she had lived to see the day when her children had to wait upon themselves, and she likewise. The Yankees had taken possession, and her posterity were on an equality with the black man. Mr. Lewis despised the Irish, and often declared he would board at the hotel before he would employ Irish help, but he now has a dissipated Irish cook. When I was his slave I was obliged to keep away every fly from the table, and not allow one to light on a person. They are now compelled to brush their own flies and dress themselves and children. Mr. Lewis' brother Benjamin was a more severe slave master than the one who owned me. He was a tobacconist and very wealthy. As soon as the war commenced he turned Unionist to save his property. He was very severe in his punishments. He used to extend his victim, fastened to a beam, with hands and feet tied, and inflict from fifty to three hundred lashes, laying their flesh entirely open, then bathe their quivering wounds with brine, and, through his nose, in a slow rebel tone he would tell them "You'd better walk a fair chalk line or else I'll give yer twice as much." His former friends, the guerrillas, were aware he only turned Union to save his cash, and they gave those persons he had abused a large share of his luxury. They then, in the presence of his wife and another distinguished lady, tortured him in a most inhuman manner. For pretending Unionism they placed him on a table and threatened to dissect him alive if he did not tell them where he kept his gold. He immediately informed them. They then stood him against the house and fired over his head. From that, they changed his position by turning him upside down, and raising him two feet from the floor, letting him dash his head against the floor until his skull was fractured, after which he lingered awhile and finally died. There was a long piece published in the paper respecting his repentance, benevolence, & c. All the slaves who ever lived in his family admit the Lord is able to save to the uttermost. He saved the thief on the cross, and perhaps he saved him.

When I made my escape from slavery I was in a query how I was to raise funds to bear my expenses. I finally came to the conclusion that as the laborer was worthy of his hire, I thought my wages should come from my master's pocket. Accordingly I took twenty-five dollars. After I was safe and had learned to write, I sent him a nice letter, thanking him for the kindness his pocket bestowed to me in time of need. I have never received any answer to it.

When I complete my education, if my life is spared, I shall endeavor to publish further details of our history in another volume from my own pen.

CHRISTIANITY

Christianity is a system claiming God for its author, and the welfare of man for its object. It is a system so uniform, exalted and pure, that the loftiest intellects have acknowledged its influence, and acquiesced in the justness of its claims. Genius has bent from his erratic course to gather fire from her altars, and pathos from the agony of Gethsemane and the sufferings of Calvary. Philosophy and science have paused amid their speculative researches and wonderous revelations, to gain wisdom from her teachings and knowledge from her precepts. Poetry has culled her fairest flowers and wreathed her softest, to bind her Author's "bleeding brow." Music has strung her sweetest lyres and breathed her noblest strains to celebrate His fame; whilst Learning has bent from her lofty heights to bow at the lowly cross. The constant friend of man, she has stood by him in his hour of greatest need. She has cheered the prisoner in his cell, and strengthened the martyr at the stake. She has nerved the frail and sinking heart of woman for high and holy deeds. The worn and weary have rested their fainting heads upon her bosom, and gathered strength from her words and courage from her counsels. She has been the staff of decrepit age, and the joy of manhood in its strength. She has bent over the form of lovely childhood, and suffered it to have a place in the Redeemer's arms. She has stood by the bed of the dying, and unveiled the glories of eternal life; gilding the darkness of the tomb with the glory of the resurrection.

Christianity has changed the moral aspect of nations. Idolatrous temples have crumbled at her touch, and guilt owned its deformity in her presence. The darkest habitations of earth have been irradiated with heavenly light, and the death shriek of immolated victims changed for ascriptions of praise to God and the Lamb. Envy and Malice have been rebuked by her contented look, and fretful Impatience by her gentle and resigned manner.

At her approach, fetters have been broken, and men have risen redeemed from dust, and freed from chains. Manhood has learned its dignity and worth, its kindred with angels, and alliance to God.

To man, guilty, fallen and degraded man, she shows a fountain drawn from the Redeemer's veins; there she bids him wash and be clean. She points him to "Mount Zion, the city of the living God, to an innumerable company of angels, to the spirits of just men made perfect, and to Jesus the Mediator of the new Covenant," and urges him to rise from the degradation of sin, renew his nature and join with them. She shows a pattern so spotless and holy, so elevated and pure, that he might shrink from it discouraged, did she not bring with her a promise from the lips of Jehovah, that he would give power to the faint, and might to those who have no strength. Learning may bring her ample pages and her ponderous records, rich with the spoils of every age, gathered from every land, and gleaned from every source. Philosophy and science may bring their abstruse researches and wonderous revelations—Literature her elegance, with the toils of the pen, and the labors of the pencil—but they are idle tales compared to the truths of Christianity. They may cultivate the intellect, enlighten the understanding, give scope to the imagination, and refine the sensibilities; but they open not, to our dim eyes and longing vision, the land of crystal founts and deathless flowers. Philosophy searches earth; Religion opens heaven. Philosophy doubts and trembles at the portals of eternity; Religion lifts the veil, and shows us golden streets, lit by the Redeemer's countenance, and irradiated by his smile. Philosophy strives to reconcile us to death; Religion triumphs over it. Philosophy treads amid the pathway of stars, and stands a delighted listener to the music of the spheres; but Religion gazes on the glorious palaces of God, while the harpings of the blood-washed, and the songs of the redeemed, fall upon her ravished ear. Philosophy has her place; Religion her important sphere; one is of importance here, the other of infinite and vital importance both here and hereafter.

Amid ancient lore the Word of God stands unique and pre-eminent. Wonderful in its construction, admirable in its adaptation, it contains truths that a child may comprehend, and mysteries into which angels desire to look. It is in harmony with that adaptation of means to ends which pervades creation, from the polypus tribes, elaborating their coral homes, to man, the wonderous work of God. It forms the brightest link of that glorious chain which unites the humbles [sic] work of creation with the throne of the infinite and eternal Jehovah. As light, with its infinite particles and curiously blended colors, is suited to an eye prepared for the alterations of day; as air, with its subtle and invisible essence, is fitted for the delicate organs of respiration; and, in a word, as this material world is adapted to man's physical nature; so the word of eternal truth is adapted to his moral nature and mental constitution. It finds him wounded, sick and suffering, and points him to the balm of Gilead and the Physician of souls. It finds him stained by transgressions and defiled with guilt, and directs him to the "blood that cleanseth from all unrighteousness and sin." It finds him athirst and faint, pining amid the deserts of life, and shows him the wells of salvation and the rivers of life. It addresses itself to his moral and spiritual nature, makes provision for his wants and weaknesses, and meets his yearnings and aspirations. It is adapted to his mind in its earliest stages of progression, and its highest state of intellectuality. It provides light for his darkness, joy for his anguish, a solace for his woes, balm for his wounds, and heaven for his hopes. It unveils the unseen world, and reveals him who is the light of creation, and the joy of the universe, reconciled through the death of His Son. It promises the faithful a blessed re-union in a land undimmed with tears, undarkened by sorrow. It affords a truth for the living and a refuge for the dying. Aided by the Holy Spirit, it guides us through life, points out the shoals, the quicksands and hidden rocks which endanger our path, and at last leaves us with the eternal God for our refuge, and his everlasting arms for our protection.

CHRONOLOGY OF SYLVIA DUBOIS 1768(?)–1888

1756 (March 5)—Dominicus "Minical" Dubois born Somerset County, New Jersey, fourth child of Abraham Dubois Sr. and Jannetje Van Dyke.

1768 (March 5)—Alleged birth date of Sylvia Dubois, in Hillsborough Township, Somerset County, New Jersey.

1779—Dominicus Dubois marries Marie Pittinger (d. April 3, 1786).

1782 (April 1)—Most probable birth date of Sylvia Dubois.

1791 (September 21)—Dubois and Seth Putnam purchase 601 acres of ground south of the Susquehanna River in Lackawanna (now Susquehanna) County, Pennsylvania, from Benajah Strong; Dubois soon moves his family including slaves to establish a tavern and a ferry.

1793—Dominicus Dubois marries Elizabeth Scudder.

Circa 1806—Judith (Roberts), daughter of Sylvia, born in Great Bend, Pennsylvania.

1808—Sylvia "whipts" her mistress, Elizabeth Dubois; Minical frees Sylvia, who walks back to New Jersey (with an eighteen-month-old baby girl in her arms) from Great Bend.

1812 (February 28)—Harry Compton, Sylvia's grandfather, purchases two adjacent tracts on Sourland Mountain at a spot called Cedar Summit in Amwell Township (now East Amwell Township), Hunterdon County, New Jersey, where he establishes a crossroads tavern ("Put's Old House") that becomes notorious as a rowdy place. Sylvia soon joins her grandfather to help in running the establishment; she soon establishes her homestead adjacent to the tavern; raises corn and pigs.

1815—Charlotte (Moore), daughter of Sylvia, born near Blawenburg, New Jersey.

Circa 1825—Elizabeth (Alexander), daughter of Sylvia, born near Blawenburg, New Jersey.

Circa 1827—Rachel (Conover), daughter of Sylvia, born in Montgomery Township, Somerset County, New Jersey.

1830s—Sylvia "Deboice" and her two youngest daughters are brought into court a number of times for disturbance of the peace; assault; operation of an unlicensed house.

1837 (January 10)—Cornelius Wilson Larison born Lambertville, New Jersey.

Circa 1840—Sylvia Dubois's tavern and home burns to the ground. Arson is suspected but never proven. She soon loses her property for nonpayment of taxes and is near destitute for the rest of her life.

1883 (January)—Dr. C. W. Larison travels to Cedar Summit to interview Sylvia Dubois.

1883 (November)—Dr. C. W. Larison visits Sylvia Dubois for second time.

1883 (December 30)—Dr. C. W. Larison travels again to Cedar Summit to interview Sylvia Dubois.

1888 (May 27)—Sylvia Dubois dies at her daughter Elizabeth's home in the Sourland Mountains.

Sylvia Dubois
(Now 116 Years Old),

A Biography of the Slave Who Whipped Her Mistress and Gained Her Freedom

C. W. LARISON, M.D.

SYLVIA DUBOIS AND DAUGHTER, ELIZABETH ALEXANDER,
CIRCA 1883.

PREFACE

As much interest always attaches to one who lives to a very great age, and as a Negress so old as Sylvia Dubois is seldom known, I have thought that an outline biography of her might be desired by the reading public. The more so, because while getting the biography of the heroine, a vast amount of the customs and manners of the people with whom she lived is also acquired, and a knowledge of the ways of folks of a hundred years ago gained.

In writing this sketch, I have been as brief as circumstances would allow. As much of the matter entering into the composition of this book was gotten from her, in a colloquial manner, and as this was put upon paper, in shorthand, just as she spoke it, and as by giving her own words in the order and style in which she spoke them, portrays more of the character, intelligence, and force of the heroine than can possibly be given in any other way, I have written the most essential parts of it, exactly as she related the facts to me.

The narrative abounds in profanity, an element that is foreign to me, and one that I most cordially despise, and sincerely deprecate. But, Sylvia is a profane Negress; her language always abounds in profanity; and, terse and forcible as it is, castigate it of its profane words, and it is flat and meaningless, and utterly fails to convey the idea intended, or to reveal her character. In the narrative, my aim is more to show the character, force and spirit of independence of the heroine, than to make out a long line of years; or to tell with whom she dwelt. To accomplish this, I must use those words and phrases peculiar to herself, which alone are adequate to the task before me. This then is my apology for the profanity that so abundantly exists in this story.

In the orthography of the book, I have, in the main, aimed to follow the rules of the Spelling Reform. That in some instances I have failed, there is no doubt. But, in many instances in which I have not followed the advice of the Philologic Society, I have done so because I thought the advice of that body, respecting these particular instances not well founded (as in using ŏ for o in the word or), or else not practiced at the present time. In the future, perhaps, some of the changes to which I allude will be practiced. And when the reading people are prepared for them, none will be more ready to adopt them than I. Indeed, I long to see the time when one character will represent but one phone; and one phone is represented by one character.

But, while I am not willing to adopt, in every instance, just now, every measure recommended by the Committee on the Reform of English Spelling, there are many measures, not recommended by the committee, that are much needed, and that I shall at once adopt.

To follow the spelling now in vogue, is utterly absurd. Such a meaningless, jumbling of characters as occur in the printing or writing of words as found in most books and newspapers is unpardonable, and insulting to the taste and judgment of all readers of culture. A few years ago, writers could not safely do otherwise than to follow this censurable spelling; but, since this widespread concerted action of the Spelling Reformers—men of the highest and broadest culture, and so famously known as critics and teachers in our Colleges and Universities, there is, at the best, but poor excuse for continuing to spell words with aphonic characters.

As it may happen that some who are not acquainted with the Reformed spelling of the English language may read this book, to help them to learn the new orthography, and to facilitate their progress in reading these pages, I here introduce the rules submitted in the "Report of the American Committee on the Reform of English Spelling." In stating these rules, so far as it suits my purpose, I use the language of Dr. F. A. March, author of the report cited.

RULES OF THE COMMITTEE ON THE REFORM OF ENGLISH SPELLING

1. e.—Drop silent e when phonetically useless, as in live, liv; vineyard, vinyard; believe, belev; bronze, bronz; single, singl; engine, engin; granite, granit; eaten, etn; rained, rand, etc.

2. ea.—Drop a from ea having the sound of e, as in feather, fether; leather, lether; jealous, jelus, etc.

3. eau.—For beauty, use the old beuty—buty.

4. eo.—Drop o from eo having to the sound of e, as in jeopardy, jepardy; leopard, lepard. For yeoman, write, yoman.

5. i.—Drop I of parliament to parlament.

6. o.—For o having the sound of u in but, write u, as in above, abuv; dozen, duzn; some, sum; tongue, tung, etc. For women, restore wimen.

7. ou.—Drop o from ou having the sound of u, as in journal, jurnal; nourish, nurish; trouble, trubl; rough, ruf; tough, tuf, etc.

8. u.—Drop silent u after g before a, and in native English words, as in guarantee, garante; guard, gard; guess, ges; guild, gild; guilt, gilt.

9. ue.—Drop ue in apologue, apology; catalogue, catalog; demagogue, demagog, etc.

10. y.—Spell rhyme, rime—rim.

11. Double consonants may be simplified: Final b, d, g, n, r, t, f, l, x, as in ebb, eb; add, ad; egg, eg; inn, in; purr, pur; butt, but; bailiff, balif; dull, dul; buzz, buz; (not all). Medial before another consonant, as in battle, batl; ripple, ripl; written, ritn. Initial unaccented prefixes, and other unaccented syllables, as in abbreviate, abreviat; accuse, acus; affair, afar; traveller, traveler.

12. b.—Drop aphonic b in bomb, bom; crumb, crum; debt, det; doubt, dout; dumb, dum; lamb, lam; limb, lim; numb, num; plumb, plum; subtle, sutl; succumb, sucum; thumb, thum.

13. c.—Change c back to s in cinder, sinder; expence, expens; fierce, fers; hence, hens; once, wuns; pence, pens; scarce, scars; since, sins; source, sors; thence, thens; tierce, ters; whence, hwens.

14. ch.—Drop the h of ch in chamomile, camomil; cholera, colera; choler, coler; melancholy, melancoly; school, scol; stomach, stumac.

15. d.—Change d and ed final to t when so pronounced, as in crossed, crost; looked, lokt, etc.

16. g.—Drop g in feign, fan; foreign, foren; sovereign, soveren.

17. gh.—Drop h in aghast, agast; burgh, burg; ghost, gost.

Drop gh in haughty, haty; though, tho; through, thru.

Change gh into f where it has that sound, as in cough, cof; enough, enuf; laughter, lafter; tough, tuf.

18. l.—Drop l in could, cud.

19. p.—Drop p in receipt, recet.

20. s.—Drop s in aisle, il; demesne, demen; island, iland.

Change s into z in distinctive words, as in abuse, abuz (verb); house, houz (verb); rise, riz (verb), etc.

21. sc.—Drop c in scent, sent; scythe, syth.

22. tch.—Drop t as in catch, cach; pitch, pich; witch, wich, etc.

23. w.—Drop w in whole, hol.

24. ph.—Write f for ph, as in philosophy, filosofy; sphere, sfer, etc.

The above rules greatly aid us in improving English spelling; yet there are many difficulties that they do not help us solve. To surmount these, I add a few that seem to me quite as necessary as those made by the above named philologists:

1. Silent vowels.—Drop all silent or aphonic vowels, as in goose, gos; loose, los; food, fod; book, bok; great, grat; gain, gan.

2. i.—Write I for e or ee when so sounded, as in been, bin.

3. a.—Write e for a when a has the sound of e, as in any, eny; many, meny.

4. e.—Write a for e when e has the sound of a, as in eight, at; they, tha.

5. w.—Use w only as a consonant. Write u for w in diphthongs in which w has the sound of u, as in new, neu; stew, steu.

6. o.—Use o as a vowel only. When o has the sound of w, write w, as in one, wun; once, wuns.

7. u.—When u is equivalent to w, writ w, as in language, langwag; lingual, lingwal.

8. i.—Write y for i when i has the sound of y, as in pinion, pinyun; minion, minyun.

9. c, t, s.—Write sh for c, t, and s when c, t and s has the sound of sh, as in ocean, oshun; social, soshal; nation, nashun; notion, noshun; mission, mishun; passion, pashun.

10. f.—Write v for f when f has the sound of v, as in of, ov.

The above rules, good as they are, if used, will make an English orthography very little better than the one hitherto in use. Indeed, to do much, in the improvement of English orthography, we must have a better alphabet. The one in general use is not sufficient. In our alphabet there should be at least one character for every simple phone; and each character should always be called by the sound, or phone, it is intended to represent. But, in our language there are thirty-seven well defined phones; while in our alphabet there are only twenty-six characters. And, what makes the matter worse, four of these characters, a, i, u and x, represent compound phones—a beginning with a sound heard only in the initial and essential of a, and then ending in a sound heard in the essential and vanish of e. I is equal to äe; u is equal to yu;

x is equal to ks or gs. Hence, in reality, we have twenty-two characters to represent thirty-three simple phones, and four characters that represent compound phones.

To improve the alphabet, then we must enlarge it. This we do by using each of the vowel characters in the old alphabet, without diacritic marks to represent the sound, or phone, heard in uttering it; that is, we use its name sound. Hence when any vowel has no diacritic mark, it has its name sound, as a in ape—ap; e in eve—ev; u in tune—tun; o in old, i in unite—unit; But, to represent other vowel phones, these vowel characters modified by diacritic marks are used. Thus, ä represents the vowel phone in the word ask, ạ in all, ạ in what, ă in at; ĕ in met; ĭ in it; ŏ in not, ọ in boot—bọt; ọ in book—bọk; ŭ in but, ụ in rude—rụd; ụ in full—fụl; ÿ in cÿst; y in my.

Some of the consonant characters represent more than one phone. Such are c, g, n, s, th, x, z; as for instance, c in corn and c in ced; g in gun—gŭn, and g in gem—ġĕm; n in no, and n in link—lĭnk, or sing; s in sin—sĭn, and s in his—hĭs; th in them—tҺĕm and th in thing—thĭng; x in fix—fĭx, and x in exist—exĭst; z in zone—zon, and z in azure—ăzhur.

The first sound above instance is the one which is more frequently heard. Hence, we may call it the first sound. To represent this (the first sound) we will use the several consonant characters, here cited without diacritic marks; and to indicate the second sound of each of the same characters, we will use certain marks. Thus, to represent the second sound of c, we will use c marked thus ç; and to represent the second sound of g, we will use g marked thus ġ; the second sound of n we will indicate thus ṉ; and of th thus ҭh, (the first sound being represented by th); and of x thus ҳ; and of z thus zh. Hence, our alphabet will appear as the arrangement of characters below.

ALPHABET USED IN THE ORTHOGRAPHY OF THIS BOOK

Vowel Characters

a   ale, fate,==al, fat
ă   ădd, făt,==ăd, făt
ä   ärm, fäther

å   åsk, glåss
ą   ąll, tąlk
ą   whąt, wąnder

e   eve, mete—ev, met
ĕ   ĕnd, mĕt

i   içe, fine—iç, fin
ĭ   ĭn, fĭn

o   old, note—not
ŏ==ą ŏdd==ŏd, nŏt, whąt
ǫ   prǫve==prǫv, dǫ, tǫ
ǫ   wǫlf, wǫl, bǫok—bǫk

u   us̲e, tube==us̲, tub
ŭ   ŭs, tŭb
ų==ǫ rųde—rųd, dǫ
ų==ǫ bųll—bųl, pųt, wǫlf

y==i fl**y**, iç,==iç
y̆==ĭ cy̆st, pĭn

Consonant Characters and the Sounds or Phones They Represent

b   barn, rob
c   cąll, colt
ç   çede, traçe
~~ch~~ ~~ch~~ild, mu~~ch~~
d   dale, săd
f   fame, leaf
g   go, găg
ġ   ġĕm, ġĭn
h   hąll, hăt
j==ġ jär, joke, ġĕm
k==c keep, kĭng, cąll
l   lĕft, bĕll

m make, aġe

n nĕt, tĕn

n̲ lĭn̲k, ŭn̲cle, same

p pay, ape

q̶u̶ q̶ueen, cŏnq̶uĕst

r rĭp, fär

s same, yĕs, çede

s̲ hăs̲, åmuse

s̶h̶ s̶hĕlf, flĕs̶h̶

t tone, nŏt

t̶h̶ t̶hĭng, brĕat̶h̶

t̶h̶ t̶hine, wĭt̶h̶

v vane, wave

w wĕt, wạs

hw hweat, hweel

x expĕct, fŏx—fŏks

x̲ exĭst==ĕgs̲ĭst

y yạwn, yĕt

z zone, maze

z-h azure==azhure

In printing the book, I have used the diacritic type prepared to print my book entitled Elements of Orthoepy. This makes the spelling of the words—as the spelling of every word should be—phonic. (For a discussion of phonics and phonic spelling, see my "Elements of Orthoepy," or my Phonic Speller and Syllabater.)

By using the diacritic type and following the phonic orthography, the number of pages, in the book is about one fifth less than would be, had I followed the aphonic spelling. By using the diacritic type, no doubt is left respecting the pronunciation of any word; by this method, each phone in a word is represented by a suitable character; and with few exceptions there is no character in a word that does not represent a phone.

C. W. LARISON.

Academy of Science and Art,
Ringos, N. J., August 1st, 1883.

THE BIOGRAPHY OF SYLVIA DUBOIS

The twenty seventh of January 1883 dawned frosty and dreary. The mercury pointed to 20° above zero. The sky was overcast and soon the weather appeared threatening. Hills and dales, mountains and valleys, uplands and less, were covered with snow; and, save the numerous bold areas of woods and the spreading bows of leafless orchards, the prospect was quite arctic.

The chilly air caused the cattle to remain in their stalls, or to snuggle together upon the lea-side of buildings. The poultry refused to descend from their roost. The sparrow hovering its little frost-bitten feet, uttered its sharp chirp in a plaintive way. While the snow bird, in quest of weed-seed, busily hopped over the frozen crust, or diligently flitted among the dead branches of ambrosia, scarcely taking the time to utter his shrill notes—che-dee-dee-dee—so eager was he to find food for his morning meal, and then to hasten to his sheltered haunt.

But, the sleighing was good and the cares of busy life forced many a cotter from his home to brave the frigid air of the chilly morning. Horses stepped quick, light and free, and the jingle of sleigh bells echoed from the fore corners of the horizon. But, the fury muffs covering the heads and faces of the well robed passengers told well that no one left his home that morning to sleigh-ride for pleasure.

It was Saturday; and, as the duties of the school-room did not demand our labor for the day, we turned our attention to the abject, and the aged. Accordingly, about 7 o'clock A. M., we adjusted our wrappings, mounted the sleigh and directed our way to Cedar Summit, the most elevated portion of the Sourland Mountain. Rapidly we sped along. And, as we reached the brow of the mountain, for a moment we passed to survey the landscape. Toward the west, north and east, the view was unobstructed, and the prospect was grand.

Elevated 400 feet above the Redshale Valley, we scanned the basin of the Raritan from the source of the stream to its exit into the sea. The bold mountains that skirt it on the north, rose gently up and seemed to slope so gradually toward the north that they seemed knolls and hills. The plain, though rolling and rigid, seemed entirely level. Everywhere was snow. Indeed, the dreary sameness of the snowy fleece was only relieved by sparse areas of wood lands, and the long line of peering fences. Even the distant villages could hardly be described, so completely were they enveloped in the fleece of snow. But, nearer by, from the chimney of many a farm-house ascended the sooty smoke, in curling festoons.

Onward we hastened, over a road that meandered now amid umbrageous forest, now amid rocky areas over-grown with cedars, now amid the small rocky fields of the mountain farmer. Everywhere the feathery bows of the cedars that skirted the way were pendant with snow—a beautiful spectacle. The branches of the great oaks maintained their light somber gray, adding dreariness to the winter scene. The oval backs of the huge rocks lifted a mound of snow, like the houses of the Eskimos. The mountaineers huts, far removed from the road, away back near some spring, or upon the brink of some plashing rill, exhibited no signs of life, save the sooty column of curling smoke that lazily ascended amid the forest bows.

From the main road to each mountaineers hut, or to sparse groups of squalid settlements, footpaths, or narrow by-ways, extend back, sometimes, for miles, meandering amid huge rocks, thickets of cedars, umbrageous forests, through marshes and swamps, and, over streams that are not everywhere forded. These by-ways are best known to the mountaineers. Their stock of geographic knowledge consists mainly in an acquaintance of these winding ways. And, while each mountaineer, in the darkest night follows each, and any one of these by-ways, with as much certainty and as much dexterity as a cat traverses a beam in the night, or her meandering path through a gloomy hay-mow, a person not skilled in the ways of the mountaineers, would, at mid-day, be not more successful in his journeying here than in the labyrinth of Egypt, or of Corinth. Accordingly, when we had arrived at the corner at which the road extends east-ward to Rock Mills, to lead our way to the hut of Sylvia Dubois, we employed one who professed to be acquainted with these meandering paths.

To me, the site at which we left the main road to go in to Sylvia's mansion looked no more like a road than did any other half rod of ground upon the same side of the road, for the last half mile. But, faith in our guide, induced us to follow him implicitly wherever he led. The way was very crooked. Perhaps, not a single rod of the path extended in the same direction. Nor, could we see far ahead of us, sometimes not a rod. But, on we moved, around huge rocks, between large trees, over large stones, through narrow and dangerous pass ways, now amid a thicket of cedars, or a growth of brambles, or a copse of bushes, or a sparse forest of umbrageous oaks and hickories. Sometimes the road was rutty, sometimes sidling, sometimes up a sharp knoll, sometimes down a steep bank; never level; sometimes stony, and always dangerous. But, by and by a vista appeared. We were on a slight eminence. Opening up before us was an area of land cleared of trees, the property of Elizabeth, the youngest daughter of Sylvia Dubois. Upon it, her modest mansion rises, a hut ten feet square, built of logs, roofed with boards, unadorned with porch, piazza, colonnade or verandah. Primitive simplicity enters into every phase of architecture. It contains not an element that is not absolutely needed. Near by stands the scraggling branches of a dead apple tree, and beneath it is the shelter of the faithful dog. Around the area is a fence built in the most economic way;—in some places it is made of crutches with one pole, in some places with crutches and two poles, in some places there are two stakes and a rider, in other places it is made of rails so arranged that one end rests upon the ground while the other is elevated by means of stakes fixed across another inclining rail.

Peering above the snow, here and there, were stacks of maze, cabbage, bean-vines, pea-brush and other evidences that the enclosed area, during the spring summer and autumnal months, had been tilled, and had yielded a sparse supply to the tenants of the soil.

When from the eminence we had surveyed the hut and its environs, we descended to the fence that enclosed the lot, fastened, and blanketed our horses and advanced toward the habitation.

The door is double—consisting of an upper and a nether part. The upper part stood ajar, and in the center of the opening appeared the full round face of a large, buxom Negress,—the owner and proprietor of the mansion which we visited, and youngest daughter of Sylvia Dubois, the lady of whom we had heard so much talk. Our visit was a surprise. Yet, with marked complaisance and that hospitality that characterizes the fearless mountaineer, we were invited in, and bade to be seated by the stove.

The room was not well lighted. And as I was sitting down, I noticed, sitting upon a chair, a dusky form closely snuggled up in the narrow space, between the stove and the wall. As my eyes became accommodated to the dress of lightness of the room, I saw that this dusky form was the elderly lady that we desired to see,—that she had fixed herself here in the warmest part of the room, and that she was asleep.

I scanned her closely. Though sitting, her sleep was as tranquil as that of a babe. Her head, tide up with a handkerchief, after the usual manner of colored ladies, was bowed forward, so that the chin rested upon her fleshy chest. Her hands were folded upon her lap. Her feet were extended beneath the stove. Her countenance was severe, but serene.

Her apparel was not Parisian: yet, it was reasonably whole, and not dirty. Their seemed to be enough of it, and adjusted entirely in accordance with the genius of the African race. Indeed, the spectacle was such that it elicited the expression (thought, not made): "Well! You are at home in the enjoyment of life, just as you would have it."

Cautiously, but critically, I surveyed the room and the furniture. The logs composing the wall were not entirely straight, and the interspaces between them, in some places were large. At one time, these interspaces had been filled with mud,—and then, no doubt, the house was comparatively warm. But, now, in many places, by frost and rain, and by bug and mouse, the mud has crumbled and fallen out; and the openings admit alike the light and the wind. Within reach of my chair, I could pass my hand between the logs, until it was entirely out of doors; and in some places, I could see light through a crevice two feet long; in others, I could pass my fingers along an open space between the logs from ten to fifteen inches. Through these open spaces, the wind was passing at a rapid rate.

The inner surface of the wall was not even. Each log showed its barky contour, and each interspace its clay ledge, or its open space. Calcimine and white-wash did not appear; and wall-paper with gilded border was wanting. The ceiling is wanting. In its stead is the bare roof, or the splintery surface of some rails that extend from wall to wall, for the support of such things as are in the way, if lying upon the floor.

In erecting the edifice, the logs in the southern façade had been laid up to the height of 4½ feet, with an open space near the center, to serve as a door. The next layer of logs extend entirely around, forming the plates for the roof and the lintel of the door. From these log-plates ascend, at a sharp inclination, to the ridge-pole, the rafters, which in some places are covered with shingles; in others, with boards or bark.

Upon either side of the door, from the log-plate that caps the front wall, to its counterpart upon the back wall, extend oak rails, with the flat splintery side downwards. This forms, upon either side of the door, a small loft, upon which are piled bundles of clothes, bed-clothes and bedding, and I know not what else. To get upon these lofts, there are neither steps nor ladder; and yet they are handy. Standing upon the floor, a tall person can reach almost to any part of them, and take down, or put away, anything desired. I noticed that the chairs that were not in use had been placed upon one of these lofts, out the way.

So low is the lintel, that in the act of entering the door, a person is obliged to stoop; and when rising up, after entering, were he not careful to be in the open space between the lofts, he would bang his head against the rail floor. Although this was my first visit, I was fortunate enough, upon entering to be in the right position. But, I was not a little surprised as I looked about and found that while my feet and legs, and the lower part of my body were down stairs, my shoulders, arms and head were up stairs. However, the surprise did not unfit me for surveying the lofts, their arrangements and their contents. Perhaps, I would have surveyed these apartments and their contents longer, and more critically; but, when well engaged in viewing these things, the thought occurred: What may they be doing below; may my nether parts not be in some danger; or at the least, may they not demand my attention. Accordingly I stooped down, accepted a proffered chair, and seated myself in a space that seemed to be the most out of the way and began, as aforesaid, a critical survey of the environs of my position.

The floor seemed to be made of boards and split wood, laid upon the ground, and perhaps pounded upon, until nearly level. I saw no puddles of standing water, and yet the floor was not entirely dry. The interspaces between the floor-boards would easily have allowed me to ascertain the quality of the soil upon which the house is built. Although these interspaces were tolerably well filled with clay, yet the floor somewhat reminded me of the appearance of a corduroy road.

The logs out of which this house is built, served a term of years in the wall of an older house. The primitive house which was an earlier mansion on this lot, was built a long while ago. In the course of time the ends of the logs of that house rotted off, and the edifice became unsafe. Thereupon, one afternoon about eighteen years ago, Elizabeth convoked her neighbors, the capacity of a frolic, as such gatherings are here called, to reconstruct her mansion. According to her plan, they took down the old building, notched the logs back a suitable distance from the end, and piled them up in such a way that, out of the useable material of the old house they constructed the present edifice. We are told that the old house was somewhat larger on the ground, somewhat higher, and in every way more stylish than the present mansion.

The household furniture—so far as I could see—consisted of an old-time cook stove, a dinner pot, a water pail, six chairs, a small cupboard and some bed-clothes that appeared to have been long in use, and not well protected from dirt.

The cook stove is one of that pattern which was in use from thirty to forty years ago. It was made for burning wood. It is now much the worse for wear. There is yet remaining of what it once was, a part of each fire-door, and a considerable of the top plates. But, the fire is well aired; it has an abundance of draft from every side. It stands close up in the southwest corner, in a diagonal manner, in such a way that the pipe-end is toward the corner, and the fire-end toward the center of the house. The smoke finds exit through two joints of pipe, that extend from the stove almost to the roof. From the roof upwards extends a kind of chimney, made of a piece of sheet-iron, bent almost into a cylinder, with fantastic scallops around the top—whether the work of an artisan, or the result of the disintegrating influence of rust, I do not know. Although the space between the pipe and the chimney is large, somehow the sparks and the smoke—that is some of them—follow this interrupted flue up and out of the house.

Although I saw, out of doors, no pile of wood from which they could draw—and I think I saw not a single stick, the stove was well fed, the sparks rushing up the interrupted smoke-way furiously. And, although my back was a little cold, my shins and knees were about as hot as I have ever had them, and my eyes were as well filled with smoke as they have ever been, not excepting the times during which I have been attending a fire in a smoke-house.

The dinner-pot was ample, and appeared to have seen service. Of course, it was upon the stove—the water in it, boiling furiously; but from it, I failed to detect any odor of seething pottage—beef or mutton, pork or chicken.

The chairs were bottomed with rush, and they were in good repair.

Along the wall, upon the west side of the room, stood a box or cupboard, about 3 feet long, eighteen inches wide and two and one half feet high, painted and armed with doors. Upon it was a tin kerosene lamp that burned without a chimney; and judging from the crust of soot and lamp-black upon the railing directly above the place it occupied, it smoked well—even if it failed to light the room.

These were the only articles of furniture that I saw. That there were others, excepting such as may have been in the cupboard, is hardly possible.

During the time I was making the survey, there was not silence. All the while we conversed. Our talk ran sociably, and our host was as complacent as a French belle.

At length, we announced that we had come to interview the aged lady, Mrs. Sylvia Dubois. Hereupon, her daughter aroused her mother, told her that parties had called to see her, and introduced us to our heroine. Our greetings were not very formal, nor much prolonged. But while exchanging salutes, our host, for a moment, freed from entertaining us, adjusted things about the room, made ineffable apologies respecting the appearance of the apartment, and extended to us such politeness and such attention, as made us feel that we were welcome guests.

I had seen Sylvia on a former occasion, and knew something of her idio-syncrasies. Indeed, I had, during a former interview, heard her relate many of the most important instances of her life. So, what follows, in this colloquy, to some extent, I had heard her relate before, and was at this time, drawn out, by a series of prepared questions, in the order in which it is here stated, so that to the reader it would be somewhat coherent.

Sylvia is large of stature. In her palmy days, she has been not less than five feet ten inches high. She informs me that she usually weighed more than two hundred pounds. She is well proportioned, of a nervo-lymphatic tem-perament, and is still capable of great endurance. Years ago, she was known to be the strongest person in the settlement, and the one who had the great-est endurance. She was industrious, and was usually in great request during the house-cleaning and soap making season of the year. Everybody wanted Sylvia to help clean house, and to help make soap. She was so strong she could lift anything that needed to be moved and could carry anything that had to be toted; and she was so willing to use her strength that her popular-ity was ineffable. So Sylvia went everywhere, and everybody knew her—especially the children, who, as a rule, were wonderfully afraid of her.

According to her own account, to children she was not very wooing. On the contrary, she used to take delight in telling them goblin stories, and in making them afraid of her. She used to tell them that she would kidnap them and that she would swallow them alive; and, it is said, to children, she looked as if she might do such things.

Usually, children kept out of her way. Usually, when they saw her coming, they sought refuge in the company of older folks,—in some secluded place,—or in a foot-race. As a joke, she tells a story respecting an occurrence in the boy-hood of a certain individual now well advanced in years. He, a little more bold than the average boy of ten years, on one occasion, ventured to be a little sassy to her, and for the time, kept out of her way. But a few days after, while he was busy playing in a garden, around which was a high picket fence, Sylvia entered the gate about the time the lad saw her. To try his metal, she exclaimed: Now I'll have you, sir! Up he bounced! Every limb was in motion! The high pail-fence was a trifling barrier—one awful yell he gave, and then through the raspberry briers and over the fence he went like a cat; and, howling lustily as he ran, disappeared from view, by creeping under an old barrack.

Her love of freedom is boundless. To be free is the all-important thing with Sylvia. Bondage, or even restraint, is too near akin to death for Sylvia. Freedom is the goal; freedom of speech, freedom of labor, freedom of the passions, freedom of the appetite—unrestrained in all things. To enjoy this, she would go to any extremes—even to the extremes of living upon the charity of her acquaintances, in the hut in which we found her,—away from civilization and culture, with but little to eat, with less to wear, and the poorest kind of shelter. Thus she gains the object of her desire. And, she is indeed free—every passion is free, every desire is gratified. Less restraint I have never saw in any person-nor indeed could there be.

The old lady did not awake from her slumber quickly. Nor did she quickly comprehend that she had visitors. But, as aged folks usually do, she awoke slowly,—a part of her at a time, as it were. At first, she moved her hands and arms; then her feet and legs; then rubbed her face; then she moved her body upon the chair; and in the course of some minutes, she began to realize that she had guests, and that she must entertain them. Thereupon, adjusting her clothes, and quickly turning her head toward me, she ejaculated: "Who are these?" To this interrogation her daughter replied: "Why, mommy! Dr. Larison, his daughter, and Miss Prale. They want to see you—they want to talk with you."

Quickly and sternly she replied: "Want to see me! I don't know why they should want to see me; such an old thing as I am,—pretty near dead now, and God knows I ought to have been dead long ago."

Hereupon, I began to inquire about her health. She informed me that she was well—and that she was always well; except sometimes she suffered "colds." She said that she had never had a spell of severe sickness, and did not intend to have; that "taint no use to be sick; folks don't feel well when them sick; they feel best when them well."

"Just so, Sylvia," I replied; "but, it seems that folks can't always be well—sickness will come sometimes."

To this comment the old lady hastily replied: They wouldn't be sick half so much if they'd behave 'em selves, and stay at home, and eat plain victuals. They want to run all over, and be into all kind of nigger shines, and stuff 'emselves with all kinds of things; and their guts won't stand it. Then they get sick; and like enough send for a doctor—and when he comes, if they're not pretty careful, they'll have a hell of a time; for he's sure to go right for the guts, fust pass; never knew one of 'em to miss. A big dose of calomel and jalap to begin business, and then the war is begun. These doctors, they've got no mercy on you, 'specially if you're black. Ah! I've seen 'em, many a time, but, they never come after me, I never gave 'em a chance—not the fust time.

When I had grown quiet from a fit of laughter, provoked by the old woman's style, as much from the matter spoken, I told her that I had come to talk with her—to learn what I could respecting her great age, her course of life, the history of her family, the customs of the people who lived a century or more ago, her present welfare and her future prospects.

With this statement Sylvia seemed pleased, and announced that she was ready and willing to inform me respecting matters as far as she was able. At once, she assumed an attitude, and an air that showed she was "all attention" and ready to talk. I had provided myself with paper and pencil to take down in short-hand, her language as it fell from her mouth. Respecting this, I informed her, and requested the privilege that I might print and publish anything that she told me. To this request she replied: "Most of folks think that niggers ain't no account but, if you think what I tell you is worth publishing,

I will be glad if you do it. 'T won't do me no good but maybe 't will some-body else. I've lived a good while, and have seen a good deal, and if I should tell you all I've seen, it would make the hair stand up all over your head."

By this time, it had fully appeared that Sylvia, in her own way, was not a little religious, and was well used to speaking the name of the Supreme Being; and what is more remarkable in a woman, she seemed to be so famil-iar with all those words expressive of the attributes of God. Indeed, I have seldomly known a clergyman, even when an excellent Hebrew and Greek scholar, to be more familiar with these terms than Sylvia, nor more in the habit of using them. And yet, between Sylvia and a clergyman, there seemed to be a marked difference in the way in which each used them. For, while the clergyman uses these terms mainly in speaking of the goodness and omnipo-tence of God, and in invoking His blessing, Sylvia seemed to use them in an interjectional, or adjectival way to embellish her language, and to give force to her expressions. And, of all that I have ever listened to, I have not heard any one handle these terms more rhetorically, or yet more in accordance with the principles of elocution. And, as it will detract very greatly from the merits of her discourse, in case I omit this part of her language, I beg my readers the privilege of leaving the words in her phrases, just as she uttered them, as much as is bearable.

While Sylvia's familiarity with the titles with which Jehovah is want to be addressed, is exceedingly great, her knowledge of that utter being called the Devil, is, by no means limited. If his character has ever been better portrayed by any other person, or if he has ever been addressed by, or known by, any other terms, than those she used, it has not come to my knowledge. Indeed, it seemed that every title, appellation, and epithet, that had ever been used in reference to his Satanic Majesty, she handled with peculiar freedom and ease. Indeed, the prolificness of her mind, in this direction, is transcendent. For where rotes with the most exquisite prefixes and suffixes, fail to serve her purposes, she extemporaneously and without hesitation, coins an overflow of self-explaining compounds, that seem to fully meet the demand even of her own extreme cases.

Nor is she barren of ideas respecting those imaginary beings, called by the learned Faeries, Nymphs, Sprites, Elves, Demons, and the like. To her, every grot and corner, every wood and swamp, hill and meadow, is inhabited by these imaginary beings, who are ceaselessly plying their arts in interfering with human affairs—working to this person wealth and happiness—to that one, poverty and woe.

THE COLLOQUY

I began my interrogations by saying, "I expect you have always been pretty well acquainted with the people living upon this mountain." To this remark she quickly replied:

"Yes! And I tell you that they are the worst set of folks that has ever lived; they lie and steal, and cheat, and rob, and murder, too. Why, you wouldn't believe how bad they are; they'd cheat the very devil, if he was on earth; and they'd lie him out of his possessions, too. Why, a person is in danger of his life up here, and he can't keep nothin'. They'd steal the bread out of a blind nigger's mouth, and then murder him if he told of it. That's the way it goes up here—they're worse then the devil himself."

"But," I replied, "there must be some good ones among them." To this she ejaculated: "No, there ain't; not one; they're all bad, and some are worse. You never seen such folks; they're the damnedest that ever lived."

"Well, then how do they live?" said I.

"Live! Why, they don't live—they only stay—and hardly that; a good many of them don't stay long in the same place, neither; they're a set of damned turtles; they carry all they've got on their backs—and that ain't much, neither—and then they're ready to get up and get out, any time; and you catch 'em if you want to."

"Well, if they are so bad, do any of them live together, or does each one live alone?" I inquired.

To this she replied: "Live together! Guess they do; too many of 'em. Why, in some of them shanties there are a dozen or more—whites and blacks, and all colors—and nothin' to eat, and nothin' to wear, and no wood to burn—and what can they do—they have to steal."

"And then there is no distinction of color up here?" said I.

"No, not a bit. The niggers and whites all live together. The whites are just as good as the niggers, and both are as bad as the devil can make 'em."

"Well, then, do the Negroes marry the whites?"

"When they want to; but, they don't do much marrying up here—they don't have to—and then it's no use—it's too much trouble."

"Well, then, how about the children, are there any?"

"Yes; a plenty of 'em; and all colors—black, and white, and yellow—and any other color that you have ever seen, but blue; there ain't no blue ones yet."

"Well, if their parents are not married, how do they bring up the children?"

"Bring 'em up! They don't bring 'em up. Why, as soon as they are born, every devil of 'em is for himself, and the devil's for 'em all. That's how that goes. And I tell you, they have a blamed hard time of it, too."

"And then how do they name the children?"

"Name 'em! Why, they name 'em after their daddies, to be sure—if they know who they are. But, that don't make any odds; 'cause, before they are grown up, half of 'em don't know their own young ones from anybody else's, and the other half of 'em wouldn't own 'em if they did; and the young ones ain't know better—they often swear they had no daddies. You see, just as soon as they get big enough, they travel out to get something to eat, and if the feed is pretty good, maybe they'll stay—never get back; and if they come back, they find so many more in the nest, they can't stay if they want to. Why, none of 'em that's good for anything ever stays here. They go away when they are small, and get work and stay. You'll find folks born on this mountain, live in Princeton, New Brunswick, and Trenton, in New York, and the devil knows where all; and if they are driving team for big-bugs, or are waiters in some great hotel, they'll never own they were born on this mountain, not a bit of it. They know better. But, if one turns out to be a poor devil and gets into some bad scrape—that fellow is sure to come back to the mountain. That's the way they keep the ranks full—full of the scoundrels that can't stay anywhere else; that's the way it goes with the folks here."

"Have you always lived on this mountain, Sylvia?"

"No; I was born on this mountain in an old tavern that used to stand near the Rock Mills; it stood upon the land now owned by Richard Scott. The old hotel was owned and kept by Richard Compton; it was torn down a long while ago, and now you can't tell the spot on which it stood. My parents were slaves; and when my master moved down to Neshanic, I went along with them; and, when my master went to Great Bend, on the Susquehanna, I went with him there. Afterwards I lived in New Brunswick, and in Princeton, and in other places. I came back to the mountain because I inherited a house and lot of land, at my father's death. That's what brought me back to the mountain."

"Who was your father?"

"My father was Cuffy Bard, a slave to John Bard. He (Cuffy) was a fifer in the Battle of Princeton. He used to be a fifer for the minutemen, in the days of the Revolution."

"Who was your mother?"

"My mother was Dorcas Compton, a slave to Richard Compton, the proprietor of the hotel and Rock Mills. When I was two years old, my mother bought her time of Richard Compton—Minical Dubois going her security for the payment of the money. As my mother failed make payment at the time appointed, she became the property of Minical Dubois. With this failure to make payment, Dubois was greatly disappointed, and much displeased, as he did not wish to fall heir to my mother and her children as slaves to him. So he treated mother badly—often times cruelly. On one occasion, when her babe was but three days old, he whipped her with an ox-goad, because she didn't hold a hog while he yoked it; it was in March; the ground was wet and slippery, and the hog proved too strong for her, under the circumstances. From the exposure and the whipping, she became severely sick with puerperal fever; but, after a long while she recovered.

"Under the slave laws of New Jersey, when the slave thought the master too severe, and the slave and the master did not get along harmoniously, the slave had a right to hunt a new master. Accordingly, my mother, Dorcas went in quest of a new master; and as Mr. Wm. Bard used to send things for her and her children to eat, when Dubois neglected, or refused to furnish enough to satisfy their craving stomachs, she asked him (Bard), to buy her. This he did. And she liked him well; but she was ambitious to be free. Accordingly, she bought her time of Bard, but failed to make payment, and returned to him his slave.

"She was then sold to Miles Smith, who was a kind master, and a good man. But she was ambitious to be free—so of Smith she bought her time, and went away to work, and to live with strangers. But, as she failed to make payment at the appointed time, she was taken back a slave, and spent the remainder of her days with him, and was buried about 45 years ago upon his homestead.

"Of course, I remained a slave to Minical Dubois. He did not treat me cruelly. I tried to please him, and he tried to please me; and we got along together pretty well—excepting sometimes I would be a little refractory, and then he would give me a severe flogging. When I was about five years old, he moved upon a farm near the village of Flagtown. While there, I had good times—a plenty to eat, a plenty of clothes, and a plenty of fun—only my mistress was terribly passionate, and terribly cross to me. I did not like her, and she did not like me; so she used to beat me badly. On one occasion, I did something that did not suit her. As usual, she scolded me. Then I was sassy. Hereupon, she whipped me until she marked me so badly that I will never lose the scars. You can see the scars here upon my head, today; and I will never lose them, if I live another hundred years.

"When I was about ten years old, the Battle of Monmouth occurred. I remember very well when my master come home for that battle. Cherries were ripe, and we were gathering harvest. He was an officer; but I do not know his rank. He told great stories about the battle, and of the bravery of the New Jersey militia; and about the conduct of General Washington. He said they whipped the British badly—but it was a desperate fight. He told us that the battle occurred on the hottest day he ever saw; he said he came near perishing from the excess of heat and from thirst; and that a great many did die for the want of water.

"I also remember when my father and others returned from the Battles of Trenton and Princeton—but I was younger then, and only remember that it was winter, and that they complained that they had suffered so much from cold and exposure.

"Before the Battle of Princeton, my master had been a prisoner of war. He had been captured while fighting on the water, somewhere near New York. I used to hear him tell how he and several others were crowded into a very small room in the hold of a vessel—the trap-door securely fastened down, and the supply of fresh air so completely shut off, that almost all who were thus imprisoned, died in a few hours. In this place they were kept two days. Dubois, by breathing with his mouth in close contact with a nail-hole, held out until he was removed. Two or three others were fortunate enough to

find some other defects in the wood-work, through which a scanty supply of
air came.

"When I was in my fourteenth year, my master moved from Flagtown to
his farm along the Susquehanna River. This farm is the land on which the
village called Great Bend has been built. When we moved upon the farm,
there was but one other house in the settlement for the distance of several
miles. These two houses were built of logs. The one upon my master's farm
had been kept as a tavern; and when he moved into it, he kept it as a tavern.
The place was known as Great Bend. It was an important stopping place for
travelers on their way to the Lake Countries, and to other places westward.
Also, it was a place much visited by boatmen going down and up the river.
Here, too, came great numbers of hunters and drovers. In fact, even in these
days, Great Bend was an important place.

"In moving to Great Bend, we went in two wagons. We took with us
two cows; these I drove all the way there. After we crossed the Delaware at
Easton, the road extended through a great forest, with only here and there a
cleared patch, and a small log hut. Even the taverns were only log huts—
sometimes with but one room down stairs and one up stairs. Then there
would be two or three beds in the room upstairs, and one in the room down
stairs.

"The great forest was called the Beech Woods. It was so big that we was
six days in going through it. Sometimes we would go a half a day without
passing a house, or meeting a person. The woods was full of bears, panthers,
wild-cats and the like. About these I had heard a great many wild stories. So
I made sure to keep my cows pretty close to the wagons.

"Usually, we stopped over night at a hotel. But, as the houses were small,
often it would happen that others had stopped before we arrived, and the
lodging rooms would all be occupied. Then we would sleep in our wagons,
or in the out-buildings. In those days, travelers had to get along the best way
they could.

"As my master saw that the sight upon which he lived was favorable to
business, during the third summer after our arrival, he erected a large new
frame house—the first house, not built of logs, in Great Bend. Then, he
began to do a large business, and became a very prominent man there, as he
was while he lived in New Jersey.

"Already several people had moved to the neighborhood, had erected log houses, cleared the lands, and begun to cultivate fields, and raise stock. Very soon, in the village, store-houses and mills were built. Indeed, Great Bend began to be the center of a large and thriving settlement.

"At this time hunters used to come to this point to trade; to sell deer-meat, bear-meat, wild turkeys and the like, and to exchange the skins of wild animals for such commodities as they wished. At our tavern, they used to stay; and they were a jolly set of fellows; I liked to see them come—there was fun then.

"There was a ferry across the Susquehanna at Great Bend. The boat upon our side was owned by my master; the one upon the other side was owned by Captain Hatch. I soon learned to manage the boat as well as anyone could, and often used to ferry teams across alone. The folks who were acquainted with me used to prefer me to take them across, even when the ferrymen were about. But, Captain Hatch did not like me. I used to steal his customers. When I landed my boat upon his side, if any body was there that wanted to come over to the Bend, before he knew it, I would hurry them into my boat and push off from the shore, and leave him swearing. You see the money I got for fetching back a load was mine; and I stole many a load from old Hatch; I always did, every time I could.

"Along with the ferry boat, always were one or two skiffs. These we took along to have in readiness in case of accident. When the load was heavy, or when it was windy, two or more ferrymen were required. At such times, I would help them across, but I always come back alone in a skiff. In this way I got so that I could handle the skiff first rate, and was very fond of using it. Often times I used to take single passengers over the ferry in a skiff; some-times two or more at once. This I liked, and they used to pay me well to do it. I had a good name for managing the skiff—they used to say that, in using the skiff I could beat any man on the Susquehanna—and I always did beat all that raced with me.

"Oftentimes when the ferrymen were at dinner, someone would come to the ferry to cross. They would holler to let us know that someone wanted to cross. Then there would be a race. I'd skip out and down to the wharf so soon that I'd have 'em loaded and pushed off before anyone else could get there—and then I'd get the fee. I tell you, if they did not chuck knife and fork, and run at once, 'twas no use—they couldn't run with me—the fee was gone. I've got many a shilling that way, and many a good drink, too."

I asked: "Was your master willing that you should cheat the ferryman out of his fees in that way?"

She replied: "He did not care; he thought I was smart for doing it. And sometimes, if I had not been in the habit of hurrying things up in this way, people would have waited at the ferry by the hour—but you see they didn't have to wait when I was about, and this is why they liked me, and why my master like me, too."

"Well, Sylvia, what kind of times did you have while at Great Bend?"

"What kind of times? Why, first rate times! There were plenty of frolics, and I used to go and dance all night—folks could dance then. Why, there were some of the best dances up there that I ever saw; folks knew how to dance in those days."

"Then you think that the young folks of this neighborhood don't know how to dance?"

"I know they don't; I've seen 'em try, and they can't dance a bit. They've got no step."

"Have you seen anybody try to dance very lately?"

"Yes, last winter they made a party over here, at one of the neighbors and they invited me over, and I went. They had a fiddle, and they tried to dance—but they couldn't—not a damned a one of 'em."

"Well, what was the matter?"

"What was the matter! Why, they had no step—you can't dance unless you have the step; and they were as awkward as the devil; and then they were so damned clumsy. Why, if they went to cross their legs, they'd fall down."

"Then you think that to dance well, it is necessary to cross the legs?"

"Sometimes it is—nobody can dance much without crossing the legs; but they couldn't do it—they'd get tangled in the rigging and capsize. Why, they cantered over the floor like so many he goats."

"Well, did you show them how to dance?"

"Well, yes; I took a step or two; but I couldn't do it as I used to when I was young. They thought I did well; but they don't know—they've never seen good dancing. Why, when I was young, I'd cross my feet ninety-nine times in a minute, and never miss the time, strike heel or toe with equal ease, and go through the figures as nimble as a witch. But now they're so clumsy that when one takes a foot off from the floor, somebody has to hold him up while he shakes it. And then when they reel they push and crowd like a yoke of young steers, and they bang each other until they are in danger of their lives."

"Yes, Sylvia, the art of dancing has fallen into decline, and I am sorry for it."

"The young folks of this generation are not only clumsy and awkward, but they are bad figures; there is nothing in their sports to develop a good form, and as a consequence, this generation is characterized by bad development—weak bodies with ugly faces, and poor minds."

Hereupon Sylvia began to say:

"But, they think they're great things and very handsome. But they ain't; they're poor scrawny mortals—make no appearance and can't do nothing. Why, the men of the age of my master looked brave. They were tall and commanding, and stout of limb, and graceful and handy; they had good faces, great high foreheads—and large bright eyes and broad mouths with good teeth. They stood up straight, and walked with freedom and ease. I tell you, in those old times, there were good looking men—brave looking men, they were all so; General Washington was, Lafayette was, and my master was and all the great men that I ever saw were, and they were all good dancers; and danced whenever they had a chance. They used to say that General Washington was the most beautiful dancer in America—that he could even beat the Marquis de Lafayette.

"The big Yankees from York State and New England used to come to our house, and they were very fine looking men—all of 'em were. And they were very tall, and very straight, and very dignified; and their wives were well formed and beautiful, and very dignified women. And they were all very polite—had the best of manners—were the most accomplished folks I ever saw. And they were all good dancers—the best of dancers—and they never got tired of dancing. Even the old men and old women danced—and they were just as good figures as you ever saw, and very graceful."

"I see, Sylvia, that you had good times when at the Great Bend."

"Guess we had! When my master moved into his new house, we had a big time. All the grand folks were there, and I tell you, things were lively. We had a plenty of brandy, and they used it, too—a big time I tell you; aye, aye, the biggest kind of a time."

"Did you use any brandy?"

"Well, I did; but not till toward night; I had too much to do; I had to see to the rest; I knew where everything was, and I had to help them get them. But, I looked out for myself. There was one keg of brandy that I knew was made very good, for I helped make it; we used to make our own brandy, and I always helped my master make it, and knew just as well how to do it as anybody.

"I left this keg till it was the last thing to be moved; then, when I and a certain fellow began to move it, we concluded that we would see if it had kept well; we had no cup, so we drawed it out in an earthen pot; and then he drank; and then I drank—till we drank all we could; but still there was some left in the pot, and we couldn't get it back in the keg, for we had no funnel; we didn't want to throw it away, that looked too wasteful; so, we concluded we'd drink it up; so, he drank and I drank, till it was gone. This made us pretty full; but we started with the keg; by and by it begun to be too heavy— and then it got down, and then we got down; and then I knew there'd be a time, because I knew if my master saw me, I'd get a hell of a lickin'. And some of the rest knew that too. And they didn't want to see me licked, so they got me up, and helped me off toward the house to put me to bed.

"I used to be subject to the cramps, and sometimes I used to have it very bad,—so that my mistress used to give me medicine for it; and once a little while before, I was so bad with it that she thought I was going to die with it. Well, I thought now I had better have the cramp, and then maybe I wouldn't get licked. So I began to have pain—and soon it got pretty bad—worse than I'd ever had it before; anyhow, I made more fuss than I ever had before, and yelled a good deal louder.

"Pretty soon they called missy, and she was awfully frightened; she thought I would die, sure; she said she'd never seen me so weak with it before.

"So she had me carried and placed upon the trundle-bed, in her own room, and attended to me nicely. She gave me some medicine which she thought helped me amazingly; but before the medicine could do any good the rum stopped all my yelling, and grunting too; in fact, I was so drunk that I couldn't see, hear, nor feel. For awhile, I thought I was dead; but by and by the brandy began to wear off, and I began to see. I cautiously squirmed around to see whether anybody was about, and there sat missy, fanning me. I cautiously opened my eyes just the least bit, to see how she looked; she looked very pitiful—I was too drunk to laugh; but 'My God,' thought I, 'if you only knew what I am doing, you'd throw that fan away and give me hell.'

"At night, my master came to bed very late. When he came in to undress, I was making believe that I was asleep. I didn't dare to get well too soon. At once, mistress began to tell him how sick I was; and how near I came to dying—but I didn't fool him. He looked at me a little, and then went to bed. He said: 'Pa! She's only drunk—she's been drinking with the men. Go to sleep—she'll be all right in the morning.' And so I was, too; but, that cured me of drinking."

"Then you never drank after that?"

"I never got drunk after that. Sometimes when others have been drinking, I have taken a dram, too; but, I didn't get drunk—I never do. I know my measure, and I take no more."

"Did your mistress ever find out that you were deceiving her when you were drunk?"

"I guess not; if she had, she'd a killed me—if she could; but, I have laughed about it a great many times. I spoiled her fun for that night—she had to leave her company and take care of me,—it was pretty hard for her; for she had a great deal of big company there, that night, and she was hell for company."

"Well, your mistress was always kind to you, wasn't she?"

"Kind to me; why, she was the very devil himself. Why, she'd level me with anything she could get hold of—club, stick of wood, tongs, fire-shovel, knife, axe, hatchet; anything that was handiest;—and then she was so damned quick about it, too. I tell you, if I intended to sass her, I made sure to be off a ways."

"Well, did she ever hit you?"

"Yes, often; once she knocked me till I was so stiff that she thought I was dead; once after that, because I was a little sassy, she leveled me with the fire-shovel and broke my pate. She thought I was dead then, but I wasn't."

"Broke your pate?"

"Yes, broke my skull; you can put your fingers here, in the place where the break was, in the side of my head, yet. She smashed it right in—she didn't do things to the halves."

Hereupon I examined Sylvia's head, and found that, at some time, long ago, the skull had been broken and depressed for a space not less than three inches; that the depressed fragment had not been elevated, as surgeons now do, and that in consequence, there is, to this day, a depression in which I can bury a large part of the index finger.

Upon her head, I found numerous other scars most of which Sylvia says, are the result of wounds inflicted by her mistress. But she says some of them are not. These are, according to her tale, the results of wounds incurred during other wars,—waged after she gained her freedom. For, in the struggle for life, Sylvia incurred many a combat; and, although she always came off from the field victorious, sometimes she did not come off unscathed.

In her fights, it is said, she engaged alike man or woman, black or white—beast or bird—anything but God or devil.

According to her tale, she cared but little for fist or foot; but sometimes when they came down upon her with wood and steel, she did wince a little. But woe to the combatant that dared to resort to those unfair implements of war. At best, even with these, they could only wound her,—just enough to exasperate her to do justice to the occasion. For, when rigid for a fist fight, never enough stood before her, nor gathered around her, to discomfit her, or to keep her upon the sod.

Respecting her prowess, Sylvia's testimony is not all that I have gathered. Different men, whose venerable looks show that they are old enough to remember scenes that they witnessed sixty and seventy years ago, tell me that they have seen Sylvia in battle many a time, and that her courage, and her ability was always adequate to any emergency.

However, tradition states, that Sylvia was neither quarrelsome nor aggressive. On the contrary, she was decidedly a peace-maker; and some of her most noteworthy feats were accomplished when suppressing a row, or, parting combatants; indeed, her presence often prevented a fight. Because, if the fight began contrary to her will, oftentimes she, to make them more obedient in the future, and to terrify others of a quarrelsome or pugilistic nature, would severely whip both the combatants.

Nor was she less likely to interfere in cases where there was a free fight. In cases in which from five to ten were in a fight, Sylvia has often been known to wade in, to seize wherever hand-holt was easiest, and to throw one Negro in one direction, and another in another direction, until the last fellow was hurled from the arena of fight; and oftentimes she threw them with such force, that the dash upon the ground unfitted them for further action, or for returning to the battle; such feats, owing to her great size, and greater strength, she accomplished with ease; and, it is said, that such were her deliberations, that she would return from such scenes in the utmost composure.

"Well, Sylvia, what did your master say about such as was done by your mistress?"

"Say? Why, he knew how passionate she was. He saw her kick me in the stomach one day so badly that he interfered. I was not grown up then; I was too young to stand such. He didn't tell her so when I was by, but I have heard him tell her when they thought I was not listening that she was too severe—that such work would not do—she'd kill me next."

"Well, did his remonstrating with her make her any better?"

"Not a bit—made her worse—just put the devil in her. And then, just as soon as he was out of the way, if I was a little sassy, or a little neglectful, I'd catch hell again.

"But I fixed her—I paid her up for all her spunk. I made up my mind that when I grew up I would do it, and when I had a good chance, when some of her grand company was around, I fixed her."

"Well, what did you do?"

"I knocked her down, and blamed near killed her."

"Well, where and how did that happen?"

"It happened in the barroom; there was some grand folks stopping there, and she wanted things to look pretty stylish; and so she set me to scrubbing up the barroom. I felt a little grum, and didn't do it to suit her; she scolded me about it, and I sassed her; she struck me with her hand. Think's I, it's a good time now to dress you out, and damned if I won't do it; I set down my tools, and squared for a fight. The first whack, I struck her a hell of a blow with my fist. I didn't knock her entirely through the panels of the door; but her landing against the door made a terrible smash, and I hurt her so badly that all were frightened out of their wits, and I didn't know myself but that I'd killed the old devil."

"Were there anyone in the barroom, then?"

"It was full of folks; some of them were Jersey folks, who were going from the Lake Countries home to visit their friends; some were drovers, on their way to the west, and some were hunters and boatmen staying a while to rest."

"What did they do when they saw you knock your mistress down?"

"Do! Why, they were going to take her part, of course; but I just sat down the slop bucket and straightened up, and smacked my fists at 'em, and told 'em to wade in, if they dared, and I'd thrash every devil of 'em; and there wasn't a damned one that dared to come."

"Well, what next?"

"Then I got out, and pretty quick, too. I knew it wouldn't do to stay there; so I went down to Chenang Point; and there went to work."

"Where was your master, during this fracas?"

"He! He was gone to tend court at Wilksbarre. He was grand jury man, and had to be gone a good many days. He often served as a grand jury man, and then he was always gone a week or two. Things would have gone better if he had been home."

"When he came home, what did he do?"

"He sent for me to come back."

"Did you go?"

"Of course, I did, I had to go; I was a slave, and if I didn't go, he would have brought me, and in a hurry, too; in those days, the masters made the niggers mind; and when he spoke, I knew I must obey.

"Them old masters, when they got mad, had no mercy on a nigger—they'd cut a nigger all up in a hurry—cut 'em all up into strings, just leave the life—that's all; I've seen 'em do it, many a time."

"Well, what did your master say when you came back?"

"He didn't scold me much; he told me that, as my mistress and I got along so badly, if I would take my child and go to New Jersey, and stay there, he would give me free; I told him I would go. It was late at night; he wrote me a pass, gave it to me, and early the next morning I set out for Flagtown, N. J."

"It seems that you got along with your master much better than you did with your mistress?"

"Yes, I got along with him, first rate; he was a good man; and a great man, too; all the grand folks liked Minical Dubois. When the great men had their meetings, Minical Dubois was always invited to be with 'em; and he always went, too; he was away from home a great deal; he had a great deal of business, and he was known all over the country. I liked my master, and everybody liked him.

"He never whipped me unless he was sure that I deserved it; he used to let me go to frolics and balls, and to have good times away from home, with other black folks, whenever I wanted to; he was a good man and a good master; but, when he told me I must come home from a ball at a certain time, when the time came, the jig was out—I knew I must go; it wouldn't do to disappoint Minical Dubois."

"Did parties often occur?"

"Yes, and I always went, too; Old Minical would always let me go, because I was a good Negress, and always tried to please him; I had good times when he was around, and he always done things right; but you mustn't get him mad.

"In the long nights of winter, we often had frolics, almost every week; we'd hardly get over one frolic when we'd begin to fix for another.

"Then there was the holidays—Christmas, and New Year, and Easter, and the Fourth of July, and General Training. But, the biggest of 'em all was general training. That was the biggest day for the niggers—I tell you that was the biggest day. The niggers were all out to general training—little and big—old and young; and then they'd have some rum—always had rum at general trainings—and then you'd hear 'em laugh a mile—and when they got into a fight, you'd hear 'em yell more than five miles."

"Did the niggers yell when they fought?"

"The cowards did—worse than anything you ever heard—worse than anything but a cowardly nigger."

"Where did you hold your frolics?"

"There was a great many niggers around the neighborhood of Great Bend, and sometimes we'd meet at one master's house, and sometimes at another's. We was sure to have a fiddle, and a frolic, and a first rate time; but none of 'em had a better time than myself—I liked frolics. I could dance all night, and feel as jolly as a witch all next day. I never tired at frolics—not I; nor at general training, neither."

"Did you say your master used to make his own brandy?"

"Yes, he often made it—always made his peach brandy; any one can make peach brandy—the best that was ever drunk; you just burn about four pounds of dried peaches until you can rub them to powder in your hands; you must burn 'em in a pot that has a very tight cover on. Then rub 'em fine in your hands; or, if some pieces are too hard for that, pound them fine with a hammer. Then put this powder of burnt peaches into a barrel of new apple whiskey, and in four weeks, if you shake the barrel every day, you will have a barrel of peach brandy good enough for anybody.

"You make apple brandy in almost the same way; you burn about four pounds of apples dried with the skins on. Make them into powder, and put 'em in a barrel of new apple whiskey, and shake the barrel every day for four weeks. In four weeks, you have a barrel of apple brandy better than any you ever saw. A little of that will make a fellow talk—and won't burn his guts out neither. Folks used to drink brandy right along—drank it every day—drank a plenty of it, and didn't get the man-a-poche, nor the delirium tremens, neither.[1] Why, the brandy used to be good—tasted good and was pleasant to drink; you can't get none such now—not a bit of it. A drink of brandy now, burns like fire—burns all the way down—goes through the guts worse than a sheet of red-hot sand paper."

SYLVIA, A FREE NEGRESS

"How did you go to Flagtown?"

"On foot, to be sure; I came right down through the Beech Woods, all alone, excepting my young one in my arms; sometimes I didn't see a person for a half a day; sometimes I didn't get half enough to eat, and never had any bed to sleep in; I just slept anywhere. My baby was about a year and a half old, and I had to carry it all the way. The wood was full of panthers, bears, wildcats, and wolves; I often saw 'em in the daytime, and always heard 'em howling in the night. Oh! That old panther—when he howled, it made the hair stand up all over my head.

"At Easton, I went on board of a raft to go down the Delaware. A man by the name of Brink, had his wife and family on board of a raft, bound for Philadelphia; I went on board to help the wife, for my passage; they were nice folks, and I had a good time; I left the raft not far from Trenton, but I do not know exactly where—there was no town at the place at which I got off the raft.

"Then I proceeded directly to Flagtown, to see my mother; I did not find her there—she had moved to New Brunswick. On my way, a man called to me, asking me, 'Whose nigger are you?' I replied, 'I'm no man's nigger—I belong to God—I belong to no man.'

"He then said: 'Where are you going?' I replied, 'That's none of your business—I'm free; I go where I please.'

"He came toward me; I sat down my young one, showed him my fist, and looked at him; and I guess he saw 't was no use; he moseyed off, telling me that he would have me arrested as soon as he could find a magistrate.

"You see that in those days, the Negroes were all slaves, and they were sent nowhere, nor allowed to go anywhere without a pass; and when anyone met a Negro who was not with his master, he had a right to demand of him whose Negro he was; and if the Negro did not show his pass, or did not give good evidence whose he was, he was arrested at once, and kept until his master came for him, paid whatever charges were made, and took him away. You see, in those days, anybody had authority to arrest vagrant Negroes. They got pay for arresting them, and charged for their keeping till their master redeemed them. But, he didn't arrest me—not a bit.

"When I got to New Brunswick, I found my mother; soon after, I went to work, and remained in New Brunswick several years. From New Brunswick I went to Princeton to work for Victor Tulane. I remained in his family a long while; I worked for him when Paul Tulane was a child; I worked there when he was born.[2] Victor Tulane was a great man, and a good man; and he used his servants well; and Paul was a nice boy, and Madame Tulane was a good woman; and I liked 'em all, and all the servants liked 'em.

"After a long while, I visited my grandfather, Harry Compton, who lived at the forks of the road, near this place; he was then an old man; they say he was more than a hundred years old, and I guess he was; but he was yet quite active; he wanted me to stay with him and take care of him, and I stayed; and at his death, I inherited his property. I lived on the old homestead until a few years ago, when them damned democrats set fire to my house, and burned up my home and all that I had. Since that time, I have lived at this place, with my youngest daughter."

"Well, Sylvia, you have lived a long while, and have suffered a great many hardships, and, I expect that you are tired of living."

"No, I ain't; I'd like to live another hundred years yet—and I don't know but I will, too; my teeth are good, and if I can get enough to eat, I don't know why I should die; there's no use in dying—you ain't good for anything after you are dead."

"Well, Sylvia, I expect you are well acquainted with this mountain, and with all the folks that live on it."

"Yes, I know every foot of it—every hole and corner of it; every place where anybody lives or ever has lived. And I know the folks, too; and some of 'em are pretty bad ones, too; in fact, they are all bad, and some of them are worse. What the devil will ever do with them when he has to take 'em, I don't know. Surely he don't want 'em, and wouldn't have 'em if he could help it. The only reason that some of these folks up here don't die sooner than they do is, the devil won't have them; he just puts off taking them, because he knows what a time he'll have when he gets 'em. Why! Some of them are starved to death long enough before they die; but, they can't die—there's no place for them to go after they are dead. They ain't fit to go to heaven, and the devil won't have 'em, and so they have to stay here. Why, this mountain is worse than hell itself. Why, if some of these folks don't behave better, after they go into the infernal regions than they do while here, the devil will have a time of it. He'll never manage 'em; he'll have to call a congress and have an amendment fixed to the constitution. A brimstone fire won't do; it will never faze 'em; it don't here. I've seen it tried, and it don't do at all—only makes 'em worse."

"Well, Sylvia, you tell a pretty hard story about your neighbors."

"Tell a hard story! I tell the truth; and I could tell more of it; why, you don't know 'em; there is more folks killed up here than anybody knows of; and you know somebody is killed up here every year; and nobody is ever hanged for it; and it gets worse and worse. If they kill anybody up here, they just take the murderers off to Flemington and keep them in jail awhile till they have a trial, and then they turn 'em out to come back here, and then they are worse than they were before; they just kill anybody then.

"And they steal! Why, you wouldn't believe how much they steal; they don't steal much of one another, because that wouldn't do; if they were caught at that, they'd get killed damned soon, and then they ain't got much to be stoled. But they go off from the mountain, down into the valleys, and there they steal anything they can find—sheep and chickens, and grain, and meat, and clothes—and anything else that they can eat or wear; and, nobody can find anything that has been stolen by the folks up here, for, when anything is to be stolen, they all know about it, and they all lie for each other, and they all know where it is to be hid, and they all help to keep folks from finding it; so it does no good to hunt up here for stolen goods. And then they know so damned well how to hide things, too; they don't hide what they steal, in their houses, until all the houses have been searched; when they steal anything they hide it in some hole that nobody but mountaineers know of; or else under some rocks, or under some wood, where nobody but the mountaineers would think of looking. That is the way they do business up here; and if you tell 'em of it, they'll kill you—damned if they won't."

"And Sylvia, you have lived right here, in the midst of them for fifty years without falling into their ways?"

"Yes, and longer, too. I know 'em; I've been to 'em—but they have never troubled me much—they know it wouldn't do; they know I'd give 'em that."

(So saying, she brought her right fist into her left hand until the smack could be heard fifty yards.)

"Well, Sylvia, what do you think ought to be done with these bad folks?"

"Ought to be done with 'em? Why, some of 'em ought to be hanged right up by the neck; and some of 'em ought to be tied up and licked nearly to death—tied right up to a post and licked till within an inch of the life. That's what ought to be done with 'em—that's the way I'd serve 'em. I'd take 'em up to Flemington, and lick 'em till they'd never want to be licked again."

"Have you ever been to Flemington, Sylvia?"

"Been where?"

"Been to Flemington?

"Been to that damned Flemington? Yes, I've been there; and it is the damnedest place in the world."

"Why, Sylvia, what have you got against Flemington?"

"I've got enough against it. You can't get anything there without money; nobody is considered anything there unless he has money; nobody will tell you anything there unless you give 'em money; if you ask a lawyer anything, he won't tell you a bit until he gets your money. You can't get justice there unless you have some money; and you can't get it then— because, if another person has more money than you have, they'll all of 'em—every damned lawyer, the judge, and the jury, go for him, and a poor body has no show at all. I know 'em—I've been to 'em—they're a bad set."

"Have you been to the lawyers at Flemington, Sylvia?"

"Yes, I have—but, it didn't do any good; these damned S___'s have been trying to get my property away from me for many years, and I wanted to consult a lawyer to get him to put these devils through; but I couldn't; not a damned lawyer would take my case, because I had no money; they said they could not talk without money; they couldn't do anything for me unless I paid 'em some money."

"Why didn't you pay them some money?"

"Pay 'em! I couldn't—I hadn't a cent to my name."

"Well, Sylvia, how did you feel when they told you that they could do nothing for you without you gave them some money?"

"Feel! I felt like kicking their damned tripes out.[3] They think they are so damned big because they are dressed up a little; and they are too damned proud to be decent. If they'd come over on the mountain we'd show 'em; we'd skin every devil of 'em—I'd do it myself, as old as I am. I'd just like to put my fist against their eyes."

(So saying, she brought the fist against the hand, until it smacked aloud.)

"Were you ever at Flemington when you were not consulting lawyers?"

"Yes, often. I used to go whenever there was any doings there; whenever there was general training, and whenever the big men had their meetings there. All the niggers used to go to Flemington on those big days; and then they'd get licked—good God, how they'd get licked! Why, they'd tie 'em right up and lick'm to death—cut 'em into pieces—cut 'em all into strings."

"Did you ever see them whip the Negroes?"

"See 'em! Yes, I have; see 'em lick a dozen of 'em at a time. Tie 'em right up to a post, and give 'em hell, right on the bare back—fetch the blood every time; and they'd holler! Good God! They'd howl till you could hear 'em a mile; and then, when they had cut the back all in slits, they'd put salt in the gashes; and then they'd howl. Lord God! No panther in the beech woods ever made half so much noise.

"That's the way they fixed the nigger in old times, them damned Flemingtoners—they think they are so damned big."

"What did the Negroes do, that they whipped them so badly?"

"Why, of course they'd get some whiskey, and then they'd get into a canticoy, and make a noise perhaps; they'd get into a row or a fight, and then somebody would get hurt; and then the one that got hurt would complain to the authorities, and then the constables would be after the niggers; and when they caught'm, they'd tie 'em right up without judge or jury, and pull off the shirt, and put it right on the bare hide.[4] My God, how they lick 'em—cut the hide all in gashes.

"That's the way they used to fix the old slaves; give 'em a holiday to have a little sport, and then if they had any fun, lick 'em till they'd have a sore back till the next holiday come."

"Well, Sylvia, would they want to go to the next holiday?"

"Yes, the niggers always wanted to go, back sore or well; never knew one to miss when his master told him he could go. Then he'd be sure to get licked worse than he was before, because some niggers couldn't have a holiday without getting into a fight, then he'd be sure to get tied up and licked."

During the time Sylvia was answering the last few questions, she became so excited, so eloquent in her own way, and so indulgent in her profane epithets, that I feared that I would not be able to take down all that she said, nor be able to fit up for the press what I did take down. Indeed, when she began to tell about the treatment of the Negroes during the days of slavery, she at once waxed eloquent, and soon became so vehement, that I did not know whether it was wise to prosecute my inquiries any further in this direction. At almost the first question, I thought I smelt the fumes of brimstone; and as we proceeded, the sulfurous odor became so strong, that I feared that by her powerful gesticulation and the peals of terrific language, she had rent the crust of the earth somewhere near where she sat, and the fumes from the infernal regions were ascending through the fissure into the apartment in which we sat. Indeed, the atmosphere was decidedly choky, and I should have asked for a better ventilation, but for the fact that, whichever way I looked, the open spaces between the logs allowed me to see the swaying forest trees, and gave the piercing wind a free current to my chilly back and to my chillier ears.

Reflecting that this, then, naturally would be a little exciting to an old slave, I concluded to run the risk of the swing of her big fist, and the increasing chokiness of the sulfurous atmosphere, and proceeded as follows:

"Were you at Flemington when the little Negro was hanged for murdering his mistress?"

"Yes, and that was the damnedest time I ever saw. The niggers quarreled and fought, and pounded each other, and bit each other's ears off; and then pounded each other's noses down, bunged each other's eyes and some got blamed near killed. And then them damned Flemingtoners got after 'em, and they tied 'em up, and licked 'em without mercy—cut 'em all up —cut 'em all in strings; just left the life—no more.

"That was a great time, I'll never forget that."

"Well, Sylvia, did the Negroes not deserve to be whipped sometimes?"

"Yes, sometimes—most always, I expect. They had to lick 'em, there was no other way; they had to make 'em mind; the niggers that behaved well never got licked; but some wouldn't behave; they'd always get into a row, or steal something, and then they'd be sure to get licked."

"Sylvia, they say that you are very old, over a hundred years old—Do you know how old you are?"

"Not exactly—can't tell exactly; they didn't used to keep a record of the birth of niggers; they hardly kept a record of the birth of white children; none but the grand folks kept a record of the birth of their children—they didn't no more keep the date of a young nigger, than they did of a calf or a colt; the young niggers were born in the Fall or in the Spring, in the Summer or in the Winter; in cabbage time, or when cherries were ripe; when they were planting corn, or when they were husking corn; and that's all the way they talked about a nigger's age."

"But, Sylvia, is there no way to tell approximately when you were born?"

"To be sure there is; and that's what makes folks say that I am a hundred and fifteen years old. They tell this by the record of the birth of Richard Compton. My mother and many other old folks, used to tell me that, when my mother was a slave to Richard Compton, there was born to him a son, whom they called Richard, after his father. When this son Richard was two days old, I was born; so there is but two days difference between the date of Richard Compton's birth and my birth.

"In an old Bible which is now in possession of Mr. Richard Gomo, who lives near Rock Mills, is the record of the Compton family. By referring to this record they tell how old I am. But I do not know how old I am—I can't read; but I expect they tell me right. I know that I am older than anybody else around here—older than their parents were; and in most cases, I knew their great-grandparents.

"I remember that while we were small children, I and Richard Compton were about of a size, and that we used to play together. My mother and his mother used to tell me that we both nursed the same breast, alternately, the same day; as we were so near the same age, when his mother wished to go away to visit, or upon business, Richard was left in the care of my mother; and while his mother was away, he used to nurse my mother with me. Once, Mrs. Compton and one of the neighbors was gone to the city a whole week; and while gone, Richard was left in charge of my mother. Then she used to take us both upon her lap, and while he was nursing one breast, I was nursing the other. They used to say that this was the reason Richard and I got along so well together. As long as he lived, he always claimed to be about my age, and we always visited, and we used to talk over the circumstance that we used to be together when we were babies, and when we were children, and that we had always visited, and always intended to visit.

"A great many old folks used to tell me that they had seen me nurse my mother at the same time that Richard Compton was nursing her, and that he and I were about the same in age. As we lived at a tavern, I expect folks saw us more, and that more folks noticed us than would have done so, in a less public place."

To verify the statements above made, respecting Sylvia's age, I visited Mr. Gomo to consult the ancient record of the Compton family. I soon learned that Mrs. Gomo was a niece of Richard Compton; that she was the daughter of Richard Compton's sister Deborah, who was born January 5th, 1793. This lady, Deborah Compton, had married Vanlieu, by whom she had Mrs. Gomo. After Vanlieu's death, she married D. Danbury. After Danbury's death, she lived with her daughter, Mrs. Gomo, to whom she used to tell that her brother Richard, and Sylvia Dubois, were about of an age. Mrs. Gomo, now an old lady, informs me, that several old folks used to tell her when a girl, that her Uncle Richard and Sylvia Dubois, were about of the same age; that they had seen both Richard and Sylvia nurse the same mother at the same time; and that her Uncle Richard used to tell that his mother used to say that he was two days older than Sylvia.

It happened that the old Bible in the possession of Mrs. Gomo, did not contain a full record of the Compton family; that the record here made dated no further back than the birth of Deborah Compton, which occurred as above stated, Jan. 5th, 1793; but, Mrs. Gomo informed me that the old Bible, having the ancient record for which I was searching was in possession of her daughter, Mrs. John Elbertson, living about two miles east of Rock

Mills. Upon visiting Mrs. Elbertson, and stating the purpose of my visit, she kindly produced the old book, and welcomed me to the hospitalities of her comfortable home. In this record, I found, among others, the following statement: Richard Compton, born March 3d, A. D., 1768; Deborah Compton, born Jan. 5th, A. D., 1793; Hence, we learn that, were Richard Compton still living, he would be almost 115 years old. Then, if tradition is true, and, in this case it is corroborated in so many ways that I cannot doubt it, Sylvia Dubois will be 115 years old upon the 5th day of March, 1883.

Sylvia is in good health, and in good condition of mind. Her memory is excellent; and she is as much interested in the affairs of life as is the most of people at thirty-five. She looks as if she might live many years yet.

Unto Sylvia have been born six children: Moses, Judith, Charlotte, Dorcus, Elizabeth and Rachel. Rachel lives in Princeton. Lizzie owns, and resides upon the lot described in this article. With her, now lives her aged mother. She is a large and stout woman, and looks as if she might live to be as old as her mother. She is well proportioned and very active. It is said that it is not easy to find even among the "bullies," a man that is a match for her, in a hand to hand conflict, or in a fist fight. Perhaps she is as near like her mother, in build, prowess and endurance, as a daughter can be; she seems mild, complacent and courteous. But, rumor says that she has taken part in many a prize fight; that she has never been particular whether the champion who was to meet her was male or female; and that she has seldom, if ever, come out of the contest second best. It is also told that she has sometimes gone a long distance to meet the champion who dared to challenge her, or to provoke her ire.

Lizzie Dubois is far famed as a fortune teller. To hear her descant upon the events of his life, many a young fellow winds his way to the humble hut of this sable lady, and, elated with the information gained, drops his piece of silver into Lizzie's hand, hastes away to watch secretly, the unfolding of every mystery. Nor is her stock of lore barren of witchery. From afar, the votaries of witchcraft go to Lizzie in quest of knowledge respecting stolen goods, and other things that are supposed to be known only to those who are in communication with the spirits of the nether abodes.

Lizzie is about 78 years of age; but she is so well preserved that she would pass for a Negress of 40. Her chances to live to be 120 years old, are very good.

"Sylvia, you have an unusually strong frame, and you have lived to an exceedingly great age; you must have been very properly fed in childhood, or else these things could not be. Upon what did they used to feed you, that you have grown so large and so strong?"

"They gave us Indian dumplings, samp, porridge, corn bread, potatoes, pork, beef, mush and milk, and nigger butter; and we didn't get a bellyful of these, sometimes—I've often gone to bed hungry, but, 't was no use to complain—you had your measure and you got no more. That's the way they fed young niggers, in old times, but they made 'em grow."

"Tell me how the dumplings, porridge, corn bread, and nigger butter were made."

"To make Indian dumplings, scald the Indian meal, work it into a ball, and then boil until done, in the liquor that meat—pork or beef—has been boiled in. These were eaten without any dip, butter or sauce.

"To make samp porridge: boil equal parts of beef and pork together, until done; remove the meat and stir into the liquor in which the meat was boiled, course Indian meal, and boil till done.[5]

"Corn bread was made by mixing equal measures of Indian meal and rye meal together, and baking in an oven.

"Nigger butter was made by mixing two parts of lard with one part of molasses.

"This nigger butter was what we had to use on our bread; and we did well if we didn't have to spread it deuced thin. The bread was so hard that it needed greasing; and this was all that we had to grease it with—we had no gravy.

"We used to have pies occasionally. Sometimes they were made out of sweet apples; sometimes out of sour ones, without any sugar or molasses; didn't feed niggers sugar and molasses much in those days; the white folks didn't get much of 'em—their pies were almost as sour as ours; and there was very little sugar in their coffee, and the sugar that they used was as black as my hide.

"We never drank coffee or tea. Sometimes we got some cider. The white folks only drank tea and coffee on Sunday, or when they had company.

"They used to boil, or roast our potatoes, with the skins on, and then we didn't take the skins off, we ate 'em skins and all. And the white folks ate theirs just so; but they had gravy, or butter, to put on theirs. The white folks didn't eat wheat bread only on Sunday, or when they had company. They ate rye bread; they didn't cultivate much wheat, 't wouldn't grow; never had more than enough to make pie-crust and cakes, out of. They ate a great deal of mush and samp porridge, and Indian cakes, and these were good enough if you had a plenty of good milk and butter, and gravy to eat with 'em.

"I expect folks nowadays, think that this was hard fare, but 't was good enough—when we had enough of it; but sometimes we didn't get a belly-ful—that went a little hard. If the folks nowadays would live as we used to, they'd be a good deal stronger, more healthy, and wouldn't die so soon. They eat so many dainties; too much sugar, too many sweet puddings and pies, too much rich cake, and too much fresh bread; and they drink too much coffee and tea; and they don't dress warm enough; that calico ain't the thing for health. We used to wear woolen underclothes, and our skirts were always made of linsey-woolsey. Our stockings were woolen and our shoes were made of good thick leather, so heavy that you could kick a man's tripe out with 'em.

"This is the way we used to dress, and it was a good way too. The old masters knew how to take care of their niggers.

"We had good beds to sleep in; the ticks were filled with straw, and we had plenty of woolen blankets, and coverlets, as they used to call 'em. The fires were all made of wood, and usually they were big. The fireplaces usually extended entirely across one end of the kitchen—fifteen to twenty feet wide, with large stone jambs that made 'em three or more feet deep, provided with a chimney that 2 or 3 could climb up and stand in, side by side. In the back part of this huge fireplace a large back-log—as much as two or three could carry—was placed, and upon the handirons another log called a fore-stick, as much as a man could carry, was placed; and then between this back-log and fore-stick was piled smaller wood, until it made a fire that would scare the young folks of this generation out of their wits. This big fire not only warmed, but it also lighted the room. As a rule, the niggers had no other light, and no other fire than this—they had to stay in the kitchen—this was their part of the house, and here they had good times, too. The white folks were in another part of the house, where the fireplace was not quite so big. Sometimes the white folks had stoves; and then they lighted their room with tallow candles; there was no kerosene then, nor any coal; they didn't know how to use such things."

Thus ended our colloquy with Sylvia Dubois. As the day was far spent, we gathered our utensils, dropped into the hand of our aged hostess an expression of our charity toward her, bade her good-bye, mounted our sleigh and set off to visit Richard Gomo, at Rock Mills, to examine the records of the Compton family. When the records had been examined, the night was fast coming on, and we hastened toward Ringos. We arrived home after the shades of night had fully supervened, tired and hungry, but delighted with the acquisitions of the day. The aged and careworn visage of Sylvia Dubois, her humble hut and sparse furniture, her shrill, stern voice, her pert replies, her quick answers, her cheerful disposition and her contentment with her lot, has formed a picture in our minds so indelible, that time will never erase it.

APPENDIX

Eleven months have elapsed since the writing of the preceding pages, and still Sylvia Dubois lives—hale, hearty, witty, and as pious as ever. The flash of her eye still is like a gleam of a falcon. Her gait is firm, her voice clear, her hearing acute, her vision excellent. She eats well, drinks well, and smokes better. Her memory is excellent, and she takes as much interest in passing events, as would one of forty years. She enjoys a joke as well as ever; and tells one with exceeding grace. Her laugh is as indicative of merriment as that of a wench of eighteen. Indeed, Sylvia is alive yet.

Sylvia's good spirits do much toward prolonging her days. Her matter-of-fact way of viewing life, prevents worry, and keeps the machinery of her system from friction. That which wears out the machinery of the human frame more than any other one thing (I had almost said more than all else combined) is worry. From this Sylvia is ever free; she has that firm reliance upon Providence that entirely prevents any anxiety about the future. To find one better bottomed upon the Calvinistic faith, is not easy; she says she grew up among the Old School Presbyterians, that she saw their ways were good and that she adopted them—that is, those of their ways that suit her; she says: "If one will only do right, Providence will provide for him. 'T ain't no use to worry—it only makes things worse; let come what will, you've got to bear it—'tain't no use to flinch. Providence knows best—He sends to you whatever He wants you to have, and you've got to take it and make the best of it. I've always got along somehow, and I always will—but sometimes it's pretty damned hard sledding, I tell you."

Sylvia never fidgets. When she sits, her hands rest in her lap, and she is as motionless as a statue. When she stands, she is as firm as a tree. When she walks, her gait is precise and adroit. While talking, she gesticulates not a little; but in the maneuvering of her hands, there is much grace and marked propriety; she is a hearty laugher, but her laugh is agreeable—and not very Africanic—entirely free from that labial Guinea-Negro laugh—wah, wah, wah, wah! Or that palatal laugh so peculiar to the Negro: yah, yah, yah, yah! In the act of laughing, her whole frame is in motion, so much so, that one might think she'd shake the soles from her shoes.

With all her vivacity, she shows decline. During her last year, she has grown old rapidly—has become emaciated and somewhat bowed. Farther, her mind shows decline, and her conversation indicates that she is verging toward the end of life; she talks much of death, and of dying, and seems willing to die. In the course of conversation, she remarked: "None of us have a lease of life; but, I know I am old, and according to the way it has been with everybody else, I see I must die; I may die very suddenly—when none are expecting it—such old folks sometimes die very suddenly, but, there's no telling about that."

Upon the first of November last, I called at the humble mansion in which Sylvia resides, to inquire after her health, her wants, etc., etc. It was evening and the shades of night had well nigh prevented me from following my way; so, to make matters sure, I was escorted over the rocky, winding path, by a guide. After several stumbles, and scratches by cedar bushes, in the distance appeared a faint light. To this, I saw our guide was aiming. It was the lamp that illuminates the hut of our heroine; soon we arrived at the door, was welcomed in, entered and stated the reason of our errand. The old lady sat in her accustomed place—in the niche between the stove and the west wall. Beside her, I placed a proffered chair, and began conversation. She distinctly remembered my visit upon the twenty-seventh of January, 1883, and much that we talked about—faulted me for not having come to see her sooner, and inquired after the welfare of those who were with me during my last visit.

Upon inquiry, she informed me that she had enjoyed good health—that she was strong and still could walk a long way—that she had just returned from Harlingen—a distance of four and one half miles. To be certain as to the manner of returning from Harlingen, I asked her:

"Who brought you from Harlingen?"

To this, in her peculiar style, she replied: "Brought myself—nobody brought me!"

"What! Did you walk home from Harlingen this afternoon?"

"To be sure I did. How else would I get here?"

"What! A woman one hundred and sixteen years old, walk four and a half miles in an afternoon?"

"Yes, there's no other way—I had to walk."

"How long were you upon the way?"

"About two hours, I guess—we came slow—had a good deal to carry—and I can't walk fast anymore."

"Are you not very tired?"

"No, I ain't much tired—I'm a little tired, to be sure—and a little hungry."

Her daughter (with whom Sylvia lives) seemed to be gathering her winter store; and in the little hut were more pieces of furniture and boxes than I had seen before. A table, a barrel or two, and a pile of cheese-boxes, were crowded in the back part of the room, and the space in the loft seemed very full. Indeed, the little house seemed so full that there was hardly sitting room or standing room.

Elizabeth, as usual, was lavish with apology. Her house was not in order—it needed repairing—she'd had a carpenter to view it to see what could be done; mammy's dress was old and ragged, and needed washing; the fire was poor—she'd not yet got her winter wood, and her stove had almost given out—and I know not what there was for which she did not apologize.

To make arrangements for the photograph of our heroine, upon the 20th of November, I again called at her daughter's home. I found Sylvia in her accustomed niche—with her head and face very much swollen and very much muffled with rags and poultices. She had suffered a severe quinsy, and had not yet fully recovered her health. She was feeble and needed supporting treatment. Accordingly, I prescribed for her, and advised her daughter how to manage her poultices, etc., etc. While I was fixing her medicine, Sylvia remarked: "I didn't used to get quinsy, nor any other kind of sore throat, but now I'm old and my teeth are out, and the wind blows right down my throat, and I take cold. Why, sometimes it blows clear down to my stomach, and further, too; why, it blows clear through me. When I had teeth, it didn't used to do so."

Arrangements were made with Sylvia to sit for her photograph as soon as she was well enough to ride to the Artist's Gallery. Upon telling her that a carriage would be ready to take her at any time, she replied:

"I want you to inform me in time for me to fix myself, and get on some decent clothes—them folks at Lambertville are a proud set—and I don't want to go down there looking just anyhow; I want to look pretty sniptious."

I replied: "I see, Sylvia, you are somewhat proud in your old days."

"I always was proud—and liked to appear decent; and I always did appear decent, when I could, but I never dressed beyond my means—I wouldn't do that!"

At ten o'clock, upon the thirtieth of November, Sylvia sat for her photograph. Although well nigh 116 years old, this was her first experience in looking into the artist's camera. But, the frontispiece of this volume gives some idea of the gracefulness of her manner at these advanced years. The picture shows that she was a little tired. This will be expected by everyone when informed that the old lady had rode about nine miles between the time of breakfasting and that of entering into the Artist's Gallery. It is not likely that so old a woman has ever before set for a photograph; and it is not likely that so old a one will ever present her face to the artist's camera.

Immediately after taking the negative for Sylvia's picture, the artist adjusted the camera to the face of Elizabeth, the youngest daughter and constant companion of our heroine. Thus a woman in the 78th year of her age, and her mother in the 116th year of age, were photographed on the same day.

GLEANINGS

About twenty-one years ago, the practice of medicine brought me into acquaintance with many of the most aged people living in the southern part of Hunterdon and Somerset Counties, and the northern part of Mercer. Since that time, it has been my fortune to maintain an acquaintance with nearly all the old folks for many miles around. As I have always had an ear for history, and especially a deep interest in all that relates to the history of my native county, and of the people who dwell here, I have ever listened to, and often made notes of, the stories that the aged have told me. Hence, I have slowly accumulated a store of facts, such as every lover of history cannot well forget—even if he wanted to.

Of these facts, some relate to the fairest phases of life—to heroic patriotism, to high-sold philanthropy, to untiring devotion to the Christian cause, to filial affection and the like; some, to the darkest, dreariest phases of human life—to scenes of revelry, acts of debauchery, to squalid poverty, to abject degeneracy, and to heinous crimes. But facts are facts; and, it has taken each and all of these, and thousands that are yet untold to form the lives of the citizens of our county—the doings of the people among whom we live; and no history of our county can be complete, nor of much value as a record of the lives of a people, that does not chronicle, at the same time, the doings of the great and the small, the rich and the poor, the proud and the humble, the exalted and the abject, the virtuous and the vicious, the frugal and the squalid. Too often, what is called history is but the records of the fairest facts of a single famous individual, or of a favored few, which look well upon paper and are pleasing to the ear, but which only represent the scintillations of society, or of some favored individual, entirely ignoring the doings of the masses, and shunning with disdain the deeds, the patience and the sufferings of the poor. Too often we forget that it takes the peasant as well as the priest and the president to make society, to form the Constituency of the State. Too often we forget that the degenerate, and the abject are indispensable parts of society—that they have rights and privileges—and that they are but the counterparts of the best of the citizens of a commonwealth.

On this occasion, it is my business to record the acts and sayings of one who has not been illustrious for philanthropic deeds. But, a study of this record—of these acts and sayings—is worthy, and will well repay anyone who wishes to know the results of a life of dissoluteness; who wishes to see what unbridled passions lead to; who wishes to know how abject and squalid a person can be, and yet live not far from the fairest phases of civilized life.

That my readers may the better comprehend the life of the heroine of this tale, I will give a brief sketch of an ancient mountain tavern, once famous for ill fame. This house, tradition says, stood upon the north side of the road that extends westward from the Rock Mills, near its intersection with the road that extends from Wertsville to Hopewell. It was the property of a manumitted Negro, and was called Put's Tavern—afterwards, Put's Old Tavern; a property that Sylvia Dubois inherited from her grandfather, Harry Compton.

The founder of this house, and for many years its proprietor, was the character who figures in the colloquy, in this book, as Harry Compton, the fifer, of note in the army of the Revolution. Harry was a slave to General Rufus Putnam, who sold him to Captain Riener States, who sold him to Richard Compton, from whom he bought his time and became free. As General Rufus Putnam was his first master, and more distinguished than either of the other two masters, Harry was often called after his first master, Harry Putnam; indeed, this name he preferred. Accordingly, when he became the proprietor of a hotel, and a man of note as a mountain tavern keeper, for short, they called him Harry Put; and the house that he kept was usually called Put's Tavern.

Harry Putnam's house, although far famed and much frequented, especially by sporting characters, was never licensed. In early times, the selling of whiskey and other intoxicating liquors as a beverage was allowed to almost everyone—unless, by doing so, the vender became very offensive. In the place in which Harry's house was built, even an extravagance in the sale of liquor, in the demonstrations consequent upon the use of it, was less likely to be complained of, than to be encouraged. Consequently, in peace and prosperity, he managed his business, accumulated wealth and became renowned. His house, far removed from the gaze of the cultured, and the pious, became the scene of cockfights, fox-chases, hustling matches, prize-fights, etc, etc. Indeed, Put's Tavern became famous as a place of resort for all such as indulged in such games, or liked to be present where such things transpired. It was the center for the dissolute. From afar, renowned gamesters came— and tradition says, many were the pounds, shillings and pence they carried off with them; and many were the young men and young women ruined in that house.

At Put's House, culture was but little regarded. Blacks and whites, alike, partook in the pastimes, or the business of the occasion. That the blacks were regarded equal with the whites, there may be some doubt; but that the blacks were as good as the whites, there is not question. But be these things as they may, they pretended to associate upon terms of equality—too much so for the well being of their posterity.

Twenty years ago I was physician to several old gamesters, the maladies of whom were incurred by frequenting this celebrated house of ill fame, and the consequent intercourse with such as congregated there. Although the mishaps leading to disease occurred during boyhood, or early manhood, the materes morbi were never eradicated, and these old offenders of Nature's laws, as they grew older, constantly needed the care of a medical advisor.[6] Although they were wont to curse the day they learned to fond, and deplored the shame and misery which their offenses had brought them, yet often, while I was engaged in preparing medicine for them, they used to delight in telling me of the grand old times they used to have in their young days, at Put's old tavern. Not one of these numerous bits of history is fit to be recorded in this narrative; everyone of them was revolting to people of culture; most of them would shock the modesty of a Hottentot, and many of them would blanch the cheek and chill the blood of the most dissolute. They were scenes perpetrated by intellectual but lewd men, of the basest passions, fired by whiskey and hilarity, in an atmosphere entirely free from decency or shame. Thus let loose, in company with their peers, their passions worked out such things as could be done only by the most daring, the most lustful, and the most wanton. To those who know only a fragment of the history of this ancient house, it is not a wonder that there are so many shades of color in the population of the neighborhood of Cedar Summit, nor that in those of lighter shades, there is so much tendency to vice and crime.

Harry Put had an instinctive desire to be free. Being industrious, frugal and honorable, he managed to buy his time of his master, Richard Compton. Charcoal being much in demand in those times, he turned his attention to the burning of coalpits, and at the business, accumulated a little money. With his earnings he purchased a site and erected a house. His social qualities, and the supply of liquor always on hand, made his house a popular place of resort. Soon he found it necessary to enlarge—so rapidly did his patronage increase; and finally, he found it necessary to rebuild.

The new house, tradition says, was somewhat pretentious. It consisted of four large rooms upon the first floor, and a half story, suitably divided into rooms above. Along the entire front was a porch; and the windows and doors were ample. Nearby stood the sheds and other necessary outbuildings; the whole surrounded by a virgin forest that extended for miles in every direction.

It is hardly to be supposed, that Harry Put, a slave, whose high spirit prompted him to make the sacrifices necessary to purchase his freedom, had a vicious tendency. It is easier to believe that he was an industrious, easy-going, flexible, far-seeing Negro, who unschooled in ethics, and freshly liberated from bondage, had not a just appreciation of freedom and morality; and withal, a strong greed for gain, and a desire to be popular. Thus constituted, he became a fit tool for such as desired to frequent a house so far removed from the gaze of the law-abiding and the pious, that while there, their passions could be unbridled, their acts unseen by the virtuous, and their deeds unknown, except to the basest of men.

The guests that visited Put's House were not all from the mountain, nor yet from the adjacent valleys. Far from it—from Trenton they came, and from Princeton, and New Brunswick, and New York, and Philadelphia, and even from cities farther away. The news of a cockfight, and old gamester says, usually spread through a community and reached the ears of gamblers, in olden times, faster than the stink of a skunk traverses the air of a valley. The same old wit used to say, the ear of a gamester is as sharp to hear the report of a cockfight as the nose of a vulture is to scent a dead horse.

So, whenever the air of the mountain became polluted with the concoction of a cockfight, every gamester that sniffed the air for a hundred miles around winded the game, and, with his wench or his drab, set out for the mountain. As a consequence, a speckled host assembled. The Negro of the mountain was there; and there too, was the Negro of the valleys round about. The mountain bandit was there; and there too, were the banditti of the adjacent valleys, and of the nearer cities. And there too, was every gambler who dwelt within a radius of many a mile, who could walk or ride, that could possibly leave home. The Negress in rags, and the drab in brocade and in satin; the Negro with his patch coat; the city bandit in his beaver suit; the farmer gamester in his linsey-woolsey; the mechanic in satinette, drinking and talking, laughing and shouting, intermingled as though every element of distinction had been removed, and the business of life was only hilarity.

I recall a statement made many years ago, by a very worthy patient, respecting a cockfight that he witnessed at this place, that occurred in his boyhood. The story—or that part of it which I venture to tell—runs thus: When about eighteen years old, I was sent by my father to see a certain man respecting a certain business. When I arrived at his house, I was informed that he was not at home—that he had gone to Put's Old Tavern to attend a cockfight. Accordingly I directed my way thitherward; and, when near the house, I saw a great concourse of people—of all colors, of all sizes, and of both sexes. They were in the wood, a little way from the house. Some were well dressed, some were superbly dressed, some were badly dressed, and some were hardly dressed at all. They were intimately mixed—the raged and the dandy. Here a wench with hardly enough patches to keep the flies off stood talking to a man dressed in costly broadcloth; there a thick lipped Negro, ragged and dirty, and drunk, stood talking with women dressed in brocade, and decked with the most gaudy jewels. Here a group boisterous in making bets—there a bunch hilarious with fun and rum; yonder a ring formed around two bullies—one a white man, the other black—fighting for no other reason than to see which could whip. While in this group and in that were white men and Negroes, white women and wenches, with scratched faces and swollen eyes—the results of combats that had grown out of jealousy, whiskey, or the intrigues of shrewd men who liked to see fights.

The wood was vocal with Negro laugh—ya, ya, ya, ya—and wa, wa, wa, wa; and with shouts of mirth and merriment, of indecent songs, and of boisterous profanity. A more appalling and more disgusting scene, I never witnessed. I was upon a horse; I did not dismount. I inquired for, and found, the man I was sent to see, transacted my business, and ran my horse toward the road, and left the wood in utter disgust.

Of all the incidents respecting Put's House, that have come to my ears, the above is the mildest. But the above is only a part of the story; the rest is too dark to be told.

That the house was better kept after it descended into the hands of our heroine; or that the guest that frequented it were of a higher order, is much to be doubted. However, its popularity waned, and its patrons were those of less note. As the demand for timber increased, the wood upon the side and the top of the mountain was cut away; the sun shone in upon places that hitherto were dark, the land in places was tilled, civilization and virtue encroached upon the environs of the scene of the dissolute; Put's Tavern became a thing of opprobrium, and in the year of 1840, it was burned to ashes. Such is the history of the house that was the arena, tradition says, of the vilest deeds that were ever perpetrated in Hunterdon County.

Sylvia much complained of the loss of property incurred by the conflagration. All that she had was in this building; beds, chairs, books, culinary
apparatus, and whatever else is necessary to an outfit to keep a mountain
tavern. The conflagration occurred during her absence. She states that she is
satisfied that the house was plundered before it was fired. In evidence of this,
she states that several articles of furniture and several books—one a Bible
containing the family record—were found scattered over the mountain,
some in one house, some in another. But it seems she was never able to
reclaim one of these things.

In Sylvia's day, Put's Tavern was regarded only as a cake and beer house.
But that other drinks could often be got there, there seems to be an abundance of evidence. Indeed, on one occasion, it is said the house was visited
by an officer of the law, and the proprietor, free of charge, enjoyed a ride to
the county seat.

In her day, Sylvia was somewhat famous as a breeder of hogs. For this
business, the great unfenced mountain forest was very favorable. Her herd
was often very large and her stock very noted. Often, to improve his breed, a
farmer would go a long way to Sylvia's herd, to buy a hog. Nor did he expect
to purchase her stock at a low figure. She well knew the value of hogs, and
always got a fair price.

After the burning of Put's Tavern, I am told that Sylvia erected another
house, and dwelt upon the land that she had inherited. This house, it is said,
was built of cedars. The architecture was primitive. The poles of which it was
made were cut about as long as a rail and arranged somewhat after the pattern followed in building the frame of a wigwam. These poles were covered
with cedar brush, and the like, arranged somewhat after the manner of fixing
straw in thatching a roof.

What the furniture of the house was, I have failed to learn. But that it
was ample, and that the edifice was spacious, and comfortable, there can be
no doubt. Nor can it be doubted that Sylvia was ever selfish, or inhospitable.
Even her sow and pigs, it is said, shared with her the comforts of her mansion. Nor did she compel her chickens to go to an outbuilding, or a tree to
roost; but considerate and conservative, she made each one feel at home
beneath her hospitable roof.

Thus at peace with beast and fowl, Sylvia, for a while, spent her days.
But perpetual and unsullied happiness has not been bequeathed to any

mortal. During her absence, some vile incendiary fired her domicile, and Sylvia again was houseless. Advanced in years, penniless and dismayed, she accepted an invitation to abide with her daughter, and with her daughter she still lives.

OUR LAST VISIT

Excepting the pages written under this head, the matter of this book is now in type, ready for the press, and, but for the printing of the pages that I am now writing, Dec. 21st, 1883, the last form of this book would go to press today. But, certain circumstances seem to warrant a delay until I can pen a few pages, and my printer can put them in type. These circumstances are as follows:

Upon the nineteenth of December, occurred a severe storm, and during it the snow fell to the depth of seven inches. To everyone it seemed that winter had begun with extreme vigor, and the thoughtful began to meditate respecting the preparations they had made for the bleak days and the frigid nights of these trying winter months. Our thoughts were not entirely con- fined to our own condition, nor to the preparations that we had made for ourselves alone. Among the destitute that occurred to our mind was that aged lady, the heroine of this volume, Sylvia Dubois, who dwells with her faithful daughter Lizzie in that Little Old Hut near the top of the mountain. To visit her, to encourage her, and to learn her needs, was quickly deter- mined upon, and the morning of the 20th of December, 1883, was the time appointed to pay our respects to her aged ladyship.

The sleighing was good, the air salubrious, and the scenery inviting. Although the sky was overcast, the day was delightful. It much resembled those quiet cloudy days that I used to see so often follow a heavy snowstorm in northern New York and in Canada.

Not willing to enjoy the sleighing alone, nor the treat of visiting the home of these aged mountaineers, on my way, about 9 in the morning, I called upon two of my patients, Mrs. Rebecca Prall and Miss Eliza Prall, whom I invited to share with me the events of the day. Soon we were ascend- ing the slope of the mountain. The prospect was delightful—a cheerful winter scene. High up the hill, upon a favorable spot, we stopped to view.

The snow-clad plain beneath us stretched away so gently that we could detect neither ridge nor meadow, neither the course of the roads nor the meandering streams. The villages that were but a few miles away could hardly be distinguished, while those which were but little farther off could not be descried—so completely were all things covered with the new-fallen snow. Toward the northeast, the plain seemed interminable—stretched away without hill or vale until the snowy expanse seemed bounded by the eastern sky. But, over against us, fifteen miles away, rose up the graceful form of Long Ridge, which lifts its graceful crests and its bold summits to relieve the view and beautify the landscape.

Soon we reached the crest of Cedar Summit. The scenery here was especially delightful. The cedars covered with snow seemed things of art, while the huge round rocks with snowy backs, looked like the pictures of houses in Arctic scenes. Through the winding way we wended our course, amid a forest mostly of cedar, until at once a mountain vista came to view, and we looked eastward, far out over a delightful plain that stretches away until it is bounded by the sea. But soon the vista was past, and again we wound around huge rocks and through thickets of cedars, until—There! What is that? That squalid hut built of logs and roofed with boards, windowless and chimney-less, and is fast yielding to decay?

That! Why, that's the mansion—the home of Lizzie Dubois. That's the house you've longed to see.

We dismounted from the sleigh; but ere we reached the house, Joe, the faithful dog, gave a few shrill barks, and out came the hostess to see what was disturbing the quiet of their secluded home. She met us with a smile, and bade us go in. We entered, were seated near a very warm stove, found Sylvia in her accustomed place—between the stove and the west wall—began to chat, and the time passed pleasantly. Directly, we inquired after the health of our host and her aged mother, and after their supplies for the winter. We were informed that they were destitute—that they were in want of many things, but especially they were in want of wood. They had employed some hands to cut their winter wood, but so far they had failed to find teams to haul it home. But, while talking, someone drove up with a load of wood, and then there was great rejoicing; the old woman exclaimed, "Thank heaven! I'm so glad—now we will be able to keep warm."

Sylvia had quite regained her health, was very cheerful, and much inclined to talk. She inquired after the health of many of her old acquaintances, and in all respects showed that she was alive to the affairs of the day. She talked of the coming holidays, and told us what good times they used to have during Christmas and New Year, how many parties she used to attend, how they used to dance, etc., etc.

I remarked: "Did I understand you to say that you used to dance on Christmas?"

She replied, "To be sure, we did! Why, the old slaves no more knew the meaning of Christmas than the hogs in the pen! They only knew that it was a holiday, and that they were turned loose for some fun, and of course they had it; to be sure they danced. In those days they could dance, too."

I said: "Then you think they can't dance nowadays?"

She replied: "No, not a bit; they think they can; they stomp and jump and hop and run, and like enough turn heels over head, and they call it dancing; but it isn't dancing; they don't know how to dance; they've got no steps—they don't know any steps."

"What steps did you like best when you used to dance?"

"Well, I liked the eleven times, the twelve times, and the thirteen times: these were the best steps for me; these were the steps my grandfather, Harry Compton, used to like, and all other good dancers."

"Was Harry Compton a good dancer?"

"Well, he was! He was considered the best dancer on the mountain, or that has ever been on this mountain, or anywhere in these parts. I have seen him when he was old, dance at Princeton, and everybody who saw him said he was the best dancer they ever saw."

"Was Harry Compton a large man?"

"No, he was short, but very stout, and very strong; he was considered the strongest man on the mountain, and they used to say he was the strongest Negro that ever lived, and he was very active; he could put any man upon the ground—white or black."

"Sylvia, do you think you could dance yet?"

"Yes, I could dance yet—only had a good fiddle—I like music. A good fiddle always starts the Negro, even if he's old."

"Well! Do you think you'll dance this Christmas?"

"Guess not; guess I'd better think about something else; folks of my age had better think about dying. But I like to see 'em dance—it looks good."

In the course of conversation, Sylvia adverted to the difficulty she had had with certain folks who tried to sell her land from her. Her eyes soon began to sparkle, her voice grew loud, and her words more bulky and a little sulfurous; she soon coined some pretty hard epithets, and used them with no little force.

I asked her: "Is the gentleman who tried to sell your land from you living yet?"

Turning her face toward me, in a very positive manner, she replied: "He's no gentleman—he's a damned rascal!"

I said: "Well, is he living?"

She replied: "I don't know whether the devil has sent for him yet or not; if he hasn't yet, he will some of these days. He pretends he's so damned good, but he'll never get to heaven. When he buried his father, he wanted to show his piety, and he had cut upon the ornament (monument, I suppose) that he placed upon his grave, a hand with one finger pointing towards heaven. That looks pretty well, but he ought to have had a bottle of whisky engraved just above the end of the finger; that would look better, would be more significant—'specially to those of us who knew him."

"Why, was his father a bad man, too?"

"No, his father was not a bad man, but he did like a dram of whisky most desperate well; and he could take such a soaker, too."

"Really, his father was a good man—was very good to the poor—and we all liked him. He was as much to be liked for his goodness, as his son is to be despised for his badness. The trouble is, when the old man died, he took all the goodness of the family with him; what is left behind is nothing but damned trash. His son is worse than the devil himself, and will cheat anybody he can."

While talking, I heard the voices of chickens. They seemed to be directly behind the chair of one of our party. To let my companions see how mountaineers care for their poultry, I said, "Don't I hear some chickens?"

"Yes, I guess you do," replied Lizzie. "We have to fetch our chickens into the house at night, to keep them from thieves. They steal everything up here when they can. So I just put my chickens in this box and bring them in. As it is snowy today, I have not put them out; they are nice ones—you can see 'em." So saying, she raised the lid of a large box, and there stood the birds as sleek as doves and as docile as children.

"Sylvia, do you ever attend church?"

"Yes, sometimes. When I was young, I used to go to church very often; but now I don't go very often. There is no church near us, and I can't walk so far any more. I used to walk a good ways to meeting—to Pennington, to Princeton, to Hopewell, and to Harlingen, and to camp meeting, but I can't walk, so far any more. We used to have meeting near by, and then I always went. But the white trash broke our meeting up, and now I don't hear preaching any more—but I'd like to."

"Did you say you used to go to camp meeting?"

"Yes, I always went to camp meeting—'specially when I was young. That was the best kind of meeting for me—I liked that. I'd walk ten miles to a camp meeting—further, too.

"They used to have great times at camp meetings. They'd turn out from everywhere—both blacks and whites. I've seen two thousand folks at one meeting. There was a camp meeting about seventy-five years ago, about four miles below Trenton, near a place called Crosswicks; and I and some more of our color, went down, we walked down. That was the biggest camp meeting I ever attended, and the nicest one, too. The campground was a mile long—and they had such good order; there was nobody drunk, and there were no fights, and there was no noise of any kind, except what the meeting folks made—and they had a big time—the biggest kind of a time. They hollered and shouted till you'd think the devil was in 'em. I never heard such shouting—you could hear 'em to Trenton. There were four pulpits—a good way apart—and four preachers were preaching all the time. And they hollered, and the folks hollered—good God, how they hollered; I never saw such a time—I guess nobody did. I went to stay all the week, but in about three days I got a bellyful of it, and more too, and then I started home. And when I got home, I guess I was glad—I guess no nigger was ever so glad to get home. I got enough camp meeting in those three days to last a year. But the next year I heard of another camp meeting, and I wanted to go just as bad as ever."

"Did you say the white folks disturbed your meeting?"

"Yes, they broke it up. We used to have a good meeting over here, near the Rock Mills; but this white trash around here couldn't behave; they'd come into the meetinghouse and talk right out in meeting and call each other's names—and do anything to disturb us. And when quarterly meeting came, the white trash from all over came and filled the house and the space around the house, and behaved so badly and made so much noise out of doors, that we couldn't have our meeting any more."

"Well, Sylvia, this is a hard story. It's a disgrace to the more respectable white people of the neighborhood that they have not protected the colored church. Certainly, there is much need of a church just here; indeed, I know of no place where one is more needed. The people of this mountain certainly need preaching to, and if the colored people try to have a church here, there ought to be respectable white people enough to enforce the law and see that their meetings are not disturbed. This matter must be looked after; we'll see if this church can't be reorganized."

When the time arrived for us to draw our visit to a close, we bade Sylvia adieu, and proceeded toward the sleigh. The paths were not shoveled, and in Lizzie's opinion there was some danger that the ladies, in walking to the sleigh, would get their shoes snowy, and as a consequence, before they arrived home, would suffer cold feet. To obviate this difficulty, the kind woman took a board from the side of the house, extended it from the door-sill to the sleigh, and thus secured us against the effects of the snow.

NOTES

This text is essentially a translation into standard English spelling of Larison's pho-netically spelled original narrative. In addition to translating the text, the editors have inserted quotation marks to indicate Dubois's and Larison's voices.

1. According to the *Oxford English Dictionary* "mania a potu" is "a mental disor-der attributed to alcoholic consumption, usually thought to be characterized by extreme excitement and violent behaviour, but sometimes identified with delirium tremens." See http://dictionary.oed.com/cgi/entry/00333369?single=1&query_type =word&queryword=mania+a+potu&first=1&max_to_show=10. Here Sylvia Dubois uses the local colloquial form of the term.

2. As an adult, Paul Tulane moved to New Orleans where he opened a general merchandise store. With the fortune from the store and investments, Tulane became a philanthropist and donated $363,000, the seed money to found Tulane University

of Louisiana to educate "white young persons." Tulane's segregationist beliefs were well known, particularly in Louisiana.

3. The tripe is the lining of the stomach, the term is usually used in reference to bovines.

4. A canticoy was a social gathering with dancing. The term originates from Native American cultures.

5. Samp porridge is a dish unique to the New York-New Jersey area. Made from ground Indian corn, a meal is pounded in "samp mortars." The corn thus pounded is called 'samp'—they put the corn the night before in a weak ley of wood ashes, to take off the husk of the grain. This preparation they use in making their celebrated 'samp porridge'" (Moore 226). For more one samp porridge see Frank Moore, ed. *Antiquities of Long Island by Gabriel Furman, to Which is Added a Bibliography by Henry Onderdonk, Jr.* New York: John W. Bouton, 1874. 226–28.

6. Materes morbid is Latin for a medical term referring to a germ or a microbe; something that could cause disease.

SILVIA DUBOIS,

BORN MARCH 5th, 1768.

PREFAC.

As mŭch ĭntĕrĕst ạlwas ătăchĕs tọ wŭn whŏ lĭvs tọ à vĕrȳ grat aġ, ănd ạs à negrĕs so old ạs Sĭlvĭà Dụbois ĭs sĕldŭm non, I hăv thŏt thăt ăn outlin biŏgrafȳ ŏv hĕr mit be desird bȳ the redĭng pŭblĭc. The mor so, becạs whil gĕtĭng the biŏgrafȳ ŏv the heroin, à vàst àmount ŏv the cŭstŭms ănd mănĕrs ŏv the pepl wĭth hwọm she lĭvd ĭs ạlso ăequird, ănd ä knŏlĕdg ŏv the was ŏv folks ŏv à hŭndrĕd yers àgo gand.

In ritĭng thĭs, skĕtch, I hăv bĭn ạs bref ạs çĭreŭmstánçĕs wŭd álou. As mŭch ŏv the mbăttĕr ĕntĕrĭng ĭntọ thĕ cŏmposĭshŭn ŏv thĭs bọk was gŏtĕn frŏm hĕr, ĭn à cŏloquĭàl mănnĕr, ănd ạs thĭs was put ŭpŏn papĕr, ĭn short-hănd, jŭst ạs she spok ĭt, ănd ạs by gĭvĭng hĕr on wŭrds ĭn the ordĕr ănd styl ĭn whĭch she spok thĕm, portras mor ŏv the cărăctĕr, ĭntĕllĭġĕnç, ănd forç ŏv the heroin thăn căn pŏsibly be gĭven ĭn anȳ ŭthĕr wa, I hăv rĭtĕn the

most ĕsĕnshȧl pärts ŏv ĭt, ĕxăctlȳ ăṣ she re-
latĕd the făets tọ me.

The năratĭv ȧbounḏṣ ĭn profănĭtȳ, ăn ĕlemĕnt
thăt ĭṣ fŏrĕn tọ me, ănd wŭn thăt I most eor-
dyălȳ despiṣ, ănd sĭnçerlȳ dĕprecat. Bŭt,
Sĭlvĭȧ ĭṣ ȧ profan negrĕs; hĕr lăngwaġ ạlwaṣ
ȧbounḏṣ ĭn profănĭtȳ; ănd, tĕrs ănd forçibl ăṣ
ĭt ĭṣ, căstigat ĭt ŏv ĭts profan wŭrḏṣ, ănd ĭt ĭṣ
flăt ănd menĭngĕs, ănd ŭtĕrlȳ fȧls tọ conva the
ideȧ ĭntĕnĕd, or tọ revel hĕr căractĕr. In the
năratĭv, mȳ am ĭṣ mor tọ sho the căractĕr, forç
ănd spĭrĭt ŏv ĭndepĕndĕnç ŏv the heroin, thăn
tọ mak out ȧ lŏng lin ŏv yerṣ; or tọ tĕl wĭth
họm she dwĕlt. Tọ ăeŏmplĭsh thĭs, I mŭst
uṣ thos wŭrḏṣ ănd fraṣĕṣ peculĭȧr tọ hĕrsĕlf,
hwĭeh ȧlon är ădequat tọ the tȧsk befor me.
Thĭs thĕn ĭṣ mȳ ăpŏloġȳ for the profănĭtȳ thăt
so ạbŭndȧntlȳ ĕxĭst ĭn thĭs storȳ.

In the orthŏgrafȳ ŏv thĭs bọk, I hăv, ĭn the
man, amd tọ fŏlo the ruḷṣ ŏv the Spĕlĭng Reform. Thăt ĭn sŭm ĭnstȧnçĕṣ I hav fȧld, thĕr
ĭṣ no doubt. Bŭt, ĭn mĕnȳ ĭnstȧnçĕṣ ĭn hwĭeh
I hav nŏt fŏlod the ădvis ŏv the Fĭlolŏġĭc
Soçietȳ, I hăv dŭn so becạs I thŏt the ădvis ŏv
thăt bŏdȳ, respĕetĭng thes pärtĭculȧr ĭnstȧnçĕṣ
nŏt wĕl foundĕd (ăṣ ĭn usĭng ŏ for o ĭn the

würd or), or ĕls nŏt prăctĭc ăt thĕ prĕsĕnt
tim. In the futur, pĕrhăps, sŭm ŏf thĕ
changĕs to hwĭeh I alu̯d wĭl be prătic. And
hwĕn the redĭng pepl är prepard for thĕm,
nŭn wĭl be mor rĕdy̆ to̯ ȧdŏpt thĕm thăn I.
Indĕd, I lŏng to̯ se thĕ tim hwĕn wŭn cărăctĕr
wĭl rĕprezĕnt bŭt wŭn fon; ănd wŭn fon ĭs
rĕpresĕntĕd by̆ wŭn cărăctĕr.

Bŭt, hwil I ăm nŏt wĭlĭng to̯ ȧdŏpt, ĭn ĕvĕry̆
ĭnstȧnç, jŭst nou, ĕvĕry̆ masu̯r rĕcŏmĕndĕd by
the Cŏmĭte ŏn thĕ Reform ŏv Ęnglĭsh Spĕlĭng, thĕr är mĕny̆ masu̯rs, nŏt rĕcŏmĕndĕd by
the cŏmĭte, thăt a̯r mŭch nedĕd, ănd thăt I
shăl ăt wŭnç ȧdŏpt.

To̯ fŏlo thĕ spĕlĭng nou ĭn vog, ĭs ŭtĕrly̆
ăbsŭrd. Sŭeh à menĭnglĕs, jŭmblĭng ŏv cărăctĕrs ăs ŏcŭr ĭn the prĭntĭng or ritĭng ŏv
würds ăs found ĭn most bo̯ks ănd neuspapĕrs
ĭs ŭnpȧrdŭnȧbl, ănd ĭnsŭltĭng to̯ the tast ănd
jŭdġmĕnt ŏv a̯ll redĕrs ŏv eŭltur. A feu yers
à go, ritĕrs cu̯d nŏt safly̆ do̯ ŭthĕrwis thăn to̯
fŏlo thĭs çĕnsurȧbl spĕlĭng; bŭt, sĭnç thĭs
wid-sprĕd cŏnçĕrted ăcshŭn ŏv the Spĕlĭng
Reformĕrs—mĕn ŏf thĕ hiĕst ănd bra̯dĕst eŭltur, ănd so famu̯sly̆ non ăs crĭtĭcs ănd teehĕrs
ĭn our Colĕġĕs ănd Unĭvĕrsĭtĭs, thĕr ĭs, ăt thĕ

bĕst, bŭt po̦r ĕxcus for cŏntĭnuĭng to̦ spĕl wŭrds wĭth áfonĭc cărăctĕrs.

As ĭt ma hăpĕn thăt sŭm ho̦ är nŏt ăcqwantĕd wĭth thĕ Reformd spĕlĭng ŏv the Englĭsh lăngwaġ ma red thĭs bo̦k, to̦ hĕlp thĕm to̦ lĕrn thĕ neu orthŏgrafy̆, ănd to̦ façĭlitat thar prŏgrĕs ĭn redĭng thes paġĕs, I her ĭntrŏduç the ru̦ls su̦bmĭtĕd ĭn the "Report ŏv the Amĕricán Cŏmĭte ŏn thĕ Reform ŏv Englĭsh Spĕlĭng." In statĭng thes ru̦ls, so fär ăs ĭt suts mȳ pŭrpŭs, I us thĕ lăngwaġ ŏv Dr. F. A. March, ạthŭr ŏv thĕ rĕpŏrt çitĕd.

RULS OV THE COMITE ON THE REFORM OF ENGLISH SPELING.

1. e.—Drŏp silĕnt e hwĕn fŏnĕtĭcály̆ uslĕs, ăs ĭn live, lĭv; vineyard, vĭnyȧrd; believe, belev; bronze, brŏnz; single, sĭngl; engine, ĕnġĭn; granite, grănĭt; eaten, etn; rained, rand, etc.

2. ea.—Drŏp a frŏm ea hăvĭng thĕ sound ŏv ĕ, ăs ĭn feather, fĕthĕr; leather, lĕthĕr; jealous, jĕlŭs, etc.

3. eau.—For beauty, us thĕ old beuty̆,—buty.

4. eo.—Drŏp o frŏm eo hăvĭng thĕ sound ŏv ĕ, ăs ĭn jeopardy, jĕpȧrdy̆; leopard, lĕpȧrd. For yeoman, rit yomȧn.

5. i.—Drŏp i ŏv parliament, pärlȧmĕnt.

6. o.—Fŏr o hăvĭng the sound ŏv ŭ ĭn bŭt, rit ŭ, ăṣ ĭn above, ȧbŭv; dozen, dŭzn; some, sŭm; tongue, tŭng, etc. For women, restor wĭmĕn.

7. ou.—Drŏp o frŏm ou hăvĭng thĕ sound ŏv ŭ, ăṣ ĭn journal, jŭrnȧl; nourish, nŭrĭsh; trouble, trŭbl; rough, rŭf; tough, tŭf, etc.

8. u.—Drŏp silĕnt u ȧftĕr g befor ă, ănd ĭn nătĭv Englĭsh wŭrds, ăṣ ĭn guarantee, gărȧnte; guard, gärd; guess, gĕs; guild, gĭld; guilt, gĭlt.

9. ue.—Drŏp ue ĭn apologue, ăpolŏg; catalogue, cătȧlŏg; demagogue, dĕmȧgŏg, etc.

10. y.—Spĕl rhyme, rime,—rim.

11. Dŭbl cŏnsonȧnts ma be sĭmplĭfid: Fĭnȧl b, d, g, n, r, t, f, l, x, ăṣ ĭn ebb, ĕb; add, ăd; egg, ĕg; inn, ĭn; purr, pŭr; butt, bŭt; bailiff, balĭf; dull, dŭl; buzz, bŭz; (not all). Medial befor ănŭthĕr cŏnsonȧnt, ăṣ ĭn battle, bătl; ripple, rĭpl; written, rĭtn. Inĭshȧl ŭnăccĕntĕd prefĭxĕṣ, ănd ŭthĕr ŭnăccĕntĕd sўlȧblṣ, ăṣ ĭn abbreviate, ȧbrevĭat; accuse, ȧcŭṣ; affair, ȧfar; traveller, trăvĕlĕr.

12. b.—Drŏp ȧfonĭc b ĭn bomb, bŏm; crumb, crŭm; debt, dĕt; doubt, dout; dumb, dŭm;

lamb, lam ; limb, lĭm ; numb, nŭm ; plumb, plŭm ; subtle, sŭtl ; succumb, sŭcŭm ; thumb, thŭm.

13. c.—Chang̣ c băk tọ s ĭn cinder, sĭndĕr ; expence, ĕxpĕns ; fierce, fers ; hence, hĕns ; once, wŭns ; pence, pĕns ; scarce, scars ; since, sĭns ; source, sors ; thence, thĕns ; tierce, ters ; whence, hwĕns.

14. ch.—Drŏp thĕ h ŏv ch ĭn chamomile, cămomil ; cholera, cŏlerà ; choler, cŏlĕr ; melancholy, mĕlàncŏlў ; school, scọl ; stomach, stŭmâc.

15. d.—Chang̣ d ănd ed finàl tọ t hwĕn sọ pronounçt, ăṣ ĭn crossed, crŏst ; looked, lọkt, etc.

16. g.—Drŏp g ĭn feign, fan ; foreign, fŏrĕn ; sovereign, sŏvĕrĕn.

17. gh.—Drŏp h ĭn aghast, àgăst : burgh, bŭrg : ghost, gost.

Drŏp gh ĭn haughty, hạtў : though, tho : through, thrụ.

Chang̣ gh ĭntọ f hwar ĭt hăṣ thăt sound, ăṣ ĭn cough, cŏf : enough, enŭf : laughter, lạftĕr : tough, tŭf.

18. l.—Drŏp l ĭn could, cụd.

19. p.—Drŏp p ĭn receipt, recet.

20. s.—Drŏp s ĭn aisle, il : demesne, demen : island, ilánd.

Chang̣ s intọ z in dĭstĭnctĭv wŭrdṣ, ăṣ ĭn abuse, ábuz (verb) : house, hoᴜz (verb): rise, riz (verb): etc.

21. sc.—Drŏp c ĭn scent, sĕnt : scythe, sȳth.

22. tch.—Drŏp t ăṣ ĭn catch, căch; pitch, pĭch; witch, wĭch, etc.

23. w.—Drŏp w ĭn whole, hol.

24. ph.—Rit f for ph, ăṣ in philosophy, fĭl-ŏsofȳ; sphere, sfer, etc.

Thĕ ábŭv rᴜḷṣ gratlȳ ăd ŭs ĭn ĭmprọvĭng English spĕlĭng; yĕt thĕr är mĕnȳ dĭficŭltĭs thăt tha dọ nŏt hĕlp ŭs sŏlv. Tọ sŭrmount theṣ, Ī ăd à feu thăt sem tọ me quit ăṣ nĕçĕs-arȳ ăṣ thoṣ mad by thĕ ábŭv namd filŏloġĭsts :

1. Silĕnt vouĕls.—Drŏp ạll silĕnt or áfonĭc vouĕlṣ, ăṣ ĭn goose, goṣ; loose, lọṣ; food, fọd; book, bọk; great, grat; gain, gan.

2. i.—Rit ĭ for e or ee hwĕn so soundĕd, ăṣ ĭn been, bĭn.

3. a.—Rit ĕ for a hwĕn a hăs the sound ŏv ĕ ăṣ in any, ĕnȳ; many, mĕnȳ.

4. e.—Rit a for e whĕn e hăṣ thĕ sound ŏv a, ăṣ ĭn eight, at; they, tha.

5. w.—U<u>s</u> w onl<u>ў</u> ăs á cŏnsonánt. Rit u̥ for w ĭn dĭf<s>thŏngs</s> ĭn hwi<s>ch</s> w hă<u>s</u> <s>thĕ</s> souud ŏv u̥, ăs in new, neu̥; stew, steu̥.

6. o.—U<u>s</u> o ă<u>s</u> á vou̯ĕl onl<u>ў</u>. Hwĕn o hă<u>s</u> <s>thĕ</s> sound ŏv w, rit w, ă<u>s</u> ĭn one, wŭn; once, wŭn<u>s</u>.

7. u.—Hwĕn u ĭ<u>s</u> eqi̯ĭválĕnt to̥ w, rit w, ă<u>s</u> ĭn language, lă<u>n</u>gwa<u>ġ</u>; lĭngŭal, lĭ<u>n</u>gwál.

8. i.—Rit y for i hwĕn i hă<u>s</u> <s>thĕ</s> sound ŏv y, ă<u>s</u> ĭn pinion, pĭnyŭn; minion, mĭnyŭn.

9. c, t, s.—Rit <s>sh</s> for c, t, and s, hwĕn c, t and s hă<u>s</u> <s>thĕ</s> sound ŏv sh, ă<u>s</u> ĭn ocean, oshŭn; social, soshál; nation, nashŭn; notion, noshŭn; mission, mĭshŭn; pa<u>ss</u>io<u>n</u>, păshŭn.

10. f.—Rit v for f hwĕ<u>n</u> f hă<u>s</u> <s>thĕ</s> sound ŏv v, ă<u>s</u> ĭn of, ŏv.

The ábŭv ru̥l<u>s</u>, go̥d ă<u>s</u> <s>tha</s> är, ĭf u<u>s</u>d, wĭl mak ăn Englĭ<s>sh</s> orthŏgraf<u>ў</u> vĕr<u>ў</u> lĭtl bĕtĕr <s>than</s> <s>thĕ</s> wŭn hĭthĕrto̥ ĭn us. Inded, to̥ do̥ <s>much</s>, ĭn <s>thĕ</s> ĭmpro̥vmĕnt ŏv Englĭ<s>sh</s> orthŏgraf<u>ў</u>, we mŭst hăv á bĕtĕr ălfabĕt. Thĕ wŭn ĭn ġĕnĕrál us ĭ<u>s</u> nŏt sŭfĭshĕnt. In our ălfabĕt <s>thĕr</s> shu̥d be ăt lest wŭn cărăctĕr for ĕvĕr<u>ў</u> <s>zi</s>mpl fon; ănd e<s>ch</s> cărăctĕr shu̥d ḁlwa<u>s</u> be cḁld <s>by</s> the sound, or fon, ĭt ĭ<u>s</u> ĭntĕndĕd to rĕpre<u>s</u>ent. Bŭt, ĭn our lă<u>n</u>gwa<u>ġ</u> thĕr är thĭrt<u>ў</u>-sĕvĕn

wĕl defind fons; hwil ĭn our ălfabĕt thĕr är
onlỹ twĕntỹ six cărăctĕrs. And, whạt maks
thĕ mătĕr wŭrs, for ŏv thes cărăctĕrs, a, i, u and x,
rĕpresĕnts cŏmpound fons---a begĭnĭng with
á sound hĕrd onlỹ ĭn thĕ ĭnĭshál ănd ĕsĕnshál
ŏv a, ănd thĕn ĕndĭng ĭn á sound hĕrd ĭn the
ĕsĕnshál ănd vănĭsh ŏv e. i ĭs equál to äe;
u ĭs equál to yu, x is equal to ks or gs. Hĕnç,
ĭn reălitỹ, we hăv twĕntỹ-tu cărrăctĕrs tọ rĕpresĕnt thĭrtỹ-thre sĭmpl fons, ănd for cărăctĕrs
thăt rĕpresĕnt cŏmpound fons.

Tọ ĭmprọv thĕ ălfàbĕt, thĕn we mŭst ĕnlärġ
ĭt. Thĭs we dọ by usĭng eeh ŏv thĕ vouĕl
cărăctĕrs ĭn thĕ old ălfàbĕt, without diácrĭtĭç
märks tọ rĕpresĕnt thĕ souund, or fon, hĕrd
ĭn ŭttĕrĭng ĭt; thăt ĭs, we use ĭts nam sound.
Hĕnç whĕn ĕnỹ vouĕl hăs no diácrĭtĭc märk, ĭt
hăs ĭts nam sound, ăs a ĭn ape,—ap; e ĭn eve,—
ev; u ĭn tune,—tun; o ĭn old, i ĭn unite,—unit;
Bŭt, tọ rĕpresĕnt ŭthĕr vouĕl fons, thes vouĕl
cărăctĕrs mŏdifid by diácrĭtĭc märks är usd.
Thŭs, á rĕpresĕnts thĕ vouĕl fon ĭn thĕ wŭrd
àsk, ạ ĭn ạll, ạ ĭn whạt, ă ĭn ăt; ĕ ĭn mĕt; ĭ ĭn
ĭt; ŏ ĭn nŏt, ọ ĭn boọt,—boṭ; ọ ĭn boọk,—boḳ;
ŭ ĭn bŭt, ụ ĭn rụde,—rụd; ụ ĭn fụll,—fụl; ỹ ĭn
çỹst; ȳ ĭn mȳ.

Sŭm ŏv the cŏnsonȧnt cărăctĕrṣ rĕpreṣĕnt mor thăn wŭn fon. Sŭeh är c, g, n, s, th, x, z; ăṣ for ĭnstȧnç, c ĭn corn and c ĭn ced; g ĭn gun,—gŭn, and g ĭn gem=ġĕm; n ĭn no, ănd n ĭn link,—lĭnk, or sing; s ĭn sin,—sĭn, ănd s ĭn his,—hĭṣ; th ĭn them,—thĕm ănd th ĭn thing—, thĭng; x ĭn fix,—fĭx, ănd x ĭn exist,—exĭst; z ĭn zone,—zon, ănd z ĭn azure,—ăzhur.

The fĭrṣt sound ȧbŭv ĭnstȧnçt ĭs thĕ wŭn hwĭeh ĭs thĕ mor frequĕntlȳ hĕrd. Hĕnç, we ma çȧl ĭt thĕ fĭrst sound. Tọ rĕpreṣĕnt thĭs (the fĭrst sound) we wĭl uṣ the sĕvĕrȧl cŏnsonȧnt cărăctĕrṣ, her çĭtĕd wĭthout diȧcrĭtĭc märks; ănd tọ ĭndicat the sĕcŏnd sound ŏv eeh ŏv the sam cărăctĕrṣ, we wĭl uṣ çĕrtĭn märks. Thŭs, tọ rĕpreṣĕnt the sĕcŏnd sound ŏv c, we wĭl uṣ c märdt thŭs ç; ănd tọ rĕpreṣĕnt the sĕcŭnd sound ŏf g, we wĭl uṣ g märkt thŭs ġ; the secŭnd sound ŏv n we wĭl ĭndicat thŭs n; ănd ŏv th thus th, (the fĭrst sound being rĕpreṣĕntĕd by th); ănd ov x thŭs x; ănd ov z thŭs zh. Hĕnç, our ălfabĕt wĭl ăper ăṣ the ărangmĕnt ŏv căracterṣ belo.

13

ALFABET USD IN THE ORTHOGRAFY OV
THIS BOK.

VOUEL CARACTERS.

---

a	ale, fate,=al, fat.
ă	ădd, făt,=ăd, făt.
ä	ärm, fäthĕr.
à	àsk, glàss.
a̤	a̤ll, ta̤lk.
a̢	wha̢t, wa̢nder.
e	eve, mete=ev, met.
ĕ	ĕnd, mĕt.
i	içe, fine=iç, fin.
ĭ	ĭn, fĭn.
o	old, note=not.
ŏ=a̢	ŏdd=ŏd, nŏt, wha̢t.
o̤	pro̤ve=pro̤v, do̤, to̤.
o̢	wo̢lf, wo̢l, bo̢ok=bo̢k.
u	uşe, tube=uş, tub.
ŭ	ŭs, tŭb.
ṳ=o̤	rṳde=rṳd, do̤.
u̢=o̢	bu̢ll=bu̢l, pu̢t, wo̢lf.
ȳ=i	flȳ, içe=iç.
y̆=ĭ	cy̆st, pĭn.

14

CONSONANT' CARACTERS, AND THE SOUNDS
OR FONS THA REPRESENT.

------

b	bärn, rob.
c	call, colt.
ç	çede, traçe.
ch	child, much.
d	dale, săd.
f	fame, leaf.
g	go, găg.
ġ	ġĕm, ġĭn.
h	hall, hăt.
j=ġ	jär, joke, ġĕm.
k=c	keep, kĭng, call.
l	lĕft, bĕll.
m	make, aġe.
n	nĕt, tĕn.
n̤	lĭnk, ŭncle, same
p	pay, ape.
qu	queen, cŏnquĕst.
r	rĭp, fär.
s	same, yĕs, çede.
s̤	hăs̤, ámus̤e,
sh	shĕlf, flĕsh.
t	tone, nŏt.
th	thĭng, brĕath.
th	thine, wĭth.
v	vane, wave.
w	wĕt, was̤.

hw	hweat, hweel.
x	expĕct, fŏx=fŏks.
x̲	exĭst= ĕgs̲ĭst.
y	yạwn, yĕt.
z	zone, maze.
z-h	azure= azhure.

In prĭntĭng the bọk, I hăv us̲d the diàcrĭtĭc tȳp prepard tọ prĭnt mȳ bọk ĕntitld Elements ŏv Orthoepy. Thĭs maks the spĕlĭng ŏv the wŭrds̲—ăs the spĕlĭng ŏv ĕvĕrȳ wŭrd shụd be —fonĭc. (For à discŭshŭn ŏv fonĭcs ănd fonĭc spĕlĭng, se mȳ "Elements ŏv Orthoepy," or mȳ Fonĭc Spĕlĕr and Sȳlàbatĕr.)

Bȳ us̲ĭng the diàcrĭtĭc tȳp ănd fŏloĭng the fonĭc orthŏgràfȳ, the nŭmbĕr ŏv pàgĕs̲, ĭn the bọk ĭs̲ àbout wŭn fĭfth lĕs thăn wụd be, hăd I fŏlod the àfonĭc spĕlĭng. By us̲ĭng the diàcrĭtĭc tȳp, no doubt ĭs̲ lĕft respĕctĭng the pronŭnçĭashŭn ov ĕnȳ wŭrd; by thĭs mĕthŏd, eeh fon ĭn à wŭrd ĭs rĕpres̲ĕntĕd bȳ à sutàbl càràctĕr; ănd wĭth feu ĕxçĕpshŭns̲ thĕr ĭs̲ no càràctĕr ĭn à wŭrd thăt dŭs nŏt rĕpres̲ĕnt à fon.

C. W. LARISON.

Academy ov Sienc and Art,

Ringos, N. J., Agust 1st, 1883.

THE BIOGRAFY

OF

SILVIA DUBOIS.

The twĕntў sĕvĕnth ŏv Jănuarў 1883 dạnd frŏstў ănd drerў. The mĕrcŭrў pointĕd tọ 20° ȧbŭv zero. The skȳ waṣ ovĕrcăst ănd sọn the wĕthĕr ăperd thrĕtĕnĭng. Hĭlṣ ănd dalṣ, mountĭnṣ ănd vălўṣ, ŭplȧndṣ ănd lĕs, wĕr cŭvĕrd wĭth sno; ănd, sav the numĕrŭṣ bold arĕȧs ŏv wọdṣ ănd the sprĕdĭng boṇs ŏv leflĕs orchȧrdṣ, the prŏspĕct wȧṣ quit ȧrctĭc.

The chĭllў ar cạṣd the cătl tọ reman ĭn thar stalṣ, or tọ snŭgl tọgĕthĕr ŭpŏn the le-sid ŏv bĭldĭngṣ. The poltrў refuṣd to deçĕnd frŏm thar rọst. The spȧro hŭvĕrĭng ĭts lĭtl frŏst-bĭtĕn fet, ŭtĕrd ĭts shȧrp chĭrp ĭn ȧ plantĭv wa. Whil the sno bĭrd, ĭn quĕst ŏv wed-sed, bĭsilў hŏpt ovĕr the frozĕn crŭst, or dĭligĕntlў flĭtĕd ȧmŭṇg the dĕd brănchĕs ŏv ămbrosĭå, scarçlў takĭng the tim to ŭtĕr hĭs shrĭl nots---ehe-de-de-de---so egĕr waş he to find fod for hĭs mornĭng mel, ănd thĕn to hastĕn to hĭs shĕltĕrd hant.

Bŭt, thĕ slaĭng waş god ănd the carş ŏv bĭsў lif forçt mĕnў å cŏtĕr frŏm hĭs hom to brav the frĭgĭd ar ŏv the ehĭlў mornĭng. Horsĕş stĕpt quĭk, lit ănd fre, ănd the jĭngl ŏv sla bĕlş ĕcod frŏm the for cŏmĕrş ŏv the horizŭn. Bŭt, the fŭrў mŭfs cŭvĕrĭng the hĕds ănd façĕş ŏv the wĕl robd păsĕngĕrş told wĕl thăt no wŭn lĕft hĭs hom thăt mornĭng to sla-rid for plaşur.

It waş Sătŭrda; ănd, ăş the dutĭş ŏv the scol-rom dĭd nŏt demănd our labor for the da, we tŭrnd our ătĕnshŭn to the ăbjĕct, ănd the agĕd. Acordĭnglў, åbout 7 o'clŏk A. M., we ădjŭstĕd our răpĭngş, mountĕd the sla ănd dĭrĕctĕd our wa to Cedár Sŭmmĭt, the most ĕlevatĕd, porshŭn ŏv the Sourlánd.Mountĭn. Răpĭdlў we spĕd ålŏng. And, ăş we reeht the brou ŏv the mountĭn, for å momĕnt we paşd to sŭrva the lăndscap. Toward the wĕst, north ănd est, the viu waş ŭnŏbstrŭetĕd, ănd the prŏspĕet wàş grănd.

Ĕlĕvatĕd 400 fĕt åbŭv thĕ Rĕdshal Văllў, wĕ

scānnd thĕ basĭn ŏv the Răritàn frŏm the sorç
ŏv the strem tọ ĭts ĕxĭt ĭnto the se. The bold
mountĭns thăt skĭrt ĭt ŏn the north, roṣ ġĕntlў
ŭp ănd semd tọ slop so ġrăduàlў towàrd the
north thăt tha semd nols ănd hĭllṣ. The
plan, tho rolĭ̲ng ănd rĭġd, ṣemd ĕntirlў lĕvĕl.
Evĕrўhwăr wạṣ sno. Inded, the drerў samnĕs
ŏv the snoў fleç wạṣ onlў relevd by spärç areàṣ
ŏv wọd làndṣ, ănd the lŏ̲ng line ŏv perĭ̲ng
fĕnçĕṣ. Evĕn the dĭstànt vĭlaġĕṣ cụd härdlў
be descrid, so cŏmpletlў wĕr tha ĕnvĕlopt ĭn
the fleç ŏv sno. Bŭt, nerĕr by, frŏm the chĭmnў ŏv mĕnў à färm-hous ăsçĕndĕd the ṣọtў
smok, ĭn cŭrlĭ̲ng fĕstọnṣ.

Onwàrd we hăstĕnd, over à rod thăt meăn-
dĕrd nou àmĭd ăn ŭmbraġŭs fŏrĕst, nou
àmĭd rŏkў areàṣ over-gron wĭth çedàrṣ, nou
àmĭd the smạl rŏkў fĕldṣ ŏv the mountĭn
färmĕr. Evĕrўhwĕr the fĕthĕrў bouṣ ŏv the
çedàrṣ thăt skĭrtĕd thĕ wa wĕr pĕndànt wĭth
sno---à bĕutĭfụl spĕctàcl. The brånchĕṣ ŏv
the grat oks mantand thar lit sŏmbr gra,
ădĭ̲ng drerĭnĕs tọ the wĭntĕr sĕn. The ovàl
băks ŏv the huġ rŏks lĭftĕd à mound ŏv sno,
lik the houṣĕṣ ŏv the Esquĭmos. The mountĭnĕrṣ hŭts, fär remọvd frŏm the rod, àwa băk

ner sŭm sprĭng, or ŭpŏn the brĭnk ŏv sŭm
plăshĭng rĭl, ĕxhĭbĭtĕd no sins ŏv lif, sav the
sŏtẙ cŏlŭm ŏv cŭrlĭng smok thăt lazilẙ ăscĕnd-
ĕd àmĭd the fŏrĕst boᵤs.

Frŏm the man rod tọ eeh mountĭnĕrs hŭt,
or tọ spärç grọps ŏv squălĭd sĕttlmĕnts, fọt-
páths, or năro bẙ-was, ĕxtĕnd băk, sŭmtims,
for mils, meăndĕrĭng àmĭd huġ rŏks, thĭkĕts
ŏv çedárs, ŭmbraġŭs fŏrĕsts, thrᵤ märshĕs ănd
swạmps, ănd, ovĕr strems thăt är nŏt ĕvĕrẙ-
hwĕr fordĕd. Thĕs by-was är bĕst non tọ
thĕ mountĭnĕrs. Thar stŏk ŏy ġeogrăfĭc nŏl-
ĕdġ cŏnsĭsts manlẙ ĭn ăn ăcquantànç ŏv thes
windĭng was. And, whil eeh mountĭnĕr, ĭn
the därkĕst nit fŏlos eeh, ănd ĕnẙ wŭn ŏv thes
bẙ-was, wĭth ăs mŭeh çĕrtĭntẙ ănd ăs mŭeh
dĕxtĕrĭtẙ ăs à căt trăvĕrsĕs à bem ĭn the nit,
or hĕr meăndĕrĭng páth thrᵤ à glọmẙ ha-mou,
à pĕrsŭn nŏt skĭld ĭn the was ŏv the mountĭnĕrs, wụd, ăt mĭd-da, be nŏt mor sŭcçĕsful
ĭn hĭs jŭrnẙĭng her thăn ĭn the lăbẙrĭnth ŏv
Eġẙpt, or ŏv Cŏrĭnth. Acordĭnglẙ, hwĕn wẹ
hăd ărivd ăt the eornĕr ăt hwĭeh the rod ĕxtĕnds est-wàrd tọ Rŏk Mĭls, tọ led our wa tọ
thĕ hŭt ŏf Sẙlvĭà Dᵤbois, we ĕmployd wŭn

ho profèst to be ăcquantĕd wĭth thes meăndĕrĭng päths.

To me, the sit ăt whĭch we lĕft the man
rod to go ĭn to Sȳlvĭă's mănshŭn lòkt no mor
lik à rod thăn dĭd ĕnȳ ŭthĕr hàlf rŏd ŏv ground
ŭpŏn the sam sid ŏv the rod, for the làst hàlf
mil. But, fath ĭn our gid, ĭnduct ŭs to fŏlo
hĭm ĭmplĭcĭtlȳ whĕrĕvĕr hĕ lĕd. The wa was
vĕrȳ crokĕd. Pĕrhăps, nŏt à sĭngl rŏd ŏv the
pàth ĕxtĕndĕd ĭn the same dĭrĕcshŭn. Nor,
cud we se fär àhĕd ŏv ŭs, sŭmtims nŏt ä rŏd.
Bŭt, ŏn we movd, ăround hug rŏks, betwen
lärġ tres, over lärġ stons, thru năro ănd dănġĕrŭs pàs was, nou àmĭd à thĭkĕt ŏv cedárs,
or à groth ŏv brămbls, or à cŏps ŏv bushĕs, or
à spàrs fŏrĕst ŏv ŭmbraġŭs oks ănd hĭkorĭs.
Sŭmtims the rod was rŭtȳ, sŭmtims sidlĭng,
sŭmtĭms ŭp à shärp nol, sŭmtims doun à step
bănk; nĕvĕr lĕvĕl; sŭmtĭms stonȳ, ănd alwas dănġĕrŭs. Bŭt, by ănd by à vĭstà ăp-
perd. We wĕr ŏn à slit ĕmĭnĕnc. Opĕnĭng
ŭp befor ŭs wàs ăn areà ŏv lănd clerd ŏv tres,
bushĕs ănd brămbls, fĕnct ănd färmd. It ĭs
thĕ prŏpĕrtȳ ŏv Elĭzábĕth, the yŭnġĕst dater
ŏv Sȳlvĭà Dubois. Upŏn ĭt, hĕr mŏdĕst mănshŭn risĕs, à hŭt tĕn fet squar, bĭlt ŏv lŏgs,

rǫft wĭth bordṣ, ŭnȧdornd wĭth poreh, pĭȧzȧ, cŏlonad or vĕrȧndȧ. Prĭmȧtĭv sĭmplĭ̢çĭtў ĕn- tĕrṣ ĭntǫ ĕvĕrў faṣ ŏv ĭts ȧrcitĕtcur. It cŏn- tans nŏt ȧn ĕlemĕnt thȧt ĭṣ nŏt ȧbsolutlў nĕdĕd. Ner ᴐў stȧndṣ the scrȧglĭng branehĕṣ ŏv ȧ dĕd ȧpl tre, ȧnd beneth ĭt ĭṣ the shĕltĕr for the fathfǫl dŏg. Around the areȧ ĭṣ ȧ fĕnç bĭlt ĭn thĕ most econŏmĭc wa ;—ĭn sŭm plaçĕṣ ĭt ĭṣ mad ŏv crŭtehĕṣ wĭth wŭn pol, ĭn sŭm placᵔṣ wĭth crŭtehĕṣ ȧnd tǫ polṣ, ĭn sŭm plaçĕṣ thĕr ȧr tǫ staks ȧnd ȧ ridĕr, ĭn ŭthĕr plaçĕṣ ĭt ĭṣ mad ŏv ralṣ so ȧranġd thȧt wŭn ĕnd rĕsts ŭpŏn thĕ ground whil the ŭthĕr ĭṣ ĕlevatĕd bў menṣ ŏv stȧks fĭxt ȧcrŏs ȧnŭthĕr inclinĭng ral.

Perĭng ȧbŭv the sno, her ȧnd thar, wĕr stȧks ŏv maz, cȧbag, ben-vinṣ, pe-brŭsh ȧnd ŭthĕr ĕvidĕnçĕṣ thȧt the ĕncloṣd areȧ, durĭng the sprĭng sŭmĕr ȧnd ȧtŭmnȧl mŭnths, hȧd bĭn tĭld, ȧnd hȧd yeldĕd ȧ spȧrç sŭplў tǫ the tĕnȧnts ŏv the soil.

Wĕn frŏm the ĕminĕnç we hȧd sŭrvad the hŭt ȧnd ĭts ĕnvironṣ, we deçĕndĕd tǫ the fĕnç thȧt ĕncloṣd the lŏt, fȧstĕnd, ȧnd blankĕtd our horsĕṣ ȧnd ȧdvȧnçt towȧrd the hȧbĭtashŭn.

Thĕ dōr ĭs dŭbl——cŏnsĭstĭng ŏv ȧn ŭpĕr ȧnd

á nĕthĕr pärt. The ŭpĕr pärt stǫd ájär, ănd
ĭn the çĕntĕr ŏv the opĕnĭng ăpĕrd the fǫl,
round faç ŏv à lärġ, bŭxŭm negrĕs,—the onĕr
ănd proprietor ŏv thĕ mănshŭn whĭeh we vĭsĭtĕd,
ănd the yŭngĕst dǫghtĕr ŏv Sĭlvĭá Dǫbois, the
ladỹ ŏv hǫm we hăd hĕrd so mŭeh tǫlk. Our
vĭsĭt wạs à sŭrprṣ. Yĕt, wĭth märkt eŏmpla-
sánç ănd that hŏspĭtălĭtỹ that cặráctĕrizeṣ the
ferlĕs mountĭner, we wĕr ĭnvĭtĕd ĭn, ănd băd
tǫ be setĕd bỹ the stov.

The rǫm wạs nŏt wĕl litĕd. And ăṣ I wạs
sĭtĭng down, I notĭçt, sĭtĭng ŭpŏn à ehar, à
dŭskỹ form closlỹ snŭgld ŭp ĭn the năro
spaç, betwĕn the stov ănd the wạl. Aṣ mỹ yṣ
(eyes) becam ăeŏmodatĕd tǫ the degre ŏv
litnĕs ŏv the rǫm, I sạ that thĭs dŭskỹ form
wạs the ĕldĕrlỹ ladỹ that we deṣird tǫ se,--that
she hăd fĭxt hĕrsĕlf her ĭn the wạrmĕst pärt ŏv
the rǫm, ănd that she wạs áslep.

I scănd hĕr closlỹ. Tho sĭtĭng, her slep wặṣ
ăṣ trănquĭl ăṣ that ŏv à bab. Hĕr hĕd, tid ŭp
wĭth à hăndkĕrehĭf, áftĕr the uṣuál mănĕr ŏv
cŭlŭrd ladĭṣ, wạs boud forwàrd, so that the
ehĭn rĕstĕd ŭpŏn hĕr flĕshỹ ehĕst. Hĕr hănds̱
wĕr foldĕd ŭpŏn hĕr lăp. Hĕr fĕt wĕr ĕxtĕndĕd

beneth the stov. Hĕr countenànç wąs sever, bŭt seren.

Hĕr ăpărĕl wąs nŏt Parĭşĭàn: yĕt, ĭt wàs rĕşŭnàblў hol, ănd nŏt dĭrtў. Thĕr semd tǫ be enŭf ŏv ĭt, ănd ădjŭstĕd ĕntirlў ĭn ăcordànç wĭth the genyŭs ŏv the Afrĭeàn raç. Indĕd, the spĕctàcl wàs sŭeh thăt ĭt elĭçĭtĕd the ĕxprĕshŭn (thŏt, nŏt mad): " Wĕl! yu är ăt hom ĭn the ĕnjoymĕnt ŏv lif, jŭst ăş yu wǫd hăv ĭt."

Cąshŭslў, bŭt crĭtĭcàlў, I sŭrvad the rǫm ănd the fŭrnitur. The lŏgṣ cŏmposĭng the wąl wĕr nŏt ĕntirlў strat, ănd the ĭntĕrspaçĕṣ betwen thĕm, ĭn sŭm plaçĕṣ, wĕr larġ. At wŭn tim, thĕṣ ĭntĕrspaçĕṣ hăd bĭn fĭld wĭth mŭd,— ănd thĕn, no doubt, the hous wąs cŏmpăratĭvlў wąrm. Bŭt, nou, ĭn mĕnў plaçĕṣ, bȳ frŏst ănd ran, ănd bȳ bŭg ănd mouç, the mŭd hăṣ crŭmbld ănd fąlĕn out; ănd, the opĕnĭngṣ ădmĭt àlik the lit ănd the wĭnd. Wĭthĭn reeh ŏv mȳ ehar, I cŭd pàs mȳ hănd betwen the lŏgṣ, ŭntĭl ĭt wąṣ ĕntirlў out ŏv dorṣ; ănd, ĭn sŭm plaçĕṣ, I cǫd se lit thru à crĕvĭç tǫ fet lŏng; ĭn ŭthĕrṣ, I cǫd pàs mȳ fĭngĕrṣ àlŏng ăn opĕn spaç betwen the lŏgṣ frŏm tĕn tǫ fĭften ĭnehĕṣ. Thru thĕṣ opĕn spaçĕṣ, the wĭnd wąṣ pàsĭng ăt à răpĭd rat.

The ĭnĕr sŭrfȧç ŏv the wạl wạs nŏt evĕn. Eeh lŏg shod ĭts bärkў cŏntųr, and eeh ĭntĕr-spaç ĭts claў lĕdġ, or ĭts opĕn spaç. Călçimĭn ănd whit-wạsh dĭd nŏt ăper; ănd wạl-papĕr wĭth gĭldĕd bordĕr wạs wạntĭng. The çelĭng ĭs wạntĭng. In ĭts stĕd ĭs the bar rọf, or the splĭntĕrў sŭrfȧç ŏv sŭm ralṣ thăt ĕxtĕnd frŏm wạl tọ wạl, for the sŭpport ŏv sŭeh thĭngṣ ăṣ är ĭn the wa, ĭf lўĭng ŭpŏn the flor.

In erĕctĭng the ĕdifĭc, the lŏgṣ ĭn the sŭth-ĕrn fȧçad hăd bĕn lad ŭp tọ the hit ŏv 4½ fet, wĭth ăn opĕn spaç ner the çenter, tọ sĕrv ăṣ ȧ dor. The nĕxt laĕr ŏv lŏgṣ ĕxtĕnd ĕntirlў ăround, formĭng the plats for the rọf ănd the lĭn-tĕl ŏv the dor. Frŏm theṣ lŏg-plats ăsçĕnd, ăt ȧ shărp ĭnçlinashŭn, tọ the rĭdġ-pol, the râftĕrṣ, hwĭeh ĭn sŭm plaçeṣ är cŭvĕrd wĭth shĭnglṣ; ĭn ŭthĕrṣ, wĭth bordṣ or bärk.

Upŏn ethĕr sid ŏv the dor, frŏm the lŏg-plat thăt căps the frŏnt wạl, tọ ĭts countĕrpárt ŭpŏn the băk wạl, ĕxtĕnd ok ralṣ, wĭth the flăt splĭntĕrў sid downwȧrdṣ. Thĭs formṣ, ŭpŏn ethĕr sid ŏv the dor, a smạl lŏft, ŭpŏn hwĭeh är pild bŭndlṣ ŏv clothṣ, bĕd-clothṣ ănd bĕdĭng, ănd I no nŏt hwạt ĕls. Tọ gĕt ŭpŏn theṣ lŏfts, thĕr är nethĕr stĕps nor ladĕr; ănd yet tha är hăndў. Stăndǐng ŭpŏn the flŏr, á tạl pĕrsŭn căn reeh ạlmost tọ ĕnў pärt ŏv thĕm, ănd take doun, or pụt áwa, ĕnўthǐng dĕṣird. I notǐct thăt the ehars thăt wĕr nŏt ǐn us hăd bǐn plaçt ŭpŏn wŭn ŏv theṣ lŏfts, out ŏv the wa.

So lo ǐṣ the lǐntĕl, thăt ǐn the ăct ŏv ĕntĕrǐng the dor, á pĕrsŭn ǐṣ obliġd tọ stọp; ănd, hwĕn riṣǐng ŭp, áftĕr ĕntĕrǐng, wĕr he nŏt carfụl tọ be ǐn the opĕn spaç betwen the lŏfts, he wụd băng hǐṣ hĕd áganst the ral flor. Altho thǐs waṣ mў fǐrst vǐsǐt, I waṣ fortunat enŭf, ŭpŏn ĕntĕrǐng, tọ be ǐn the rit poṣǐshŭn. Bŭt, I wás nŏt á lǐtl sŭrpriṣd ăṣ I lọkt ábout ănd found thăt hwil mў fĕt ănd lĕgṣ, ănd the loĕr pärt ŏv mў bŏdў wĕr doun starṣ, mў sholdĕrṣ, ärmṣ ănd hĕd wĕr ŭp stars. Houĕvĕr, thĕ sŭrpriṣ dǐd nŏt ŭnfǐt me for sŭrvaǐng the lŏfts, thar ărangmĕnts ănd thar cŏntĕnts. Pĕrhăps, I wụd hăy sŭrvad theṣ ápärtmĕnts ănd thar cŏntĕnts lŏngĕr, ănd mor crǐtǐcálў; bŭt, whĕn wĕl ĕngaġd ǐn veuǐng theṣ thǐngṣ, the thŏt ŏeŭrd: Whăt ma tha be dọǐng belo; ma mў nĕthĕr pärts nŏt be ǐn sŭm dangĕr; or ăt the lest, ma tha nŏt demănd mў ătĕnshŭn. Acŏrdǐnglў I stọpt doun, ăçĕptĕd á prŏfĕrd ehar, ănd setĕd mўsĕlf ǐn á spaç thăt semd tǫ be the most out ŏv the wa, ănd begăn, ăṣ ăforsĕd, á crĭtĭcál sŭrva ŏv the ĕnvirŭns ŏv mȳ poṣĭshŭn.

The flor semd tǫ be mad ŏy bordṣ ănd splĭt wǫd, lad ŭpŏn the ground, ănd pĕrhăps poundĕd ŭpŏn, ŭntĭl nerlȳ lĕvĕl. I sǎ no pŭdlṣ ŏv stăndĭng wǎtĕr, ănd yĕt thĕ flor wǎṣ nŏt ĕntirlȳ drȳ. The ĭntĕrspaçĕṣ betwen the flor-bords wǫd ĕsilȳ hăv áloud me tǫ ăsçĕrtan the quǎlĭtȳ ŏv the soil ŭpŏn whĭeh thĕ hous ĭṣ bĭlt. Altho theṣ ĭntĕrspaçĕṣ wĕr tŏlĕráblȳ wĕl fĭld wĭth cla, yĕt the flor sŭmhwǎt remindĕd me ŏv the ăperánç ŏv á cordǫroy rod.

The lŏgṣ out ŏv hwĭeh thĭs hous ĭṣ bĭlt, sĕrvd á tĕrm ŏv yers ĭn the wǎl ŏv ăn ŏldĕr houṣ. The prĭmatĭv hous hwĭeh wǎṣ ăn ĕrlĭĕr mănshŭn ŏn thĭs lŏt, wǎṣ bĭlt á lŏng hwil ágo. In the cors ŏv tim the ĕndṣ ŏv the lŏgṣ ŏv thǎt hous rŏtĕd ŏf, ănd the ĕdifĭç beeam ŭnsaf. therŭpŏn, wŭn áftĕrnǫn about 18 yers ágo, Elĭzábĕth cŏnvokt hĕr nabŭrṣ, ĭn the capăeĭtȳ ŏv á frŏlĭc, ăṣ sŭeh găthĕrĭugṣ är her cǎld, tǫ recŏnstrŭct hĕr mănshŭn. Acordĭng tǫ hĕr plăn, tha tǫk doun the old bĭldĭng, nŏteht the lŏgṣ băk á sutábl dĭstánç frŏm the ĕnd, ănd pild thĕm ŭp ĭn sŭeh á wa thăt, out ŏv the uṣábl matĕrĭál

ŏv the old hous tha cŏnstrŭctĕd the prĕsĕnt
ĕdifĭc. We är told thăt the old hous wăs sŭmhwạt lärgĕr ŏn the ground, sŭmhwạt hiĕr, ănd
in ĕvĕrÿ wa mor stÿlĭsh thăn the prĕsĕnt man-
shŭn.

The houshold fŭrnitur—so fär ăs I cụld se—
cŏnsĭstĕd ŏv ăn old-tim cọk stov, a dĭnĕr pŏt,
a wạtĕr pal, sĭx chars, a smal cŭbärd ănd sŭm
bĕd-cloths thăt ăperd tọ hăv ʋĭn lŏng ĭn us, ănd
nŏt wĕl protĕctĕd frŏm dĭrt.

The cọk stov ĭs wŭn ŏv thăt pătĕrn hwĭch
wăs ĭn us frŏm 30 tọ 40 yers ago. It wạs
mad for bŭrnĭng wọd. It ĭs nou mŭch the
wŭrs for war. Thĕr ĭs yĕt remänĭng ŏv hwạt
it wŭns wạs, a pärt ŏv ceh fir-dŏr, ănd a cŏn-
sĭdĕrábl ŏv the top plats. Bŭt, the fir ĭs wĕl
ard; ĭt hăs ăn ábŭndánç ŏv dräft frŏm ĕvĕrÿ sid
It stănds clos ŭp ĭn the southwest cornĕr, ĭn a
diăgonàl mănĕr, ĭn sŭch a wa thăt the pip-ĕnd
ĭs toärd the cornĕr, ănd the fir-ĕnd toärd the
çĕntĕr ŏv the hous. The smok finds exĭt thrụ
tụ joints ŏv pip, thăt ĕxtĕnd frŏm the stov ạlmost tọ the rọf. Frŏm the rọf ŭpwàrd ĕxtĕnds
a kĭnd ŏv chĭmnÿ, mad ŏv a peç ŏv shet-irŏn,
bĕnt ạlmost ĭntọ a çÿlĭndĕr, wĭth făntăstĭc
scŏlŏps áround the tŏp—wĕthĕr the wŭrk ŏv

ăn ärtiṣan, or the rĕsŭlt ŏv the dĭsĭntĕgratĭng ĭnflṵĕnç ŏv rŭst, I dọ nŏt no. Altho the spac betwen the pip ănd the chĭmnў ĭṣ lärġ, sŭmhow the spärks ănd the smok—thăt ĭṣ sŭm ŏv thĕm—folo thĭs ĭntĕrŭptĕd flu ŭp ănd out ŏv the hous.

Altho I sạ, out ŏv dorṣ, no pil ŏv wod frŏm hwĭch tha cụd drạ—ănd I thĭnk I sạ nŏt à sĭṇgl stĭck, the stov wạṣ wĕl fĕd, the spärks rŭshĭng ŭp the ĭntĕrŭptĕd smok-wa furĭuslў. And, altho mў băk wạṣ à lĭtl cŏld, mў shĭnṣ ănd neṣ wĕr about ăṣ hŏt ăṣ I hăv ĕvĕr hăd thĕm, ănd mў ўs (eyes) wĕr ăṣ wĕl fĭld wĭth smọk ăṣ tha hăv ĕvĕr bĭn, nŏt ĕxçĕptĭṇg the tims durĭṇg hwĭch I hăv bĭn ătĕndĭṇg à fir ĭn à smok-hous.

The dĭner-pŏt wạṣ ămpl, ănd ăpĕrd tọ hăv sen sĕrvĭç. Of cours, ĭt wạṣ ŭpŏn the stov—the wạtĕr ĭn ĭt, boilĭṇg furĭuslў; bŭt frŏm ĭt, I fald tọ detĕct ĕnў odŭr ŏv sething pŏtag—bef or mŭtŭn, pork or chĭkĕn.

The chars wĕr bŏtŭmd wĭth rŭsh, ănd tha wĕr ĭn gọd repar.

Alŏṇg thĕ wạl, ŭpŏn the wĕst sid ŏv the rọm, stọd à bŏx or cŭbärd, about 3 fet lŏṇg, 18 ĭnches wid ănd 2½ fet hi, pantĕd ănd ärmd wĭth

dors. Upŏn ĭt wặs á tĭn kĕrosen lămp thăt
bŭrnd wĭthout á ehĭmnỹ ; ănd, jŭdġĭng frŏm
the crŭst ŏv sọt ănd lămp-blăk ŭpŏn the ral-
çelĭng dirĕctlỹ ábŏv the plaç ĭt ŏcupyd, ĭt
smokt wĕl—ĕvĕn ĭf ĭt fald tọ lĭt the rọm.

Thes wĕr the onlỹ ärtĭcls ŏv fŭrnitur thăt I
sạ. Thăt thĕr wĕr ŭthĕrs, ĕxçĕptĭng sŭeh ăs
ma hăv bĭn ĭn the cŭbärd, ĭs härdlỹ pŏsibl.

Durĭng the tim I wăs mäkĭng the sŭrva,
thĕr wặs nŏt sĭlenç. All the hwĭl we cŏnvĕrst.
Our tạlk rán sŏsháblỹ, ănd our host wặs ăs
cŏmpláçĕnt ăs á Frĕneh bĕl.

At lĕngth, we ănounçt thăt we hăd cŭm
tọ ĭntĕrvew thĕ aġĕd ladỹ, Mrs. Sĭlvĭá Dụbois.
Herŭpŏn, hĕr dạtĕr ároụsd hĕr mŭthĕr, told hĕr
thăt pärtĭs hăd eạld tọ se hĕr, ănd ĭntrodŭçt ŭs
tọ our heroin. Our gretĭngs wĕr nŏt vĕrỹ formál,
nor mŭeh prolŏngd. Bŭt hwĭl ĕxehàngĭng sá-
luts, our hŏst, for á mŏmĕnt, frcd frŏm ĕntĕrtan-
ĭng ŭs, adjŭstĕd thĭngs ábout the rọm, mad ĭn-
ĕfàbl ăpŏlogĭs respĕctĭng the ăperánç ŏv the
ápärtmĕnt, ănd ĕxtĕndĕd tọ ŭs sŭeh politnĕs
ănd sŭeh ătĕnshŭn, ăs mad ŭs fel thăt we wĕr
wĕlcŭm gĕsts.

I hăd sen Sĭlvĭá ŏn á formĕr ocàshŭn, ănd

neu sŭmthĭng ŏv hĕr ĭdĭosy̆ncrasĕs. Indĕd, I
hăd, durĭng à former ĭntĕrvu, hĕrd hĕr relat
măny̆ ŏv the most ĭmportȧnt ĭnstȧnçĕs ŏv hĕr
lif. So, hwạt fŏloṣ, ĭn thĭs cŏloquy̆, tụ sŭm
ĕxtĕnt, I hăd hĕrd hĕr relat befor, ănd wạṣ, ȧt
thĭs tim, drạn out, bȳ à serĭṣ ŏv prepȧrd qwĕs-
yŭns, ĭn the ordĕr ĭn hwĭeh ĭt ĭṣ her statĕd, so
thăt tọ the redĕr ĭt wụd be sŭmhwạt coherĕnt.

Sĭlvĭá ĭṣ lärġ ŏv statur. In hĕr pämy̆ daṣ,
she hăṣ bĕn nŏt lĕs thăn 5 fet 10 ĭnehĕs hi. She
ĭnformṣ me thăt she usuȧly̆ wad mor thăn 200
lbs. She ĭs wĕl proporshŭnd, ŏv à nĕrvo-ly̆m-
fătĭc tĕmpĕrȧmĕnt, ănd ĭṣ stĭl capabl ŏv grat
ĕndurȧnç. Yers ȧgo, she wạṣ non tọ be the
strŏngĕst pĕrsŭn ĭn the sĕtlmĕnt, ănd the wŭn
họ hăd the gratĕst ĕndurȧnç. She wạṣ ĭndŭstrĭŭs, ănd wạṣ usuȧly̆ ĭn grat reqwĕst durĭng
the hous-clenĭng ănd sop makĭng seṣŭn ŏv the
yer. Evĕry̆ bŏdy̆ wäntĕd Sĭlvĭá tọ hĕlp clen
hous, ănd tọ hĕlp mak sop. She wạṣ so strŏng
she cụd lĭft ĕny̆thĭng thăt nedĕd tọ be mọvd,
ănd cụd căry̆ ĕny̆thĭng thăt hăd tọ be totĕd;
ănd she wạṣ so wĭlĭng tọ ŭṣ hĕr strĕngth thăt
hĕr pŏpulărĭty̆ wạṣ ĭnĕfȧbl. So Sĭlvĭá wĕnt
ĕvĕry̆hwĕr, ănd ĕvĕry̆ bŏdy̆ neu hĕr—ĕspĕshȧly̆

the childrěn, ho, ăs a rul, wěr wŭnděrfulў afrad ŏv hěr.

Acording to hěr on ăcount, to childrěn she was nŏt věrў woing. On the cŏntrarў, she usd to tak delit ĭn tělĭng thěm gŏblĭn storĭs, ănd ĭn makĭng thěm afrad ŏv hěr. She usd to těl thěm thăt she wŭd kidnăp thěm, ănd thăt she wŭd swalo thěm aliv; ănd, ĭt ĭs sěd, to childrěn, she lŏkt ăs ĭf she mit do sŭch thĭngs.

Usualў, childrěn kěpt out ŏv hěr wa. Usualў, hwěn tha sa hěr cŭmĭng, tha sat rěfug ĭn the cŭmpánў ŏv olděr folks,—ĭn sŭm secludŭd plaç,— or ĭn à fot-raç. As a jok, she těls a storў respěctĭng ăn ŏcŭrěnç ĭn the boy-hod ŏv a çěrtĭn ĭndivĭduál nou wěl ădvánçt ĭn yers. He, a lĭtl mor bold thăn the ăvěrag boy ŏv 10 yers, ŏn wŭn ŏcashŭn, věnturd to be à lĭtl sasў to hěr, ănd for the tim, kěpt out ŏv hěr wa. Bŭt a fěw das áftěr, hwil he was bĭsў plaĭng ĭn a gärděn, ăround hwĭch wás a hi pĭckět fenç, Silvĭá ěntěrd the gat ábout the tim the lăd sa hěr. To trў hĭs mětál, she ěxclamd: Nou I'll hăv yu, sĭr! Up he bounçt! Evěrў lĭmb wás ĭn moshŭn! The hi pal-fěnç was a triflĭng barĭěr—wŭn áful yěl he găv, ănd thěn thru the răsběrў brĭěrs ănd ověr the fěnç he wĕnt lik á cát; ănd, houlĭng lŭstilȳ ăş he răn, dĭsăpĕrd from veu, bȳ crepĭng ŭndĕr ăn old bărak.

Hĕr lŭv ŏv fredŭm ĭş boundlĕs. Tọ be fre ĭş the ạl-ĭmportánt thĭng wĭth Sĭlvĭá. Bŏndaġ, or evĕn restrant, ĭş tọ ner ákĭn tọ dĕth for Sĭlvĭá. Fredŭm ĭş the gol; fredŭm ŏv speeh, fredŭm ŏv labŭr, fredŭm ŏv thĕ păshŭnş, fredŭm ŏv the ăpetit—ŭnrestrand ĭn ạl thĭngş. Tọ ĕnjoy thĭs, she wụd go tọ ĕnȳ ĕxtremş— evĕn tọ the ĕxtremş ŏv lĭvĭng ŭpŏn the ehărĭtȳ ŏv hĕr aqwantánçĕş, ĭn the hŭt ĭn hwĭeh we found hĕr,—áwa frŏm çĭvĭlizashŭn ănd cŭltur, wĭth bŭt lĭtl tọ et, wĭth lĕs tọ war, ănd the porĕst kind ŏv shĕltĕr. Thŭs she ganş the ŏbjĕct ŏv hĕr desĭr. And, she ĭş ĭnded fre—ĕvĕrȳ păshŭn ĭş fre, ĕvĕrȳ desĭr ĭş grătifĭd. Lĕs restránt I nĕvĕr sạ ĭn ĕnȳ pĕrsŭn—nor ĭnded cụd thĕr be.

The old ladȳ dĭd nŏt áwak frŏm hĕr slŭmbĕr qwĭklȳ. Nor dĭd she qwĭklȳ cŏmprehĕnd thăt she hăd vĭsĭtorş. Bŭt, ăş aġĕd foks uşuálȳ dọ, she áwok slolȳ,—á pärt ŏv hĕr ăt á tim, ăş ĭt wĕr. At fĭrst, she mọvd hĕr hăndş ănd ärmş; thĕn hĕr fet ănd lĕgş; thĕn rŭbd hĕr faç; thĕn she mọvd hĕr bŏdȳ ŭpŏn the ehar; ănd ĭn the cors ŏv sŭm mĭnĭts, she begăn tọ reàliz thăt she hăd gĕsts, ănd thăt she mŭst ĕntĕrtan thĕm. Tharŭpŏn, àdjŭstĭng hĕr cloths, ănd qwĭklў tŭrnĭng hĕr hĕd toàrd me, she ejăculatĕd: "Họ är thes?" Tọ thĭs ĭntĕrogashŭn hĕr dạtĕr replid: "Hwy, mŏmў! Dr. Lärison, hĭs dạtĕr, ănd Mĭs Pral. Tha wạnt tọ se yu —tha wạnt tọ tạk wĭth yu."

Qwĭklў ănd stĕrnlў shĕ replid: "Wạnt tọ se me! I don't no hwȳ tha shụd wạnt tọ se me; sŭch ăn old thĭng ạs I ăm,—prĕtў ner dĕd nou, ănd Gŏd nos I ạt tọ hăv bĭn dĕd lŏng àgo."

Herŭpŏn, I begàn tọ ĭnqwir àbout hĕr hĕlth. She ĭnformd me thăt she wạs wĕl—ănd thăt she wạs ạlwas wĕl; ĕxçĕpt sŭmtims she sŭfĕrd "colds." She sĕd thăt she hăd nĕvĕr hăd à spĕl ŏv sever sĭknĕs, ănd dĭd nŏt ĭntĕnd tọ hăv; thăt "tant no ụs tọ be sĭk; foks don't fel wĕl wĕn tham sĭk; tha fel bĕst wĕn tham wĕl."

"Jŭst so, Sĭlvĭà," I replid; "bŭt, ĭt sems thăt foks căn't ạlwas be wĕl—sĭknĕs wĭl cŭm sŭmtims."

Tọ thĭs cŏmmĕnt the old ladў hastĭlў replid: Thă wŭdĕnt be sĭk hàf so mŭch ĭf tha'd behav 'ĕm sĕlvs, ănd sta ăt hom, ănd et plan vĭtàls. Tha wạnt tọ rŭn ạll ovĕr, ănd be ĭntọ ạll kind

ŏv nĭgàr shins, ănd stŭf 'ĕmsĕlvs wĭth all kinds
ŏv thĭngs ; ănd thar gŭts wont stănd ĭt. Thĕn
tha gĕt sĭk ; ănd lik enŭf sĕnd for à dŏctŏr—
ănd whĕn he cŭms, ĭf thar nŏt prĕtў carfụl,
tha'l hăv à hĕl ŏv à tim ; for he's shur tọ
go rit for the guts, fŭst păs ; nĕvĕr neu wŭn ŏv
'ĕm tọ mĭs. A bĭg dos ŏv calomĕl ănd jäläp
tọ begĭn bĭsinĕs, ănd thĕn thĕ war ĭs begŭn.
Thĕs dọctŏrs, tha'v gŏt no mĕrcў ŏn yu, 'spĕsh-
âlў ĭf yur blăk. Ah ! I'v sen 'ĕm, mĕnў à tim,
bŭt, thay nĕvĕr cŭm áftĕr me, I nĕvĕr gav 'ĕm
à chănc,—nŏt the fŭst tim.

When I hăd gron qwiĕt frŏm à fĭt ŏv láftĕr,
provokt bӯ the old wọmàn's stӯl, ăs mŭch ăs
frŏm the mătĕr spokĕn, I told hĕr thăt I hăd
cŭm tọ tak wĭth hĕr,—tọ lĕrn hwat I cŭd respĕctĭng hĕr grat aġ, hĕr cors ŏv lif, the hĭstorў
ŏv hĕr fămilў, the cŭstŭms ŏv the pepl họ
lĭvd à cĕnturў or mor ágo, hĕr prĕsĕnt wĕlfar
ănd hĕr futur prŏspĕcts.

Wĭth thĭs statmĕnt Sĭlvĭà semd plesd, ănd
ănounct thăt she was rĕdў ănd wĭlĭng tọ ĭn-
form me respĕctĭng mătĕrs ăs fär ăs she was
abl. At wŭns, she ăsumd ăn ătitud, ănd ăn ar
thăt shod she was " all ătĕnshŭn " ănd rĕdў tọ
tak. I hăd provĭdĕd mӯsĕlf wĭth papĕr ănd

pĕnçil tọ tak doun ĭn short-hănd, hĕr lăṇgwaġ
ăṣ ĭt fĕl frŏm hĕr mouth. Respĕctĭṇg thĭs, I
ĭnformd hĕr, ănd reqwĕstĕd the prĭvĭlĕġ thăt I
might prĭnt ănd pŭblĭsh ănÿthĭṇg thăt she told
me. Tọ thĭs reqwĕst she replid: "Most ŏv
foks thĭnk thăt nĭgĕrs hăn't no ăcount; bŭt,
ĭf yu thĭnk hwạt I tĕl yu ĭṣ wŭrth pŭblĭshĭṇg,
I wĭl be glăd ĭf yu dọ ĭt. T'wont dọ me no
gọd; bŭt ma be 'twĭl sŭmbŏdÿ ĕls. I'v lĭvd
à gọd hwil, ănd hăv sen à gọd del, ănd ĭf I
shụd tĕl yu ạl I'v sen, ĭt wụd mak the har
stănd ŭp ạl ovĕr yur hĕd."

Bȳ thĭs tim, ĭt hăd fụlÿ ăperd thăt Sĭlvĭà,
ĭn hĕr on wa, wạṣ nŏt à lĭtl relĭġŭs, ănd wạṣ
wĕl uṣd tọ spekĭṇg the nam ŏv the Suprem
Beĭṇg; ănd hwạt ĭṣ mor remärkàbl ĭn à wọmăn,
she semd tọ be so famĭlyàr wĭth ạll thoṣ wŭrdṣ
ĕxprĕsĭv ŏv the ătrĭbuts ŏv Gŏd. Inded, I hăv
sĕldŭmlÿ non à clĕrġÿmàn, ĕvĕn hwĕn ăn ĕxçĕlĕnt Hebrụ ănd Grek scŏlàr, tọ be mor famĭlyàr wĭth theṣ tĕrmṣ thăn Sĭlvĭà, nor mor ĭn the
hăbĭt ŏv uṣĭṇg thĕm. And yĕt, betwen Sĭlvĭà
ănd à clĕrġÿmàn, thĕr semd tọ be à märkt dĭfĕrĕnç ĭn the wa ĭn hwĭch ech uṣd thĕm. For,
hwil the clĕrġÿmàn uṣĕṣ theṣ tĕrmṣ manlÿ ĭn
spekĭṇg ŏv the gọdnĕs ănd ŏmnĭpotĕnç ŏv Gŏd,

ănd ĭn ĭnvokĭng Hĭs blĕsĭng, Sĭlvĭà semd tọ
uş thĕm ĭn ăn ĭntĕrjĕcshŭnál, ŏr ăn ădjĕctĭvàl
wa tọ ĕmbĕlĭsh hĕr lăngwaġ, ănd tọ gĭv forç tọ
hĕr ĕxprĕshŭns.   And, ŏv ạl thăt I hăv ĕvĕr
lĭsĕnd tọ, I hăv nŏt hĕrd ĕnў wŭn hăndl theş
tĕrmş mor retŏrĭcálў, or yĕt mor ĭn ăcordánç
wĭth the prĭnçĭpls ŏv ĕlocushŭn. And, ăş ĭt wĭl
detrăct vĕrў gratlў frŏm the mĕrĭts ŏv hĕr dĭs-
cors, ĭn cas I omĭt thĭs pärt ŏv hĕr lăngwàg, I
bĕg mў redĕrş the prĭvĭlĕġ ŏv levĭng the wŭrdş
ĭn hĕr frázĕş, jŭst ăş she ŭtĕrd thĕm, ăş mŭeh
ăş ĭş baràbl.

Hwil Sĭlvĭà'ş famĭlĭărĭtў wĭth the titls wĭth
hwĭeh Jehová ĭş wŭnt tọ be ădrĕst, ĭş ĕxçed-
ĭnglў grat, hĕr nolĕdġ ŏv thăt ŭthĕr beĭng cạld
the Dĕvĭl, ĭş, bў no menş lĭmĭtĕd.   If hĭş
cărăctĕr hăş ĕvĕr bĭn bĕtĕr portrad bў ĕnў
ŭthĕr pĕrsŭn, or ĭf he hăş ĕver bĭn ădrĕst bў,
or non bў, ĕnў ŭthĕr tĕrmş thăn thoş she uşd,
ĭt hăş nŏt cŭm tọ mў nolĕdġ. Inded, ĭt semd
thăt ĕvĕrў tĭtl, ăpĕlashŭn, ănd ĕpithĕt, thăt
hăd ĕvĕr bĭn uşd ĭn rĕfĕrĕnç tọ hĭş Satănĭc
Măjĕstў, she hăndld wĭth peculĭàr fredŭm ănd
eş. Inded, the prolĭfĭcnĕs ŏv hĕr mind, ĭn thĭs
dĭrĕcshŭn, ĭş trănsĕndànt. For hwĕr rots wĭth
the most ĕxqwĭşĭt prefĭxĕş ănd sŭfĭxĕş, fal tọ

sĕrv hĕr pŭrpos, she ĕxtĕmporaneŭslў ănd wĭthout hĕsitashŭn, coin̲s ăn ovĕrflo ŏv sĕlf-ĕx-
planĭn̲g cŏmpound̲s, thăt sem to fulў met the
demănd ĕvĕn ŏv hĕr on ĕxtrem casĕ̲s.

Nor i̲s she bărĕn ŏv ideà̲s respĕctĭng tho̲s
ĭmăgĭnarў bein̲g̲s, cald bу the lĕrnĕd, Fari̲s,
Nўmf̲s, Sprit̲s, Elfs,. Demon̲s, ănd the lik. To
hĕr, ĕvĕrў grŏt ănd cornĕr, ĕvĕrу wod ănd
swa̲mp, hĭl ănd mĕdo, i̲s ĭnhăbĭtĕd bу thĕ̲s ĭm-
agĭnĕrў bein̲g̲s, ho är çeslĕslу plуĭn̲g thar ärts
ĭn ĭntĕrferĭn̲g wĭth humàn àfar̲s—workĭn̲g to
this pĕrsŭn wĕlth ănd hapĭnĕs,—to thăt wŭn,
povĕrtу ănd wo.

THE COLLOQUY.

I begăn mȳ ĭntĕrogashŭn̠s bȳ saĭn̠g, I ĕx-pĕct yu hăv a̠lwas̠ bĭn prĕtȳ wĕl ăcquantĕd wĭth the pepl lĭvĭn̠g ŭpŏn thĭs mountĭn. To̠ thĭs remărk she quĭklȳ replid:

Yes! And I tĕl yu thăt tha är the wŭrst sĕt ŏv folks thăt hăs̠ ĕvĕr lĭvd; thĕȳ lȳ ănd stel, ănd chet, ănd rŏb, and mŭrdĕr, to̠. Hwȳ! yu wu̠d'nt belev hou băd tha är; tha'd chet the vĕrȳ dĕvĭl, ĭf he wa̠s̠ on ĕrth; ănd tha'd lȳ hĭm out ŏv hĭs̠ posĕshŭn̠s, to̠. Hwȳ, à pĕrsŭn ĭs̠ ĭn dan̠gĕr ŏv hĭs̠ lif ŭp her, ănd he căn't kep nŏthĭn'. Tha'd stel the brĕd out ŏv à blind nĭgĕr's̠ mouth, ănd thĕn mŭrdĕr hĭm ĭf he told ŏv ĭt. Thăt's the wa ĭt gos̠ ŭp her—tha'r wŭs thăn the dĕvĭl hĭmsĕlf.

Bŭt, I replid, thĕr mŭst be sum go̠d wŭn̠s ămŭn̠g thĕm. To̠ this she ejăculatĕd: No, ther ant; nŏt wŭn; thar äl bad, ănd sŭm är wŭs̠. Yu nĕvĕr sen such folks; thar the dămdĕst thăt ĕvĕr lĭvd.

Wĕl, thĕn, hou dọ tha lĭv? sĕd I.

Liv! Hwȳ, tha don't lĭv—tha onlў sta—ănd hărdlў thăt; à gọd mĕnў ŏv thĕm don't sta lŏng ĭn the sam plaç, nethĕr; tha'r à sĕt ŏf dămd tŭrtls; tha cărў al tha'v gŏt ŏn thar băks —ănd thăt ant mŭeh, nethĕr,—ănd thĕn thar rĕdў tọ gĕt up ănd gĕt out, ĕnў tim; ănd yu căeh 'ĕm ĭf ўu wạnt tọ.

Wĕl, ĭf tha är so băd, dọ ĕnў ŏv thĕm lĭv togĕthĕr, or dŭs eeh wŭn lĭv àlon? I ĭnqwird.

Tọ thĭs she replid: Lĭv togĕthĕr! Gĕs tha dọ; tọ mĕnў ŏv 'em. Hwy! ĭn sŭm ŏv thĕm shăntĭs thĕr är à dŭzĕn or mor,—hwits ănd blăks, ănd al cŭlŭrs—ănd nŏthn' tọ et, ănd nŏthn' tọ war, ănd nọ wọd tọ bŭrn,—ănd hwạt căn tha dọ—thà hăv tọ stel.

And thĕn thĕr ĭs no dĭstĭncshŭn ŏv cŭlŭr ŭp her? sĕd I.

No, nŏt à bĭt. The nĭgĕrs ănd whits al lĭv togĕthĕr. The hwits är jŭst ăs gọd ăs the nĭgĕrs, ănd both är ăs băd ăs the dĕvĭl căn mak 'ĕm.

Wel, thĕn, dọ the negros mărў the whits?

Hwĕn tha wạnt tọ; bŭt, tha don't dọ mŭeh mărўĭng ŭp her—tha don't hăv tọ—ănd thĕn ĭts no us,—ĭts tọ mŭeh trŭbl.

Wĕl, thĕn, hou àbout the chĭldrĕn, är thĕr ĕnў?

Yĕs; à plĕntў ŏv 'ĕm; ănd al cŭlŭrs—blăk, ănd whit, ănd yelo—ănd ĕnў ŭthĕr cŭlŭr thăt yu hăv ĕvĕr sen, bŭt blu; thĕr ant no blu wŭns yĕt.

Wĕl, ĭf thĕr parĕnts är nŏt mărĭd, hou do tha brĭng ŭp the chĭldrĕn?

Brĭng 'ĕm ŭp! Tha don't brĭng 'ĕm ŭp. Hwy, ăs son ăs tha är born, ĕvĕrў dĕvĭl ŏv 'ĕm ĭs for hĭmsĕlf, ănd the dĕvĭl's for 'ĕm al. Thăt's hou thăt gos. And I tĕl yu, tha hăv à blamd hărd tim ŏv ĭt, to.

And thĕn, hou do tha nam the chĭldrĕn?

Nam 'ĕm! Hwy, tha nam 'ĕm ăftĕr thar dădĭ's, to be sur—ĭf tha no ho tha är. Bŭt, thăt don't mak ĕnў ŏds; cas, befor tha är gron ŭp, hăf ŏv 'em don't no thar on yŭng wŭns from ĕnўbŏdў ĕls's, ănd the ŭthĕr hăf ŏv 'ĕm wudn't on 'ĕm ĭf tha dĭd; ănd the yŭng wŭns ant no bĕtĕr—tha ŏfĕn swar tha hăd no dădĭs'. Yu se, jŭst ăs son ăs tha gĕt bĭg enŭf, tha trăvĕl out to gĕt sŭmthĭng to et, ănd ĭf the fed ĭs prĕtў god, ma be tha'l sta—nĕvĕr gĕt băk; ănd ĭf thà cŭm băk, tha find so mĕnў mor ĭn the nĕst, tha căn't sta ĭf tha want to. Hwў! nŭn

ŏv 'ĕm thăt's gŏd for ĕnýthĭng ĕvĕr stas her.
Tha go àwa hwĕn tha är smal, ănd gĕt wŭrk
ănd sta. Yu'l find foks born ŏn thĭs mountĭn,
lĭv'n ĭn Prĭnctŭn, Neu Brŭnswĭk, ĭn Trĕntŭn,
ĭn Neu York, ănd the dĕvĭl nos hwĕr al; ănd
ĭf tha är driv'n tem for sŭm bĭg-bŭgs, or är wa-
tĕrs ĭn sŭm grat hotĕl, tha'l nĕvĕr on tha wĕr
born on thĭs mountĭn, nŏt à bĭt ŏv ĭt. Tha no
bĕtĕr. Bŭt, ĭf wŭn tŭrns out to be à por dĕvĭl,
ănd gĕts ĭnto sŭm băd scrap—thăt fĕlo is sur
to cŭm băk to the mountĭn. Thăt's the wa tha
kep the rănks ful—ful ŏv the scoundrĕls thăt
căn't sta ĕný hwĕr els; thăt's the wă ĭt gos
wĭth the foks her.

Hàv yu alwas lĭvd ŏn thĭs mountĭn, Sĭlvĭà?
No; I was born ŏn thĭs muontĭn ĭn ăn old
tăvĕrn thăt usd to stănd ner the Rŏk Mĭls; ĭt
stod ŭpŏn the lănd nou ond bȳ Rĭehàrd Scŏt.
The old hotĕl was ond ănd kĕpt bȳ Rĭehàrd
Cŭmptŭn; ĭt was torn doun à lŏng hwil àgo,
ănd nou yu căn't tĕl the spŏt ŏn hwĭeh ĭt stod.
Mȳ parĕnts wĕr slavs; ănd hwĕn mȳ màstĕr
movd doun to Neshănĭc, I wĕnt alŏng wĭth
thĕm; ănd, hwĕn mȳ màstĕr went to Grat Bĕnd,
ŏn the Sŭsqwehănà, I wĕnt wĭth hĭm thar.
Aftĕrwàrds I ĭvd lĭn Neu Brŭnswĭk, ănd ĭn

Prĭnçtŭn, ănd ĭn ŭthĕr placĕş. I cam băk tọ
the mountĭn becạş I ĭnhĕrĭtĕd à hous ănd lŏt ŏv
lănd, ăt mȳ fäthĕr'ş dĕth. Thăt's hwạt brŏt me
băk tọ the mountĭn.

Ho wạş yur fathĕr?

Mȳ fäthĕr wạş Cŭfȳ Bard, à slav tọ Jŏn
Bard. He (Cŭfȳ) wạş à fifĕr ĭn the bătl ŏv
Prĭnçtŭn. He uşd tọ be à fifĕr for the mĭnĭt
mĕn, ĭn the daş ŏv the Rĕvolushŭn.

Ho wäş yur mŭthĕr?

Mȳ mŭthĕr wàş Dorcŭs Cŭmptŭn, à slav tọ
Rĭehard Cŭmptŭn, the proprietor ŏv the hotĕl,
ăt Rŏk Mĭlş. Hwĕn I wạş tọ yerş old, mȳ
mŭthĕr bŏt hĕr tim ŏv Rĭehàrd Cŭmptŭn,—
Mĭnĭcàl Dụbois goĭng hĕr securĭtȳ for the pamĕnt ŏv the mŭnȳ. Aş mȳ mŭthĕr fald tọ mak
pamĕnt ăt the tim àpointĕd, she becam the prŏpĕrtȳ ŏv Mĭnĭcàl Dụbois. Wĭth thĭs falur tọ
mak pamĕnt, Dụbois wạş gratlȳ dĭsàpointĕd,
ănd mŭeh dĭspleşd, ăş he dĭd nŏt wĭsh tọ fạl ạr
tọ mȳ mŭthĕr ănd hĕr ehĭldrĕn, ăş slavş tọ hĭm.
So he tràtĕd mŭthĕr bădlȳ—ŏfĕn tĭmş cruĕlȳ.
On wŭn ŏcạşyŭn, hwĕn hĕr bab wạş bŭt thre
dàş old, he whĭpt hĕr wĭth ăn ŏx-găd, becạş
she dĭdn't hold à hŏg hwil he yokt ĭt; ĭt wạş
ĭn Märeh; the ground wạş wĕt ănd slĭpĕrȳ,

ănd the hŏg prọvd tọ strŏng for hĕr, ŭndĕr the çĭrcŭmstănçĕs. Frŏm the ĕxpọsyur ănd the whĭpĭng, she becȧm severlў sĭk wĭth puĕrperȧl fevĕr; bŭt, ȧftĕr ȧ lŏng hwil she recŏvĕrd.

Undĕr the slav lạs ŏv Neu Jĕrsў, hwĕn the slav thŏt the mästĕr tọ sever, ănd the slav ănd the mästĕr dĭd nŏt gĕt ȧlọng harmonĭŭslў, the slav hăd ȧ rit tọ hŭnt ȧ neu mästĕr. Acordĭnglў, mȳ mŭthĕr Dọrcŭs, wĕnt ĭn qwĕst ŏv ȧ neu mästĕr; ănd, ạs Mr. Wm. Bard uṣd tọ sĕnd thĭngs for hĕr ănd hĕr chĭldrĕn tọ et, hwĕn Dubois nĕglĕctĕd, or refuṣd tọ fŭrnĭsh enŭf tọ sătĭsfy thar cravĭng stŭmăcs, she ȧskt hĭm (Bard), tọ bȳ hĕr. Thĭs he dĭd. And she likt hĭm wĕl; bŭt she wạs ămbĭshŭs tọ be fre. Acordĭnglў, she bŏt hĕr tim ŏv Bard, bŭt fald tọ mak pamĕnt, ănd retŭrnd tọ hĭm hĭṣ slav.

She wạs thĕn sold to Milṣ Smith, ho wạs ȧ kind mästĕr, ănd ȧ gọd măn. Bŭt, she wạs ămbĭshŭs tọ be fre—so ŏv, Smĭth she bŏt hĕr tim, ănd wĕnt ȧwa tọ wŭrk, ănd tọ lĭv wĭth strängĕrṣ. But, ạs she fald tọ mak pamĕnt ăt the ăpointĕd tim, she wạs takĕn băk ȧ slav, ănd spĕnt the remandĕr ŏv hĕr daṣ wĭth him, ănd wạs bĕrĭd ȧbout 45 yerṣ ȧgo ŭpŏn hĭṣ homsted.

Ov corṣ, I remand ȧ slav tọ Mĭnĭcȧl Dụbois.

He dǐd nǒt tret me crṳelў. I trid tọ pleṣ hǐm, ǎnd he trid tọ pleṣ me; ǎnd we gǒt álọng tog̃ěthěr prětў wěl—ěxçěptǐng sumtimṣ I wṳd be á lǐtl refrǎctorў, ǎnd then he wṳd gǐv me á sever flŏgǐng. Hwěn I wạṣ ábọut fiv yerṣ old, he mọvd ǔpǒn á färm ner the vǐlaǵ ǒv Flagtoun. Hwil ther, I hǎd gọd timṣ—á plěntў tọ et, á plěntў ǒv clothṣ, ǎnd á plěntў ǒv fun— onlў mȳ mǐstrěs wạ̀ṣ těriblў pǎshunạt, ǎnd těriblў croṣ tọ me. I dǐd nǒt lik hěr, ǎnd she dǐd nǒt lik me; so she uṣd tọ běat me bǎdlў. On wun ǒcaṣhun, I dǐd sumthǐng thǎt dǐd not sut hěr. Aṣ uṣuàl, she scolděd me. Then I wạṣ sáçў. Herupǒn, she whǐpt me untǐl she mǎrkt me so bǎdlў thǎt I wǐl něvěr loṣ the scärṣ. Yu cǎn se the scärṣ her upǒn mȳ hed, tọ-da; ǎnd I wǐl něvěr loṣ them, ǐf I lǐv ǎnuthěr hundrěd yerṣ.

Hwěn I wạṣ ábọut těn yerṣ old, the bǎtl ov Mǔnmuth ǒcurd. I reměmběr věrў wěl hwěn mȳ mästěr cum hom frǒm thǎt bǎtl. Chěrǐs wěr rip, ǎnd we wěr g̃ǎthěrǐng härvěst. He wạṣ ǎn ǒffiçěr; but I dọ nǒt no hǐṣ rǎnk. He told grat storǐṣ ábọut the bǎtl, ǎnd ǒv the bravěrў ǒv the Neu Jěrsў mǐlǐshá; ǎnd ábọut the cǒnduct ǒv Gěněràl Wȧshǐngtun. He sěd

tha whĭpt the Brĭtĭsh bădlў—but ĭt wạs à dĕspĕrat fit. He told us thăt the bătl ŏcurd ŏn
the hŏtĕst da he ĕvĕr sạ; he sĕd he cam ner
pĕrĭshĭng frŏm thĕ ĕxçĕs ŏv het ănd from thĭrst;
ănd thăt à-grat mĕnў dĭd di for the wạnt ŏv
wạtĕr.

I ạlso remĕmbĕr hwĕn mў făthĕr ănd uthĕrs
returnĕd frŏm the bătls ŏv Trĕntun ănd Prĭnçtun,—but I wạs yungĕr thĕn, ănd onlў remĕmbĕr thăt ĭt wạs wĭntĕr, ănd thăt tha cŏmpland
thăt tha hăd suffĕrd so much frŏm cold ănd
ĕxposur.

Befor the bătl ŏv Prĭnçtun, mў mästĕr hăd
bĭn à prĭsunĕr ŏv wạr. He hăd bĭn căpturd
hwil fitĭng ŏn the wạtĕr, sumwhĕr ner Neu
York. I usd tọ her hĭm tĕl hou he ănd sĕvĕràl
uthĕrs wĕr croudĕd ĭntọ à vĕrў smạl rọm ĭn
the hold ŏv à vĕsĕl—the trăp-dor securlў fàst-
ĕnd doun, ănd the suplў ŏv frĕsh ar so com-
pletlў shut ŏf, thăt almost ạl họ wĕr thus ĭm-
prĭsund, did ĭn à fĕw hours. In thĭs plaç tha
wĕr kĕpt tụ das. Dụbois, bў brethĭng wĭth
hĭs mouth ĭn clos cŏntăct wĭth à nal-hol, hĕld
out untĭl he wàs removd. Tụ or thre uthĕrs
wĕr fortunat enuf tọ find sum uthĕr defĕcts ĭn

the wọd-wurk, thru hwĭch á scăntẙ suplẙ ŏv ar
cam.

Hwĕn I wàṣ ĭn mẙ 14th yer, mẙ mästĕr
mọvd frŏm Flăgtoun tọ hĭṣ färm álọng the Sus-
qwhăná Rĭvĕr. Thĭs färm ĭṣ the länd ŏn hwĭch
the yĭlag cạld Grat Bĕnd häṣ bĭn bĭlt. Hwĕn
we movd upŏn the färm, thĕr wàṣ but wun
uthĕr hous ĭn the sĕtlmĕnt for the dĭstánç ŏv
sĕyĕrál milṣ. Theṣ tu houseṣ wĕr bĭlt ŏv lŏgṣ.
The wun upŏn mẙ mästĕrṣ färm hăd bĭn kĕpt
ăṣ á tăvĕrn; ănd hwĕn he mọvd ĭntọ ĭt, he kĕpt
ĭt ăṣ á tăvĕrn. The plaç waṣ non ăṣ Grat
Bĕnd. It waṣ ăn ĭmportánt stŏpĭng plaç for
trăvĕlĕrṣ on thar wạ tọ the Lak Cuntrĭṣ, ănd
tọ uthĕr plaçṣ wĕstwàrd. Alsọ, ĭt wàṣ á plaç
muçh vĭsĭtĕd bẙ botmĕn goĭng doun ănd up
the rĭvĕr. Her, tọ, cam grat numbĕrs ŏv hun-
tĕrṣ ănd drovĕrṣ. In făct, ĕvĕn ĭn theṣ daṣ,
Grat Bĕnd waṣ ăn ĭmportánt plaç.

In mọvĭng tọ Grat Bĕnd, we wĕnt ĭn tu
wăgunṣ. We tọk wĭth uṣ tu couṣ; thĕṣ I
droy ạl the wa thar. Aftĕr we crŏst the Dĕláwar ăt Estun, the rod ĕxtĕndĕd thru á grat
fŏrĕst, wĭth onlẙ her ănd thar á clerd pătçh,
ănd á smạl lŏg hut. Eyĕn the tăvĕrnṣ wĕr
onlẙ lŏg huts—sumtimṣ wĭth but wun rọm

doun stars̱ ănd wŭn ŭp stars̱. Thĕn thĕr wu̇d be tu̱ or thre bĕds̱ ĭn the ro̱m ŭp stars̱, ănd wŭn ĭn the ro̱m doun stars̱.

The grat fŏrĕst was̱ cạld the Bĕeh Wo̱ds̱. It was̱ so bĭg thăt we was̱ sĭx das̱ ĭn goĭng thru̱ ĭt. Sŭmtims̱ we wu̱d go à hȧlf da wĭthout pȧsĭng à hous̱, or metĭng à pĕrsŭn. The wo̱ds̱ was̱ fu̱l ŏv bars̱, pănthĕrs̱, wild-căts ănd the lik. About thes̱ I hăd hĕrd à grat mĕnÿ wild storĭs̱. So I mad shur to̱ kep mȳ cous̱ prĕtÿ clos to̱ the wăgŭns̱.

Usuȧlÿ, we stŏpt ovĕr nit ăt à hotĕl. Bŭt, ăs̱ the housĕs̱ wĕr smạl, ŏfĕn ĭt wu̇d hăpĕn thăt ŭthĕrs̱ hăd stŏpt befor we ărivd, ănd the lŏdġĭng ro̱ms̱ wu̱d a̱l be ŏcupid. Thĕn we wu̱d slep ĭn our wăgŭns̱, or ĭn the out-bĭldĭngs̱. In thos̱ das̱, trăvĕlĕrs̱ hăd to̱ gĕt ȧlŏng the bĕst wa tha cu̱d.

As̱ mȳ mästĕr sa̱ thăt the sit ŭpŏn whĭeh he lĭvd was̱ favŭrȧbl to̱ bĭsinĕs̱, durĭng the thĭrd sŭmĕr ȧftĕr our ărivȧl, he erĕctĕd à lärġ neu fram hous—the fĭrst hous, nŏt bĭlt ŏv lŏgs̱, ĭn Grat Bĕnd. Thĕn, he begăn to̱ do̱ à lärġ bĭsinĕs̱, ănd becam à vĕrÿ prŏminĕnt măn thar, ăs̱ he was̱ hwil he lĭvd ĭn Neu Jĕrsÿ.

Alrĕdÿ sĕvĕrȧl pĕpl hăd mo̱vd to̱ the nabŭrhod, hăd erĕctĕd lŏg housĕs, clerd the lănds, ănd begŭn tọ cŭltivat felds, ănd ras stŏk. Vĕrȳ sọn, ĭn the vĭlag, stor-housĕs ănd mĭls wĕr bĭlt. Inded, Grat Bĕnd begăn tọ be the cĕntĕr ŏv à lärg ănd thrivĭng sĕtlmĕnt.

At thĭs tim hŭntĕrs usd tọ cŭm tọ thĭs point tọ trad ; tọ sĕl der-met, bar-met, wĭld tŭrkȳs ănd the lĭk, ănd tọ ĕxchàng the skĭns ŏv wild ănimàls for sŭch cŏmŏditĭs ăs tha wĭsht. At our tăvĕrn, tha usd tọ stạ ; ănd tha wĕr à jŏlȳ sĕt ŏv fĕlọs ; I likt tọ se thĕm cŭm—thĕr wàs fŭn thĕn.

Thĕr wạs à fĕrȳ àcrŏs the Sŭsqwehănà ăt Grat Bĕnd. The bot ŭpŏn our sid wàs ond bȳ mȳ mästĕr ; the wŭn ŭpŏn the ŭthĕr sid wàs ond bȳ Căptĭn Hatch. I sọn lĕrnd tọ mănag the bot ăs wĕl ăs ĕnȳ wŭn cụd, ănd ŏfĕn usd tọ fĕrȳ tems àcrŏs àlon. The foks họ wĕr ăc- qwantĕd wĭth me, ŭsd tọ prĕfĕr me tọ tak thĕm àcrŏs, ĕvĕn hwĕn the fĕrȳmĕn wĕr àbout. Bŭt, Căptĭn Hătch dĭd nŏt lik me. I usd tọ stel hĭs cŭstŭmĕrs. Hwĕn I lăndĕd mȳ bot ŭpŏn hĭs sid, ĭf ĕnȳ bŏdȳ wàs thar thăt wạntĕd tọ cŭm over tọ the Bĕnd, bĕfor he neu ĭt, I wụd hŭrȳ thĕm ĭntọ mȳ bot ănd push ŏf frŏm the shor, ănd lev hĭm swarĭng. Yụ se the

mŭnў I gŏt for fĕtehĭng băk à lod was min;
ănd, I stol mĕnў à lod frŏm old Hăteh; I alwas
dĭd, ĕvĕrў tim I cud.

Alŏng wĭth the fĕrў bot, alwas wĕr wŭn or
tu skĭfs. Thes we tok àlŏng to hăv ĭn rĕdĭnĕs
ĭn cas ŏv acĭdĕnt. Hwĕn the lod was hĕvў, or
hwĕn ĭt was wĭndў, tu or mor fĕrўmĕn wĕr re-
qwird. At sŭeh tims, I wud hĕlp thĕm àcrŏs,
bŭt I alwas cŭm băk àlon ĭn à skĭf. In this
wa I gŏt so thăt I cud hăndl the skĭf fĭrst rat,
ănd was vĕrў fŏnd ŏv usĭng ĭt. Ofĕn tims I
usd to tak sĭngl păsĕngĕrs ovĕr the fĕrў ĭn à
skĭf; sŭmtims tu or mor ăt wŭnc. Thĭs I likt,
ănd tha usd to pa me wĕl to do ĭt. I hăd à god
nam for mănagĭng the skĭf—tha ŭsd to sa thăt,
ĭn usĭng the skĭf I cud bet ĕnў măn ŏn the
Susqwehănà,—ănd I alwas dĭd bet al thăt ract
wĭth me.

Ofĕntims hwĕn the fĕrўmĕn wĕr ăt dĭnĕr,
sŭm wŭn wud cŭm to the fĕrў to crŏs. Tha
wud hŏlo to lĕt ŭs no thăt sŭm wŭn wantĕd
to crŏs. Thĕn thĕr wud be à rac. I'd skĭp
out, ănd doun to the wharf so son thăt I'd hăv
'ĕm lodĕd ănd pusht ŏf befor ĕnў wŭn ĕls cud
gĕt thar—ănd thĕn I'd gĕt the fe. I tĕl yu, ĭf
tha dĭd nŏt ehŭk nif ănd fork, ănd rŭn ăt wŭnc,

'twas no us—tha cųd'nt rŭn wĭth me,—the fe
wȧs gŏn.   I'v gŏt mĕnў ȧ shĭlĭng that wa, ănd
mĕnў ȧ gọd drĭnk, tọ.

I ȧskt: Wạs yur mästĕr wĭlĭng thăt yu shụd
ehet the fĕrўmȧn out ŏv hĭs feṣ ĭn thăt wa?

She replid: He dĭd nŏt car; he thŏt I wạs
smärt for doĭng ĭt.   And sŭmtims, ĭf I hăd nŏt
bĭn ĭn the hăbĭt ŏv hŭrўĭng thĭngs ŭp ĭn thĭs
wa, pepl wụd hăv watĕd ăt the fĕrў bȳ the
hour,—bŭt yu se tha dĭd'nt hăv tọ wat hwĕn I
wȧṣ ȧbout, ănd thĭs ĭṣ hwȳ tha likt mĕ, ănd
hwȳ mȳ mästĕr likt me, tọ.

Wĕl, Sĭlvĭȧ; hwȧt kind ŏv timṣ dĭd yu hăv
hwil ăt Grat Bĕnd?

Whạt kĭnd ŏv timṣ?   Hwȳ, fĭrst rat timṣ!
Thĕr wĕr plĕntў ŏv frolĭcs, ănd I uṣd tọ go
ănd dȧnç ạl nit,—foks cụd dȧnç thĕn.   Hwȳ!
thĕr wĕr sŭm ŏv the bĕst dȧnçerṣ ŭp thar thăt
I ĕvĕr sạ; foks neu hou tọ dȧnç ĭn thoṣ daṣ.

Thĕn yu thĭnk thăt the yŭng foks ŏv thĭs
naborhọd don't no hou tọ dȧnç?

I no tha don't; I'v sen 'ĕm trȳ, ănd tha
căn't dȧnç ȧ bĭt.   Tha'v gŏt no stĕp.

Hăv yu sen ĕnўbŏdў trȳ tọ dȧnç vĕrў lȧtlў?

Yĕs; lȧst wĭntĕr tha mad ȧ pärtў ovĕr

her, ăt wŭn ŏv the nabŭrs, ănd tha ĭnvītĕd me
ovĕr; ănd I wĕnt. Tha hăd á fĭdl, ănd tha
trid to dànç—bŭt tha cud'nt—nŏt á dămd á
wŭn ŏv 'ĕm.

Wĕl!! hwạt wạs the mătĕr?

Hwạt wạs the mătĕr! Hwȳ! tha hăd no
stĕp,—yu căn't dànç ŭnlĕs yu hăv the stĕp;
ănd tha wĕr ăs ạkwàrd ăs the dĕvĭl; ănd thĕn
thà wĕr so dămd clŭmsȳ. Hwȳ, ĭf tha went
to crŏs thar lĕgs, tha'd fạl do̟un.

Thĕn yu thĭnk thăt to dànç wĕl, ĭt ĭs nĕçes-
arȳ to crŏs the lĕgs?

Sŭmtims ĭt ĭs,—nobŏdȳ căn dànç mŭch
wĭthout crŏsĭng the lĕgs; bŭt tha cudn't do ĭt
—tha'd gĕt tăngld ĭn the rĭgĭn ănd căpsiz.
Hwȳ! tha căntĕrd ovĕr the flor lik so mĕnȳ
he gots.

Wĕl, dĭd yu sho thĕm ho̟u to dànç?

Wĕl, yĕs; I to̟k á stĕp or tu; bŭt I
cudn't do ĭt ăs I usd to hwĕn I wạs yŭng.
Tha thŏt I dĭd wĕl; bŭt tha don't no—tha'v
nĕvĕr sen gọd dànçĭng. Hwȳ! hwĕn I wạs
yŭng, I'd crŏs mȳ fet nĭntȳ-nin tims ĭn ạ mĭnĭt,
ănd nĕvĕr mĭs the tim, strĭk hel or to wĭth
eqwàl es, ănd go thru the fĭgurs ăs nĭmbl ăs á
wĭtch. Bŭt no̟u tha'r so clŭmsȳ thăt hwĕn

wŭn taks á fọt ŏf frŏm the flor, sŭmbŏdў hăş to hold hĭm ŭp hwil he shaks ĭt. And thĕn hwĕn tha rel tha pụsh ănd croud lik á yok ŏv yŭng sterş, ănd tha băng eeh ŭthĕr ŭntĭl tha är ĭn dangĕr ŏv thar livş.

Yes, Sĭlvĭá, the ärt ŏv dánçĭng hăş fạlĕn ĭntọ declin, ănd I ăm sŏrў tor ĭt. The ўŭng foks ŏv thĭs gĕnĕrashŭn är nŏt onlў clŭmşў ănd ạkwàrd, bŭt tha är băd fĭgurş; thĕr ĭş nŭthĭng ĭn thar sports tọ devĕlŏp á gọd form, ănd ăş á cŏnseqwĕnç, thĭs gĕnĕrashŭn ĭş cărăctĕrizd bў băd devĕlŏpmĕnt—wek bŏdĭş wĭth ŭglў façes, ănd pọr mindş.

Herŭpŏn Sĭlvĭá bgăn tọ sa:

Bŭt, tha thĭnk thar grat thĭngs ănd vĕrў hăndsŭm. Bŭt tha ant; thar pọr, scrŏnў mortáls—mak no ăperànç, ănd căn't dọ nŏthĭng. Hwў! the mĕn ŏv the aǥ ov mў mästĕr, lọkt brav. Tha wĕr tạl ănd cŏmăndĭng, ănd stout ŏv lĭmb, ănd ǥraçfụl ănd hăndў; tha hăd gọd façes, grat hi forhĕdş—ănd lärǥ brit ўs (eyes) ănd brŏd mouthş wĭth gọd teth. Tha stọd ŭp strat, ănd wạlkt wĭth fredŭm ănd eş. I tĕl yu, ĭn thos ŏld tims, thĕr wĕr gọd lọkĭng mĕn,— brav lọkĭng mĕn, tha wĕr ạl so; Gĕnĕràl Washĭngtŭn wạş, ănd Láfaĕt wạş, ănd mў mästĕr wạş

ănd ạl the grat měn thặt I ěvěr sạ wěr, ănd
tha wěr ạl gọd dànçers; ănd dànçt hwěněvěr
tha hăd à chànç. Tha usd tọ sà thặt Gěněrál
Washịngtŭn wạs the most beutǐfụl dạnçěr ǐn
Aměricà—thặt he cụd ěvěn bet the Marcŭs de
Làfaět.

The big yankǐs fròm York Stat ănd Neu
Englànd, usd tọ cŭm tọ our hous, ănd tha wěr
věrў fin lọkǐng měn—ạl ǒv 'ěm wěr. And tha
wěr věrў tạl, ănd věrў strat, ănd věrў dǐgnǐfid;
ănd thàr wivs wěr wěl formd ănd beutǐfụl, ănd
věrў dǐgnǐfid wiměn. And tha wěr ạl věrў
polit—hăd the best ǒv măněrs—wěr the mǒst
acǒmplǐsht foks I ěvěr sạ. And tha wěr ạl
gọd dànçěrs—the best ǒv dànçěrs—ănd tha
něvěr gǒt tǐrd ǒv dànçǐng. Ěvěn the old měn
ănd old wiměn dànçt—ănd tha wěr jŭst ặs gọd
figurs ặs yu ěvěr sạ, ănd věrў graçfụl.

I se, Sǐlvǐà, thặt yu hăd gọd tims hwěn ặt
the Grat Běnd.

Ges we hăd! Hwěn mȳ mästěr mọvd ǐntọ
hǐs neu hous, we hăd à bǐg tim. Al the grănd
foks wěr thar, ănd I těl yu, thǐngs wěr livlў.
We hăd à plěntў ǒv brăndў, ănd tha usd ǐt, tọ
—à bǐg tim I těl yu; ăȳ! ăȳ! the bǐgěst kind
ǒv à tim.

Dĭd yu us̱ ĕnȳ brăndȳ?

Wĕl, I dĭd; bŭt nŏt tĭl towárds̱ nit; I hăd
tọ mŭeh tọ dọ; I hăd tọ se tọ the rĕst; I neu
hwĕr ĕvĕrȳthĭṉg wạs̱, ănd I hăd tọ hĕlp thĕm
gĕt thĕm. Bŭt, I lọkt out for mȳsĕlf. Thĕr
wạs̱ wŭn kĕg ŏv brăndȳ that I neu wạs̱ mad
vĕrȳ gọd, for I hĕlpt mak ĭt; wĕ us̱d tọ mak
our on brăndȳ, ănd I ạlwas̱ hĕlpt mȳ mästĕr
mak ĭt, ănd neu jŭst ás̱ wĕl hou tọ dọ ĭt ăs̱
ĕnȳbŏdȳ.

I lĕft this kĕg tĭl ĭt wạs̱ the làst thĭṉg tọ
be mọvd; then, hwĕn I ănd á çĕrtĭn fĕlo begăn
tọ mọv ĭt, we cŏnclụdĕd that we wụd se ĭf ĭt
hăd kĕpt wĕl; we hăd no cŭp, so we drạwd ĭt
out ĭn ăn ĕrthĕn pŏt; ănd then he drănk; ănd
then I drănk—tĭl we drănk ạl we cụd; bŭt stĭl
thĕr wạs̱ sŭm lĕft ĭn the pŏt, ănd we cụdn't gĕt
ĭt băk ĭn the kĕg, for we hăd no fŭnĕl; we
dĭdn't wạnt tọ thro ĭt áwa, that lọkt tọ wastfụl;
so, we cŏnclụdĕd we'd drĭnk ĭt ŭp; so, he drănk
ănd I drănk, tĭl ĭt wạs̱ gŏn. This mad ŭs
prĕtȳ fụl; bŭt we stärtĕd wĭth the kĕg; bȳ
ănd bȳ ĭt begŭn tọ be tọ hevȳ—ănd then ĭt
gŏt doun, ănd then we gŏt doun; ănd then I
neu thĕr'd be á tim, becạs̱ I neu ĭf mȳ mästĕr sạ
me, I'd gĕt á hĕl ŏv á lĭk'n. And sŭm ŏv the

rĕst neu thăt tọ. And tha dĭdn't wạnt tọ se
me lĭkt, sọ tha gŏt me ŭp, ănd hĕlpt me ŏf tọ-
wärd the hous tọ pụt me tọ bed.

I uṣd tọ be sŭbjĕct tọ the crămps, ănd sŭmtims I uṣd tọ hăv ĭt vĕrȳ băd,—so thăt mȳ
mĭstrĕs uṣd tọ gĭv me mĕdiçĭn for ĭt ; ănd, wŭns
â lĭtl hwĭl befor, I wạs so bàd wĭth ĭt thăt
she thŏt I wạs goiṇg tọ di wĭth ĭt. Wĕl, I
thŏt nou I hăd bĕtĕr hăv the crămp, ănd thĕn
mabe I wụdn't gĕt lĭkt. So I begăn tọ hăv
pan—ănd sọn ĭt gŏt prĕtȳ băd—worṣ thăn I'd
ĕvĕr hăd ĭt befor; ănȳhou, I mad mor fŭs thăn
I ĕvĕr hăd befor, ănd yĕld ă gọd del loudĕr.

Prĕtȳ sọn tha cạld mĭsȳ, ănd she wạs awfụlȳ
fritĕnd ; she thŏt I wụd di, shur ; she sĕd she'd
nĕvĕr sen me so wek wĭth ĭt befor.

So she hăd me cărĭd ănd plaçt ŭpŏn the
trŭndl–bĕd, ĭn hĕr on rọm, ănd ătĕndĕd tọ me
niçlȳ. She gav me sŭm mĕdiçĭn hwĭeh she
thŏt hĕlpt me àmazĭṇglȳ ; bŭt befor the mĕdiçĭn cụd dọ ĕnȳ gọd the rŭm stŏpt ạl mȳ yĕlĭṇg,
ănd grŭntĭng tọ ; ĭn fäçt, I wạs so drŭnk thăt
I cụdn't se, her, nor fel. For âhwil, I thŏt I
wạs dĕd ; bŭt bȳ ănd bȳ the brăndȳ begăn tọ
war ŏf, ănd I begăn tọ se. I cạshŭslȳ sqŭrmd
àround tọ se wĕthĕr ĕnȳbŏdȳ wạs àbout, ănd

thar săt mĭsȳ, fănĭng me. I cạshŭlȳ opĕnd mȳ
ȳs (eyes) jŭst the lest bĭt, tọ se hou she lọkt;
she lọkt vĕrȳ pĭtȳfụl—I wạs tọ drŭnk tọ läf;
bŭt "Mȳ God," thŏt I, "ĭf yu onlȳ neu hwàt
I ăm dọĭng, yu'd thro thăt făn àwa ănd gĭv
me hĕl."

At nit, mȳ mästĕr cam tọ bĕd vĕrȳ lat.
Hwĕn he cam ĭn tọ ŭndrĕs, I wạs makĭng bĕ-
lev thăt I wạs àslep. I dĭdn't dar tọ gĕt wĕl
tọ sọn. At wŭns, mĭstrĕs begăn tọ tĕl
hĭm hou sĭk I wạs; ănd hou ner I cam tọ dy-
ĭng,—bŭt I dĭdn't fọl hĭm. He lọkt ăt me à
lĭtl, ănd thĕn wĕnt tọ bĕd. He sed: "Pạ!
she's onlȳ drŭnk—she's bĭn drĭnkĭng wĭth the
men. Go tọ slep—she'l be ạl rit ĭn the mornĭng." And so I wạs, tọ; bŭt, thăt cụrd me
ŏv drĭnkĭng.

Thĕn yu nĕvĕr drănk àftĕr thăt?

I nĕvĕr gŏt drŭnk àftĕr thăt. Sŭmtims
hwĕn ŭthĕrs hăv bĭn drĭnkĭng, I hăv takn à
drăm, tọ; bŭt, I dĭdn't gĕt drŭnk—I nĕvĕr dọ.
I no mȳ mạsụr, ănd I tak no mor.

Dĭd yur mĭstrĕs ĕvĕr fĭnd out thăt yu wĕr
deçevĭng hĕr hwĕn yu wĕr drŭnk?

I ges nŏt; ĭf she hăd, she'd à kĭld me—ĭf
she cụd; bŭt, I hăv läft ạbout ĭt à grat mĕnȳ

tims. I spoild hĕr fŭn for thăt nit—she hăd tọ
lev hĕr cŭmpánў ănd tak car ŏv me,—ĭt wạṣ
prĕtў härd for hĕr; for she hăd á grat del ŏy
bĭg cŭmpánў thar thăt nit, ănd she wạṣ hĕl for
cŭmpạnў.

Wĕl; yur mĭstrĕs wạṣ álwaṣ kĭnd tọ yu,
wạṣn't she?

Kĭnd tọ me; hwỹ, she wạṣ the vĕrў dĕvĭl
hĭmsĕlf. Hwỹ, she'd lĕvĕl me wĭth ĕnўthĭng
she cụd gĕt hold ŏv—clŭb, stĭk ŏv wọd, tŏngṣ,
fir-shŭvĕl, nif, ăx, hătehĕt; ĕnўthĭng thăt wạṣ
hăndўĕst; ănd thĕn she wạṣ so dămd qwĭk
ábout ĭt, tọ. I tĕl yu, ĭf I ĭntĕndĕd tọ sạç hĕr,
I mad shur tọ be ŏf áwạṣ.

Wĕl; dĭd she ĕvĕr hĭt yu?

Yes, ŏfĕn; wŭnṣ she nŏçt me tĭl I wạṣ so
stĭf thăt she thŏt I wạṣ ded; wŭnṣ áftĕr thăt,
becạṣ I wạṣ á lĭtl sạçў, she lĕvĕld me wĭth the
fir-shŭvĕl ănd brok mỹ pat. She thŏt I wạṣ
ded thĕn, bŭt I wạṣn't.

Brok yur pat?

Yĕs; brok mỹ skŭl; yu cán pụt yur fĭngĕrṣ
her, ĭn the plaç hwar thĕ brak wạṣ, ĭn the sid
ŏv mỹ hĕd, yĕt. She smăsht ĭt rit ĭn—she
dĭdn't dọ thĭngṣ tọ the hálvṣ.

Herŭpŏn I ĕxămīnd Sīlvĭà's hĕd, ănd found thăt, ăt sŭm tim, lŏng àgo, the skŭl hăd bĭn brokĕn ănd deprĕst for a spaç nŏt lĕs thăn thre ĭnehĕs ; thăt the deprĕst frăgmĕnt hăd nŏt bĭn ĕlevatĕd, ăs sŭrgĕns nou do, ănd thăt ĭn cŏnseqwĕnç, thĕr ĭs, to this da, à deprĕshŭn ĭn hwĭeh I căn bĕrў à lärg pärt ŏv the ĭndĕx fĭnger.

Upŏn hĕr hĕd, I found numĕrŭs ŭthĕr scärs most ŏv hwĭeh Sīlvĭà sĕs, är the reşult ŏv wounds ĭnflĭctĕd bў hĕr mĭstrĕs Bŭt she sĕs sŭm ŏv them är nŏt.   Thes är, ăcordĭng to hĕr tĕl, the reşults ŏv wounds ĭncŭrd durĭng ŭthĕr wars,—wagd ăftĕr she gand hĕr fredŭm.   For, ĭn the strŭgl for lif, Sīlvĭà ĭncŭrd mĕnў à cŏmbăt ; ănd, altho she älwas căm ŏf frŏm the feld vĭctorĭŭs, sŭmtĭms she dĭd nŏt cŭm ŏf ŭnscăthd.

In hĕr fits, ĭt ĭs sĕd, she ĕngagd àlik măn or womàn, blăk or hwit—best or bĭrd—ĕnўthĭng bŭt Gŏd or dĕvĭl.

Acordĭng to hĕr tĕl, she card bŭt lĭtl for fĭst or fot ; bŭt sŭmtĭms hwĕn tha cam doun ŭpŏn hĕr wĭth wod ănd stel, she dĭd wĭnç à lĭtl. Bŭt wo! to the cŏmbătànt thăt dard to reşort to thos ŭnfar ĭmplemĕnts ŏv war.   At bĕst, ĕvĕn wĭth thes, tha cud onlў wound hĕr,—jŭst enuf

tọ ĕxăspĕrat hĕr tọ dọ jŭstĭç tọ the ŏcashun.
For, hwĕn rĭgd for ạ fĭst fit, nĕvĕr enŭf stọd
befor hĕr, nor găthĕrd àround hĕr, tọ dĭscŭmfĭt
hĕr, or tọ kep hĕr ŭpŏn the sọd.

Respectĭng hĕr prowĕs, Sĭlvĭà's tĕstimonỹ ĭs
nŏt ạl thăt I hăv găthĕrd. Dĭf'ĕrĕnt mĕn, whŏs
vĕnĕràbl lŏks sho thăt tha är old enŭf tọ remĕmbĕr sens thăt tha wĭtnĕst sĭxtỹ ănd sĕv-
ĕntỹ yers àgo, tĕl me thăt tha hăv sen Sĭlvĭà ĭn
bătl mĕnỹ à tim, ănd thăt hĕr cŭraǥ, ănd hĕr
àbĭlĭtỹ wạs ạlwạs ădeqwat tọ ĕnỹ ĕmĕrǥĕnçỹ.

Houĕvĕr, tradĭshŭn stats, thăt Sĭlvĭà wạs
nĕthĕr qwärĕlsŭm nor ăgrĕsĭv. On the cŏntrarỹ, she wạs deçidĕdlỹ à peç-makĕr; ănd sŭm
ŏv hĕr most notwŭrthỹ fets wĕr ăcomphlĭst
hwĕn sŭprĕsĭng à rou, or, pärtĭng cŏmbătànts;
ĭnded, hĕr prĕẹĕnç ŏf ĕn prĕvĕntĕd à fit. Be-
càṣ, ĭf the fit begăn cŏntrarỹ tọ hĕr wĭl, ŏfĕn-
tims she, tọ mak thĕm mor obedĭĕnt ĭn the
futur, ănd tọ tĕrifỹ ŭthĕrṣ ŏv à qwạrelsŭm or
à puǥĭlistĭc natur, wụd sevĕrlỹ whĭp both the
cŏmbătànts.

Nor wạs she lĕs liklỹ tọ ĭntĕrfer ĭn casĕs
hwĕr thĕr wạs à fre fit. In casĕs ĭn hwĭeh frŏm
fiv tọ tĕn wĕr ĭn à fit, Sĭlvĭà hăṣ ŏfĕn bĭn non
tọ wad ĭn, tọ sez wĕrĕvĕr hand-holt wạs cṣĭĕst,

ănd tǫ thro wŭn negro ĭn wŭn dĭrĕcshŭn, ănd
ănŭthĕr ĭn ănŭthĕr dĭrĕcshhŭn, untĭl the làst
fĕlo wąs hŭrld frŏm the àrenà ŏv fit ; ănd, ŏfĕn
tims she thrų thĕm wĭth sŭeh forc, thăt the
dăsh ŭpŏn the ground ŭnfĭtĕd thĕm for fŭrthĕr
àcshŭn, or for retŭrnĭng tǫ the batl; sŭeh fets,
oĭng tǫ hĕr grat siz, ănd gratĕr strĕnth, she
ăcŏmplĭsht wĭth ez ; ănd, ĭt ĭz sed, thăt sŭeh
wĕr hĕr delĭbĕrashŭns, thăt she wųd retŭrn
frŏm sŭeh sens ĭn the ŭtmost cŏmpoʂur.

Wĕl, Sĭlvĭà, hwăt dĭd yur mästĕr sa àbout
sŭeh ăs wąs dŭn bȳ yur mĭstrĕs ?

Sa ! hwȳ he neu hou păshŭnat she wąs. He
sa hĕr kĭk me ĭn the stŭmăc wŭn da sǫ bădlȳ,
thăt he ĭntĕrferd. I wąs nŏt gron ŭp, thĕn ; I
wås tǫ yung tǫ stănd sŭeh. He dĭdn't tĕl hĕr
sǫ hwĕn I wąs bȳ ; bŭt, I hăv hĕrd hĭm tĕl hĕr
hwĕn tha thŏt I wąs nŏt lĭstĕnĭng, thăt she wąs
tǫ sever—thăt sŭeh wŭrk wųd nŏt dǫ—she'd
kĭl me nĕxt.

Wĕl, dĭd hĭz remŏnstràtĭng wĭth hĕr mak hĕr
ĕnȳ bĕtĕr ?

Nŏt à bĭt ; mad hĕr wŭrs—jŭst pųt the dĕvĭl
ĭn hĕr. And thĕn, jŭs ăs sǫn ăs he wąs out ŏv

the wa, ĭf I wạṣ à lĭtl sạçy̆, or à lĭtl neglĕctfụl,
I'd cătẹh hĕl àgĕn.

Bŭt I fĭxt hĕr—I pad hĕr ŭp for ạl hĕr
spŭnk; I mad ŭp mȳ mind thăt hwĕn I grụ
ŭp I wụd dọ ĭt; ănd hwĕn I hăd à gọd ẹhánç,
hwĕn sŭm ŏv hĕr grănd cŭmpàny̆ wạṣ àrou̇nd,
I fĭxt hĕr.

Wĕl, hwăt dĭd yu dọ?

I nŏkt hĕr dou̇n, ănd blămd ner kĭld hĕr.

Wĕl; hwar ănd hou̇ dĭd thăt hăpĕn?

It hăpĕnd ĭn the bär-rọm; thar wạṣ sŭm
grănd foks stŏpĭng thar, ănd ṡhe wạntĕd thĭngṣ
tọ lọk prĕty̆ stȳlĭṡh; ănd sọ ṡhe sĕt me tọ scrŭb-
ĭng ŭp the bär-rọm. I fĕlt à lĭtl grŭm, ănd
dĭdn't dọ ĭt tọ sut hĕr; ṡhe scoldĕd me àbou̇t
ĭt, ănd I sạçt hĕr; ṡhe strŭk me wĭth hĕr hănd.
Thĭnk's I, ĭt's à gọd tĭm nou̇ tọ drĕs yu ou̇t,
ănd dămd ĭf I wŏn't dọ ĭt; I sĕt dou̇n mȳ tọlṣ,
änd sqwàrd for à fit. The fĭrst hwăk, I strŭk
hĕr à hĕl ŏy à blo wĭth mȳ fĭst. I dĭdn't nŏk
hĕr ĕntirly̆ thrụ the pănĕlṣ ŏv the dọr; bŭt hĕr
lándĭng àgănst the dor mad à tĕrĭbl smăṡh, ănd
I hŭrt hĕr so bădly̆ thăt ạl wĕr fritĕnd ou̇t ov
thar wĭts, ănd I dĭdn't no mȳsĕlf bŭt thăt I'd
kĭld the old dĕvĭl.

Wĕr thĕr ĕny̆ wŭn ĭn the bär-rọm, thĕn?

It waṣ ful ŏv foks ; sŭm ŏv thĕm wĕr Jĕrsȳ foks, họ wĕr goīng frŏm the Lak Cŭntrĭṣ hom, tọ vĭsĭt thar frĕndṣ ; sŭm wĕr drovĕrṣ, ŏn thar wa tọ the wĕst, ănd sŭm wĕr hŭntĕrṣ ănd botmĕn staīng à hwil tọ rĕst.

Hwạt dĭd tha dọ hwĕn tha sạ yu nŏk yur mĭstrĕs doun ?

Do! hwȳ, tha wĕr goīng tọ tak hĕr pärt, ŏv corṣ ; bŭt I jŭst săt doun the slŏp bŭkĕt ănd stratĕnd ŭp, ănd smăkt mȳ fĭsts ăt 'ĕm, ănd tŏld 'ĕm tọ wad ĭn, ĭf tha dard, ănd I'd thráśh ĕvĕrȳ dĕvĭl ŏv 'ĕm ; ănd thĕr waṣn't à dămd à wŭn thăt dard tọ cŭm.

Wĕl, hwăt nĕxt ?

Thĕn I gŏt out, ănd prĕtȳ qwĭk, tọ. I neu ĭt wụdn't dọ tọ sta thar ; so I wĕnt doun tọ Chenăng Point ; ănd thar wĕnt tọ wŭrk.

Hwar waṣ yur mästĕr, dŭrĭng thĭs fracŭs ?

He! he waṣ gŏn tọ tĕnd cort at Wilksbar. He waṣ à grănd-jŭry-màn, ănd hăd tọ be gŏn à gọd mĕnȳ daṣ. He ŏfĕn sĕrvd ăṣ grănd jurȳ-màn, ănd thĕn he waṣ àlwaṣ gŏn à wek or tụ. Thĭngṣ wụd hăv gŏn bĕtĕr ĭf he hăd bĭn hom.

Hwĕn he cam hom, hwạt dĭd he do ?

He sĕnt for me tọ cŭm băk.

Dĭd yu go ?

Ov cors, I dĭd, I hăd to go; I was á slav,
ănd ĭf I dĭdn't go, he wu̯d hăv brŏt me, ănd ĭn
á hŭrў, to; ĭn thos das, the mästĕrs mad the
nĭgĕrs mind; ănd hwĕn he spok, I neu I mŭst
oba.

Thĕm old mästĕrs, hwĕn tha gŏt măd, hăd
no mĕrcў on á nĭgĕr—tha'd cŭt á nĭgĕr a̯l ŭp
ĭn á hŭrў—cŭt 'ĕm a̯l ŭp ĭnto strĭngs, jŭst lev
the lif—thăt's a̯l; I'v sen 'ĕm do ĭt, mĕnў á
tim.

Wĕl, hwăt dĭd yu̯r mästĕr sa hwĕn yu cam
băk?

He dĭdn't sco̯ld me mŭeh; he told me thăt,
ăs mў mĭstrĕs ănd I gŏt álŏng so bădlў, ĭf I
wu̯d tak mў ehild ănd go to Neu Jĕrsў, ănd
sta thar, he wu̯d gĭv me fre; I told hĭm I wu̯d
go. It was lat ăt nit; he rot me á pás, gav ĭt
to me, ănd ĕrlў the nĕxt mornĭng I sĕt out for
Flăgtoun, N. J.

It sems thăt yu gŏt along wĭth yu̯r mästĕr
mŭeh bĕtĕr thăn yu dĭd wĭth yu̯r mĭstrĕs?

Yĕs; I gŏt álŏng wĭth hĭm, fĭrst rat; he
was á go̯d măn; ănd á grat măn, to; a̯l the
gränd foks lĭkt Mĭnĭcál Du̯bois. Hwĕn the
grat mĕn hăd thar metĭngs, Mĭnĭcál Du̯bois
was a̯lwas ĭnvitĕd to be wĭth 'ĕm; ănd he a̯lwas

wĕnt, to̱ ; he wa̱s áwa frŏm hom á grat del ; he hăd á grat del ŏv bĭs̱nĕs, ănd he wa̱s non a̱l ovĕr the cŭntrȳ. I likt mȳ mästĕr, ănd ĕvĕrȳ bŏdȳ likt hĭm.

He nĕvĕr whĭpt me ŭnlĕs he wa̱s s̱hur tẖăt I desĕrvĕd ĭt ; he u̱s̱d to̱ lĕt me go to̱ frŏlĭcs ănd ba̱ls, ănd to̱ hăv go̱d tims̱ áwa frŏm hom, wĭtẖ ŭtẖĕr blak foks, whĕnĕvĕr I wa̱ntĕd to̱ ; he wa̱s á go̱d măn ănd á go̱d mästĕr ; bŭt, hwĕn he told me I mŭst cŭm hom frŏm á ba̱l ăt á çĕrtĭn tim, hwĕn tẖe tim cam, tẖe jĭg wa̱s out—I neu I mŭst go ; ĭt wu̱dn't do̱ to̱ dĭs-ăpoint Mĭnĭcál Du̱bois.

Dĭd pärtĭs̱ ŏfĕn ŏcŭr?

Yĕs ; ănd I a̱lwas̱ wĕnt, to̱ ; Old Mĭnĭcál wu̱d a̱lwas̱ lĕt me go, becau̱s̱ I wa̱s á go̱d ne-grĕs̱, ănd a̱lwas trid to̱ ples̱ hĭm ; I hăd go̱d tims̱ hwĕn he wa̱s áround, ănd he a̱lwas̱ dŭn tẖĭng̱s̱ rit ; bŭt yu mŭstn't gĕt hĭm măd.

In tẖe lŏṉg nits ŏv wĭntĕr, we ŏfĕn hăd frŏl-ĭcs, a̱lmŏst ĕvĕrȳ wek ; we'd härdlȳ gĕt ŏvĕr wŭn frŏlĭç wĕn we'd begĭn to̱ fĭx for ánŭtẖĕr.

Tẖĕn tẖĕr wa̱s tẖē holĭdas̱—Crĭstmàs, ănd Neu Yĕr, ănd Estĕr, ănd tẖe Fortẖ ov Jŭlȳ, ănd Gĕnerál Tranĭng. Bŭt, tẖe bĭgĕst ŏv 'ĕm a̱l wa̱s̱ gĕnerál tranĭng. Tẖăt wa̱s̱ tẖe bĭgĕst da for the nĭgĕrs—I tĕl yu thăt wạs the bĭgĕst da. The nĭgĕrs wĕr ạl out tọ gĕnerȧl tranĭng —lĭtl ănd bĭg—old ănd yung; ănd thĕn tha'd hăv sŭm rŭm—ạlwas hăd rŭm ăt gĕnerȧl tranĭngs—ănd thĕn yu'd hĕr 'ĕm lȧf ȧ mil—ănd hwĕn tha gŏt ĭntọ ȧ fit, yu'd hĕr 'em yĕl mor thăn fiv milṣ.

Dĭd the nĭgĕrs yĕl hwĕn tha fạt?

The couȧrds dĭd—wŭrs than ĕnȳthĭng yu ĕvĕr hĕrd—wŭrs thăn ĕnȳthĭng bŭt ȧ couȧrdlȳ nĭgĕr.

Hwar dĭd yu hold yur frŏlĭcs?

Thĕr wạs ȧ grat mĕnȳ nĭgĕrs ȧround the nabŭrhọd ŏv Grat Bĕnd, ănd sŭmtims wĕ'd met ăt wŭn mästĕr'ṣ hous, ănd sŭmtims ăt ănŭthĕr'ṣ. We wạs shụr tọ hăv ȧ fĭdl, ănd ȧ frŏlĭk, ănd ȧ fĭrst rat tim; bŭt nŭn ŏv 'ĕm hăd ȧ bĕtĕr tim thăn mȳsĕlf—I likt frŏlĭçs. I cụd dȧnç ạl nit, ănd fel ăṣ jŏlȳ ăṣ ȧ wĭch ạl nĕxt da. I nĕvĕr tird ăt frŏlĭçs—nŏt I; nŏr ăt gĕnerȧl tranĭng, nethĕr.

Dĭd yu sa yur mästĕr uṣd tọ mak hiṣ on brăndȳ?

Yĕs; he ŏfĕn mad ĭt—ạlwas mad hĭs peeh brăndȳ; ĕnȳ wŭn căn mak peeh brăndȳ—the bĕst thăt wạs ĕvĕr drŭnk; yu jŭst bŭrn ȧbout

for pounds ŏv drid pĕehĕs ŭntĭl yu căn rŭb
thĕm tọ poudĕr ĭn yur hănds; yu mŭst bŭrn
'ĕm ĭn å pŏt thăt hăs å vĕrў̆ tĭt cŭvĕr ŏn. Thĕn
rŭb 'ĕm fin ĭn yur hănds; or, ĭf sŭm peçĕs är
tọ härd for thăt, pound thĕm fin wĭth å hămĕr.
Thĕn pụt thĭs poudĕr ŏv bŭrnt pĕehĕs ĭntọ å
bărĕl ŏv neu ăpl hwĭskў̆, ănd ĭn for wĕks, ĭf yu
shak the bărĕl ĕvĕry da, yu wĭl hăv å bărĕl ŏv
peeh brăndў̆ gọd ĕnŭf for ĕnў̆ bŏdў̆.

Yu mạk ăpl brăndў̆ ĭn almost the sam wa;
yu bŭrn åbout for pounds ŏv ăpls drid wĭth the
skĭns ŏn. Mak thĕm ĭntọ poudĕr, ănd pụt 'ĕm
ĭn å bărĕl ŏv neu ăpl hwĭskў̆, ănd shak the
bărĕl ĕvĕrў̆ da for for weks. In for weks, yu
hăv å bărĕl ŏv ăpl brăndў̆ bĕtĕr thăn ĕnў̆ yu
ĕvĕr sạ. A lĭtl ŏv thăt wĭl mak å fĕlo tạlk—
ănd wŏn't bŭrn his gŭts out, nĕthĕr. Foks
uṣd tŏ drĭnk brăndў̆ rit ålŏng—drănk ĭt ĕvĕrў̆
da—drănk å plĕntў̆ ŏv ĭt, ănd dĭdn't gĕt the
măn-å-poehe, nor the delĕrĭŭm trĕmĕns, nethĕr.
Hwȳ, the brăndў̆ uṣd tọ be gọd—tastĕd gọd,
ănd wạs plĕṣent tọ drĭnk; yu căn't gĕt nŭn
sŭeh nou—nŏt å bĭt ŏv ĭt. A drĭnk ŏv brăndў̆
nou, bŭrns lik fir—bŭrns ạl the wa doun—gọs
thrụ the gŭts wŭrs thăn å shet ŏv rĕd-hŏt sănd
păpĕr.

SILVIA A FRE NEGRES.

Hou dĭd yu go tọ Flăgtoun?

On fọt, tọ be shụr; I cam rit doun thrụ the Beẹh Wọds, ạl àlon, ĕxçĕptĭng mȳ yuṇg wŭn ĭn mȳ ärmṣ; sŭmtimṣ I dĭdn't se à pĕrsŭn for à háf à da; sŭmtimṣ I dĭdn't gĕt half enŭf tọ et, ănd nĕvĕr hăd ĕnȳ bĕd tọ slep ĭn; I jŭst slept ĕnȳhwar. Mȳ babȳ wạṣ ăbout à yer ănd à háf old, ănd I hăd tọ cărȳ ĭt ạl the wa. The wọd wạṣ fụl ŏv pănthĕrṣ, barṣ, wild-căts ănd wọlvṣ; I ŏfĕn sạ 'ĕm ĭn the datim, ănd ạlwaṣ hĕrd 'ĕm houlĭṇg ĭn the nit. O! thăt old pănthĕr—hwĕn he hould, ĭt mad the har stănd ŭp ạl ovĕr mȳ hĕd.

At Estŭn, I wĕnt on bord ov à ràft tọ go doun the Dĕláwar. A măn bȳ the nạm ŏv Brĭnk, hăd hĭṣ wif ănd fămĭlȳ ŏn bord ŏv à ràft, bound for Filádĕlĭfá; I wĕnt ŏn bord tọ hĕlp the wĭf, for mȳ păsaġ; tha wĕr niç foks, ănd I hăd à gọd tim; I lĕft the ràft nŏt fär

frŏm Trĕntŭn, bŭt I dọ nŏt no ĕxăctlў hwar—
thar wąs no toun ăt the plàç ăt hwїeh I gŏt ŏf
the ráft.

Thĕn I proçedĕd dirĕctlў tọ Flăgtoun, tọ se
mў mŭther; I dĭd nŏt fĭnd hĕr thar—she hăd
mọvd tọ Neu Brŭnswĭk. On mȳ wa, à măn
cąld tọ me, ăskĭng me, "Họs nĭgĕr är yu?"
I replid, I'm no măn'ş nĭgĕr—I belŏṉg̣ tọ Gŏd
—I belŏṉg tọ no măn.

He thĕn sĕd: Hwar är yu goĭṉg? I replid:
Thăt's nŭn ŏv yur bĭşnĕs—I'm fre; I go hwar
I pleş.

He cam towärd me; I săt doun mȳ yuṉg
wŭn, shod hĭm mȳ fĭst, ănd lọkt ăt hĭm; ănd I
gĕs he sạ t'wąs no us; he mozed ŏf, tĕlĭṉg me
thăt he wụd hăv me ărĕstĕd ăş sọn ăş he cụd
fĭnd à măg̣ĭstrat.

Yu se thăt ĭn thoş daş, the negroş wĕr ąl
slavs, ănd tha wĕr sĕnt nohwar, nŏr ăloud tọ
tọ go ĕnȳhwar wĭthout à pás; ănd hwĕn ĕnȳ-
wŭn mĕt à negro whọ wàs nŏt wĭth hĭş mästĕr, he hăd à rit tọ dĕmănd ŏv hĭm họş negro
he wąs; ănd ĭf the negro dĭd nŏt sho hĭş pás,
or dĭd nŏt g̣ĭv gọd ĕvidĕnç họş he wąs, he
wąs ărĕstĕd ăt wŭnş, ănd kĕpt ŭntĭl hĭş mästĕr cam for hĭm, pàd hwatĕvĕr ehärg̣ĕs wĕr

mad, ănd tọk hǐm àwa. Yu se, ǐn thọṣ daṣ, ĕnȳbŏdȳ hăd ạthŏrǐtȳ tọ ărĕst vagrànt negrọṣ. Tha gŏt pa for ărĕstǐng thĕm, ănd chärgd for thar kepǐng tǐl thar mästĕr redemd thĕm. Bŭt, he dǐdn't ărĕst me—nŏt à bǐt.

Hwĕn I gŏt tọ Neu Brŭnṣwǐk, I found mȳ mŭthĕr; sọn àftĕr, I wĕnt tọ wŭrk, ănd remànd ǐn Neu Brŭnṣwǐk sĕvĕràl yerṣ. Frŏm Neu Brŭnṣwǐk I wĕnt tọ Prǐnçtŭn tọ wŭrk for Victŏr Toulan. I remand ǐn hǐṣ fămǐlȳ ă lŏng hwil; I wŭrkt for hǐm hwĕn Paŭl Toulan waṣ à child; I wŭrkt thar hwĕn he waṣ born. Victŏr Toulan waṣ à grat măn, ănd à gọd măn; ănd he uṣd hǐṣ sĕrvànts wĕl; ănd Paul waṣ à niç boy, ănd Mădàm Toulan waṣ à gọd wụmàn; ănd I likt 'ĕm ạl, ănd ạl the sĕrvànts likt 'ĕm.

Aftĕr à lŏng hwil, I vǐsǐtĕd mȳ grăndfàthĕr, Hărȳ Cŭmptŭn, họ lǐvd ăt the forks ŏv the rod, ner thǐs plaç; he waṣ thĕn ăn old măn; tha sa he waṣ mor thăn à hŭndrĕd yerṣ old, ànd I gĕs he waṣ; bŭt he waṣ yĕt qwit ăctǐv; he wạntĕd me tọ sta wǐth hǐm ănd tak çar ŏv hǐm, ănd I stad; ănd ăt hǐṣ dĕth, I ǐnherǐtĕd hǐṣ prŏpĕrtȳ. I lǐvd ŏn the old homstĕd ŭntǐl à feu yerṣ àgo, hwĕn thĕm dămd dĕmocrăts set fir to mȳ hous, ănd bŭrnd ŭp mȳ hom and ạl thăt I hăd. Sīnç thăt tim, I hăv līvd ăt thĭs plaç, wĭth mȳ yuᶇgĕst dạtĕr.

Wĕl, Sīlvĭă, yu hăv līvd à lŏᶇg hwil, ănd hăv sŭfĕrd à grat mĕnȳ hărdshĭps, ănd, I expĕçt thăt y̆u är tird ŏv līvĭᶇg.

No, I ant; I'd lik to līv ănŭthĕr hŭndrĕd yers̰ y̆ĕt—ănd I dŏn't no bŭt I wĭl, to; mȳ teth är gọd, ănd ĭf I căn gĕt enŭf to et, I dŏn't no hwȳ I shụd di; thĕr's no us ĭn diᶇg—yu ant gọd for ĕnȳthĭᶇg áftĕr yu är dĕd.

Wĕl, Sīlvĭă, I ĕxpĕçt yu är wĕl ăqwantĕd wĭth thĭs mountĭn, ănd wĭth ạl the foks thăt līv on ĭt.

Yĕs, I no ĕvĕrȳ fọt ŏv it—ĕvĕrȳ hol ănd cornĕr ŏv ĭt; ĕvĕrȳ plaç hwar ĕnȳbŏdȳ līvs̰, or ĕvĕr hăs̰ līvd. And I no the foks, to; ạnd sŭm ŏv 'ĕm är prĕtȳ băd wŭns̰, to; ĭn făct, tha är ạl băd, ănd sŭm ŏv thĕm är wŭrs. Hwạt the dĕvĭl wĭl ĕvĕr dọ wĭth thĕm hwĕn he hăs̰ to tạk 'ĕm, I dŏn't no. Shurlȳ he dŏn't wạnt 'ĕm, ănd wụdn't hăv 'ĕm ĭf he cụd help ĭt. The onlȳ resụn thăt sŭm ŏv thĕs̰ foks ŭp her dŏn't di sonĕr thăn tha dọ ĭs̰, the dĕvĭl wŏn't hăv thĕm; He jŭst pụts ŏf tăken thĕm, becạs̰ he nos̰ hwạt à tim he'l hăv hwĕn he gĕts 'ĕm. Hwȳ! sŭm

ŏv thĕm är stärvd tọ dĕth lŏ̤ng enŭf befor tha
di; bŭt, tha căn't di—thĕr's no plaç for thĕm
tọ go tọ áftĕr tha är dĕd. Tha ȧn't fit tọ go tọ
hĕvĕn, ănd the dĕvĭl wŏn't hăv 'ĕm, ănd so tha
hăv tọ sta her. Hwȳ, thĭs mọuntĭn ĭs̤ wŭrs thăn
hĕl ĭtsĕlf; hwȳ, ĭf sŭm ŏv thes̤ foks don't behav bĕtĕr, áftĕr tha go ĭntọ the ĭnfĕrnȧl regṳ̆ng
thăn tha do hwil her, the dĕvĭl wĭl hăv ȧ tim ŏv
ĭt. He'l nĕvĕr mănȧġ 'ĕm; he'l ̇hăv tọ çạl ȧ
cŏngrĕs ănd hăv ăn ȧmĕndmĕnt fĭxt tọ the
cŏnstitushŭn. A brĭmston fir won't dọ; ĭt wĭl
nĕvĕr faz 'ĕm; ĭt don't her. I'v sen ĭt trĭd, ănd
ĭt don't dọ ăt ạl—onlȳ maks 'ĕm wŭrs.

Wĕl, Sĭlvĭȧ, yu tĕl ȧ prĕtȳ härd storȳ ȧbout
yur nabŭrs̤.

Tĕl ȧ härd storȳ! I tĕl the truṭh; ănd I cụd
tĕl mor ŏv ĭt; hwȳ, yu dont no 'ĕm; thĕr ĭs̤
mor foks kĭld ŭp her thăn ĕnȳbŏdȳ nos̤ ŏv; ănd
yu no sŭmbŏdȳ ĭs̤ kĭld ŭp her ĕvĕrȳ yer; ănd
nobŏdȳ ĭs̤ ĕvĕr hăṳgd for ĭt; ănd ĭt gĕts wŭrs
ănd wŭrs. If tha kĭl ĕnȳbŏdȳ ŭp her, tha jŭst
tak the mŭrdĕrĕrs̤ ŏf tọ Flĕmĭṳgtŭn ănd kĕp
'ĕm ĭn jal ȧhwil tĭl tha hăv ȧ triȧl, ănd then tha
tŭrn 'ĕm out tọ cŭm băk her, ănd thĕn tha är
wŭrs thăn tha wĕr befor; tha jŭst kĭl ĕnȳbŏdȳ
thĕn.

And tha stel! hwȳ, yu wŭd'nt belev hou mŭeh tha stel; tha don't stel mŭeh ŏv wŭn ănŭthĕr, becaṣ thăt wŭldn't do; if tha wĕr cat ăt thăt, tha'd gĕt kīld dămd son, ănd thĕn tha 'ant gŏt mŭeh to be stold. Bŭt tha go ŏf frŏm the mountĭn, doun īnto the vălīṣ, ănd thar tha stel ĕnȳthīng tha căn find—shĕp ănd ehĭckĕnṣ, ănd gran, ănd met, ănd clothṣ—ănd ĕnȳthīng ĕls thăt tha căn et or war; ănd, nobŏdȳ căn find ĕnȳthīng thăt hăṣ bĭn stolĕn bȳ the foks ŭp her, for, hwĕn ĕnȳthīng īṣ to be stolĕn, tha al no ábout ĭt, ănd tha al lȳ for eeh ŭthĕr, ănd tha al no hwar ĭt iṣ to be hĭd, ănd tha al hĕlp to kep foks frọm findīng ĭt; so ĭt dŭṣ no gọd to hŭnt ŭp her for stolĕn gọdṣ. And thĕn tha no so dămd wĕl hou to hid thĭngṣ, to; tha don't hid hwạt tha stel, ĭn thar houṣĕṣ, ŭntĭl al the houṣĕṣ hăv bĭn sĕreht; hwĕn tha stel ĕnȳthīng tha hid ĭt ĭn sŭm hol thăt nobŏdȳ bŭt mountĭnĕrṣ no ŏv; or ĕls ŭndĕr sŭm rŏks, or ŭndĕr sŭm wọd, hwar nobŏdȳ bŭt the mountĭnĕrṣ wụd thĭnk ŏv lọkĭng. Thăt īṣ the wa tha do bĭṣnĕs ŭp her; ănd īf yu tĕl 'em ŏv ĭt, tha'l kĭl yu—dămd īf tha won't.

And Sīlvĭä, yu hăv līvd rit her, ĭn the mĭdst

ŏv thĕm for fĭftȳ yers̱ wĭthout fa̤lĭṉg ĭnto̤ thar was̱?

Yĕs; ănd lŏṉgĕr to̤. I no 'ĕm; I'v bĭn to̤ 'ĕm—bŭt tha hăv nĕvĕr trŭbld me mŭch—tha no ĭt wụd'nt do̤; tha no I'd gĭv 'ĕm thăt.

(So saĭṉg, she brŏt hĕr rit fĭst ĭnto̤ hĕr lĕft hănd ŭntĭl the smăk cụd be hĕrd fĭfty yärds̱.)

Wĕl, Sĭlvĭȧ, hwa̤t do̤ yu thĭnk ŏt to̤ be dŭn wĭth thĕs̱ băd foks?

Ot to̤ be dŭn wĭth 'ĕm? Hwȳ, sŭm ŏv 'ĕm ŏt to̤ be hăṉgd rit ŭp bȳ the nĕk; ănd sŭm ŏv 'ĕm ŏt to̤ be tid ŭp ănd lĭkt nerlȳ to̤ dĕth—tid rit ŭp to̤ ȧ post ănd lĭkt tĭl wĭthĭn ăn ĭnch ŏv the lif. Thăt's hwa̤t ŏt to̤ be dŭn wĭth 'ĕm—thăt's the wa I'd sĕrv 'ĕm. I'd tak 'ĕm ŭp to̤ Flĕmĭṉgtŭn, ănd lĭk 'ĕm tĭl tha'd nĕvĕr wa̤nt to̤ be lĭkt ȧgĕn.

Hăv yu ĕvĕr bĭn to̤ Flĕmĭṉgtŭn, Sĭlvĭȧ?

Bĭn hwar?

Bĭn to̤ Flĕmĭṉgtŭn?

Bĭn to̤ thăt dămd Flĕmĭṉgtŭn?—yĕs, I'v bĭn thar; ănd ĭt ĭs̱ the dămdĕst plaç ĭn the wŭrld.

Hwȳ, Sĭlvĭȧ, hwa̤t hăv yu ȧgĕnst Flĕmĭṉgtŭn?

I'v gŏt enŭf ȧgĕnst ĭt. Yu căn't gĕt ĕnȳthĭṉg thar wĭthout mŭnȳ; nobŏdȳ ĭs̱ cŏnsĭd-

ĕrd ĕnȳthȋng thar ŭnlĕs he hăs mŭnȳ ; nobŏdȳ
wĭl tĕl yu ĕnȳthȋng thar ŭnlĕs yu gȋv 'ĕm
mŭnȳ ; ȋf yu ȧsk ȧ la̤yĕr ĕnȳthȋng, he won't
tĕl yu ȧ bȋt ŭntȋl he gĕts yur mŭnȳ.   Yu căn't
gĕt jŭstȋc thar ŭnlĕs yu hăv sŭm mŭnȳ ; ănd
yu căn't gĕt ȋt thĕn—beca̤s, ȋf ănŭthĕr pĕrsŭn
hăs mor mŭnȳ thăn yu hăv, tha'l a̤l ŏv 'ĕm—
ĕvĕrȳ dămd la̤yĕr, the jŭdg, ănd the jury, go
for hȋm, ănd ȧ po̤r bŏdȳ hăs no sho ăt a̤l. I no
ĕm—I'v bȋn to̤ 'ĕm—thar ȧ băd sĕt.

Hăv yu bȋn to̤ the la̤yĕrs ăt Flĕmȋngtŭn,
Sȋlvȋȧ ?

Yes, I hăv—bŭt, ȋt dȋdn't do̤ ĕnȳ go̤d ; thes
dămd S——'s hăv bȋn trȳȋng to̤ gĕt mȳ prŏpĕrtȳ ȧwa frŏm me for mĕnȳ yers, ănd I wa̤ntĕd
to̤ cŏnsŭlt ȧ la̤yĕr to̤ gĕt hȋm to̤ pṳt thes dĕvȋls
thrṳ ; bŭt I cṳdn't ; nŏt ȧ dămd ȧ la̤yĕr wṳd tak
mȳ cas, bĕca̤s I hăd no mŭnȳ ; thă sĕd tha cṳd
nŏt ta̤lk wȋthout mŭnȳ ; tha cṳdn't do̤ ĕnȳthȋng for me ŭnlĕs I pad 'ĕm sŭm mŭnȳ.

Hwȳ dȋdn't yu pa thĕm sŭm mŭnȳ ?

Pa 'ĕm ! I cṳdn't—I hădn't ȧ cĕnt to̤ mȳ
nam.

Wĕl, Sȋlvȋȧ, hou dȋd yu fel hwĕn tha told yu
thăt tha cṳd do̤ nŭthȋng for yu wȋthout yu
gav thĕm sŭm mŭnȳ ?

Fel! I fĕlt lik kĭkĭng thar dămd trips out. Tha think tha är so dămd bĭg becas tha är drĕst ŭp a lĭtl; ănd tha är to dămd proud to be decĕnt. If tha'd cŭm over ŏn the mountĭn we'd sho 'ĕm; we'd skĭn ĕvĕrў dĕvĭl ŏv 'em —I'd do ĭt mўsĕlf, ăs old ăs I ăm. I'd jŭst lik to put mў fĭst agĕnst thar ўs (eyes).

(So saĭng, she brŏt the fĭst agĕnst the hănd, ŭntĭl ĭt smăkt aloud.)

War yu ĕvĕr ăt Flĕmĭngtŭn hwĕn yu wĕr nŏt cŏnsŭltĭng layĕrs?

Yĕs, ŏ fĕn. I usd to go hwĕnĕvĕr thĕr was ĕnў doĭngs thar; hwĕnĕvĕr thĕr was gĕnĕrăl tranĭng, ănd hwĕnĕvĕr the bĭg mĕn hăd thar mĕtĭngs thar. Al the nĭgĕrs usd to go to Flĕmĭngtŭn ŏn thos bĭg das; ănd thĕn thad gĕt lĭkt—god Gŏd, hou thad gĕt lĭkt! Hwў, thad ti'm rit ŭp ănd lĭck'm to dĕth—cŭt 'ĕm ĭnto pecĕs—cŭt 'ĕm al ĭnto strĭngs.

Dĭd yu ĕvĕr se thĕm hwĭp the negros?

Se 'ĕm! yĕs, I hăv; se 'ĕm lĭk a dŭzĕn ŏv 'ĕm ăt a tim. Ti 'ĕm rit ŭp to a post, ănd gĭv 'ĕm hĕl, rit ŏn the bar-băk—fĕteh the blod ĕvĕrў tim; ănd tha'd hŏlĕr! God Gŏd! tha'd houl tĭl yu cud her 'ĕm a mil; ănd thĕn, hwĕn tha hăd cŭt the băk al ĭn slĭts, tha'd put salt

ĭn the găshĕs ; ănd thĕn tha'd houl, Lord Gŏd!
no pănthĕr ĭn the bĕeh wǫds ĕvĕr mad hálf so
mŭeh noiṣ.

Thăt's the wa tha fĭxt the nĭgĕr ĭn old timṣ,
thĕm dămd Flĕmĭngtŏnĕrṣ—tha thĭnk tha är
so dămd bĭg.

Hwǫt dĭd the negroṣ dǫ, thăt tha hwĭpt thĕm
so bădlў ?

Hwȳ, ŏv cǫrs tha'd gĕt sŭm hwĭskў, ănd thĕn
tha'd gĕt ĭntǫ á kĭntў-koy, ănd mak ă noiṣ pĕrhăps; tha'd gĕt ĭntǫ á rou or á fit, ănd thĕn sŭmbŏdў wǫd gĕt hŭrt ; ănd thĕn the wŭn thăt
gŏt hŭrt wǫd cŏmplan tǫ the athŏritĭṣ, ănd
thĕn the cŏnstáblṣ wǫd be áftĕr the nĭgĕrṣ ;—
and hwĕn tha cǫt'm tha'd ti 'ĕm rit ŭp wĭthout
jŭdg or jǫrў, ănd pǫl ŏf the shĭrt, ănd pǫt ĭt
rit ŏn the bar hid.   Mȳ Gŏd, hou tha'd lĭk 'ĕm
—cŭt the hid ạl ĭn găshĕs.

That's the wa tha uṣd tǫ fĭx the old slavṣ ;
gĭy 'ĕm á hŏlidá tǫ hăv á lĭtl sport, ănd thĕn
ĭf tha hád ĕnў fŭn, lĭk 'ĕm tĭl tha'd hăv á sor
băk tĭl the nĕxt hŏlida cŭm.

Wĕl, Sĭlvĭa, wǫd tha wạnt tǫ go tǫ the nĕxt
hŏlidá ?

Yes, the nĭgĕrṣ ạlwaṣ wạntĕd tǫ go, băk sor
or wĕl ; nĕvĕr neu wŭn tǫ mĭs hwĕn hĭṣ mästĕr

told hĭm he cŭd go.   Thĕn he'd be shur to gĕt
lĭkt wŭrs thăn he was befor; becas sŭm nĭgĕrs
cŭdn't hăv á hŏlidá wĭthout gĕtĭng ĭnto á fit,
thĕn he'd be shur to gĕt tid ŭp ănd lĭkt.

Durĭng the tim Sĭlvĭá was ănsĕrĭng the lást
few qwĕstyŭns, she becam so ĕxcĭtĕd, so ĕloqwĕnt ĭn hĕr own wa, ănd so ĭndŭlgĕnt ĭn hĕr
profan ĕpithĕts, thăt I ferd thăt I wud nŏt be
ábl to tak doun al thăt she sĕd, nŏr be ábl to
fĭt ŭp for the prĕs hwat I dĭd tak doun.   Inded, hwĕn she begăn to tĕl ăbout the tretmĕnt
ŏv the negros durĭng the das ŏv slavĕrў, she
ăt wŭns wăxt ĕloqwĕnt, ănd son becam so ve-
hemĕnt, thăt I dĭd nŏt no hwĕthĕr ĭt was wis
to prŏsecut mў ĭnqwirўs ĕnў fŭrthĕr ĭn thĭs dirĕcshŭn.   At almost the fĭrst qwĕstyŭn, I thŏt
I smĕlt the fŭms ŏv brĭmston; ănd ăs we procedĕd, the sulfŭrŭs odŭr becam so strŏng, thăt
I ferd thăt bў hĕr pouĕrful gĕstĭculáshŭn ănd
the pels ŏv hĕr tĕrĭfĭc lăngwaġ, she hăd rĕnt
the crŭst ŏv the erth sŭmhwĕr ner hwar she
săt, ănd the fums frŏm the ĭnfĕrnál regŭns wĕr
ăscĕndĭng thru the fĭshŭr ĭnto the ápártmĕnt
ĭn hwĭch we săt.   Inded, the ătmŏsfer was dĕ-
cĭdĕdlў chokў, ănd I shud hăv áskt for á bĕtĕr

vĕntĭlashŭn, bŭt for the făct thăt, hwĭehĕvĕr
wa I lǫkt, the opĕn spaçĕs betwen the lŏg̣s áloud
me tǫ se the swaĭng fŏrĕst treṣ, ănd gav the
perçĭng wĭnd á fre cŭrĕnt tǫ mȳ ehĭlȳ băk ănd
tǫ mȳ ehĭliĕr erṣ.

Reflĕctĭng thăt thĭs, thĕn, năturálȳ wŭd be
á lĭtl ĕxçitĭng tǫ ăn old slav, I cŏncluḍĕd tǫ
rŭn the rĭsk ŏv the swĭng ŏv hĕr bĭg fĭst, ănd
the ĭncresĭng ehŏkȳnĕs ŏv the sŭlfŭrŭs ătmŏsfer, ănd proçedĕd ăṣ folos :

Wĕr yu ăt Flĕmĭngtŭn hwĕn the lĭtl negro
waṣ hăng̣d for mŭrdĕrĭng hĭṣ mĭstrĕs?

Yĕs ; ănd thăt waṣ the dămdĕst tim I ĕvĕr
sạ. The nĭgĕrṣ qwärĕld ănd fout, ănd poundĕd
eeh ŭthĕr, ănd bĭt eeh ŭthĕrṣ erṣ ŏf; ănd thĕn
poundĕd eeh ŭthĕrṣ nosĕṣ doun, bŭngd eeh
ŭthĕrṣ ȳṣ (eyes) ănd sŭm gŏt blamd ner kĭld.
And thĕn thĕm dămd Flĕmĭngtŏnĕrṣ gŏt áftĕr
'ĕm, ănd tha tid 'ĕm ŭp, ănd lĭkt 'ĕm wĭthout
mĕrcȳ—cut 'ĕm ạl ŭp—cŭt 'ĕm ạl ĭn strĭngṣ ;
jŭst lĕft the lif—no mor.

Thăt waṣ á grat tim, I'l nĕvĕr forgĕt thăt.

Wĕl, Sĭlvĭá, dĭd the negroṣ nŏt desĕrv tǫ be
hwĭpt sŭmtĭmṣ?

Yĕṣ, sŭmtĭmṣ—mŏst ạlwaṣ, I ĕxpĕct. Tha

hăd tọ līk 'ĕm, thĕr wạs no ŭthĕr wa ; tha hăd
tọ mak 'ĕm mind ; the nīgĕrṣ thăt behavd wĕl
nĕvĕr gŏt līkt ; bŭt sŭm wụdn't behav ; tha'd
ạlwaṣ gĕt īntọ à rou, or stel sŭmthĭng, ănd
thĕn tha'd be shŭr tọ gĕt līkt.

Sīlvĭå, tha sa thăt yu är vĕrў old, ovĕr à
hŭndrĕd yerṣ old—dọ yu no hou old yu är ?

Nŏt ĕxăctlў—căn't tĕl exăctlў ; tha dĭdn't
uṣd tọ kep à rĕcŭrd ŏv the bĭrth ŏv nīgĕrṣ ;
tha hardlў kĕpt à rĕcŭrd ŏv the bĭrth ŏv hwit
chĭldrĕn ; nŭn bŭt the grănd foks kept à rĕcŭrd
ŏv the bĭrth ŏv thar chĭldrĕn—tha dĭd'nt no
mor kep the dat ŏv à yŭng nīgĕr, thăn tha dĭd
ŏv à cálf or à colt ; the yŭng nīgĕrṣ' wĕr born
īn the Fạl or īn the Sprĭng, īn the Sŭmĕr or īn
the Wīntĕr ; īn căbaġ tim, or hwĕn chĕrĭṣ wĕr
rip ; hwĕn tha wĕr plăntĭng corn, or hwĕn tha
wĕr hŭskĭng corn ; ănd thăt's ạl the wa tha
tạkt about à nīgĕr'ṣ aġ.

Bŭt, Sīlvĭå, īṣ thĕr no wa tọ'tĕl àprŏxĭmatlў
hwĕn yu wĕr born ?

Tọ be shur thĕr īṣ ; ănd thăt's hwạt maks
foks sa thăt I, ăm à hŭndrĕd ănd fīftĕn yerṣ
old. Tha tĕl thĭs bў the rĕcŭrd ŏv the bĭrth
ŏv Rīchàrd Cŭmptŭn. Mў mŭthĕr ănd mĕnў
ŭthĕr old foks, uṣd tọ tĕl me thăt, hwĕn ˌmў

mŭthĕr was a slav to Rĭehárd Cŭmptŭn, thĕr
was born to hĭm a sŭn, hom tha cąld Rĭehárd, áftĕr hĭs fąthĕr. Hwĕn thĭs sŭn Rĭehárd
was tu das old, I was born; so thĕr ĭs bŭt tu
das dĭfĕrĕnç betwen the dat ŏv Rĭehárd Cŭmptŭn's bĭrth ănd mȳ bĭrth.

In ăn old Bĭbl hwĭeh ĭs nou ĭn pŏsĕshŭn ŏv
Mr. Rĭehárd Gomo, ho lĭvs ner Rŏk Mĭls, ĭs
the rĕcŭrd ŏv the Cŭmptŭn fămĭlȳ. Bȳ refĕr-
ĭng to thĭs rĕcŭrd tha tĕl hou old I ăm. Bŭt
I do nŏt no hou old I ăm—I căn't red; bŭt I
ĕxpĕct tha tĕl me rit. I no thăt I ăm oldĕr
thăn ĕnȳbŏdȳ ĕls ăround her—oldĕr thăn thar
parĕnts wĕr; ănd ĭn most casĕs, I neu thar
grat-grănd parĕnts.

I remĕmbĕr thăt hwil we wĕr smąl ehĭldrĕn,
I ănd Rĭehárd Cŭmptŭn wĕr ábout ŏv a siz,
ănd thăt we usd to pla togĕthĕr. Mȳ mŭthĕr
ănd hĭs mŭthĕr usd to tĕl me thăt we both
nŭrst the sam brĕst, ăltĕrnatlȳ, the sam da;
ąs we wĕr so ner the sam ag, hwĕn hĭs mŭthĕr
wĭsht to go áwă to vĭsĭt, or ŭpŏn bĭsnĕs, Rĭehárd was lĕft ĭn the car ŏv mȳ mŭthĕr; ánd
whil hĭs mŭthĕr was áwa, he usd to nŭrs mȳ
mŭthĕr wĭth me. Wŭns, Mrs. Cŭmptŭn ănd
wŭn ŏv the nabors was gŏn to the cĭtȳ a hol

wek; ănd hwil gŏn, Rīehård waṣ lĕft ĭn ehårġ
ŏv mȳ mŭthĕr.   Thĕn ŝhe uṣd tọ tak ŭṣ
boŧh ŭpŏn hĕr lăp, ănd hwil he waṣ nŭrsĭng
wŭn brĕst, I waṣ nŭrsĭng ŧhe ŭŧhĕr.   Tha uṣd
tọ sa thăt thĭs waṣ ŧhe reṣŏn Rīehård ănd I
gŏt ålŏng so wĕl togĕŧhĕr.   As lŏngăs he lĭvd,
he álwaṣ clamd tọ be åbout mȳ aġ, ănd we ål-
waṣ vĭsĭtĕd, ănd we uṣd tọ tak ovĕr ŧhe cĭr-
cŭmstånç thăt we uṣd tọ be togĕŧher hwĕn we
wĕr babĭṣ, ånd hwĕn we wĕr ehĭldrĕn, ănd
thĭt we hĭd ạlwaṣ vĭsĭtĕd, ånd ạlwaṣ ĭntĕndĕd
tọ vĭsĭt.

A grat mĕnȳ old foks uṣd tọ tĕl me that ŧha
hăd seu me nŭrs mȳ mŭthĕr ăt ŧhe sam tim
thăt Rīehård Cŭmptŭn waṣ nŭrsĭng hĕr, ănd
thăt he ănd I wĕr åbout ŧhe sam ĭn aġ.   Aṣ
we lĭvd ăt å tăvĕrn, I ĕxpĕt foks sạ ŭs mor,
ănd thăt mor foks notĭçt ŭṣ ŧhăn wụd hăv dŭn
so, ĭn å lĕṣ pŭblĭc plaç.

Tọ vĕrifȳ ŧhe stătmĕnts åbŭv mad, rĕspĕctĭng Sĭlvĭa'ṣ aġ, I vĭsĭtĕd Mr. Gomo to cŏnsŭlt
ŧhe ånsĥĕnt rĕcŭrd ŏv ŧhe Cŭmptŭn fămilȳ.   I
sọn lĕrnĕd thăt Mrs. Gomo waṣ å neç ŏv Rīehård Cŭmptŭn; thăt ŝhe waṣ ŧhe dạtĕr ŏv Rīehård Cŭmptŭn's sĭstĕr Dĕbọrå, họ waṣ born

Jăn. 5th, 1793. Thĭs lădў, Dĕborȧ Cŭmptŭn, hăd mărĭd Vănlīeu, bȳ hom she hăd Mrs. Gomo. Aftĕr Vȧnlīeu's dĕth, she mărĭd D. Dănbŭrў. Aftĕr Dănbŭrў's dĕth, she lĭvd wĭth hĕr dạtĕr, Mrs. Gomo, tọ họm she uṣd tọ tĕl thăt hĕr brŏthĕr Rĭehȧrd, ănd Sĭlvĭȧ Dŭboịs, wĕr ȧbout ŏv ăn aġ. Mrs. Gomo, now ăn ŏld ladў, ĭnformṣ me, thăt sĕvĕrȧl old foks uṣed tọ tĕl hĕr hwĕn ȧ gĭrl, thăt hĕr Uncl Rĭehȧrd ănd Sĭlvĭȧ Dubois, wĕr ȧbout ŏv the sam aġ; thăt tha hăd sen both Rĭehȧrd ȧnd Sĭlvĭȧ nŭrs the sam mŭthĕr ăt the sam tim; ănd thăt her Uncl Rĭehȧrd uṣd tọ tĕl thăt hĭṣ mŭthĕr uṣd tọ sa thăt he wạṣ tụ daṣ oldĕr thăn Sĭlvĭȧ.

It hăpĕnĕd thăt the old Bĭbl ĭn the possĕshŭn ŏv Mrs. Gomo, dĭd nŏt cŏntan ȧ fụl rĕcŭrd ŏv the Cŭmptŭn fămilў; thăt thĕ rĕcŭrd her mad datĕd no färthĕr băk thăn the bĭrth ŏv Dĕborȧ Cŭmptŭn, hwĭeh ŏccŭrd ăṣ ȧbŭv statĕd, Jăn. 5th, 1793; bŭt, Mrs. Gomo ĭnfŏrmd me thăt the old Bĭbl, hăvĭng the anshĕnt recŭrd for hwĭeh I wạṣ sĕrehĭng, wạṣ ĭn pŏsĕsshŭn ŏv hĕr dạtĕr, Mrs. Jŏn Elbĕrtsŏn, lĭvĭng ȧbout tụ mils est ŏv Rŏk Mĭlṣ. Upŏn vĭsĭtĭng Mrs. Elbĕrtsŏn, ănd statĭng the pŭrpos ŏv mȳ vĭsĭt, she kĭndlў prŏdụçt the old

bǫk, ănd wĕlcŭmd me tǫ the hŏspitălitĭs̲ ŏv hĕr
cŭmfortàbl hom.   In thĭs rĕcŭrd, I found,
àmŭn̲g ŭthĕrs̲, the fŏlo-wĭn̲g statmĕnt : Rĭehárd
àrd Cŭmptŭn born Märeh 3d, A. D., 1768 ;
Dĕborá Cŭmptŭn, born Jăn. 5th, A. D., 1793 ;
Hĕnç, we lĕrn thăt, wĕr Rĭehárd Cŭmptŭn stĭl
lĭvĭn̲g, hĕ wu̲d be a̲lmost 115 yers̲ old.   Thĕn,
ĭf tradĭshŭn ĭs̲ tru̲, ănd, ĭn thĭs căs ĭt is̲ cŏrŏb-
ŏrated ĭn so mĕnў was̲ thăt I cănnŏt doubt ĭt,
Sĭlvĭá Dubois wĭl be 115 yers̲ old ŭpŏn the
5th da ŏv Märeh, 1883.

Sĭlvĭá ĭs̲ ĭn gǫd hĕlth, ănd ĭn gǫd cŏndĭshŭn
ŏv mind.   Hĕr mĕmorў ĭs̲ ĕxçĕlĕnt ; ănd she
ĭs̲ ăs̲ mueh ĭntĕrĕstĕd ĭn the àfars̲ ŏv lĭf ăs̲ ĭs̲
the mŏst ŏv pĕpl ăt thĭrtў-fiv.   She lǫks ăs̲ ĭf
she mit lĭv mĕnў yers̲ yĕt.

Untǫ Sĭlvĭá hăv bĭn born sĭx ehĭldrĕn :
Mŏsĕs̲, Judĭth, Chärlŏt, Dorcŭs, Elĭzábĕth ănd
Raehĕl.   Raehĕl lĭvs̲ ĭn Prĭnçtŭn.   Lĭzĭ ons̲,
ănd resĭds̲ ŭpŏn the lŏt dĕscrĭbd ĭn this ärtĭcl.
Wĭth hĕr, nou lĭvs̲ hĕr agĕd mŭthĕr.   She ĭs̲
á lärg ănd stout wǫmán, ănd lǫks ăs̲ ĭf she
mit lĭv tǫ be ăs̲ old ăs̲ hĕr mŭthĕr.   She ĭs̲ wĕl
prŏpŏrshŭnd ănd vĕrў ăctĭv.   It ĭs̲ sĕd thăt ĭt
ĭs̲ nŏt esў tǫ find evĕn àmŭng the "bulĭs̲," á
măn thăt ĭs̲ á măteh for hĕr, ĭn á hănd tǫ hănd

cŏnflĭct, or ĭn a fĭst fit. Pĕrhăps she ĭs ăs
ner lĭk her mŭthĕr, ĭn bĭld, prouĕs ănd ĕndur-
ânç, ăs a datĕr căn be ; she sems mĭld, cŏmpla-
çĕnt ănd cŭrteŭs. Bŭt, rumŭr ses thăt she hăs
takĕn pärt ĭn mĕnў a priz fit ; thăt she hăs
nĕvĕr bĭn pärticulár hwĕthĕr the chămpeŏn ho
was to met hĕr was mal or femal ; ănd thăt
she hăs sĕldŭm, ĭf ĕvĕr, cŭm out ŏv thĕ cŏntĕst
sĕcŭnd bĕst. It ĭs also told thăt she hăs sŭmtims gŏn a lŏng dĭstànç to met the chămpeŏn
ho dard to chălĕng hĕr, or to prevok hĕr ir.

Lĭzĭ Dubois ĭs fär famed ăs a fŏrtun tĕl-
lĕr. To her hĕr dĕscănt ŭpŏn the evĕnts ŏv
hĭs lif, mĕnў a yŭng fĕlo wĕnds hĭs wa to the
hŭmbl hŭt ŏv thĭs sabl ladў, ănd, elated wĭth
the ĭnformashŭn gand, drŏps hĭs peç ŏv sĭlvĕr
ĭnto Lĭzĭ's hănd, hăsts àwa to wătch secrĕtlў,
the ŭnfoldĭng ŏv ĕvĕrў mĭstĕrў. Nor ĭs hĕr
stŏck ŏv lor bärĕn ŏv wĭcherў. Frŏm àfär,
the vŏterĭs ŏv wĭchcráft go to Lĭzĭ ĭn qwĕst
ŏv nŏlĕg rĕspĕctĭng stolĕn gods, ănd ŭthĕr
thĭngs thăt är sŭposd to be non onlў to thos
ho är ĭn cŏmŭnĭcashŭn wĭth the spĭrĭts ŏv the
nĕthĕr àbods.

Lĭzi ĭs about 78 yers ŏv àg ; bŭt she ĭs so

wĕl prĕsĕrvd thăt she wụd pás for á negrĕs ŏv 40. Hĕr chăncĕs tọ lĭv tọ be 120 yers̱ old, är vĕrў gọd.

Sĭlvĭá, yu hăv ăn ŭnusụálў strŏng fram, ănd yu hăv lĭvd tọ ăn ĕxcẹdĭnglў grat aġ; yu mŭst hăv bĭn vĕrў prŏpĕrlў fĕd in chĭdhụd, or ĕls thĕs̱ thĭngs̱ cụd nŏt be. Upŏn hwạt dĭd tha us̱ tọ fed yu, thăt yu hăv grŏn so lärġ ănd so strŏng?

Tha găv us̱ Indĭàn dŭmplĭngs̱, sămp, pŏraġ, corn-brĕd, potatos̱, pŏrk, bef, mŭsh ănd mĭlk, ănd nĭgĕr bŭtĕr; ănd we dĭd'nt gĕt á bĕlў-fụl ŏv thes̱, sŭmtims̱—I'v ŏfĕn gŏn tọ bĕd hŭngrў, bŭt, 'twas̱ no us̱ tọ cŏmplan;—yu hăd yur masụr ănd yu gŏt no mor. Thăt's the wa tha fĕd yŭng nĭgĕrs̱, ĭn old tims̱, bŭt tha mad 'ĕm gro.

Tĕl me hou the dŭmplĭngs̱, pŏraġ, corn-brĕd ănd nĭgĕr bŭtĕr wĕr mad.

Tọ mak ĭndĭàn dŭmplĭngs̱, scạld the ĭndĭàn mel, wŭrk ĭt ĭntọ á bạl, ănd thĕn boil ŭntĭl dŭn, ĭn the lĭqọr thăt met—pork or bef—hăs̱ bĭn boild ĭn. Thes̱ wĕr etĕn wĭthout ĕnў dĭp, bŭtĕr or sạc.

Tọ mak sămp pŏraġ: Boil ĕqwàl pärts ŏv

bef ănd pork togĕthĕr, ŭntĭl dŭn; remŏv the
met ănd stĭr intọ the lĭqŏı ĭn hwĭeh thĕ met
wạs boild, cors ĭndĭản mel, ănd boil tĭl dŭn.

Corn-Brĕd wạs mad bȳ mĭxĭ͟ng eqwàl masurṣ
ŏv ĭndĭản mel ănd rȳ mel togĕthĕr, ănd bakĭ͟ng
ĭn ăn ovĕn.

Nĭgĕr bŭtĕr wạs mad bȳ mĭxĭ͟ng tụ pärts ŏv
lärd wĭth wŭn pärt ŏv molăsĕṣ.

Thĭs nĭgĕr bŭtĕr wạs hwạt we hăd tọ ŭṣ on
our brĕd; ănd we dĭd wĕl ĭf we dĭd'nt hăv tọ
sprĕd ĭt duçĕd thĭn. The brĕd wạs so härd
thăt ĭt nedĕd gresĭ͟ng; ănd thĭs wạs ạl thăt we
hăd tọ gres ĭt wĭth—we hăd no gravȳ.

We uṣd tọ hăv piṣ ŏcaṣyŭnàlȳ. Sŭmtimṣ tha
wɛr mad out ŏv swet ăplṣ; sŭmtimṣ out ŏv
sour wŭnṣ, wĭthout ɛnȳ shụgàr ŏr molăsɛṣ;
dĭd'nt fed nĭgɛrṣ shụgàr ănd molăsɛṣ mŭeh ĭn
thoṣ daṣ; the hwit foks dĭd'nt gɛť mŭeh ŏv
'ɛm—thar piṣ wɛr ạlmost ăṣ sour ăṣ ourṣ; ănd
thɛr wạṣ vɛrȳ lĭtl shụgàr ĭn thar cŏfe, ănd the
shụgàr thăt tha uṣd wạṣ ăṣ blăk ăṣ mȳ hid.

We nɛvɛr drănk cŏfe or te. Sŭmtimṣ we
gŏt sŭm çidàr. The hwit foks onlȳ drănk te
ănd cŏfe ŏn Sŭnda, or hwɛn tha hăd cŭmpànȳ.

Tha usd to boil, or rost our potatos, wĭth the skĭns ŏn, ånd thĕn wĕ dĭd'nt tak the skĭns ŏf, we at 'ĕm skĭns ănd al. And the hwit foks at thar's jŭst so; bŭt tha hăd gravў, or bŭtĕr, to put ŏn thar's. The hwit foks dĭd'nt et hwet brĕd onlў ŏn Sŭnda, or hwĕn tha hăd cŭmpånў. Tha ăt rў brĕd; tha dĭd'nt cŭltĭvat mŭeh hwet, 'twud'nt gro; nĕvĕr hăd mor thăn enŭf to mak pi-crŭst ănd caks, out ŏv. Tha at å grat del ŏv mŭsh ănd sămp pŏrag, ănd ĭndĭán caks, ănd thes wĕr god enŭf ĭf yu hăd å plĕntў ŏv god mĭlk ănd bŭtĕr, and gravy to et wĭth 'ĕm.

I ĕxpĕct foks nou-å- das, thĭnk thăt thĭs was hărd far, bŭt 'twas god enŭf—hwĕn we hăd enŭf ŏv ĭt; bŭt sŭmtims we dĭd'nt gĕt å bĕlў-ful—thăt wĕnt å lĭtl härd. If the foks nou-å-das wud lĭv ăs we usd to, tha'd be ă god del strŏngĕr, mor hĕlthў, ănd wuld'nt di so son. Tha et so mĕnў dantĭs; to mŭeh shugår, to mĕnў swet pudĭngs ănd pis, to mŭeh rĭeh cak, and to mŭeh frĕsh brĕd; ănd tha drĭnk to mŭeh cŏfe ănd te; ănd tha dŏn't drĕs warm enŭf; thăt călĭco 'ant the thĭng for hĕlth. We usd to war wolĕn ŭndĕr cloths, ănd our skĭrts wĕr alwas mad ŏv lĭndsў-wolsў. Our stŏckĭngs wĕr wolĕn ănd our shos wĕr mad ŏv god thĭck lĕthĕr, so hĕvў thăt yu cud kĭk à măn's trip out wĭth 'ĕm.

Thĭs ĭs̱ the wa we us̱d tọ drĕs, ănd ĭt was̱ à gọd wa tọ. The old mästĕrs neu hou tọ tak car ŏv thar nĭgĕrs̱.

We hăd gọd bĕds̱ tọ slep ĭn; the tĭks wĕr fïld wĭth strạ, ănd we hăd plĕntў ŏv wọlĕn blănkĕts, ănd cŭvĕrlĕts, ăs̱ tha us̱d tọ cạl 'ĕm. The firs̱ wer ạl mad ŏv wọd, ănd ŭsuảlў tha wĕr bĭg. The fir plạçĕs̱ ŭsuảlў ĕxtĕndĕd ĕntirlў ảcrŏst wŭn ĕnd ŏv the kĭtehĕn—15 tọ 20 fet wid, wĭth làrġ ston jăms̱ thăt mad 'ĕm 3 or mor fet dep, providĕd wĭth à ehĭmnў thăt 2 or 3 cud clim ŭp ănd stănd ĭn, sid bȳ sid. In the băk pärt ŏv thĭs huġ fir-plạç à làrġ băk-lŏg,—ăs̱ mŭeh ăs̱ tu or thre cud cărў—was̱ plạçt, ănd ŭpŏn the hăndirŭns̱ ănŭthĕr lŏg cạld à for-stĭk, ăs̱ mŭeh ăs̱ à măn cud cărў, was̱ plạçt; ănd thĕn betwen thĭs băk-lŏg ănd for-stĭk was̱ pild smạlĕr wọd, ŭntïl ĭt mad à fir thăt wud scar the yŭng foks ŏv́ thĭs gĕnĕra-shŭn out ŏv thar wĭts. Thĭs bĭg fir nŏt onlў wạrmd, bŭt ĭt ạlso lited the rọm. As̱ à rul, the nĭgĕrs̱ hăd no ŭthĕr lit, ănd no ŭther fir thăn thĭs—tha hăd tọ sta ĭn the kĭtehĕn—thĭs was̱ thar pärt ŏv the hous, ănd her tha hăd gọd tims, to. The hwit foks wĕr ĭn ănŭthĕr pärt ŏv the hous, hwar the fir-plaç waş nŏt qwit so bĭg. Sŭmtimş the hwit foks hăd stovş; ănd thĕn tha litĕd thar rǫmş wĭth tälo căndlş; thĕr waş no kĕrosĭn thĕn, nor ĕnў col, tha dĭd'nt no hou to uş sŭch thĭngş.

Thŭs ĕndĕd our cŏloquў wĭth Sĭlvĭá Dǫbois. Aş the da waş fär spĕnt, we găthĕrd our utĕnsĭlş, drŏpt ĭntǫ the hănd ŏv our agĕd hostĕs ăn ĕxprĕshŭn ŏv our chăritў towǎrd hĕr, băd hĕr gǫd-bў, mountĕd our sla ănd sĕt ŏf to vĭsĭt Rĭchárd Gomo, ăt Rŏk Mĭlş, to ĕxămĭn the rĕcŭrdş ŏv the Cŭmptŭn fămilў. Hwĕn the rĕcŭrdş hăd bĭn ĕxămĭnd, the nit waş fàst cŭmĭng on, ănd we hastĕnd towǎrd Rĭngoş. We ărivd hom áftĕr the shadş ŏv nit hăd fulў supervĕnd, tĭrd ănd hŭngrў, bŭt delitĕd wĭth the ăcqwisĭshŭnş ŏv the da. The agĕd ănd carworn vĭsag ŏv Sĭlvĭá Dǫbois, hĕr hŭmbl hŭt and sparç fŭrnitur, hĕr shrĭl, stĕrn voiç hĕr pĕrt replĭş, hĕr qwĭk ănsĕrş, hĕr cherful dĭspoĭshŭn ănd hĕr cŏntĕntmĕnt wĭth hĕr lŏt, hàş formd á pĭctur ĭn our mindş so ĭndĕlàbl, thăt tim wĭl nĕvĕr eras ĭt.

APENDIX.

Elĕvĕn mŭnths hăv ĕlăpst sĭnç the rītĭng ŏv the preçĕdĭng pagĕs, ănd stĭl Sĭlvĭá Dṵbois lĭvs—hal, hărtў, wĭtў, ănd ăs pĭŭs ăs ĕvĕr The flăsh ŏv hĕr ȳe (eye) stĭl ĭs lik á glem ŏv á făl-chŭn. Hĕr gat ĭs firm, hĕr voiç cler, hĕr herĭng ăcut, hĕr visyŭn ĕxçĕlĕnt. She ets wĕl, drĭnks wĕl, ănd smŏks bĕtĕr. Hĕr mĕmorў ĭs ĕxçĕl-ĕnt, ănd she taks ăs mŭch ĭntĕrĕst ĭn pásĭng evĕnts, ăs wṵd wŭn ŏv fŏrtў yers. She ĕnjoўs á jok ăs wĕl ăs ĕvĕr ; ănd tĕls wŭn wĭth ĕxçed-ĭng graç. Hĕr láf ĭs ăs ĭndĭkatĭv ŏv mĕrimĕnt ăs thăt ŏv á wĕnch ŏv aten. Inded, Sĭlvĭá ĭs álĭv yĕt.

Sĭlvĭá's gọd spĭrĭts do mŭch towạrds prŏ-lŏngĭng hĕr das. Hĕr mătĕr–ŏf–făct wa ŏv vṵĭng lif, prevĕnts wŭrў, ănd keps the măshen-ĕrў ŏv hĕr sўstĕm frŏm frĭcshŭn. Thăt hwĭch wars out the măshenĕrў ŏv the hŭmán fram mŏr thăn ĕnў ŭthĕr wŭn thĭng (I hăd álmost

sĕd mor thăn al els cŏmbind) ĭs wŭrў. Frŏm
thĭs Sīlvĭá ĭs ĕvĕr fre ; she hăs thăt fīrm rĕli-
ánç ŭpŏn Prŏvĭdĕnç thăt ĕntirlў prĕvĕnts ĕnў
ánxietў ábout the futur. Tọ find wŭn bĕtĕr
botŭmd ŭpŏn the Călvănĭstĭc fath, ĭs nŏt esў ;
she sĕs she grụ ŭp ámŏng the Olɑ Sçọl Prĕs-
bўtereáns, thăt she sạ thar was wĕr gọd ănd
thăt she ádŏptĕd thĕm—thăt ĭs, thos ŏv thar
was thăt sut hĕr ; she sĕs : If wŭn wĭl onlў dọ
rit, Prŏvĭdĕnç wĭl provid for hĭm. 'Tant no
us tọ wŭrў—ĭt onlў maks thĭngs wŭrs ; lĕt cŭm
hwát wĭl, yu'v gŏt tọ bar ĭt—'tant no us tọ
flĭneh. Prŏvĭdĕnç nos bĕst—He sĕnds tọ yu
hwạtĕvĕr He wạnts yu tọ hăv, ănd yu'v gŏt tọ
tak ĭt, ănd mak the bĕst ŏv ĭt. I'v ạlwas gŏt
álŏng sŭmhou, ănd I ạlwaўs wĭl—bŭt sŭmtims
ĭts prĕtў dămd hărd slĕdĭng, I tĕl yu.

Sīlvĭá nĕvĕr fĭdgĕts. Hwĕn she sĭts, hĕr
hănds rĕst ĭn hĕr lăp, ănd she ĭs ăs moshŭnlĕs
ăs á stătu. Hwĕn she stănds, she' ĭs ăs fīrm
ăs á tre. Hwĕn she wạks, hĕr gat ĭs prĕcis ănd
ádroit. Hwil tạkĭng, she gĕstĭculats nŏt á lĭtl ;
bŭt ĭn the manuvĕrĭng ŏv hĕr hănds, thĕr ĭs
mŭeh grac ănd märkt proprietў ; she ĭs a härtў
láfĕr, bŭt hĕr láf ĭs ágreábl—ănd not vĕrў ăf-
ricănĭc—ĕntirlў fre frŏm thăt labĭál Gīne-negro

làf—wạ, wạ, wạ, wạ! or thặt pălatál láf so pe-
culïär tọ the negro : yạ, yạ, yạ, yạ! In the ặct
ŏv làfïng, hěr hol fram ĭṣ ĭn moshŭn, so mŭch
so, thặt wŭn mit thĭnk she'd shak the solṣ ŏf
frŏm hěr shuṣ.

Wĭth ạl hěr vivặc̣ĭtў, she shoṣ declin. Durĭng the làst yer, she hăs gron old răpĭdlў—hăṣ
becŭm emáṣheatěd ănd sŭmhwạt boud. Fär-
thěr, hěr mind shoṣ declin, ănd hěr cŏnvěrsashŭn ĭndicats that she ĭṣ věrg̣ĭng towàrd the
end ŏv lif; she tạks mŭch ŏv dĕth, ănd ŏv di-
ĭng, ănd semṣ wĭlĭng tọ di. In the cors ŏv
cŏnvěrsashŭn, she remärkt : "Nŭn ŏv ŭs hăv á
les ŏv lif; bŭt, I no I ăm old, ănd ăcordĭng tọ
the wa ĭt hăṣ bĭn wĭth ĕvěrў bŏdў ĕls, I se I
mŭst di; I ma di věrў sŭdĕnlў—hwĕn nŭn är
ĕxpĕctĭng ĭt—sŭch old foks sŭmtimṣ di věrў
sŭdĕnlў, bŭt, thěrṣ no tĕlĭng àbout thặt.

Upŏn the fĭrst ŏv Novĕmběr làst, I cạld ặt
the hŭmbl mănshŭn ĭn hwĭch Sĭlvĭä reṣidṣ, tọ
ĭnqwir àftěr hěr hĕlth, hěr wạnts, &c., &c. It
wạṣ evĕnĭng, ănd the shadṣ ŏv nit hăd wĕl ni
prevĕntĕd me frŏm fŏloĭng mў wạ ; so, tọ mak
mătěrs shur, I wạṣ ĕscortĕd ověr the rọckў,
wĭndĭng pàth, bў á gid. Aftěr sěvěrál stŭm-
blṣ, ănd scrătchěs bў cĕdár bŭshěs, ĭn the dĭs-

tánç ápeŗd á fant lit. Tọ thǐs, I sạ ọur gid wạş á+mǐng. It wạş the lămp thăt ǐlụmǐnats the hŭt ŏv ọur heroǐn; sọn we ărivd ăt the dor wạş wĕlcŭmd ǐn, ĕntĕrd ănd stătĕd the reşŭn ŏv ọur ĕránd. The old ladў săt ǐn hĕr ăcŭs- tŭmd plaç—ǐn the nǐeh betwen the stov ănd the wĕst wạl. Besid hĕr, I plaçt á prŏfĕrd ehar, ănd begăn cŏnvĕrsashŭn. She dǐstǐnctlў re- mĕmbĕrd mў vǐsǐt ŭpŏn the 27th ŏv Jănuarў, 1883, ănd mŭeh thăt we tạkt ábout,—fạltĕd me for nŏt hăvǐng cŭm tọ se hĕr sọnĕr, ănd ǐn- qwird áftĕr the wĕlfar ŏv thoş họ wĕr wǐth me durǐng mў làst vǐsǐt.

Upŏn ǐnqwirў, she ǐnfŏrmd me thăt she hăd ĕnjŏўd gọd hĕlth—thăt she wạş strọng ănd stǐl cụd wạk á lŏng wa—thăt she hăd jŭst retŭrnd frŏm Härlǐngĕn—á dǐstánç ŏv 4½ milş. Tọ be cĕrtán ăş tŏ the mănĕr ŏv retŭrnǐng frŏm Härlǐngĕn, I ăskt hĕr:

Họ brŏt yu frŏm Härlǐngĕn?

Tọ thǐs, ǐn hĕr pĕculiár stўl, she replid: Brŏt mўsĕlf—nobŏdў brŏt me!

Hwạt! dǐd yu wạk hom frŏm Härlǐngĕn thǐs áftĕrnọn?

Tọ be shụr I dǐd; hou ĕls wọd I gĕt her!

Hwạt! à wọmàn 116 yers old, wạk fọ‧ ănd à
hàf mils ĭn ăn àftĕrnọn?

Yĕs; thĕrs no ŭthĕr wa—I hăd tọ wạk.

Hou lŏng wĕr yu ŭpŏn the wa?

About tụ ours, I gĕs—we cam slo—hăd à
gọd del tọ cărў—ănd I căn't wạk fäst ĕnў mor.

Ar yu nŏt vĕrў tird?

No; I 'ant mŭeh tird—I'm à lĭtl tird, tọ be
shụr—ănd à lĭtl hŭngrў.

Hĕr dạtĕr (wĭth họm Sĭlvĭà lĭvs) semd tọ be
gătherĭng hĕr wĭntĕr stor; ănd ĭn the lĭtl hŭt
wĕr mor peçęs ŏv fŭrnĭtur ănd bŏxĕs, thăn I
hăd sen befor. A tăbl, à bărĕl or tụ, ănd à pil
ŏv ehĕs-bŏxĕs, wĕr crouded ĭn the băk pärt ŏv
the rọm, ănd the spaç ĭn the lŏft semd vĕrў fụl.
Inded, the lĭtl hous semd so fụl that thĕr wạs
härdlў sĭtĭng rọm or stăndĭng rọm.

Elĭzàbĕth, ăs uşuàl, wạs lăvĭsh wĭth àpŏlogў.
Hĕr hous wạs nŏt ĭn ordĕr,—ĭt neded reparĭng
—she'd hăd à cärpĕntĕr tọ veu ĭt tọ se hwạt
cud be dŭn; mămў's drĕs wạs old ănd răgĕd,
and neded wạshĭng; the fir wạs pọr—she'd nŏt
yĕt gŏt hĕr wĭntĕr wọd, ănd hĕr stov hăd àlmost
gĭven out—ănd I no nŏt hwat thĕr wạs for
hwĭeh she dĭd nŏt àpŏlogiz.

To mak ărangménts for the Fotográf ŏv our heroin, ŭpŏn the 20th ŏv Novĕmbĕr, I ágĕn cald ăt hĕr dątĕr's hom. I found Sīlvīă ĭn hĕr ácŭstŭmd nīeh,—wĭth hĕr hĕd ănd faç vĕrӯ mŭeh swolĕn, ănd vĕrӯ mŭeh mŭfld wĭth răgs ănd poltīçĕs. She hăd sŭferd à sever qwĭnzӯ, ănd hăd nŏt yĕt fŭlӯ recŭvĕrd hĕr hĕlth. She wąs febl, ănd nedĕd sŭportĭng tretmĕnt. Acordĭngly, I prĕscrĭbd for hĕr, ănd ădvĭzd hĕr dątĕr hou tǫ mănaġ hĕr poltīçĕs, &c., &c. Hwil I wąs fīxĭng hĕr mĕdiçĭn, Sīlvīă remärkt: I dĭdn't ųsd tǫ gĕt qwĭnzӯ, nor ĕnӯ ŭthĕr kĭnd ŏv sor throt; bŭt nou I'm old, ănd mӯ teth är out, ănd the wĭnd blos rit doun mӯ throt, ănd I tak cǫld. Hwӯ! sŭmtims ĭt blos cler doun tǫ mӯ stŭmác, ănd fŭrthĕr tǫ; hwi! ĭt blos cler thru me. Hwĕn I hăd teth, ĭt dĭd'nt ųsd tǫ dǫ so.

Arangmĕnts wĕr mad wĭth Sīlvīă tǫ sĭt for hĕr fotográf ăs sǫn ăs she wąs wĕl enŭf to rid tǫ the Artīst's Gălerӯ. Upŏn tĕlĭng hĕr thăt à cărĭaġ wųd be rĕdӯ tǫ tak hĕr ăt ĕnӯ tim. she replid:

I wąnt yu tǫ īnfŏrm me ĭn tim for me tǫ fíx mӯsĕlf, ănd gĕt ŏn sŭm decĕnt clos—thĕm foks ăt Lămbĕrtvĭl är à proud sĕt—ănd I don't wąnt to go doun thar lŏkĭng jŭst ĕnў̆ hou; I wạnt to lọk prĕtў̆ snĭpshŭs.

I replid:

I se, Sĭlvĭȧ, yu är sŭmhwạt prơud ĭn yur old daṣ.

I ạlwaṣ wạṣ prơud,—ănd likt tọ ăper deçĕnt; ănd I ạlwaṣ dĭd ăper deçĕnt, wĕn I cụd; bŭt I nĕvĕr drĕst beyŏnd mȳ menṣ—I wŭd'nt dọ thăt!

At 10 o'clŏk, ŭpŏn the 30th ŏv Novĕmbĕr, Sĭlvĭȧ săt for hĕr Fotogrȧf. Altho wĕl ni 116 yerṣ old, thĭs wạṣ hĕr fĭrst ĕxperĭĕnç ĭn lọkĭng ĭntọ the ärtĭst's cămerȧ. Bŭt, the frŏntĭçpeç ŏv thĭs vŏlum, gĭvṣ sŭm ideȧ ŏv the graçfụlnĕs ŏv hĕr mănĕr ăt theṣ ȧdvȧnct yerṣ. The pĭctur shoṣ thăt she wạṣ ȧ lĭtl tird. Thĭs wĭl be ĕxpĕctĕd bȳ ĕvĕrў̆ wŭn, hwĕn ĭnformd thăt the old ladў̆ hăd rod ȧbout nin milṣ betwen the tim ŏv brĕkfȧstĭng ănd thăt ŏv ĕntĕrĭng ĭntọ the Artĭst's Gălerў̆. It ĭṣ nŏt liklў̆ thăt so old ȧ womȧn hăṣ ĕvĕr befor sĕt for ȧ fotogrȧf; ănd ĭt ĭṣ nŏt liklў̆ thăt so old ȧ wŭn wĭl ĕvĕr preṣĕnt hĕr fac tọ the ạrtĭst's cămerȧ.

Imĕdĭatlў̆ ȧftĕr takĭng the nĕgȧtĭv for Sĭlvĭȧ'ṣ pĭctur, the ärtĭst ȧdjŭstĕd the cămerȧ tọ the

99

faç ŏv Elĭzabeth, the yŭngĕst dątĕr ănd cŏn-
stánt cŏmpănўŭn ŏv our heroin. Thŭs à wǫmán ĭn the 78th yer ŏv hĕr aġ, ănd hĕr mŭthĕr
ĭn the 116th yer ŏv aġ, wĕr fotogràft ŏn the
sam da.

GLENINGS.

—

About 21 yers ȧgo, the prăctĭç ŏv mĕdĭçĭn brŏt me ĭntọ ăcqwȧntȧnç wĭth mĕný ŏv the mŏst aģĕd pepl lĭvĭng ĭn the sŭthĕrn pärt ŏv Hŭntĕrdŏn ănd Sŏmĕrsĕt Countĭs, ănd the nŏrthĕrn pärt ŏv Merçĕr. Sĭnç thăt tim, ĭt hăs bĭn mȳ fortun tọ mantan ăn ăcqwantȧnç wĭth nerlý ạl the old foks for mĕný mĭls ȧround. As I hăv ạlwas hăd ăn er for hĭstorý, ănd ĕspeshălý ȧ dep ĭntĕrĕst ĭn ạl thăt relats tọ the hĭstorý ŏv mȳ natĭv countý, ănd ŏv the pepl họ dwel her, I hăv ĕvĕr lĭstĕnd tọ, ănd ŏfĕn mad nots ŏv, the storĭs thăt the aģĕd hăv told me. Hĕnç, I hăv slolý ăcumulatĕd ȧ stor ŏv făcts, sŭch ăs ĕvĕrý lŭvĕr ŏv hĭstorý cănŏt wĕl forgĕt —ĕvĕn ĭf he wạntĕd tọ.

Ov thes făcts, sŭm relat tọ the farĕst fazĕs ŏv lif—tọ heroĭc patrĭŏtĭzm, tọ hi-sold fĭlănthropý, tọ ŭntĭrĭng devoshŭn tọ the Crĭstyȧn cas, tọ fĭlyȧl ăfĕcshŭn ănd the lik ; sŭm, tọ the

därkĕst, drerўĕst fazĕs̱ ŏv hŭmản-lif,—tọ sens̱
ŏv rĕvĕlrў, ăcts ŏv debăehĕrў, tọ sqwảlĭd pŏv-
ĕrtў, tọ ảbjĕct degĕneraçў, ănd tọ hanŭs crims̱.
Bŭt făcts ȧr făcts ; ănd, ĭt hăs̱ takĕn eeh ănd
a̤l ŏv thes̱, ănd thousȧnds̱ thăt är yĕt ŭntold
tọ form the livs̱ ŏv the çĭtizĕns̱ ŏv our countў
—the dọĭngs̱ ŏv the pepl ȧmọng họm we lĭv ;
ănd no hĭstorў ŏv our countў căn be complet,
nor ŏv mŭeh vȧlu ăs̱ ȧ rĕcord ŏv the livs̱ ŏv ȧ
pepl thăt dŭs̱ nŏt crŏnicl, ăt the sam tim, the
dọĭngs̱ ŏv the grat ănd the smȧl, the rĭeh ănd
the pọr, the proud ănd the hŭmbl, the ĕxa̤ltĕd
ănd the ăbjĕct, the vĭrtuŭs ănd the vĭçyŭs,
the frṳgȧl ănd the sqwa̤lĭd.   Tọ ŏfĕn, hwạt ĭs̱
ca̤ld hĭstorў, ĭs̱ bŭt the rĕcŭrds ŏv the farĕst
făcts ŏv ȧ sĭngl famŭs ĭndĭvĭduȧl, or ŏv ȧ fav-
ord fĕw, hwĭeh lọk wĕl ŭpŏn papĕr ănd är ples̱-
ĭng tọ the er, bŭt hwĭeh onlў rĕpres̱ĕnt the sĭn-
tĭlashŭns̱ ŏv soçietў, or ŏv sŭm favŭrd ĭndĭvid-
uȧl, ĕntirlў ignorĭng the dọĭngs̱ ŏv the măs̱ĕs̱,
ănd s̱hŭnĭng wĭth dĭsdan, the deds̱, the pashĕnts
ănd the sŭfĕrĭngs̱ ŏv the pọr.   Tọ ŏfĕn we
forgĕt thăt ĭt taks the pĕs̱ĕnt ăs̱ wĕl ăs̱ the prest
ănd the prĕsidĕnt, tọ mak soçietў, tọ fŏrm the
Cŏnstĭtuȧnçў ŏv ȧ Stat.   Tọ ŏfĕn we forgĕt
thăt the degĕnerat, ănd the abjĕct är ĭndĭspĕn-

çibl pärts to soçietў,—that tha håv rits ănd
privēlags—ănd thăt tha är bŭt the countĕrparts
ŏv the bĕst ŏv the çitizĕns ŏv a cŏmŏnwĕlth.

On this ŏcashŭn, it is mў bisnĕs to recŏrd
the ăcts ănd saings ŏv wŭn ho hăs nŏt bĕn il-
ŭstriŭs for filănthropic deds.   But, a stŭdў ŏv
this rĕcord——ŏv thes ăcts ănd saings——is
wŭrthў, ănd wil wĕl repa ĕnў wŭn ho wishĕs
to no the resŭlts ŏv a lif ŏv disolŭtnĕs; ho
wishĕs to se hwat ŭnbridld păshŭns led to; ho
wishĕs to no hou ăbjĕct ănd sqwålid a pĕrson
căn be, ănd yĕt liv nŏt fär frŏm the farĕst fazĕs
ŏv çivilizd lif.

Thăt mў redĕrs ma the bĕtĕr cŏmprehĕnd
the lif ŏv the heroin ŏv this tal, I wil giv a bref
skĕteh ŏv ăn anshĕnt mountin tăvĕrn, wŭns
famŭs for ilfam. This hous, tradishŭn sĕs,
stod ŭpŏn the north sid ŏv the rod thăt ĕxtĕnds
wĕstwàrd frŏm the Rŏck Mils, ner its intĕrsĕc-
shŭn with the rod thăt ĕxtĕnds frŏm Wĕrtsvil
to Hopwĕl. It was the prŏpĕrtў ŏv a manŭ-
mitĕd negro, ănd was cald Pŭt's Tăvĕrn—àftĕr-
wàrds, Pŭt's Old Tăvĕrn; a prŏpĕrtў thăt
Silvia Dubois inhĕritĕd frŏm hĕr grăndfàthĕr,
Hărў Cŭmptŭn.

The foundĕr ŏv this hous, ănd for mĕnў yers

ïts prŏprïetŭr, wa͟s the cărăctĕr ho fîgur͟s ïn the
cōloq-uy̆, ïn this bo̱k, ă͟s Hăry̆ Cŭmptŭn, the
fifĕr, ŏv not ïn the ärmy̆ ŏv the Rĕvoly͟shŭn,
Hăry̆ wa͟s à slav to̱ Gĕnĕràl Ry͟fŭs Pŭtnàm, ho
sold hïm to̱ Căptïn Ry̅ner Sta̱ts, ho̱ sold hïm
to̱ Rïchàrd Cŭmptŭn, frŏm ho̱m he bŏt hï͟s
tim ănd becam fre. A͟s Gĕnĕràl Ry͟fŭs Pŭtnàm wa͟s hï͟s fïrst mästĕr, ănd mor dïstïn͟g̀wïsht
thăn ethĕr ŏv the ŭthĕr tu̱ mästĕrs, Hăry̆ wa͟s
ŏfĕn ca̱ld àfter hïs fïrst mästĕr, Hăry̆ Pŭtnàm;
ïnded, this nam he prefĕrd. Acordïngly̆, hwĕn
he becam the proprietor ŏv à hotĕl, ănd à măn
ŏv not ă͟s à mountïn tăvĕrn kepĕr, for short,
tha ca̱ld hïm Hăry̆ Pŭt ; ănd the ho-us thăt he
kĕpt, wa͟s u͟sualy̆ ca̱ld Pŭt's Tăvĕrn.

Hăry̆ Pŭtnàm's ho-us, a̱ltho fär famd, ănd
mŭch freqwĕntĕd, espĕshăly̆ by̅ sportïn͟g cărăc-
tĕr͟s, wa͟s nĕvĕr liçĕnst.   In ĕrly̆ tims, the sĕlïn͟g
ŏv hwïsky̆ ănd ŭthĕr ïntŏxïcatïn͟g lïqwĕr͟s ă͟s à
bĕyerag̀, wa͟s àloud to̱ a̱lmost ĕvĕry̆ wŭn—ŭnlĕs, by̅ so do̱ïn͟g, the vendĕr becam vĕry̆ ŏfĕn-
çïv. In the plaç, ïn hwïch Hăry̆'s ho-us wa͟s
bïlt, evĕn ăn ĕxtravïgànç ïn the sal ŏv lïqwĕr,
or ïn the dĕmŏnstrashŭn͟s cŏnseqwĕnt ŭpŏn the
us ŏv ït, wa͟s lĕs likly̆ to̱ be cŏmpland ŏv,
thăn to̱ be ĕncŭrag̀d. Cŏnseqwĕntly̆, ïn peç

ănd prŏspērĭty̆, he mănagd hĭs bĭsnĕs, ăcumŭ-
latĕd wĕlth, ănd becam rĕnound. Hĭs hous,
fär removĕd frŏm the gaz ŏv the cŭlturd, ănd
the piŭs, becam the sen ŏv cŏk-fĭts, fŏx-
chasĕs, hŭslĭng machĕs, priz-fits, &c., &c. Inded, Pŭt's Tăvĕrn becam famŭs ăs à plaç ŏv
rĕsort for al sŭch ăs ĭndŭlgd ĭn sŭch gams, or
likt to be prĕsĕnt hwĕr sŭch thĭngs trănspird.
It was the çĕntĕr for the dĭsolut. Frŏm àfär,
renound gamstĕrs cam,—ănd trădĭshŭn sĕs,
mĕny̆ wĕr the pounds, shĭlĭngs ănd pĕnç tha
cărĭd ŏf wĭth thĕm; ănd mĕny̆ wĕr the yŭng
mĕn ănd yŭng wĭmĕn ruĭnd ĭn thăt hous.

At Put's Hous, cŭlŭr was bŭt lĭtl regärdĕd.
Blăks ănd hwits, àlik, pärtok ĭn the pàstims,
or the bĭsnĕs, ŏv the ŏcashŭn. Thăt the blaks
wĕr regärdĕd eqwàl wĭth the hwits, thĕr ma be
sŭm dout; bŭt thăt the blăks wĕr ăs god ăs
the hwits, thĕr ĭs no qwĕstyŭn. Bŭt be thes
thĭngs ăs tha ma, tha pretĕndĕd to ăsoshĭat
ŭpŏn tĕrms ŏv ĕqwàlity̆,—to mŭch so for the
wĕl beĭng ŏv thĕr pŏstĕrĭty̆.

Twĕnty̆ yers àgo I wàs fisĭshŭn to sĕvĕrál
old gamstĕrs, the mălàdas ŏv hom wĕr ĭncŭrd
by̆ freqwĕntĭng thĭs cĕlebratĕd hous ŏv ĭlfam,
ănd the cŏnseqwĕnt ĭntĕrcors wĭth sŭch ăs

cŏngregatĕd thar. Altho the mĭshăps ledĭng
to dīsēs ŏcŭrd durĭng boy-hod, or ĕrlў măn-
hod, the màteres morbi wĕr nĕvĕr erădicatĕd,
ănd thes old ŏfĕndĕrs ŏv Natŭr's las, ăs tha
gru oldĕr, cŏnstàntlў nedĕd the car ŏv à mĕdĭ-
càl ădvisor. Altho tha wĕr wŏnt to cŭrs the
da tha lĕrnd to fŏĕnd, ănd deplord the sham ănd
mĭserў hwĭeh thar ŏfĕnçĕs hăd brŏt thĕm, yĕt
ŏfĕn, hwil I was ĕngagd ĭn prĕparĭng medĭ-
çĭn for thĕm, tha usd to delit ĭn tĕlĭng me ŏv the
grănd old tims tha usd to hăv ĭn thar yŭng
das, ăt Pŭt's old tăvĕrn. Nŏt wŭn ŏv thĕs
numĕrŭs bĭts ŏv hĭstŏrў ĭs fĭt to be recordĕd
ĭn this năràtĭv ; ĕvĕrў wŭn ŏv thĕm was rĕvolt-
ĭng to pepl ŏv cŭltur ; mŏst ŏv thĕm wud shŏk
the mŏdĕstў ŏv à Hŏtĕntŏt, ănd mĕnў ŏv thĕm
wud blàneh the ehek ănd ehĭl the blod ŏv the
mŏst dĭsolut. Tha wĕr sens pĕrpetratĕd bў in-
tĕlĕctuàl, bŭt lud mĕn, ŏv the băsĕst pàshŭns,
fĭrd bў hwĭskў ănd hilărĭtў, ĭn ăn ătmŏsfer ĕntirlў fre frŏm decĕnsў or sham. Thŭs lĕt los,
ĭn cŭmpànў wĭth ther pĕrs, thar pàshŭns wŭrkt
out sŭeh thĭngs ăs cud be dŭn onlў bў the most
darĭng, the most lŭstful, ănd the most wantŭn.
To thos ho no onlў à frăgmĕnt ŏv the hĭstorў
ŏv this ànshĕnt hous, ĭt ĭs nŏt à wŭndĕr thăt

thĕr är so mĕnў shads ŏv cŭlŭr ĭn the pŏpula-
shŭn ŏv the naburhod ŏv çedär sŭmĭt, nŏr thăt
ĭn thos ŏv litĕr shads, thĕr ĭs so mŭeh tĕndĕncў
to viç ănd crim.

Hărў Pŭt hăd ăn instĭnctĭv desir to be fre.
Beĭng ĭndŭstĭrŭs, frugál ănd hŏnorabl, he man-
agd to bў hĭs tim ŏv hĭs mäster, Rĭehárd
Cŭmptŭn. Chärcol beĭng mŭeh ĭn demănd ĭn
thos tims, he tŭrnd hĭs ătĕnshŭn to the bŭrnĭng ŏv colpĭts, ănd ăt the bĭsnĕs, ăcumulatĕd
á lĭtl mŭnў. Wĭth hĭs ĕrnĭngs he pŭrehast á
sit ănd erĕctĕd á hous. Hĭs soshál qwálĭtĭs,
ănd the sŭplў ŏv lĭqwŭr alwas on hănd, mad
hĭs hous á pŏpulár plaç ŏv resort. Son he
found ĭt nĕçĕsarў to ĕnlärg—so rapĭdlў dĭd hĭs
patrŏnag ĭncres ; ănd, fĭnálў, he found ĭt nĕçĕsarў to rebĭld.

The neu hous, tradĭshŭn sĕs, was sŭmhwat
pretĕnshŭs. It cŏnsĭstĕd ŏv for lärg roms ŭpŏn
the fĭrst flor, ănd á hálf storў, sutáblў dividĕd
ĭnto roms, ábŭv. Alŏng the ĕntir frŭnt was á
poreh ; ănd the wĭndos ănd dors wĕr ămpl.
Ner bў stod the shĕds ănd ŭthĕr nĕçĕsarў out-
bŭldĭngs ; the hol sŭroundĕd bў á vĭrgĭn fŏrĕst
thăt ĕxtĕndĕd for mils ĭn ĕvĕrў dirĕcshŭn.

It ĭs härdlў to be sŭposd, thăt Hărў Pŭt, á

slav, họ's hi spĭrĭt prŏmptĕd hĭm tọ mak the
săcrĭficĕṣ nĕcĕsárỹ tọ pŭrehaṣ hĭṣ frĕdŭm, hăd
à vĭshŭs tĕndáncỹ. It ĭṣ eṣĭer tọ belev thăt he
wạṣ ăn ĭndŭstrĭŭs, ezỹ-goĭṉg, flĕxibl, fär-seĭṉg
negro, họ, ŭnscọld ĭn ethĭks, ănd frĕṣhlỹ lĭbĕr-
atĕd frŏm bŏndaġ, hăd nŏt à jŭst ăprĕṣhĕashŭn
ŏv fredŭm ănd mŏrălĭtỹ ; ănd, wĭthạl, à strŏṉg
gred for gan, ănd à desir tọ be pŏpŭlár. Thŭs,
cŏnstĭtŭtĕd, he becam à fĭt tọl for sŭeh ăṣ desird tŏ frĕqwĕnt à hoṵs sọ fär remọvd frŏm the
gaz ŏv the lạ-àbidĭṉg ănd the piŭs, thăt, hwil
thar, thĕr păshŭṉṣ cụd be ŭnbrĭdld, thar ăets
ŭnsen bȳ the vĭrtuŭs, ănd thar dedṣ ŭn-non,
ĕxcĕpt tọ the ḃasĕst ŏv mĕn.

The ġĕsts thăt vĭsĭtĕd Pŭt's Hoṵs wĕr nŏt
ạl frŏm the moṵntĭn, nŏr yĕt frŏm the àdjạcĕnt
vălĭṣ. Fär frŏm ĭt,—frŏm Trĕntŭn tha căm,
ănd frŏm Prĭnctŭn, ănd Neṵ Brŭnṣwĭc, ănd
Neṵ York, ănd Fĭlàdĕlfĭà, ănd evĕn frŏm cĭtĭṣ
färthĕr àwa. The neṵṣ ŏv à cŏk-fit, ăn old
gamstĕr seṣ, uṣuálỹ sprĕd thrụ à cŏmŭnĭtỹ ănd
reeht the erṣ ŏv gămblĕrs, ĭn oldĕn tims, fàstĕr
thăn the stĭnk ŏv à skŭnk trăvĕrsĕṣ the ar ŏv
à vălỹ. The sam old wĭt ŭṣd tọ sa, the er ŏv
à gamstĕr ĭṣ ăṣ ṣhärp tọ her the report ŏv à

cŏk-fit, aṣ the noz ŏv á vŭltur ĭṣ to̤ sĕnt á dĕd hors.

So, hwĕnĕvĕr the ar ŏv the mountĭn becam polutĕd wĭth the cŏncŏcshŭn ŏv á cŏk-fĭt, ĕvĕrў gamstĕr thăt snĭft the ar for á hŭndrĕd milṣ ăround wĭnded the gam, ănd, wĭth hĭṣ wĕneh or hĭṣ drăb, sĕt out for the mountĭn. Aṣ á cŏnseqwĕnç, á spckld host ăsĕmbld. The negro ŏv the mountĭn waṣ thar; ănd thar to̤, waṣ the negro ŏv the valĭṣ round ábout. The mountĭn bandĭt waṣ thar; ănd thar, to̤, wĕr thĕ bandĭtĭ ŏv the ădjaçĕnt vălĭṣ, ănd ŏv the nerĕr cĭtĭṣ. And thar, to̤, waṣ ĕvĕrў gămblĕr ho̤ dwĕlt wĭthĭn á radĭus ŏv mĕnў á mil, ho̤ cṵd wăk or rid, thăt cṵd posĭblў lev hom. The nĕgrĕs ĭn răgṣ, ănd the drăb ĭn brŏcad, ănd ĭn sătĭn; the negro wĭth hĭṣ păeht cot, the cĭtў băndĭt ĭn hĭṣ bevĕr sṵt; the farmĕr gamstĕr ĭn hĭṣ lĭnsў-wo̤lsў, the mecănĭc ĭn satĭnĕt, drĭnk-ĭng ănd tạkĭng, láfĭng ănd shoutĭng, ĭntĕr-mĭngld ăṣ tho̤ ĕvĕrў elĕmĕnt ŏv dĕstĭncshŭn hăd bĭn remo̤vd, ănd the bĭṣnĕs ŏv lif waṣ onlў hilărĭtў.

I recál á statmĕnt mad mĕnў yerṣ ágo, bў á vĕrў wŭrthў pashĕnt, respĕçtĭng á cŏk-fit thăt he wĭtnĕst ăt thĭs plaç, thăt ŏcŭrd ĭn hĭṣ boy-

hod. The storў—or thăt părt ŏv ĭt hwĭeh I
vĕntur to̤ tĕl—rŭn̠s thŭs : Hwĕn about 18 yer̠s
old, I wa̤s̠ sĕnt bŷ mŷ fäthĕr to̤ se á eĕrtĭn măn
respĕctĭn̠g á cĕrtĭn bĭs̠nĕs. Hwĕn I árivd at
hĭs̠ hous, I wa̤s̠ ïnformd thăt he wa̤s̠ nŏt ăt hom
—thăt he hăd gŏn to̤ Pŭt's Old Tăvĕrn to̤ ătĕnd á cŏk-fit. Acordĭn̠glŷ I dĭrĕctĕd mŷ wa
thĭthĕrwàrd ; ănd, hwĕn ner the hous, I sa̤ á
grat cŏncors ŏv pepl—ŏv a̤l cŭlŭr̠s̠, ŏv a̤l sĭzĕs̠,
ănd ŏv both sĕx. Tha wĕr ĭn the wo̤d, á lĭtl
wa frŏm the hous. Sŭm wĕr wĕl drĕst, sŭm
wĕr sŭpĕrblŷ drĕst, sŭm wĕr bădlŷ drĕst, ănd
sŭm wĕr härdlŷ drĕst ăt äl. Tha wĕr ĭntĭ-
matlŷ mĭxt—the răgĕd ănd the dăndŷ. Her á
wĕneh wĭth härdlŷ enŭf păehĕs̠ to̤ kep the flis̠
ŏf, stṳd ta̤kĭn̠g to̤ á măn drĕst ĭn cŏstlŷ brŏd-
clŏth ; thăr á thĭk lĭpt negro, răgĕd ănd dĭrtŷ,
ănd drŭnk, stṳd ta̤kĭn̠g wĭth wĭmĕn drĕst ĭn
brŏcad, ănd dĕkt wĭth the mŏst ga̤dŷ juels̠.
Her á grṳp, boistĕrŭs̠ ĭn makĭn̠g bĕts,—thar á
bŭneh hilărĭŭs̠ wĭth fŭn ănd rŭm ; yŏndĕr á
rĭn̠g fŏrmd ăround tṳ bṳlĭs̠—wŭn á hwit măn,
the ŭthĕr blăk—fitĭn̠g for no ŭthĕr resṳn thăn
to̤ se hwĭeh cṳd hwĭp. Hwil, ĭn thĭs grṳp ănd
ĭn thăt, wĕr hwit mĕn ănd negros̠, hwit wĭmĕn
ănd wĕnehĕs̠, wĭth scrăteht facĕs̠ ănd swoĕn

ȳs (eyes),—the resūlts ŏv cŏmbăts thăt hăd gron out ŏv jĕlŭsȳ, hwĭskȳ, or the ĭntrĭgs ŏv shrụd mĕn họ likt tọ se fits.

The wọd waṣ vocál wĭth negro láf—yạ, yạ, yạ, yạ—ănd wạ, wạ, wạ, wạ; ănd wĭth shouts ŏv mĭrth ănd merĭmĕnt, ŏv ĭndeçĕnt sŏngs, ănd ŏv boistrŭs profănĭtȳ. A mor ápạlĭng ănd á mor dĭsgŭstĭng sen, I nĕvĕr wĭtnĕst. I waṣ ŭpŏn á horṣ; I dĭd nŏt dĭsmount. I ĭnqwird for, ănd found, the măn I waṣ sĕnt tọ se, trănsăctĕd, mȳ bĭṣnĕs, rand mȳ horṣ towärd the rod, ănd lĕft the wọd ĭn ŭtĕr dĭsgŭst.

Ov ạl the ĭnçĭdĕnts respĕctĭng Put's Hous, thăt hăv cŭm tọ mȳ erṣ, the ábŭv ĭṣ the mildĕst. Bŭt, the ábŭv ĭṣ onlȳ á pärt ŏv the storȳ; the rĕst ĭṣ tọ därk to be told.

Thăt the hous waṣ bĕtĕr kĕpt ăftĕr ĭt dĕçĕndĕd ĭntọ the hănds ŏv our heroin; or thăt the gĕsts thăt freqwĕntĕd ĭt wer ŏv á hiĕr ordĕr, ĭṣ mŭch tọ be doutĕd. Houĕvĕr, ĭts pŏpŭlărĭtȳ wand, ănd ĭts patrŏnṣ wĕr thoṣ ŏv lĕs not. Aṣ the demănd for tĭmbĕr ĭncrĕst, the wọd ŭpŏn the sid ănd the tŏp ŏv the mountĭn waṣ cŭt áwa; the sun shon ĭn ŭpŏn plaçĕs thăt hĭthĕrtọ wĕr därk, the lănd ĭn plaçĕs waṣ tĭld, çĭvĭlizashŭn ănd vĭrtu ĭncroeht ŭpŏn the ĕnvirŏns ŏv

the sen ŏv the dĭsolut; Pŭt's Tăvĕrn becam à
thĭng ŏv ŏprobrĭŭm, ănd ĭn the yer 1840, ĭt wạs
bŭrnd tọ ăshĕs. Sŭeh ĭṣ the hĭstorў ŏv the
hous thăt wạṣ the àrenà, tradĭshŭn sēṣ, ŏv the
vilĕst dedṣ thăt wĕr ĕvĕr pĕrpetratĕd ĭn Hŭn-
tĕrdŭn Countў.

Sĭlvĭà mŭeh cŏmpland ŏv the lŏs ŏv prŏpĕrtў ĭncŭrd bў the cŏnflăgrashŭn. Al thăt
she hăd wạṣ ĭn thĭs bĭldĭng; bĕds, eharṣ, bọks,
culĭnarў ăpàratŭs, ănd hwạtĕvĕr els ĭṣ nĕsĕsarў
tọ ăn outfĭt tọ kep à mountĭn tăvĕrn. The
cŏnflăgrashŭn ŏcŭrd durĭng hĕr ăbsĕnç. She
stats thăt she ĭṣ sătĭsfĭd thăt the hous wạṣ
plŭndĕrd befor ĭt wăṣ fird. In ĕvĭdĕnç ŏv thĭṣ,
she stats thăt sevĕràl ärtĭklṣ ŏv fŭrnitur ănd
sĕvĕràl bọks,—wŭn à bibl cŏntanĭng the fămilў
rĕcŭrd, wĕr found scătĕrd over the mountĭn,—
sŭm ĭn wŭn hous, sŭm ĭn ănŭthĕr. Bŭt, ĭt
sems, she wạṣ nĕvĕr abl tọ rĕclam wŭn ŏv thĕṣ
thĭngṣ.

In Sĭlvĭà's da, Put's Tăvĕrn wạṣ regärdĕd
onlў ăṣ ạ cak ănd ber hous. Bŭt, thăt ŭthĕr
drĭnks cụd ŏfĕn bĕ gŏt thar, thĕr sems tọ be
ăn abŭndànç ŏv ĕvĭdĕnç. Inded, on wŭn ŏcashŭn, ĭt ĭṣ sĕd, the hous wạṣ vĭsĭtĕd bȳ ăn ŏfĭ-

cĕr ŏv the la, ănd the proprietŭr, fre ŏv charg, ĕnjoyd à rid tọ the countў set.

In hĕr dà, Sĭlvĭà wạṣ sŭmhwạt famŭs ăṣ à bredĕr ŏv hŏgṣ. For this bĭṣnĕs, the grat un- fĕnct mountĭn forĕst, wạṣ vĕrў favŭràbl. Hĕr hĕrd wạṣ ŏfĕn vĕrў lärg, ănd hĕr stŏck vĕrў notĕd. Ofĕn, tọ ĭmprọv hĭṣ bred, à fàrmĕr wŭd go à lŏṉg wa tọ Sĭlvĭà's hĕrd, tọ bў à hŏg. Nor dĭd he ĕxpĕct tọ pŭrchas hĕr stŏk ăt à lo fĭgur. She wĕl neu the vălu ŏv hŏgṣ, ănd ạl- wạṣ g̣ŏt à far prịç.

Aftĕr the bŭrnĭṉg ŏv Put's Tăvĕrn, I am told, that Sĭlvĭà erĕctĕd ănŭthĕr hous, ănd dwĕlt ŭpŏn the lănd that she hăd ĭnhĕrĭtĕd. Thĭs hous, ĭt ĭṣ sĕd, wạṣ bĭlt ŏv çedärṣ. The ärcitĕctur wạṣ prĭmàtĭv. The polṣ ŏv hwĭch ĭt wạṣ mad, wĕr cŭt about ăṣ lŏṉg ăṣ à ral, ănd ărang̣d sŭmhwạt àfter the păttĕrn fŏlod ĭn bĭld- ĭṉg the fram ŏv à wĭgwạm. Theṣ polṣ wĕr cŭv- ĕrd wĭth çedär brŭsh, ănd the lik, ărang̣d sŭm- hwạt àftĕr the mănĕr ŏv fĭxĭṉg strạ ĭn thăch- ĭṉg à rụf.

Hwạt the fŭrnĭtur ŏv thĭs hous wạṣ, I hăv fald tọ lĕrn. Bŭt, that ĭt wạṣ àmpl, ănd that

113

the ĕdifiç wᴀṣ spashŭs, ănd cŭmfortábl, thĕr căn be no dout. Nor căn ĭt be doutĕd thăt Sīlvĭả wᴀ̤ṣ ĕvĕr sĕlfĭsh, or ĭnhŏspĭtábl. Evĕn hĕr sow ănd pīg̱s. ĭt ĭṣ sĕd, shard wĭth hĕr the cŭmforts ŏv hĕr mănshŭn. Nor dĭd she cŏm-pĕl hĕr chĭckĕns to go to̤ ăn out–bīldĭ̱ng, or ả tre, to̤ ro̤st; bŭt, cŏnsĭdĕrat ănd cŏnsĕrvatĭv, she mad eeh wŭn fel ăt hom beneth hĕr hospĭt-ábl ro̤f.

Thŭs ăt peç wĭth best ănd foul, Sīlvĭả, for ả hwil, spĕnt hĕr daṣ. Bŭt, pĕrpĕtuảl ănd ŭn-sūled hăpĭnĕs hăṣ nŏt bĭn bĕqwetht to̤ ĕnў mortál. Durĭ̱ng hĕr ăbsĕnç, sŭm vil ĭnçĕnduarў fird hĕr dŏmicĭl, ănd Sīlvĭả ảgĕn wᴀ̤ṣ hous-lĕs. Advảnçt ĭ. yerṣ, pĕnўlĕs ănd dĭsmad, she ăçĕptĕd ăn ĭnvitashŭn to̤ abid wĭth hĕr da̤tĕr, ănd wĭth hĕr da̤tĕr she stĭl lĭvṣ.

OUR LAST VISIT.

———

Excĕptĭn̄g the pag̣ĕṣ rītn ŭndĕr thĭs hĕd. the mătĕr ŏv thĭs ḅok ĭṣ nou ĭn tȳp, rĕdȳ for the prĕs, ănd, bŭt for the prĭntĭn̄g ŏv the pag̣ĕṣ thăt I ăm nou ritĭn̄g, Dec. 21st, 1883, the lást form ŏv thĭs ḅok wŭd go to prĕs to-da. Bŭt, çĕrtĭn çĭrcŭmstánçĕṣ sem to wärĕnt á dela ŭntĭl I căn pĕn á feu pag̣ĕṣ, ănd mȳ prĭntĕr căn pụt thĕm ĭn tȳp. Theṣ cĭrcŭmstánçĕṣ är ăṣ fŏloṣ :

Upŏn the nintĕnth ŏv Deçĕmbĕr, ŏcŭrd á sever storm, ănd durĭn̄g ĭt, á sno fĕl to the dĕpth ŏv sĕven ĭneheṣ. To ĕvĕrȳ wŭn ĭt semd thăt wĭntĕr hăd begŭn wĭth ĕxtrem vĭgŏr, ănd the thŏtfụl begăn to mĕditat respĕctĭn̄g the prĕpärashŭn̄ṣ tha hăd mad for the blĕk daṣ ănd the frĭgĭd nits, ŏv theṣ trȳĭn̄g wĭntĕr mŭnths. Our thŏts wĕr nŏt ĕntirlȳ cŏnfind to our on cŏndĭshŭn, nor to the prĕpàrashŭn̄ṣ thăt we hăd mad for ourselvṣ álon. Amŭn̄g the dĕstitut thăt ŏcŭrd to our mind, wạṣ thăt ag̣ĕd ladȳ, the heroin ŏv this vŏlum, Sĭlvĭå Dụbois, họ dwĕls̱ wĭth hĕr fathfụl dạtĕr Lĭzĭ, ĭn thăt Lĭtl Old Hŭt ner the tŏp ŏv the mountĭn. Tọ vĭsĭt hĕr, tọ ĭncŭrạg hĕr, ănd tọ lĕrn hĕr neds̱, wạs̱ qwĭklȳ detĕrmĭnd ŭpŏn, ănd the mornĭng ŏv the 20th ŏv Dec., 1883, wạs̱ the tim ăpointĕd tọ pa our respĕcts tọ hĕr agĕd ladȳshĭp.

The slaĭng wạs̱ gọd, the är sålubrĭŭs, ănd the senĕrȳ ĭnvitĭng. Altho the skȳ wạs̱ ovĕr-căst, the da wạs̱ delitfụl. It mŭch res̱ĕmbld thos̱ qwiĕt, cloudȳ das̱ thăt I us̱d tọ se sọ ŏfĕn fŏlo å hĕvȳ sno-stŏrm ĭn Northĕrn Neu Yŏrk ănd ĭn Cănáda.

Nŏt wilĭng tọ ĕnjoy the slaĭng ålon, nor the tret ŏv vĭsĭtĭng the hom ŏv thes̱ agĕd mountĭners̱, on mȳ wa, åbout 9 ĭn the mornĭng, I cạld ŭpŏn tụ ŏv mȳ pashĕnts, Mrs. Rebĕcå Prạl ănd Mĭs Elizå Prạl, họm I ĭnvitĕd tọ shar with me, the evĕnts ŏv the da. Sọn we wĕr ăscĕndĭng the slop ŏv the mountĭn. The prŏspĕct wạs̱ delitfụl—å cherful wĭntĕr sen. Hi ŭp the hĭl, ŭpŏn å favŭråbl spŏt, we stŏpt tọ yu. The sno–clăd plan beneth ŭs strĕteht åwa so gĕntlȳ thăt we cụd detĕct nethĕr rĭdg nor mĕdo, nethĕr the cors ŏv the rods̱, nor the meăndering strems̱. The vĭlages̱ thăt wĕr bŭt å feu mils awa cud härdlȳ be dĭstĭnguĭsht ; hwil thos hwĭeh wĕr bŭt lĭtl färthĕr ŏf, cud nŏt be dĕscrid—so cŏmpletlȳ wĕr äl thĭngs cuvĕrd wĭth the neu–falĕn sno. Towärd the northest, the plan semd ĭntermĭnàbl—streeht àwa wĭthout hĭl or val, ŭntĭl the snoȳ ĕxpánç semd boundĕd bȳ the estĕrn skȳ.ˈ Bŭt, ovĕr àganst ŭs, 15 mils àwa, ros ŭp the graçful form ŏv Lŏng Rĭdġ, hwĭeh lĭfts ĭts graçful crĕsts ănd ĭts bold sŭmĭts to relev the veu ănd butĭfȳ the lănd-scap.

Son we reeht the crĕst ŏv Cedär Sŭmĭt. The senerȳ her, was espĕshàlȳ dĕlitful. The cedärs cuvĕrd wĭth sno, semd thĭngs ŏv ärt ; hwil the hug round rŏks, wĭth snoȳ băks, lokt lik the pĭcturs ŏv houşĕs ĭn Arctĭç sens. Thru the windĭng wa we wĕndĕd our cors, amĭd à fŏrĕst mostlȳ ŏv çedär, ŭntĭl, ăt wŭnç, à mountĭn vĭstà căm to veu, ănd we lokt estwärd, fär out ovĕr à dĕlitful plan thàt strĕehĕs àwa ŭntĭl ĭt ĭs boundĕd bȳ the se. Bŭt son the vĭstà was pàst; ănd àgĕn we wound àround hug rŏks ănd thru thĭkĕts ŏv çedärs, ŭntĭl—Thar ! Hwat ĭs thàt? Thăt sqwalĭd hŭt bĭlt ŏv lŏgs, ănd rŭft wĭth bords—wĭndolĕs ănd ehĭmnȳlĕs, ănd ĭs fàst yeldĭng to deca ?

Thăt! Hwȳ, thăt's the mănshŭn,—the hom ŏv Lĭzĭ Dṵbois. Thăt's the hous yu'v lọngd tọ se.

We dĭṣmountĕd frŏm the sla; bŭt, er we reeht the hous, Jo, the fathfṵl dŏg, gav ă feu shrĭ̱l bärks, ănd out căm the hostĕs tọ se hwạt wạṣ dĭstŭrbĭ̱ng the qwiĕt ŏv thár seclṵdĕd hom. She mĕt ŭs wĭth á smil, ănd băd ŭs go ĭn. We ĕntĕrd, wĕr setĕd ner á vĕrȳ wạrm stov, found Sĭlvĭá ĭn hĕr ăcŭstŭmd plạç—betwen the stov ănd the wĕst wạl, begăn tọ ehat, ănd the tim pást plĕ̱ṣĕntlȳ. Dĭrĕctlȳ, we ĭnqwird áftĕr the hĕlth, ŏv our host ănd hĕr agĕd mŭthĕr, ănd áftĕr ther sŭplĭṣ for the wĭntĕr. We wĕr ĭnformd thăt tha wer dĕstitṵt;—thăt tha wĕr ĭn wạnt ŏv mĕnȳ thĭ̱ngs—bŭt ĕspĕsẖálȳ, tha wĕr ĭn wănt ŏv wọd. Tha hăd ĕmployd sŭm hănds̱ tọ cŭt thar wĭntĕr wọd—bŭt so fär, tha hăd fald tọ find temṣ tọ hạl ĭt hom. Bŭt, hwil tạkĭ̱ng, sŭm wŭn drov ŭp wĭth á lod ŏv wọd; ănd thĕn thĕr wạṣ grat rejoiçĭ̱ng; the old wọmăn ĕxclamd: Thănk hĕvĕn! I'm so glăd—nou we wĭl be abl tọ kep wạrm.

Sĭlvĭá hăd qwit regand hĕr hĕlth, wạṣ vĕrȳ cherfṵl, ănd mŭeh ĭnclind tọ tạk; she ĭnqwird áftĕr the hĕlth ŏv mĕnȳ ŏv hĕr old ăcqwantán-

çĕs, ănd ĭn al rĕspĕcts shụ thăt she was åliv tọ
the åfars ŏv thė da; she tạkĕd ŏv the cŭmĭng
holidas, ănd told ŭs hwạt gọd tims tha ụsd tọ
hăv durĭng Crĭstmàs ănd Neu Yer; hou mĕnў
pärtĭs she ụsd tọ ătĕnd, hou tha ụsd tọ dànç,
&c., &c.

I remärkt: Dĭd I ŭndĕrstănd yu tọ sa thăt
yu ụsd tọ dànç ŏn Crĭstmàs?

She replid: Tọ be shur, we dĭd! Hwў! the
old slavs no mor neu the menĭng ŏv-Crĭstmăs,
thăn the hŏgs ĭn the pĕn! Tha onlў neu thăt
ĭt was å hŏlida, ănd thăt tha wĕr tŭrnd lọs for
sŭm fŭn, ănd, ŏv cors, tha hăd ĭt; tọ be shụr
tha dànçt. In thọs das tha cụd dànç, tọ.

I sĕd: Thĕn yu thĭnk tha căn't dànç now-å-
das?

She replid: No; nŏt å bĭt; tha thĭnk tha
căn; tha stŏmp, ănd jŭmp, ănd hŏp, ănd rŭn,
ănd lik enŭf tŭrn hels over hĕd; ănd tha cạl ĭt
dànçĭng; bŭt ĭt ĭs'nt dànçĭng; tha don't no
hou tọ dànç; tha'v gŏt no stĕps—tha don't no
ĕnў stĕps.

Hwạt stĕps dĭd yu lik bĕst hwĕn yu ụsd tọ
dànç?

Wĕl; I likt the elĕvĕn tims, the twĕlv tims,
ănd the thĭrten tims; thes wĕr the bĕst stĕps

for me; thes wer the steps thăt mȳ grăndfăthĕr, Hărȳ Cŭmptŭn, uṣd tọ lik, ănd ạl ŭthĕr gọd dançĕrṣ.

Wạṣ Hărȳ Cŭmptŭn á gọd dáncĕr?

Wĕl he wạṣ! He wạṣ cŏnsĭdĕrd the bĕst dáncĕr on the mountĭn, or thặt hăṣ ĕvĕr bĭn ŏn thĭs mountĭn, or ĕnȳhwĕr ĭn theṣ pärts; I hăv sen hĭm hwĕn he wạṣ old, dánç ặt Prĭnçtun; ănd ĕvĕrȳ bŏdȳ họ sạ hĭm, sĕd he wạṣ the bĕst dáncĕr tha ĕvĕr sạ.

Wạṣ Hărȳ Cŭmptŭn á lärġ măn?

No; he wạṣ short, bŭt vĕrȳ stoŭt, ănd vĕrȳ strŏng; he wạṣ cŏnsĭdĕrd the strŏngĕst măn ŏn the mountĭn; ănd tha uṣd tọ sa thặt he wạṣ the strŏngĕst negro that ĕvĕr lĭvd; ănd he wạṣ vĕrȳ áctĭv; he cụd pụt ĕnȳ măn ŭpŏn the ground—hwit or blăk.

Sĭlvĭá, dọ yu thĭnk yu cụd dánç yĕt?

Yĕs; I cụd dánç yĕt—onlȳ had á gụd fĭdl— I lik muṣĭc. A gọd fĭdl ạlwaṣ stärts the ne- gro,—ĕvĕn ĭf he'ṣ old.

Wĕl! dọ yu thĭnk yu'l dánç thĭs Crĭstmás?

Gĕs nŏt; gĕs I'd bĕtĕr thĭnk ábout sŭm- thĭng ĕls; foks ŏv mȳ aġ hăd bĕtĕr thĭnk ábout dȳĭng. Bŭt I lik tọ se 'ĕm dánç—ĭt lọks gọd.

In the cors ŏv cŏnvĕrsashŭn, Sĭlvĭă ădvĕrtĕd tọ the dĭficŭltў she hăd hăd wĭth cĕrtĭn foks họ trid tọ sĕl hĕr lănd frŏm hĕr. Hĕr ȳs (eyes) sọn begăn tọ sparkl, hĕr voiç grụ loud, ănd hĕr wŭrds mor bŭlkў ănd à lĭtl sŭlfŭrŭs; she sọn coind sŭm prĕtў hărd ĕpithĕts, ănd uṣd thĕm wĭth no lĭtl forç.

I àskt hĕr: Iṣ thé gĕntlmàn họ trid tọ sĕl yur lănd frŭm yu, lĭvĭng yĕt?

Tŭrnĭng hĕr faç towạrd me, ĭn à vĕrў pŏsitĭv manĕr, she replid: Heṣ no gĕntlmàn!—heṣ à dămd răskl!

I sĕd: Wĕl, ĭṣ he lĭvĭng?

She replid: I don't no wĕthĕr the dĕvĭl hăṣ sĕnt for hĭm yĕt or not; ĭf he han't yĕt, he wĭl sŭm ŏv theṣ daṣ. He pretĕndṣ he'ṣ so dămd gọd; bŭt he'l nĕvĕr gĕt tọ hĕvĕn. Hwĕn he berĭd hĭṣ fäthĕr, he wăntĕd tọ sho hĭṣ pĭcty, ănd he hăd cŭt ŭpŏn the ornămĕnt (mŏnumĕnt, I sŭpoṣ) that he plaçt ŭpŏn hĭṣ grav, à hănd, wĭth wŭn fĭngĕr pointĭng towạrdṣ hĕvĕn.— That lọkṣ prĕtў wĕl; bŭt he ŏt tọ hăv hăd à bŏtl ŏv hwĭskў ĕngravd jŭst àbŭv the ĕnd ŏv the fĭngĕr; that wụd lọk bĕtĕr; wụd be mor signĭficànt —spĕshălў tọ thoṣ ŏv uṣ họ neu hĭm.

Hwȳ! waṣ hĭṣ fäthĕr á băd măn, tọ?

No; hĭṣ fäthĕr waṣ nŏt á băd măn; bŭt he dĭd lik á drăm ŏv hwĭskȳ most dĕspĕrat wĕl; ănd he cụd tak sŭeh á sokĕr, tọ.

Relȳ, hĭs fäthĕr waṣ á gọd măn,—waṣ vĕrȳ gọd tọ the pọr—ănd we ạl likt hĭm. He waṣ ăṣ mŭeh tọ be likt for hĭṣ gọdnĕs, ăṣ hĭṣ sŏn ĭṣ tọ be dĭspiṣd for hĭṣ bădnĕs. The trŭbl ĭṣ, hwĕn the old măn did, he tọk ạl thĕ gọdnĕs ŏv the fămilȳ wĭth hĭm; hwạt ĭṣ lĕft behind ĭṣ nŭthĭng bŭt dămd träsh. Hĭs sŏn ĭṣ wŭrs thăn the dĕvĭl hĭmsĕlf, ănd wĭl ehet ĕnȳbŏdȳ he căn.

Hwil tạkĭng, I hĕrd the voiçĕs ŏv ehĭkĕnṣ. Tha semd tọ be dĭrĕctlȳ behind the ehar ŏv wŭn ŏv our pärtȳ. Tọ lĕt mȳ compănyŭnṣ se hou mọuntĭnerṣ car for thar poltrȳ, I sĕd: Don't I her sŭm ehĭkĕnṣ?

"Yĕs—I gĕs yu dọ," replid Lĭzĭ. "We hăv tọ fĕteh our ehĭkĕnṣ ĭn the hous ăt nit, tọ kep thĕm frŏm thevṣ. Tha stel ĕvĕrȳthĭng ŭp her, hwĕn tha căn. So I jŭst pụt mȳ ehĭkĕnṣ ĭn thĭs bŏx, ănd brĭng thĕm ĭn. Aṣ ĭt ĭṣ snoȳ to-da, I hăv nŏt pụt thĕm out; tha är niç wŭns—yu căn se 'ĕm." So saĭng, she razd the lĭd ŏv á lärg bŏx, ănd thar stọd the bĭrds ăṣ slek ăṣ dŭvṣ, ănd ăṣ dŏçĭl ăṣ ehĭldrĕn.

Sĭlvĭă—do̤ yu ĕvĕr ătĕnd ehŭreh?

Yĕs͟; sŭmtims͟. Hwĕn I wa̤s͟ yung͟, I us͟d to̤ go to̤ ehŭreh vĕrў ŏfĕn; bŭt, no̤u I don't go vĕrў ofĕn. Thĕr ĭs͟ no ehŭreh ner ŭs; ănd I căn't wa̤k so fär ĕnў mor. I us͟d to̤ wa̤k ă go̤d wa̤s͟ to̤ metĭng͟—to̤ Pĕnĭng͟tŭn, to̤ Prĭnc̤tŭn, to̤ Hopwĕl, ănd to̤ Härlĭngĕn, ănd to̤ cămp-metĭng͟; bŭt, I căn't wa̤k so fär ĕnў mor. We us͟d to̤ hăv metĭng͟ ner bȳ, ănd thĕn I a̤lwa̤s͟ wĕnt. Bŭt, the hwit trăsh brok our metĭng͟ ŭp; ănd no̤w I don't her preehĭng͟ ĕnў mor— bŭt I'd lik to̤.

Dĭd yu sa yu us͟d to̤ go to̤ cămp-metĭng͟?

Yĕs; I a̤lwa̤s͟ wĕnt to̤ cămp-metĭng͟—spĕsh-ălў hwĕn I wa̤s͟ yŭng͟. Thăt wa̤s͟ the bĕst kind ŏv metĭng͟ for me—I likt thăt. I'd wa̤k ten mils͟ to̤ à cămp–metĭng͟—fŭrthĕr to̤.

Tha us͟d to̤ hăv grat tims͟ at cămp–metĭng͟s͟. Tha'd tŭrn out frŏm ĕvĕrўhwar—both blăks ănd hwits. I'v sen 2,000 foks ăt wŭn metĭng͟. Thĕr wa̤s͟ à cămp–metĭng͟ àbout sĕvĕntў-fiv yers͟ àgo, àbout four mils͟ belo Trĕntŭn, ner à plac̤ ca̤ld Crŏswĭks; ănd I ănd sŭm mor ŏv our cŭlŭr, wĕnt do̤un; we wa̤kt do̤un. Thăt wa̤s͟ the bĭgĕst cămp–metĭng͟ I ĕver ătĕndĕd, ănd the nicĕst wŭn, to̤. The cămp–gro̤und wa̤s͟ à

mil lŏng—ănd tha hăd sŭch gọd ordĕr ; thĕr
waṣ nobŏdў drŭnk, ănd thĕr wĕr no fits, ănd
ther waṣ no nois ŏv ĕnў kind, ĕxcĕpt hwạt the
metĭn' foks mad—ănd tha hăd ȧ bĭg tim—the
bĭgĕst kind ŏv ȧ tim ; tha hŏlĕrd ănd shouted,
tĭl yu'd thĭnk the dĕvĭl waṣ ĭn 'ĕm. I nĕvĕr
hĕrd sŭch shoutĭng—yu cud her 'ĕm tọ Trĕntŭn ; thĕr wĕr for pu̜lpĭts—ȧ gọd wa ȧpärt—
ănd for preehĕrs wĕr prĕehĭng ạl the tim. And
tha hŏlĕrd, ănd the foks hŏlĕrd—gọd Gŏd, hou
tha hŏlĕrd ; I nĕvĕr sạ sŭch ȧ tim—I gĕs nobŏdў dĭd. I wĕnt tŏ sta ạl the wek, bŭt ĭn
ȧbout thre daṣ, I gŏt ȧ bĕlўfu̜l ŏv ĭt, ănd mor
tọ—ănd then I stärtĕd hom. And hwĕn I gŏt
hom I gĕs I waṣ glăd—I gĕs no nĭgĕr waṣ ĕvĕr
so glăd tọ gĕt hom. I gŏt enŭf cămp-metĭng
ĭn thoṣ thre daṣ, tọ làst ȧ yer ; bŭt the nĕxt yer
I hĕrd ŏv ănŭthĕr cămp-metĭng, ănd I wạntĕd
tọ go jŭst ăṣ băd ăṣ ĕvĕr.

Dĭd yu sa the hwit foks dĭstŭrbd yur metĭng?

Yĕs ; tha brok ĭt ŭp. We uṣd tọ hăv ȧ gọd
metĭng over her, ner the Rŏk Mĭls ; bŭt thĭs
hwit trăsh ȧround her cu̜dn't behav ; tha'd cŭm
intọ the metĭng-hous ănd tạk rit out ĭn metĭng, ănd cạl eeh ŭthĕr's namṣ—ănd dọ ĕnўthĭng tọ dĭstŭrb us. And hwĕn qwạrtĕrlў

metĭng cam, the hwit trăsh frŏm al ovĕr cam, ănd fĭld the hous ănd the spac around the hous, ănd behavd so bădlў, ănd mad so mŭeh nois out ŏv dors, thăt we cud'nt hăv metĭng ĕnў mor.

Wĕl, Sĭlvĭå, thĭs ĭs å härd storў. It's å dis-graç to the mor respĕctåbl hwit pepl ŏv the nabŭrhod, thăt tha hăv nŏt protĕctĕd the cŭl-ŭrd ehŭreh. Cĕrtĭnlў, thĕr ĭs mŭeh ned ŏv å ehŭreh jŭst her ; ĭnded, I no ŏv no plaç, hwar wŭn ĭs mor nedĕd. The pepl ŏv thĭs mountĭn, cĕrtĭnlў ned preehĭng to ; ănd ĭf the cŭlŭrd pepl trў to hăv å ehŭreh her, thĕr ŏt to be re-spĕctåbl hwit pepl enŭf to ĕnforç the la, ănd se thăt thar metĭngs är nŏt dĭstŭrbd. Thĭs mătĕr mŭst be lokt åftĕr ; wĕ'l se ĭf thĭs ehŭreh căn't be reorgånĭzd.

Hwĕn the tim årivd for ŭs to dra our vĭsĭt to å clos, we băd Sĭlvĭå ådu, ănd procedĕd towård the sla. The päths wĕr nŏt shŭvld, ănd ĭn Lĭzĭ's opĭnyŭn, thĕr was sŭm dangĕr thăt the ladĭs' ĭn wakĭng to the sla, wud gĕt thar shos snoў, and ăs å cŏnsĕqwĕnç, befor tha årĭvd hom, wud sŭfĕr cold fet. To ŏbvĭat thĭs dĭfĭcŭltў, the kind womàn tok å bord frŏm the sĭd ŏv the hous, ĕxtĕndĕd ĭt frŏm the dor-sĭl to the sla, ănd thŭs secŭrd ŭs ågĕnst the ĕfĕcts ŏv the sno.